FRAMING CLASS

FRAMING CLASS

Media Representations of
Wealth and Poverty in America

DIANA KENDALL

ROWMAN & LITTLEFIELD PUBLISHERS, INC.
Lanham • Boulder • New York • Toronto • Oxford

ROWMAN & LITTLEFIELD PUBLISHERS, INC.

Published in the United States of America
by Rowman & Littlefield Publishers, Inc.
A wholly owned subsidiary of The Rowman & Littlefield Publishing Group, Inc.
4501 Forbes Boulevard, Suite 200, Lanham, Maryland 20706
www.rowmanlittlefield.com

PO Box 317
Oxford
OX2 9RU, UK

British Library Cataloguing in Publication Information Available

Library of Congress Cataloging-in-Publication Data

Kendall, Diana Elizabeth.
 Framing class : media representations of wealth and poverty in America /
Diana Kendall.
      p. cm.
 Includes bibliographical references and index.
 ISBN 0-7425-4167-3 (cloth : alk. paper)—ISBN 0-7425-4168-1 (pbk. : alk. paper)
 1. Mass media—Social aspects—United States. 2. Social classes—United States.
 3. United States—Social conditions. I. Title. HN90.M3K46 2005
 302.23'086'2—dc22

                                                          2005004850

Printed in the United States of America

∞™ The paper used in this publication meets the minimum requirements of
American National Standard for Information Sciences—Permanence of Paper for
Printed Library Materials, ANSI/NISO Z39.48-1992.

CONTENTS

1

CLASS ACTION IN THE MEDIA

San Francisco, California:

> They live—and die—on a traffic island in the middle of a busy down-
> town street, surviving by panhandling drivers or turning tricks. Every-
> one in their colony is hooked on drugs or alcohol. They are the harsh
> face of the homeless in San Francisco.
>
> The traffic island where these homeless people live is a 40-by-75 foot
> triangle chunk of concrete just west of San Francisco's downtown. . . .
> The little concrete divider wouldn't get a second glance, or have a
> name—if not for the colony that lives there in a jumble of shopping carts
> loaded with everything they own. It's called Homeless Island by the
> shopkeepers who work near it and the street sweepers who clean it; to
> the homeless, it is just the Island. The inhabitants live hand-to-mouth,
> sleep on the cement and abuse booze and drugs, mostly heroin. There
> are at least 3,000 others like them in San Francisco, social workers say.
> They are known as the "hard core," the people most visible on the
> streets, the most difficult to help. . . .
>
> Every effort to help the Islanders—from family, probation officers,
> drug counselors, homeless aid workers—has failed. They have been in
> and out of hospitals or methadone programs and jails . . . so many times
> even they have lost count. "We want to get off the street, but I got to tell
> you true," [Tommy, a homeless man, said]. "Unless they take people like
> us and put us somewhere we can't keep f——ing up, we're going to keep
> f——ing up."[1]

How does this excerpt from a newspaper article make you feel about
homeless people? Based on this news account, most newspaper readers
would have a hard time feeling sympathy for the inhabitants of Homeless
Island. To the contrary, a typical reaction to the situation depicted above, as

reported in a *San Francisco Chronicle* series, "Shame of the City," is one of disgust, tinged with "Yeah, that's the sort of homeless people who are the problem"—bums who sleep on the cement, abuse drugs and alcohol, and panhandle for the money it takes to support their habit.

Compare that media-generated account of San Francisco's homeless population with this one, also from a newspaper article:

> "He's OK," Michelle, 48, said of San Francisco Police Officer Matt Maciel one afternoon after he gently told them to move their carts and then asked if they had enough to eat. "He's just doing his job."
>
> Michelle remembers when she might have been the one calling the cops on people leaving needles outside her house. She was born . . . in Colorado . . . and was sexually abused as a child. Her dad was shotgunned to death young, and her mother was a drug addict gone to cancer. But before Michelle crash-landed at the Island five years ago, she worked as a home health aid and wore smart, pressed dresses.
>
> She dreams of getting back to that life. "That cop might be the guy who helps me, or maybe the jail people—it could be anybody," she said, giving Maciel a smile as he drove off. "I just need another chance."[2]

Based on this article, readers might feel some degree of sympathy for the homeless—especially for homeless persons like Michelle. Surprisingly, both of these depictions of the homeless are from the same newspaper and written by the same reporter. The two depictions show how *media framing* of a particular news story or television program often influences how we feel about the people in a story, especially when the subject of the story is related to wealth, poverty, or the future of the middle class. The manner in which class is framed by the media has a major impact on how people feel about class and inequality. For example, most people in the United States are not really *middle class* (since that would be statistically impossible), yet most of us think that we belong in this category—at least partly because the media define the middle class in such a way that most of us can easily self-identify with it.

WHY "FRAMING CLASS?"

My purpose in writing *Framing Class* is to demonstrate how newspaper articles and television entertainment programs contribute to the social construction of reality about class in the United States, including the manner in which myths and negative stereotypes about the working class and the poor create a reality that seemingly justifies the superior positions of the upper-middle and upper classes and establishes them as entitled to their privileged position in the stratification system.

Although I started this chapter with an example of how stories about homeless people—those at the bottom of the class hierarchy—are framed by the media, my initial interest in class-based media research related to the up- per- and upper-middle classes. When I was conducting research for my recent book, *The Power of Good Deeds: Privileged Women and the Social Reproduction of the Upper Class*,[3] I became aware of how little has been written about media representations of class, particularly the U.S. upper or privileged class. Though some scholars have examined media content in relation to race and gender, class is largely overlooked or deeply enmeshed in the larger race/class/gender sociological paradigm in these studies. *Framing Class* specifically focuses on class to fill in the gap about media representations of class; however, I am not sug- gesting that class is more important than race or gender in studying inequality. Rather, it reflects my belief that class as it is framed by the media, especially in television entertainment programs and national newspapers, must be consid- ered in its own right as a form of reality construction and maintenance.

Even a cursory look at the media reveals that class clearly permeates media content.[4] Regardless of whether journalists consciously acknowledge the importance of framing class in their analysis of everyday life, this process continually occurs in the millions of articles and television shows that are written and produced each year.

Prior to writing this book, I had studied the media for a number of years, and I must admit that I am an avid reader and a frequent viewer of television and films. Previously I have focused on the ways in which the me- dia discuss social problems and how the political economy of media indus- tries contributes to media content. On a more personal level, my interest in the upper classes and media emerged as I worked with the "high society" media in various cities, performing volunteer public relations work for sev- eral prestigious nonprofit organizations. In that role, I provided "fact sheets" and other information to columnists and television reporters about major charity fund-raisers such as debutante presentations, society balls, designer showhouses, and other gala events. While observing a variety of society columnists who wrote about social elites, I became aware of the complex relationship between privileged people and the paid journalists who work on the political, business, and philanthropy beats that cover elite activities. I noticed that for journalists to maintain their "inner circle" access, they typ- ically must be careful about what and how they write about the wealthy and powerful members of their communities.

Based on these observations, I began to compare information provided by the media about the upper classes with media representations of the working class and the poor. It was evident that journalists and television writers hold elites and their material possessions in greater awe—and encourage their audiences to do likewise—than they do the poor or homeless, who, at best, are portrayed as in need of our pity or, at worst, as doomed by their own shortcomings. I became convinced, in the words of the sociologist Herbert Gans, that "the news especially values the order of the upper-class and upper-middle class sectors of society."[5] Consequently, although my interest in media representations of class began with a desire to learn more about how journalists and television entertainment writers portray the rich and famous, over time my area of interest expanded. As I began systematically to gather data about the upper and upper-middle classes in the media, I saw how other socioeconomic dimensions (such as a person's school affiliation or the cost and location of his or her residence) are often used in the media as proxies for class. I realized that I should compare the framing of media stories across class lines to demonstrate fully the prevailing themes used to write about social class in this country. My primary focus remains on how the media glorify the upper classes, even when they are accused of wrongdoing, but I also demonstrate how framing of stories about the middle, working, and poverty classes may maintain and justify larger class-based inequalities in the United States.

"ALL MEDIA/ALL THE TIME" AND OUR IDEAS ABOUT CLASS

How the media portray class in the United States is a crucial issue, because so much of the typical individual's waking hours are spent with some form of the media. It is estimated that the average American spends about three hours a day watching television, or the equivalent of forty-five days per year.[6] When overall electronic media consumption, including television and radio programs, televised sports events, movies, videotapes, audio tapes and CDs, video games, and computer website materials, is taken into account, the typical person spends over three thousand hours per year as a consumer of media products.[7]

Understanding how the media portray the different social classes in our society is important, because studies have shown that the attitudes and judgments of media audiences may be affected by how the media frame certain issues.[8] Although some may argue that how class is depicted in the media does not matter because each of us can use our own experiences to balance any inaccurate portrayal that we see on television or read in a newspaper or magazine, this contention is not realistic; it assumes that we can distinguish between the realities of the U.S. class structure as it actually exists and the fictionalized version of a perceived reality of class as it is depicted by the mass media.

Framing is an important way in which the media emphasize some ideological perspectives over others and manipulate salience by directing people's attention to some ideas while ignoring others. As such, a frame constitutes a story line or an unfolding narrative about an issue.[9] These narratives are organizations of experience that bring order to events. As such, these narratives wield power, because they influence how we make sense of the world.[10] By the time readers and viewers such as ourselves gain access to media products, those products customarily have gone through an extensive process of review and filtration. In the news industry, for example, the joint efforts of reporters, writers, producers, camera operators, photographers, and many others have framed the available information and produced a construction of social reality that does not necessarily accurately reflect the *real* conditions of social life. Terms such as "spin" are used to describe how stories are framed based on organizational constraints, professional judgments, and the targeted audience for the media product. Surveying news stories in newspapers, on television, and on the Internet, we find that lead stories and their coverage of particular events are quite similar. The details are often interchangeable, and ready-made clichés are used in headlines and leads. According to the media scholar Gaye Tuchman, "The news frame organizes everyday reality and the news frame is part and parcel of everyday reality. . . . [It] is an essential feature of news."[11] Both conscious and unconscious motives of media framers play into how the news is framed.

Like framing in the news industry, the story lines in television entertainment shows are standardized and frequently repetitive. Similar story lines are found across a variety of situation comedies, the primarily differences being the location and the characters who act out the various events. Each year during the holiday season, for example, the story lines of numerous sitcoms center around a lead character who serves food at the homeless shelter or performs an act of kindness toward someone who is less fortunate.

What all of this adds up to with regard to the portrayal of class in the media is that we are not receiving "raw" information or "just" entertainment that accurately reflects the realities of life in different classes; in fact, audiences are receiving formulaic products that have been previously sanitized and schematized so that readers and viewers do not have to think for themselves and do not have to deal with the underlying problems of our society.[12] Today, media framing must be thought of as a process in which frame building and frame setting are important components of what we think of as reality. By this I mean that the framing of news articles and television story lines is not necessarily a realistic portrayal of class and how it affects our daily lives. We should not assume that what we see in the media accurately reflects class and class-based inequalities. In fact, contemporary media messages about class have a limited basis in reality. At the extreme, the French social theorist Jean Baudrillard argues that media images have replaced reality to such an extent that we are unable to distinguish between a media image of reality and reality itself.[13] He is joined by other scholars who argue that for many people the media constitute as much "reality" as anything that actually happens in the real world.

Consider, for example, how people for years have, days after episodes of such popular television series as *Seinfeld, Friends, Sex and the City,* and *Desperate Housewives,* discussed what happened to the characters, often referring to them as if they were friends or neighbors rather than highly paid television actors. According to the media scholar Todd Gitlin:

> Of all the institutions of daily life, the media specialize in orchestrating everyday consciousness—by virtue of their pervasiveness, their accessibility, their centralized symbolic capacity. They name the world's parts, they certify reality *as* reality—and when their certifications are doubted and opposed, as they surely are, it is those same certifications that limit the terms of effective opposition. To put it simply: the mass media have become core systems for the distribution of ideology.[14]

As Gitlin points out, media products not only are pervasive and widely accessible in our society but have the symbolic capacity to define the world for people and to limit the terms of debate if someone challenges ideologies implicitly or explicitly set forth in the media product.

By analyzing how the media socially construct meanings about class, we can more clearly see how ideology and everything that passes for knowledge in our society can affect our thinking about inequality and our personal identity in regard to the class structure. Based on a theoretical approach referred to as "the social construction of reality," I argue that we use the information we gain from the media to construct a picture of class and inequality that we come to accept as reality. In the words of the sociologists Peter L. Berger and Thomas Luckmann, "Human reality [is] socially constructed reality."[15] Accordingly, we learn about our world through primary and secondary socialization, which collectively serve as our induction into participation in the larger societal dialectic. According to Berger and Luckmann,[16] we learn a class-oriented view of society through the lens of the class-related perspectives of *significant others*—those persons whose care, affection, and approval are especially desired and who are most important in the development of the self:

The significant others who mediate this world to [us] modify it in the course of mediating it. They select aspects of it in accordance with their own location in the social structure, and also by virtue of their individual, biographically rooted idiosyncrasies. The social world is "filtered" to the individual through this double selectivity. Thus the lower-class child not only absorbs a lower-class perspective on the social world, he [or she] absorbs it in the idiosyncratic coloration given it by his [or her] parents (or whatever other individuals are in charge of his [or her] primary socialization). The same lower-class perspective may induce a mood of contentment, resignation, bitter resentment, or seething rebelliousness. Consequently, the lower-class child will not only come to inhabit a world greatly different from that of an upper-class child, but may do so in a manner quite different from the lower-class child next door.

In addition to the coloration that is given to class through the socialization process in the family, people also experience class-related coloration in the secondary socialization process when social institutions such as schools, churches, and the media present a highly selective (and sometimes distorted) view of how class works. Along with primary agents of socialization in the family and close friendship units that help to maintain the individual's subjective reality of class, a number of "less significant others" reaffirm a person's class location and serve as a "chorus in reality-maintenance."[17] The media are crucial agents in the chorus of reality-maintenance.

MEDIA FRAMING AND SOCIAL REALITIES

Framing is the process by which sense is made of events.[18] When we read a newspaper or watch television or a movie, we are living vicariously: We are not actually experiencing firsthand the event that we are reading about or seeing. Instead, we are experiencing a mediated form of communication in which images and words supply us with information that shapes our perceptions of the world around us. The media selectively frame the world,[19] and these frames manipulate salience, meaning that media audiences are directed to consider certain features or key points and to ignore or minimize others. The term *media framing* is used to describe the process by which information and entertainment are packaged by the media (newspapers, magazines, radio and television networks and stations, and the Internet) before being presented to an audience. This process includes factors such as the amount of exposure given to a story, where it is placed, the positive or negative tone it conveys, and its accompanying headlines, photographs, or other visual and auditory effects (if any).

Although various analysts have defined and applied the concept of framing differently,[20] early sociological views on framing by the media often were based on Erving Goffman's *Frame Analysis: An Essay on the Organization of Experience,* in which he stated:

> I assume that definitions of a situation are built up in accordance with principles of organization which govern events—at least social ones—and our subjective involvement in them; frame is the word I use to refer to such of these basic elements as I am able to identify. My phrase "frame analysis" is a slogan to refer to the examination in these terms of the organization of experience.[21]

According to Goffman, frames serve as cognitive structures that guide perception and the representation of reality. Frames denote *schemata of interpretation* that make it possible for people "to locate, perceive, identify, and label" occurrences within their life space and the world at large.[22] However, Goffman did not believe that individuals consciously *manufacture* frames; he thought that we unconsciously *adopt* frames in the course of communication so that we can deal with "reality" and attempt to choose appropriate repertories of cognition and action.[23] Thus, a key argument of Goffman's frame analysis is that individuals make sense of their everyday life by devising frames that shape and compartmentalize their experiences and help them explain the realm of objects and events around them.

Goffman's frame analysis has been applied to a wide range of studies examining issues including social movements,[24] gender politics,[25] and news coverage of terrorism.[26] For the most part, these studies shift his use of frame analysis from a focus on an individual's *personal* approach to reality to a larger view of how *other people,* and especially the media, devise frames that influence our interpretation of reality. For example, in their examination of the framing process and social movements, the sociologists Robert D. Benford and David A. Snow describe how social movement actors serve as agents who actively engage in the production and maintenance of meaning for other people through processes such as *frame amplification,* which involves "accenting and highlighting some issues, events, or beliefs as being more salient than others."[27] According to Benford and Snow, by punctuating or accenting certain elements the frame-amplification process creates a conceptual handle or peg that links together various events and issues, and "these punctuated issues, beliefs, and events may function much like synecdoches that come to symbolize the larger frame or movement of which it is a part."[28] The movement slogan "Homeless, Not Helpless" illustrates this function. Other synecdoches—such as "Angry White Males" and "Soccer Moms"—have taken on a political reality after journalists created pervasive gendered frames to describe social phenomenon, such as using the term *gender gap* to refer to differences between women and men in political preferences and voting behavior.[29]

Framing helps us make sense of social life, because facts have no intrinsic meaning. Facts "take on their meaning by being embedded in a frame or story line that organizes them and gives them coherence, selecting certain ones to emphasize while ignoring others."[30] Out of the many facts or bits of information that the news media might report on class-related issues, for example, frames are used to highlight or privilege certain items over others, thereby elevating them in *salience*—making them more noticeable, meaningful, or memorable to the audiences receiving those bits of information.[31] Factors that make bits of information more salient are their placement within a text, how often the same information is repeated, and the extent to which bits of information are associated with other symbols that are familiar to readers or viewers.[32]

Although media framing is most often discussed with regard to the news media, the concept of framing is also applicable to the processes used by television entertainment writers as they create story lines for dramas and situation comedies. According to Todd Gitlin, "Frames are principles of selection, emphasis and presentation composed of little tacit theories about what exists, what happens, and what matters."[33] As we watch a television entertainment show, we are influenced by the tacit theories that guided the writers of that program, whether we are aware of them or not. Like news reports, television entertainment programming provides "symbolic representations of society rather than literal portrayals thereof."[34] Although media audiences know that they are living vicariously as they watch fictionalized versions of life, viewers may identify with the characters and the events depicted, coming to experience the emotions of individuals whom they have never met and will never actually know. For some members of the viewing audience, for example, the line between fact and fiction is blurred by the media when those viewers come to identify strongly with the participants in television sagas or so-called reality shows. Consider, for example, the now-classic television show, *Marcus Welby, M.D.*, in which the actor Robert Young played the role of Dr. Welby. So convincing was Young's portrayal that many viewers came to view him as a "real" doctor and sent letters asking the actor Robert Young for medical advice. These viewers could not distinguish between the "real" actor Young and the "unreal" Dr. Welby. As a further indication of the difficulty in distinguishing between the real and the unreal, the actor Robert Young later "played" a doctor in television ads, recommending medical products to potential patients.[35]

Framing of news and entertainment shows is not an accidental occurrence. A basic premise of framing analysis is that the process of framing is an *active* endeavor involving patterns of selection, emphasis, and exclusion on the part of journalists and writers who determine what material might be entertaining or newsworthy for readers and viewers. In the process of selecting some topics as important, other issues are discarded. Once a topic has been selected, which aspects of that topic are to be emphasized and which minimized or excluded is largely left up to the journalist or script writer. In news stories about the middle class, for example, journalists may frame articles to show how the middle class is victimized by the rich (for instance, if wealthy individuals receive a special tax break) or by the working class (for instance, if workers are demanding higher wages that will increase prices). In framing articles to suggest that people in the middle class are victims, journalists may ignore how members of the middle class may victimize people in other classes, such as the house cleaners and yard workers who help them maintain their middle-class lifestyles but are paid very little.

Class-based media representations are often taken for granted by viewers and listeners when they see or hear the same ideas repeated frequently.[36] An example is the annual media coverage that accompanies holiday charity toward those who are "down on their luck." This coverage typically has a homogeneous media interpretation as journalists and television entertainment writers give their annual nod to the poor and homeless by writing news stories[37] or television scripts calling for the leading character to serve a Thanksgiving or Christmas meal to the homeless at the local soup kitchen. These media representations suggest that Americans are benevolent people who do not forget the less fortunate. Ironically, the rest of the story line for the "holiday" episode of major television situation comedies typically shows the characters fretting over their own extensive Christmas lists and overindulging at holiday parties, conveying a message widely divergent from the one about unselfishly helping the poor and homeless.

Images of wealth and poverty that are repeatedly depicted by the media may either reinforce readers' and viewers' beliefs about inequality, or these images may challenge those beliefs.[38] This can be true even with regard to a situation comedy or other television program that the viewer knows is fiction. As the communications scholar Linda Holtzman states, "We may say of television, music, or film, 'I know it's not real,' and yet with heavy consumption of the media the repetition of the images will influence us in spite of that understanding."[39] Positive images of wealthy people may make us believe that they are deserving of their wealth; negative images of the poor and homeless may make us believe that they are deserving of their wretched condition. In regard to wealthy celebrities who are constantly featured in media culture, the philosopher Douglas Kellner writes, "The celebrities of media culture are the icons of the present age, the deities of an entertainment society, in which money, looks, fame, and success are the ideals and goals of the dreaming billions who inhabit Planet Earth."[40] If we accept this dream of fame and fortune, we may engage in voyeurism, vicarious living, and unduly high levels of consumerism, all the while concluding that there is nothing wrong with our society and that our primary concern should be to get rich and avoid being poor—or at least to be solidly middle class but be able to show that we can live as the wealthy and famous do. According to Kellner, "The stars of the entertainment industry become fashion icons and models for imitation and emulation. In a postmodern image culture, style and look become increasingly important modes of identity and presentation of the self in everyday life, and the spectacles of media culture show and tell people how to appear and behave."[41]

By this approach, the melding of information and entertainment in the media has created an "infotainment society," in which many people cannot get enough media spectacle and are willing to participate in everything from reality TV as contestants to excessive consumerism that may bankrupt them. For these reasons, I become fascinated with the study of how the media have represented class in the United States, and as you read this book I hope that you will share my interest in this important topic.

CONDUCTING THE RESEARCH

Because little prior research has examined media and class, I began my study with newspaper databases, searching for key words such as "working class," "elites," and "middle class" to identify a range of articles in which some specific acknowledgment of class location or socioeconomic status was made. I watched thousands of hours of television entertainment shows, looking specifically for such class-related identifiers as the occupational status of characters, the types and locations of residences in which people lived, and media publicity about the shows that emphasized economic characteristics, such as *Life of Luxury* and *Rich Kids*. Although articles from many newspapers are included in the research, I found that the *New York Times* best reflected what was being printed in newspapers throughout the country; many other papers are affiliated with the *Times* syndicate and publish the same articles within a day or two. Reliance on the *New York Times* as a major source for my research is in keeping with the work of the journalism scholar Jack Lule, who has stated, "But more than any other U.S. news medium, the *New York Times* has become crucial reading for those interested in the news, national politics and international affairs. Understanding the *Times* has become a necessary part of understanding the times. Though not the biggest, it may well be the most significant newspaper in the world."[42] As Lule points out, stories are not necessarily more true if they are in the *Times,* but those that do appear in the *Times* carry great weight and are often widely cited by television reporters and others because they initially were published there.

I narrowed my research to newspaper articles and television entertainment shows, because newspapers and television programs are taken for granted as a form of information and entertainment. Although so-called reality series have become increasingly popular in recent years, I have chosen to limit my observation of such shows to those that overtly employ the idea of class, such as *The Simple Life,* which absurdly tries to show rich city girls living a working-class country life among "ordinary people," and *The Apprentice,* in which people compete for top-paying corporate positions. In fact, many "reality" shows are staged and do not indicate the true class position of participants. For instance, in the finale of the first season of ABC's *Bachelorette,* middle-class participants Trista Rehn (a physical therapist) and Ryan Sutter (a firefighter) enjoy a fully televised, multimillion-dollar wedding extravaganza that was in fact paid for by the television network and the show's sponsors.

In my attempt to gain a historical perspective on how class-related issues have been covered in newspapers over time, I found the archives of the *New York Times* particularly useful, as its articles dating back to the 1850s have been systematically organized by headline or key words and can be easily retrieved (for a fee) for full-text analysis. I carried out more recent research on newspaper and television news reports, and television entertainment shows as well, through Internet database searches. I recorded many of the television shows mentioned in this book and watched the episodes numerous times, looking each time for subtle nuances of class that I previously might have missed.

I divided all of the materials that I had gathered into categories reflecting the different components of the U.S. class structure and also the divisions set forth by well-known sociologists in the field of social stratification. Although there are a variety of views of the American class system, I find a fairly traditional model most useful for explaining the *objective view of class,* because it reflects more closely than some other models what most media typically purport to show about class divisions in this country. According to sociologists, a *class system* is a type of social stratification based on the ownership and control of resources and on the type of work people do.[43] One resource is *income*—the economic gain derived from wages, salaries, income transfers (governmental aid), and ownership of property. Income is most important to those in the middle and lower tiers of the class structure because without it they would not have the means for economic survival. By contrast, _wealth_ is the value of all a person's or family's economic assets, including income, personal property, and income-producing property. Some wealthy people do not need to work, because they possess sufficient economic resources—derived from ownership of property, including buildings, land, farms, factories, stocks, bonds, and large bank accounts—to live very well for the duration of their lives and to pass on vast estates to their children and grandchildren.

Because terminology such as "working class" and "upper-middle class" is frequently used by the media, I employed the Gilbert-Kahl model,[44] which divides the United States into six classes—the upper class, the upper-middle class, the middle class, the working class, the working poor, and the poor and homeless—as a basis for analyzing my data. The Gilbert-Kahl model identifies economic variables (such as _occupation, income,_ and _wealth_), status variables _(prestige, association, and socialization),_ and political variables _(power_ and _class consciousness),_ which I used to divide my data into categories for analysis. In regard to status variables, for example, the media often use prestige as a concept to differentiate between people on the basis of how much deference or, alternatively, condescension they receive from others. Similarly, the concept of _association_ helps to peg a person's class location with respect to the individuals or groups with whom the person associates. _Socialization_ is the process through which we learn the skills, attitudes, and customs of a particular class. In regard to the political variables of power and class consciousness, power is the ability of individuals or groups to achieve their goals despite opposition from others,[45] whereas class consciousness is the degree to which people at a similar location in the class system think of themselves as a distinctive group that shares political, economic, and social interests. All of these variables contribute to, or limit, opportunity for social mobility—the extent to which people can move up or down in the class system.[46]

At the top of the social class hierarchy is the upper (capitalist) class, which constitutes about 1 percent of the U.S. population and comprises the wealthiest and most powerful people, who control the majority of the nation's (and in some cases the world's) wealth. The investment decisions of people in this class shape national and international economies. The upper class includes "owners of substantial enterprises, investors with diversified wealth, heirs to family fortunes, and top executives of major corporations."[47]

Distinctions are sometimes made between "old money" (upper-upper) and "new money" (lower-upper) classes in the sociological literature.[48] Members of the old-money category come from prominent families that have possessed great wealth for several generations. On a national level, names like Rockefeller, Mellon, Du Pont, and Kennedy come to mind. However, many regional elites also are immensely wealthy and pass the benefits of that wealth on to children and grandchildren through gifts and legacies. By contrast, families with "new money" have accumulated vast economic resources during the lifetime of people in the current generation. More recently, this money has come from high-tech industries, investment and banking, top-earning professions, and high-profile careers in sports and entertainment.

Like the upper class, the upper-middle class (about 14 percent of the U.S. population) is identified as privileged in comparison to the middle, working, working poor, and underclasses, in that the upper-middle class is composed primarily of professionals with college and postgraduate degrees. This group includes many top managers of large corporations, business owners, lawyers, doctors, dentists, accountants, architects, and others who earn incomes far above the national average. People in the upper-middle class are often portrayed as having achieved the American Dream. Unlike many in the upper class, however, members of the upper-middle class work to earn a living, and their children must acquire the requisite education if they are to enter well-paid employment, rather than assuming that they will inherit family-owned businesses or diversified stock and bond portfolios.

As compared with the upper-middle class, people in the middle of the middle class (about 30 percent of the U.S. population) are characterized as possessing two-year or four-year college degrees, having more supervision at work, and experiencing less job stability than those in the upper-middle class. Occupational categories include lower-level managers, semiprofessionals, and nonretail sales workers. In the past, middle-class occupations were considered relatively secure and to provide opportunities for advancement if people worked hard, increased their level of education, and gained more experience on the job. Today, however, a number of factors, including escalating housing prices, occupational insecurity, blocked mobility on the job, and a cost-of-living squeeze that has penalized many workers, are causes of concern and much media analysis.

The working class (about 30 percent of the U.S. population) is made up of semiskilled workers such as machine operators in factories ("blue collar" jobs) and some service-sector workers, including clerks and salespeople whose jobs involve routine, mechanized tasks that require little skill beyond basic literacy and brief on-the-job training.[49] Few people in the working class have more than a high school diploma, and many have less, which makes job opportunities for them more scarce in the 2000s. Jobs in fast-food restaurants and "big box" chains such as Wal-Mart have been the largest growth areas of employment for the working class; the segment of the working class made up of semiskilled blue-collar workers in construction and manufacturing has shrunk since the 1950s.

Below the working class in the social hierarchy is the working-poor category (about 20 percent of the U.S. population). Members of the working poor live just above or just below the poverty line. They typically hold unskilled jobs, seasonal migrant jobs in agriculture, lower-paid factory jobs, and minimum-wage service-sector jobs (such as counter help at restaurants). As some people once in the blue-collar sector of the workforce have faced increasing impoverishment and joined the ranks of the working poor, increased media attention has been focused on service workers and the lowest-paid operatives and sales and clerical workers who, despite working full-time and often holding down more than one job, simply cannot make ends meet. At the bottom end of the working class, there is often a pattern of oscillating mobility in which people move back and forth between the working class and the working-poor category.[50]

The poor and homeless (the underclass), about 12 percent of the U.S. population, typically are individuals who are unemployed or are part-time workers caught in long-term deprivation that results from low levels of education and income and from high rates of unemployment. In this category are unskilled workers, many single parents, members of subordinate racial and ethnic groups, persons with mental or physical disabilities, and recent immigrants with low levels of educational attainment.

By using these objective criteria for class, I began to look for recurring frames that have been used over time to describe the lifestyles of people in the upper, middle, and lower classes. It was interesting to see the extent to which these recurring themes could be found, not only over decades but also over centuries in media portrayals. For example, although the harshness of representations of the poor and homeless have been cloaked in more respectable terms of political correctness in recent years, many of the same themes and framing devices are still used when describing the plight of those at the bottom of our society's social, economic, and political ladder. Over the years, there likewise has been an almost fawning acceptance of the rich and famous, even when accused of wrongdoing, that is not found in representations of the working class. By contrast, though most people choose to identify themselves as in the good, solid middle class, media portrayals of this class for the past 150 years have portrayed it as fragile and caught perilously between the rich and the poor. Media representations of the upper class seldom suggest that its members' favored location in the class structure might be short-lived, but depictions of the middle class often portray people in this class as holding on by a thin thread.

ORGANIZATION OF THE CHAPTERS

Although because most of us think of ourselves as being in the middle class, that might seem the place to start, I have organized the chapters in a different manner, one that places the framing of stories about the rich and famous next to those of the poor and homeless so that readers can more closely compare the sharply contrasting images of wealth and poverty that continually influence our attitudes and perceptions about class. In this way, I hope to demonstrate the sharp contrast between the often flattering descriptions of the rich and the pitying or derogatory descriptions of those at the bottom of the class heap.

Chapter 2, "Twenty-four-Karat Gold Frames: Lifestyles of the Rich and Famous," describes the history of media framing of the upper class, showing how discussions of the rich and famous have captured the interest of journalists from the days of the earliest newspapers to contemporary Internet websites. How the "society page" has changed over time is a reflection of larger societal changes and new information technologies, but it is not an indication that there has been diminished interest in the doings of the wealthy and famous. If anything, just the contrary is true: audiences can increasingly feed around the clock on gossip about those at the top of the economic pyramid. For this reason, chapter 2 analyzes four positive media frames and their messages: (1) the consensus frame: the wealthy are like everyone else; (2) the admiration frame: the wealthy are generous and caring people; (3) the emulation frame: the wealthy personify the American Dream; and (4) the price-tag frame: the wealthy believe in the gospel of materialism.

However, not all media representations of the top class are positive, and chapter 3, "Gilded Cages: Media Stories of How the Mighty Have Fallen," sets forth negative framing devices that are sometimes used to portray the upper class: (5) the "sour grapes" frame: the wealthy are unhappy and dysfunctional; and (6) the bad-apple frame: some wealthy people are scoundrels. Chapter 3 specifically looks at media coverage of the downfall of some top corporate executives and shows how their excessive consumption is of great interest to media audiences even as readers and viewers decry the greedy actions of these "captains of industry." The extent to which some wealthy people believe they can buy anything, including their way out of trouble, is a recurring media frame discussed in this chapter. How the media frame articles about the wealthy by showing them to be more interesting and more deserving of what they have stands in sharp contrast to portrayals of the poor and that show them as living tedious and less worthy lives.

In chapter 4, "Fragile Frames: The Poor and Homeless," I show that although some framing of persons in poverty and homelessness is sympathetic, much media coverage offers negative images of the poor, showing them as dependent on others (welfare issues) or as deviant in their behavior and lifestyle. A favorite media framing device is exceptionalism framing: "If this person escaped poverty, why can't you?" This approach tells "inspirational" stories about people who have risen from poverty or homelessness to find greater economic solvency and happiness in the class above them. Another framing device, charitable framing, is used by the media to show how we can help the poor at holidays and when disasters occur. Articles and television entertainment story lines using charitable framing focus on the need for a helping hand on "special occasions" but do not suggest that a more focused effort should be made on a daily basis to help alleviate the larger societal problems that contribute to individual problems of poverty, hunger, and homelessness.

Chapter 5, "Tarnished Metal Frames: The Working Class and the Working Poor," discusses five framing devices used by the media to portray the working class: (1) shady framing: greedy workers, unions, and organized crime; (2) heroic framing: working-class heroes and victims; (3) caricature framing number 1: white-trashing the working class; (4) caricature framing number 2: television's buffoons, bigots, and slobs; and (5) "fading blue collar" framing: out of work or unhappy at work. As these frames show, media representations of the working class typically do not provide a positive image of that class.

In chapter 6, "Splintered Wooden Frames: The Middle Class," I identify three key frames that I found frequently employed in media representations of the middle class: middle-class values framing, squeeze framing, and victimization framing. The first of these—middle-class values framing—emphasizes that the core values held by people in the middle class should be the norm for this country and that these values remain largely intact over time despite economic, political, and cultural changes. Within that frame the middle class becomes not only the nation's frame of reference but the ideal model to which people in the United States should aspire, particularly those in the working and poverty classes. However, the other two (seemingly contradictory) frames that I identified are also employed by the media to represent the middle class. Squeeze framing sends the message to media audiences that the middle class is perilously caught between the cost of a middle-class lifestyle and the ability to pay for that lifestyle, whereas victimization framing suggests that many middle-class problems are the result of actions of the upper class and the lower classes, potentially endangering the middle-class way of life.

Chapter 7, "Framing Class, Vicarious Living, and Conspicuous Consumption," looks at how the media may affect our behavior, particularly in regard to consumerism, and what we may do to combat this strong influence in the life of our family. The chapter suggests that, as readers and viewers, we have a responsibility to ourselves and our children to develop a greater awareness of how news and entertainment programming colors our views about our own class location and about wealth, poverty, and inequality in the larger society. Since the print media, television, and the Internet have become the primary storytellers of the twenty-first century, we should be concerned about the kinds of stories that are being told and how these socially constructed representations of reality contribute to how we think of ourselves and how they foster an unhealthy ideology that supports the ever-widening chasm between the haves and have-nots in the United States and around the world.

NOTES

1. Kevin Fagan, "Shame of the City: Homeless Island," *San Francisco Chronicle,* November 30, 2003, www.sfgate.com (accessed April 11, 2004).

2. Fagan, "Shame of the City: Homeless Island."

3. See Diana Kendall, *The Power of Good Deeds: Privileged Women and the Social Reproduction of the Upper Class* (Lanham, Md.: Rowman & Littlefield, 2002).

4. David Croteau and William Hoynes, *Media/Society: Industries, Images, and Audiences,* 3rd ed. (Thousand Oaks, Calif.: Pine Forge, 2003).

5. Herbert Gans, *Deciding What's News* (New York: Pantheon Books, 1979), 61.

6. Croteau and Hoynes, *Media/Society.*

7. Robert Perrucci and Earl Wysong, *The New Class Society,* 2nd ed. (Lanham, Md.: Rowman & Littlefield, 2003).

8. See, for example, Robert M. Entman and Andrew Rojecki, *The Black Image in the White Mind: Media and Race in America* (Chicago: University of Chicago Press, 2000); Todd Gitlin, *The Whole World Is Watching* (Berkeley: University of California Press, 1980); Todd Gitlin, *Media Unlimited: How the Torrent of Images and Sounds Overwhelms Our Lives* (New York: Henry Holt, 2003); Shanto Iyengar, *Is Anyone Responsible? How Television Frames Political Issues* (Chicago: University of Chicago Press, 1994); Pippa Norris, Montague Kern, and Marion Just, *Framing Terrorism: The News Media, the Government, and the Public* (New York: Routledge, 2003); Stephen D. Reese, Oscar H. Gandy Jr., and August E. Grant, eds., *Framing Public Life: Perspectives on Media and Our Understanding of the Social World* (Mahwah, N.J.: Lawrence Erlbaum, 2003).

9. William A. Gamson, David Croteau, William Hoynes, and Theodore Sasson. "Media Images and the Social Construction of Reality," *Annual Review of Sociology* 18 (1992): 373–93.

10. Robert K. Manoff, "Writing the *News*, by Telling the 'Story,'" in *Reading the News*, ed. Robert K. Manoff and Michael Schudson, 197–229 (New York: Pantheon, 1987).

11. Gaye Tuchman, *Making News: A Study in the Construction of Reality* (New York: Free Press, 1978), 193.

12. Max Horkheimer and Theodor W. Adorno, *Dialectic of Enlightenment,* trans. John Cummings (New York: Continuum International, 2002 [1944]).

13. Jean Baudrillard, *Simulations* (New York: Semiotext(e), 1983).

14. Gitlin, *The Whole World Is Watching,* 1.

15. Peter L. Berger and Thomas Luckmann, *The Social Construction of Reality: A Treatise in the Sociology of Knowledge* (New York: Anchor/Doubleday, 1967), 189.

16. Berger and Luckmann, *The Social Construction of Reality,* 131.

17. Berger and Luckmann, *The Social Construction of Reality,* 151.

18. Rebecca Ann Lind and Colleen Salo, "The Framing of Feminists and Feminism in News and Public Affairs Programs in U.S. Electronic Media," *Journal of Communication* 52 (2002): 211–28.

19. Entman and Rojecki, *The Black Image in the White Mind.*

20. See Robert D. Benford and David A. Snow, "Framing Processes and Social Movements: An Overview and Assessment," *Annual Review of Sociology* 26 (2000): 611–39; Paul D'Angelo, "News Framing as a Multiparadigmatic Research Program: A Response to Entman," *Journal of Communication* 52 (2002): 870–88; Robert M. Entman, "Framing: Toward Clarification of a Fractured Paradigm," *Journal of Communication* 43 (1993): 51–58; and Dietram A. Scheufele, "Framing as a Theory of Media Effects." *Journal of Communications* 49 (1999): 103–22.

21. Erving Goffman, *Frame Analysis: An Essay on the Organization of Experience* (Boston: Northeastern University Press, 1974), 10–11.

22. Benford and Snow, "Framing Processes and Social Movements"; Goffman, *Frame Analysis,* 21.

23. Gitlin, *The Whole World Is Watching,* 6–7.

24. Gitlin, *The Whole World Is Watching*; Benford and Snow, "Framing Processes and Social Movements"; David A. Snow, E. Burke Rochford, Steven K. Worden, and Robert D. Benford, "Frame Alignment Processes, Micromobilization, and Movement Participation," *American Sociological Review* 51 (1986): 464–81.

25. Pippa Norris, *Women, Media, and Politics* (New York: Oxford University Press, 1997).

26. Norris, Kern, and Just, *Framing Terrorism.*

27. Benford and Snow, "Framing Processes and Social Movements," 623.

28. Benford and Snow, "Framing Processes and Social Movements," 623.

29. Pippa Norris and Susan J. Carroll, "The Dynamics of the News Framing Process: From Reagan's Gender Gap to Clinton's Soccer Moms," ksghome.harvard.edu/~.pnorris.shorenstein.ksg/acrobat/carroll.pdf (accessed August 27, 2003).

30. William A. Gamson, "News as Framing: Comments on Graber," *American Behavioral Scientist* 33 (1989): 157.

31. Entman, "Framing."

32. Entman, "Framing."

33. Gitlin, *The Whole World Is Watching,* 6.

34. Tuchman, *Making News.*

35. Steven Best and Douglas Kellner, *Postmodern Theory: Critical Interrogations* (New York: Guilford, 1991).

36. See Gitlin, *The Whole World Is Watching;* Norris, Kern, and Just, *Framing Terrorism;* and Reese, Gandy, and Grant, eds., *Framing Public Life.*

37. William K. Bunis, Angela Yancik, and David Snow, "The Cultural Patterning of Sympathy toward the Homeless and Other Victims of Misfortune," *Social Problems* (November 1996): 387–402.

38. Linda Holtzman, *Media Messages: What Film, Television, and Popular Music Teach Us about Race, Class, Gender, and Sexual Orientation* (London: M. E. Sharpe, 2000).

39. Holtzman, *Media Messages,* 32.

40. Douglas Kellner, *Media Spectacle* (New York: Routledge, 2003).

41. Kellner, *Media Spectacle,* 7–8.

42. Jack Lule, *Daily News, Eternal Stories: The Mythological Role of Journalism* (New York: Guilford, 2001), 6.

43. Robert A. Rothman, *Inequality and Stratification: Race, Class, and Gender,* 5th ed. (Upper Saddle River, N.J.: Prentice Hall, 2005).

44. Joseph A. Kahl, *The American Class Structure* (New York: Rinehart, 1957); Dennis Gilbert and Joseph A. Kahl, *The American Class Structure: A New Synthesis* (Homewood, Ill.: Dorsey, 1982); and Dennis Gilbert, *The American Class Structure in an Age of Growing Inequality,* 6th ed. (Belmont, Calif.: Wadsworth, 2003).

45. Max Weber, *From Max Weber: Essays in Sociology,* ed. H. H. Gerth and C. Wright Mills (New York: Oxford University Press, 1946).

46. Gilbert, *The American Class Structure in an Age of Growing Inequality.*

47. Gilbert, *The American Class Structure in an Age of Growing Inequality,* 271.

48. W. Lloyd Warner and Paul S. Lunt, *The Social Life of a Modern Community* (New Haven, Conn.: Yale University Press, 1941); Richard P. Coleman and Lee Rainwater, *Social Standing in America: New Dimensions of Class* (New York: Basic, 1978); Kendall, *The Power of Good Deeds.*

49. Gilbert, *The American Class Structure in an Age of Growing Inequality.*

50. Gilbert, *The American Class Structure in an Age of Growing Inequality.*

2

TWENTY-FOUR-KARAT GOLD FRAMES: LIFESTYLES OF THE RICH AND FAMOUS

Champagne overflows glasses. Guests glide around wearing vintage 1920s attire—handsome men in top hats, beautiful women in flapper dresses. Laughter mixes with the sound of Glenn Miller's "In the Mood." It's Jamie Johnson's 21st birthday party and a regular ol' beer bash simply won't do. At midnight, the heir to the Johnson & Johnson pharmaceutical fortune receives the ultimate gift: inheriting more money than most people can spend in a lifetime.[1]

With this glowing description, the companion website for the Cable News Network introduced a new HBO documentary—*Born Rich*—that looks at the lives of several wealthy young people, including Jamie Johnson, Ivana Trump, and S. I. Newhouse IV (of the Condé Nast media empire), who were born into some of the richest families in the United States. In this interesting bit of cross-promotion (HBO is a division of media giant Time Warner, as is CNN), the writers utilize a popular framing technique for introducing stories about the rich in America, highlighting ways in which the rich are perceived to be different from other people. F. Scott Fitzgerald showed his mastery of this device in the opening lines of the short story "The Rich Kid": "Let me tell you about the very rich. They are different from you and me."[2]

To emphasize the differences between the rich and everyone else, media framers often provide elaborate descriptions of the social events and lifestyles on which the very wealthy spend vast amounts of money to have a good time and impress one another. Typically, both the physical setting and the personal appearance of the rich are carefully depicted in a manner that reflects their upper-crust status and their social position as "handsome" or "beautiful" people. This framing device conveys not only the message that the wealthy are different from other people but that they may be better than other people, or at least that some of them may be better.

How the media frame news stories and how television writers develop story lines for entertainment shows that include affluent characters help to shape our perceptions about the rich and famous. Communications scholars Robert M. Entman and Andrew Rojecki state that people have two paths to social information: *personal experience* from formal education, socialization, and conversation with others, and *mediated communication,* which comes from sources such as television and newspapers.[3] Although some individuals in the top economic and social tiers may choose to be highly visible to others, their wealth and privileged lifestyle make it possible—if they so desire—for them to live completely away from the gaze of the masses except for the media coverage they receive. Accordingly, most of us don't *really* know how "the other half" lives. The manner in which news and entertainment sources frame information about the upper classes therefore helps shape the way that other people view the wealthy and well connected, as well as how middle- and lower-income individuals perceive the U.S. class structure and larger issues of social inequality in general.

Media framing either reinforces or contradicts most people's previously held ideas about the wealthy, because we use mental shortcuts such as schemas—sets of related concepts that allow us to make inferences about new information based on already organized prior knowledge—across many different situations. Entman and Rojecki give this example:

> For instance, mainstream U.S. culture includes a schema stored in many Americans' minds that associates the concept of success with other ideas such as wealth, hard work, educational attainment, intelligence, status, snobbery, fancy cars, and good looks. Images representing those related concepts readily come to mind when people hear the word or see a symbol that evokes the concept of success—a picture of a BMW, a mansion, a big executive office suite.[4]

By contrast, a schema about "welfare" stirred up by a television news story on welfare reform might bring about ideas that individuals on welfare are lazy or that they are likely to be members of racial or ethnic minorities.[5]

The most popular media frames for news accounts of the rich and for television story lines for entertainment programs play on the preexisting schema within many people's minds that it is okay simultaneously to love and hate the rich. This is nothing new; fascination with the lifestyles and material possessions of the rich and well connected in the United States goes back several centuries, perhaps finding its apex during the Gilded Age, between the 1880s and 1920s, and it has always contained a mixture of both love and hate.

FROM THE SOCIETY PAGE TO THE INTERNET: A BRIEF HISTORY OF MEDIA FRAMING OF THE UPPER CLASSES

Today, news stories about the top classes are found throughout the newspaper in sections ranging from the "Top News Stories" and "Business" to "Entertainment and Leisure," "Fashion and Travel," "Food," and "Book Reviews." However, some of the earliest visible media framing of stories about the rich and famous was found in specifically designated portions of major newspapers, typically referred to as the "society page" or the "women's page."

The first society pages performed a useful function for journalists and editors who wanted to sell newspapers, but they also served a latent function for some of the wealthy and people who hoped to reach the top tiers of society. Writing during the era of the Great Depression, the social historian Dixon Wecter described the society page as a useful tool in the social aspirations of the wealthy:

> It is seldom realized how greatly the Society Page has helped create social consciousness in the United States. . . . The Society Page, which is flowered with peculiar luxuriance in American journalism, has often been sufficient to confer leadership on individuals or groups simply by printing their names, day in and day out, or ascribing to them a dictatorship which is accepted first by the gum-chewing typist and finally by the enthroned dowager.[6]

Among the first journalists in the United States to print personal notes about individuals in high society were James Gordon Bennett, Sr., and his staff at the *New York Herald* in the 1830s. No news item was too inconsequential to be included if the participants were "people we know," a designation made by many of the wealthy and well connected to refer to others whom they considered to be part of their in-group. According to social historians, plenty of individuals in the "people we *don't* know" category were excited to read about such trivial matters as the comings and goings of the privileged class on luxury ocean liners or their parties at big New York City hotels, even when the economic fates of the masses were dismal by comparison.[7]

Well-known journalists frequently advised young journalists on how important it was to cover the wealthy. Social historian Wecter reported that one well-known journalist told a class of college students, "Only the rich man is interesting."[8] Before the advent of television and other electronic media, newspapers and magazines provided people in lower classes opportunities to see "magic phantoms," such as the very wealthy Mrs. Cornelius

Vanderbilt, and to gain entry to her residence by way of tabloid reporters who routinely covered her activities and described her lifestyle in intricate detail. For those within the top class, sneaking a peak at the society page afforded an opportunity to keep score of one's position in relation to other elites. For the newly rich, being included in the society page was a reason for celebration. For people outside the top class, the society page afforded a chance for vicarious living: "The society editor rejoices in barriers, cliques, snobberies, and invidious implications, knowing that these things make news and give the humble reader a sense of being 'in the know' even though he may never dream of impinging upon that holy sphere."[9]

Although the society page reached its apex in power and readership in the Gilded Age and early to middle twentieth century, its history can be traced back several centuries. It is believed that the idea was borrowed from the European custom of reporting on the comings and goings of royalty, who at the time were treated in a dignified, low-key manner, unlike the tabloid formats that later emerged and brought great embarrassment to many royal families.[10] In the United States, however, the *New York Herald's* Bennett adopted a tell-all tabloid format in his reporting on high society in America: "No one ever attempted till now to bring out the graces, the polish, the elegancies, the bright and airy attributes of social life. . . . Our purpose has been, and is, to give to the highest society of New York a life, a variety, a piquancy, a brilliancy, an originality that will entirely outstrip the worn out races of Europe."[11]

By 1840, Bennett successfully infiltrated high society by smuggling a society reporter into a famous fancy-dress Fifth Avenue ball in New York City, with the host's reluctant approval. Following that event, the barriers between "society" columnists and upper-crust hostesses began to crumble. As Wecter notes, journalism began to "break down the old exclusiveness of a clique which once regarded its balls and dinners as no more the public's business than its bankruptcies and adulteries."[12] Eventually, the privileged class went from "anger to tolerance and thence to secret pleasure in seeing itself written up."[13]

After Bennett successfully launched the society page in the *New York Herald,* the idea of Society (with a capital *S*) as news was copied by a number of other newspapers in New York and other major cities, which began to "dish up social soufflé" to the public.[14] The job of the society reporter was often given to a widow or an unmarried woman who had the right connections and easy entrée into elite social circles.[15] Perhaps the media received greater acceptance because many reporters shifted the framing of their stories from derision and mockery to admiration for the pomp and grandeur of the rich and famous.[16]

Despite greater praise for the upper class and its lavish lifestyle by journalists of the late nineteenth and early twentieth centuries, stories typically were framed in a format that suggested deep-seated contradictions in the way that the privileged class lived. For example, in recording his impressions of a famous ball given in 1897 by the Bradley Martins, one journalist stated, "The power of wealth with its refinement and vulgarity was everywhere."[17] This ball was considered quite excessive for its time; it cost almost $370,000 for the party and to transform the ballroom of the Waldorf Astoria into a replica of a hall in the palace at Versailles (outside Paris). Ironically, the Martins allegedly had given this lavish costume ball to stimulate the U.S. economy during a time of severe economic depression, stating that they believed the event would "give an impetus to trade."[18] The end result of extensive media coverage of the ball's excesses was not praise for the Martins' charitable endeavors but their decision to relocate permanently to England, outside of the glare of negative publicity.

While some early newspaper accounts of the rich came from correspondents who entered the homes of the wealthy by getting jobs as butlers, chambermaids, or musicians, "hangers-on" who were never quite accepted into the magic circle of society were the main informants, dishing dirt on people who had snubbed them.[19] Although little has been written about how people in other classes viewed earlier media reporting of the upper class, the social historian Mary Cable states:[20]

> Annoying though this publicity may have been to its subjects, it was certainly adulation. For Society people, the nightmare was when the papers got hold of some scandalous event in their lives—a separation or divorce, a murder, an assault, a swindle, a paternity suit, a breach of promise, grand larceny, or some display of total absence of taste or common sense. The public wanted its idols to at least *appear* to behave well, and when they were found wanting, they were savaged by the process. "You can do anything you like," was the famous dictum of the actress Mrs. Patrick Campbell, "as long as you don't do it in the streets and frighten the horses." Rumors might fly, but as long as no one admitted to anything, they simply flew, like Fourth of July rockets, and fell to earth harmlessly.

However, as Cable notes, when the horses *did* stampede and an uproar ensured, newspaper sales were guaranteed to soar.

Although society scandals may have sparked a temporary upswing in sales, regular readers thrived on stories of society-page brides and debutantes, especially the coming-out parties that accompanied their debuts. Even among debutantes, there were inner and outer circles of exclusivity, and the public became enamored with young women who were given such titles as "Debutante of the Year." In addition to stories about debutantes from families with "old money" (families that had possessed great wealth for several generations), many people with "new money" became the favorite topic of a new breed of society reporter who covered "café society" by hanging around nightclubs. The blurring between the truly wealthy and the celebrity set was further enhanced by the use of women to sign endorsements and advertise such products as cosmetics, cigarettes, pianos, and whiskey.[21]

Newspaper articles about the wealthy proliferated whether or not members of the media had official entrée into the lives and social functions of the privileged class, and these articles began to show up in other sections of the newspaper, such as Fashion, Travel, Business, and the women's page. In *The Private World of High Society,* Lucy Kavaler describes how press agents in the 1950s became liaisons between the upper classes and the media because they had both society and newspaper contacts and did not hesitate to use the former on behalf of their clients.[22] Press agents not only influenced what the media reported about the privileged class but helped to frame the settings in which such media events took place. Some press agents held parties for their clients, which members of the media attended; others made sure that journalists and society columnists were invited to prestigious openings and charity events where their clients were sure to be present. Public relations people were also the facilitators of publicity tie-ins between individuals and products, as Kavaler explains:

> I was in Mr. Davis' office one day when he got a telephone call from a man who is a favorite with both the international set and society columnists. He had been approached by a lipstick manufacturer eager for a publicity tie-in. The firm was introducing a new shade, to be called "Continental," and it wanted the gentleman to be named "our favorite Continental" by a group of debutantes. They could then all be photographed together at a society hotel. Although this sounds pretty obvious, pictures of this type do appear regularly in the afternoon newspapers. Mr. Davis, of course, was expected to produce the debutantes— getting publicity in turn for his clients or their daughters.[23]

Although the daughters of old-line families might not have been interested in having this type of publicity, many of the newly wealthy families jumped at the chance. Eventually, the lines between Old Guard society, the nouveau riche, and the media were further blurred through the combined efforts of public relations agents, debutante-ball organizers, party planners, and others who wanted to capture the attention of the media. According to Kavaler's discussion of high society in the 1950s: "The society pages are taken seriously in small towns and big cities alike. People will go to great lengths to be mentioned. . . . Even in society's inner circle very few pay more than lip service to the still much-quoted cliché: 'A lady's name should appear in the newspapers three times—when she is born, when she is married, and when she dies.'"[24]

In the decades following Kavaler's writing, sociologists like G. William Domhoff have turned to the society or women's page as "a window on the ruling class." Although not strictly thought of as a society page any more, the women's page of daily newspapers became one of the central places where readers could learn about the ruling class.[25] In some papers, this section was referred to as the "people's page," but it still contained society news, gossip, and other so-called trivia about the wealthy and famous. Based on research in the women's pages of various newspapers in the 1960s and 1970s, Domhoff asserted that there indeed was a cohesive culture of the richest people and the top U.S. managers in high society. According to Domhoff, not only is the women's page useful in studying connections among people in the ruling class, but it is informative on the lifestyle of the ruling class and on its shared ideology:

> It is on the women's page we learn that our business, cultural, and government leaders, for all their public differences on specific issues, share in a deeper social community that keeps them as one on essential questions concerning the distribution of wealth and the system of property, questions that seldom become issues, questions that rarely receive attention on the straight news pages. Only on the women's page does the newspaper tell us each and every day that there is a ruling class in America.[26]

Since Domhoff's study, the women's page in daily newspapers has largely been replaced with sections on lifestyle, food, fashion, and travel. For example, a recent article ("Tacos, Stir-Fries and Cake: The Junior League at 102") in the *New York Times* food section not only gave a sales pitch for the latest Junior League cookbook and included several recipes from the book but featured an interview with Deborah C. Brittain, an African American woman who is the immediate past president of the Association of Junior Leagues International. In addition to being the official spokeswoman for the new cookbook, Brittain apparently is in charge of dispelling myths about the Junior League, which historically has been known as an organization that "doubled for decades as an exclusive social club where the blood was blue and the gloves were as white as the members."[27] According to journalist Alex Witchel:

> As for its stringent social qualifications, Ms. Brittain said, the Junior League relaxed them years ago. Not only had African Americans been

discouraged from joining, but Jews, Italians, middle-class women and older women were as well. She dispatched this unappetizing bit of history briskly. "The Junior League is good at changing, which is why we still survive," [Ms. Brittain] said. "Particularly in the 70's, they realized their history had a little baggage. But for the majority of our chapters, we've been there, done that, and it's over. Now our membership is open to all women who want to contribute to their community."[28]

Even with the changes so described in the Junior League, most middle- and working-class women and minority-group women remain unlikely candidates for membership in this organization. However, placing the story in the "Dining In/Dining Out" section of the *New York Times* gave it a more egalitarian frame than if it had been on the society page. As we examine contemporary media framing of the wealthy and social elites, we see that the top classes are now the subjects of news reports and other accounts throughout virtually all sections of major daily newspapers.

In the twenty-first century, television and the Internet are increasingly avenues by which elites keep informed of the activities of other elites. These media outlets also provide a window through which middle- and upper-middle-class individuals can vicariously participate in the comings and goings of the wealthy and famous. One example is Newyorksocialdiary.com, a website maintained by David Patrick Columbia, a society writer who has access to many in the international rich and celebrity subcultures. This website, which labels itself "Your link to society," provides party pictures of social and charity benefits attended by the wealthy, a calendar of "society" events, and a social diary describing Columbia's interactions with members of the top tiers at parties and other exclusive events. Websites like this have become popular in such cities as San Francisco (see www.nobhillgazette .com) as well, and they are perhaps one of the closest equivalents to the old society page in newspapers.

Along with "society" websites, local magazines and neighborhood newspapers in affluent sections of major cities have become popular ways in which affluent people keep up with each other. In New York City, *Avenue* magazine provides party pictures and stories about well-known socialites and elite volunteers, who typically live on the Upper East Side of Manhattan. Magazines such as this can be found in affluent enclaves throughout the country. Weekly newspapers for the privileged also serve the function of the old society page. In Dallas, Texas, for example, newspapers sold specifically in Highland Park and University Park (among the most affluent Zip codes in the central Dallas area) and available on the Internet (see www.parkci tiespeople.com) carry stories about society events in that area. Some stories highlight children's school accomplishments or neighborhood issues, but most are similar to the old society page, having party photos and articles about society events, debutante presentations, and weddings of social elites in the community. Although such publications are available to anyone who wants to purchase them, they serve as the virtual "in house" publications of affluent groups, making it possible for elites to read about each other and to keep up with social events whether or not major newspapers or television stations carry information about their activities. In this sense, the old society page is not dead; it has been reincarnated in newer technologies and in more specialized publications read primarily by the affluent and well connected and by those who aspire to join their ranks.

Most people, however, do not get their information about the upper classes from publications like these. Rather, their information primarily comes from the daily newspaper, the magazines (if any) that they read, and the television programs that they watch. It is therefore important to examine the framing mechanisms that these media sources utilize in depicting the various social classes in order to understand their effect on our perceptions of social class in the United States.

POSITIVE DEPICTIONS OF THE WEALTHY IN THE UNITED STATES TODAY

An examination of routine journalistic practices is important to determine what stories are covered, how they are covered, and what dominant cultural meanings are conveyed. According to media scholars, although each day's news events are unique in some ways, how journalists observe and report a specific occurrence is greatly influenced by how similar events have been framed in the past.[29] As a result, information about the very wealthy is often similarly framed whether it is located in various sections of the newspaper, television, or Internet news sources, or the story lines of television entertainment shows. I have identified six dominant media frames used in articles and story lines about the rich and famous that I believe influence how people in other classes view the wealthy. These media frames and their messages are:

- The consensus frame: the wealthy are like everyone else.
- The admiration frame: the wealthy are generous and caring people.
- The emulation frame: the wealthy personify the American dream.
- The price-tag frame: the wealthy believe in the gospel of materialism.
- The sour-grapes frame: the wealthy are unhappy and dysfunctional.
- The bad-apple frame: some wealthy people are scoundrels.[30]

The first four of these frames are discussed in this chapter, while the fifth and sixth are the topics of chapter 3.

CONSENSUS FRAMING:
THE WEALTHY ARE LIKE EVERYONE ELSE

The consensus frame tends to obscure inequalities between the classes, by highlighting ways in which very wealthy people are similar to people in other classes and by downplaying key differences between the wealthy and everyone else. Reading an article or a story that utilizes this frame, it is easy to believe that the very rich are just ordinary people who happen to have more money than the rest of us have and further, that if we just earned or saved a little bit more, we could be just like they are—if we wanted to be. If we are all alike, perhaps the concept of social class is outdated: the differences between us are simply gradations of accumulated wealth.

However, consensus framing largely ignores the vast differences in lifestyles and life chances—the extent to which individuals have access to such important societal resources as food, clothing, shelter, education, and health care—between the rich and the poor. According to the sociologist Dennis Gilbert, if income were a national pie that has been sliced into portions, the wealthiest 20 percent of U.S. households would receive almost 50 percent of the total income "pie," whereas the poorest 20 percent of households would receive less than 4 percent of all income.[31] In fact, the top 5 percent would receive more than 22 percent of all income—an amount greater than that received by the bottom 40 percent of all households.[32] To be in the top 1 percent of incomes, Americans had to earn a minimum of $293,000 in 2002; however, for the top tenth of 1 percent, the most prosperous 129,000 households in the United States, the average income was four million dollars, or a total income of $505 billion—an amount that is almost as much as the other nine-tenths of the top 1 percent.[33] These figures look only at income inequality; they do not take into account wealth inequality, which has also increased dramatically in recent decades. It is estimated, for example, that the top 1 percent of wealth holders in this country owned about 38 percent of net worth in 1998. As Gilbert explains, "The concentration of wealth has become so great that the net worth of the top 1 percent is roughly equal to that of the bottom 90 percent."[34] Consensus framing ignores the fact that few people in the top tiers of the upper class derive their income from a paycheck for hours worked, that the wealthy are not likely to experience the economic and psychological hardships of the unemployed or the homeless, and that wealth may afford some people more leisure time, better security, better health care, and better connections and opportunities for their children than are available to persons with less wealth.

Despite the vast differences in income and wealth across the United States, consensus framing of media stories serves the purpose of portraying the very rich as similar to everyone else or of showing how the affluent and nonaffluent should agree on certain pressing issues or social problems. Articles about terrorism and natural disasters often use this framing device to show that the rich and poor alike suffer from devastating events such as the September 11, 2001, terrorist attacks on the United States or a major disaster such as a tornado, flood, or fire. The burning of multimillion-dollar homes in California's 2003 major fires was frequently juxtaposed with the losses of middle- and lower-income families resulting from this disaster, often without adequate mention of the greater problems that the nonwealthy (especially the uninsured and the underinsured) would have in replacing their damaged or destroyed property.

Consensus ("we are all alike") framing is compatible with the ideological perspective of scholars who believe that class is no longer a meaningful analytical concept for studying social life in the United States. For example, John Pakulski and Malcolm Waters argue that advanced or postmodernist consumer culture has shifted the focus from class-based relations to relations based on "taste," "fashion," and "lifestyle," which have become key sources of social differentiation and affiliation, thereby displacing the old identity packages such as class.[35] Pakulski and Waters contend that key groupings in contemporary society are not organized around class per se but rather around noneconomic, nonclass bases, including "ethnicity, gender, value-commitment, life-style, and consumption."[36] Some analysts refer to this idea as the class convergence thesis, which is based on the assumption that differences in lifestyle between the wealthy, capitalist class, and the working class have largely diminished or disappeared.[37]

Previous assessments of how the media report on the wealthy have not examined the consensus approach to news reporting as much as they have analyzed existing media content to determine which topics are most frequently presented and to assess whether these topics are class specific or not. Many media scholars believe that news media content focuses almost exclusively on issues of concern to middle- and upper-class readers and viewers. News items of concern to the wealthy, such as stock market and other business reports, are routinely presented with a pressing urgency suggesting that most American families own stock and cannot wait for the latest reports from Wall Street and other financial markets.[38] However, the popularity of such reports primarily rests with the more affluent members of society, because, as previous studies have shown, "Most American families do not own any type of stock and four out of five families do not own stock directly. In fact, 86 percent of the nation's stock is owned by just 10 percent of the nation's families.[39] As media scholars David Croteau and William Hoynes state, "Thus, the vast majority of the public is unlikely to be interested in stock reports. Most Americans do not even understand stock listings and reports. Yet stock market reports are a prominent feature of news programs and newspapers."[40] According to Croteau and Hoynes, stock market reports vastly outnumber news stories on topics such as how to apply for welfare benefits or workers' rights to form a union.

Although he does not refer to it as media framing, sociologist Greg Mantsios argues that the media often send the message that "the wealthy are us."[41] He notes that everything from business reports to fashion pages, sports news, wedding announcements, and obituaries often have a built-in class bias that is not detected by ordinary readers and viewers. According to Mantsios, although the news as reported may have practical value to the wealthy, it has a strong ideological value in that it sends the message that "the concerns of the wealthy are the concerns of us all."[42]

Political reporting is a key area of news coverage in which the rich are sometimes portrayed as being like everyone else. Obviously, this framing technique has the approval of wealthy politicians and their spokespersons, who hope, at least for the duration of an election, to show that even though the candidate is wealthy, he or she shares important concerns and lifestyle elements with the people in other classes. *New York Times* articles offer numerous examples of the consensus framing of political reporting. For example, despite the elitist title "Off and Running for the Silk Stockings," an article on Gail Hilson's 2002 bid for the State Assembly from the Seventy-third District (one of New York City's wealthiest Zip codes) began with the idea that Hilson was a down-to-earth person interested in serving others, not just another rich socialite:

> On Gail Hilson's wish list for last January, you won't find the plans that some of her friends might have jotted down. There is no mention of skiing in Aspen, relaxing in St. Bart's or getting a little work done around the eyes. Ms. Hilson, 60, is one of New York City's social lions, a fund-raiser for causes like breast cancer. . . . This summer, in an announcement that surely sent some of her friends straight to the fourth floor of Bergdorf's for a nerve-steadying shot of cashmere, she became the Republican Party candidate for State Assembly. . . . Come January, she hopes to be loading her Saville Row suits and her gumball-size pearls into her BMW station wagon and hitting the New York State Thruway for Albany.[43]

Moreover, Sunday Style section writer Nancy Haas informs readers that Ms. Hilson does not see herself as a "bored socialite craving a bit of novelty." As the candidate herself is quoted as saying, "It's not as though I'm the sort of person who sits by the [fashion show] runway with a pad in her hand or spends her days shopping."[44] Journalist Haas points out that relatively speaking, Ms. Hilson is not extremely wealthy: "Ms. Hilson knows some people will dismiss her because her looks and demeanor connote money and privilege, but she points out that she is not particularly wealthy by local standards."[45] To support this statement, Haas continues: "[Ms. Hilson] doesn't have a house in the country and proudly declares that the Louis Vuitton umbrella in the corner is a $10 knockoff from Canal Street."[46]

This article about Ms. Hilson's political aspirations (she lost the election to Jonathan L. Bing, an attorney) was located in the Sunday Style section of the *New York Times,* but other wealthy candidates and elected officials, such as New York City's mayor, Michael R. Bloomberg, are often featured on the front page of that newspaper, especially when they are doing something that might endear them to the masses. In one article, "Bloomberg's Salon, Where the Powerful Mix over Meatloaf," journalist Jennifer Steinhauer emphasizes that multibillionaire Mayor Bloomberg, who owns not only a seventeen-million-dollar, five-story, 7,500-square-foot limestone Beaux-Arts mansion in Manhattan but sprawling homes in North Salem (New York), Vail (Colorado), Bermuda, and London,[47] likes to serve "common folk" food, including meatloaf and mashed potatoes, potpie, scrambled eggs, and grilled hotdogs to people he invites to his Manhattan mansion.[48] The article begins, "A few times a month, 20 or so New Yorkers open their closets and contemplate what to wear to eat meatloaf at the Beaux-Arts town house of the 108th mayor of New York."[49] Of course, as the article states, most people who are invited to come eat meatloaf with the mayor are celebrities, executives, and socialites who arrive for "an evening of comfort food, highbrow chitchat and networking."[50]

Articles like this typically appeal to middle- and upper-middle class readers, who are the primary purchasers of the *New York Times.* The framing of the article appears to be democratic, because the very wealthy mayor is acting like an ordinary person and the meatloaf and potpie have middle- to working-class connotations. However, the menu served by the mayor's staff also includes cocktail hors d'oeuvres, a first course of asparagus with lemon butter, a main course of meatloaf and potatoes, a dessert of berry cobbler with ice cream, an assortment of wines served throughout dinner, and after-dinner cookies decorated to reflect the interests of individual diners, including "a Labrador retriever for the dog lover, the insignia from Yale's rowing team for an alumnus, or the seal of a hospital for a generous donor."[51] Although the framing of this front-page article is built on the consensus approach ("we're all the same; even rich people eat meatloaf"), it brings into sharp contrast both the commonalities and differences of people in divergent class locations.

If the media portray the wealthy as just like everyone else ("good ole boys"), it obscures vast differences in economic conditions in the United States. If the very wealthy are viewed as down-home people who just have more money than everyone else, the invidious distinctions inherent in the capitalist economy are obscured and class-based oppression is downplayed, or appears to be nonexistent, in news accounts and entertainment programming.

As the Bloomberg example shows, one technique of consensus framing is to present extremely wealthy people as basically like people in other classes but then to set them apart from others by emphasizing their wealth or "ruling class" position in society. Using this "hook" to catch the interest of media audiences, the newspaper or television journalist initially leads readers or viewers to perceive the wealthy individual as just an average person, perhaps no different from someone in the middle class, on the basis of the individual's lifestyle or appearance. However, this down-home image is juxtaposed with an elaborate description of the person's material possessions or net worth, thereby clearly setting the wealthy subject apart from ordinary people. Consider, for example, this paragraph about S. I. Newhouse, Jr., a family "ruler" of the Condé Nast media empire:

> The lights of Midtown Manhattan still twinkle in the early-morning darkness as a man walks toward 4 Times Square, a huge office tower. He is short and moves with a shuffle, a gait that suggests he may be a bit old for punching a clock at 5 A.M. With his khakis, loafers, and a green sweatshirt that seems too big on him, he could be one of the kitchen staff showing up to prep food at the vaunted Condé Nast cafeteria, four floors up.
>
> But look closer at the sweatshirt and the outline of the *New Yorker* logo emerges. Peer closer at the man and S. I. Newhouse, Jr., is revealed, one of the world's richest men and the owner, along with the rest of his family, of a far-flung and immensely profitable media empire. As chairman of Condé Nast Publications, he presides over magazines like *Vogue, Vanity Fair* and yes, *The New Yorker*—shiny totems built to assemble wealthy readers and the advertisers who covet them.[52]

This is a typical introduction for an article about a business empire and the wealthy people who control it. When a very wealthy individual does not appear to embrace overtly the trappings of great wealth, reporters often see in this a newsworthy beginning for a story even if the majority of the article concerns the holdings of the person's business empire and personal wealth. By starting the article in this manner, members of the media build a tension or internal contradiction into the story line—juxtaposing appearance and reality—and thus showing media audiences that things are not always as they seem. This framing device allows journalists to reveal significant discrepancies between *appearance* and *reality* without questioning economic inequality, particularly the source of the wealth and how it is otherwise spent. Journalists who use this approach are more likely to get interviews and personality profiles from wealthy individuals, many of whom are leery of publications that do not always show them in a favorable light. For this reason, images of the wealthy as generous and caring people who engage in acts of philanthropy are among the most common forms of media coverage for individuals and families in the top economic tiers of society.

ADMIRATION FRAMING:
THE WEALTHY ARE GENEROUS AND CARING PEOPLE

The media also tend to serve the interests of the wealthy when they engage in admiration framing, showing the rich as generous and caring people who share their vast resources with other people and organizations. Although philanthropy, which involves a spirit of goodwill toward others as demonstrated in efforts to promote their welfare, takes place at all levels of the class structure, major contributions of money to worthy causes are uniquely identified with the upper classes, whose members can make larger financial contributions (even extremely large ones) than do those in the lower tiers of the class structure.[53] In this case, the media may serve as a public relations outlet for the wealthy, helping to take away the rough edges of their business dealings and (sometimes) unscrupulous acts by letting others know about their good deeds. Of course, some wealthy donors prefer to remain anonymous; however, taken as a whole, these individuals are fewer in number than those who desire to see their names on the buildings of well-known hospitals and universities or on the major donor lists of high-prestige nonprofit organizations.

Admiration framing is often used to publicize a high-society social event that raises money for a good cause. This type of coverage includes lavish descriptions of charity galas and other black-tie events, such as balls sponsored by hospital foundations or arts organizations. Events that raise money for the symphony or opera not only serve as fund-raising events but provide opportunities for the wealthy and well connected to socialize; media reports typically describe the duality between raising money for the cause and spending vast amounts of money to stage the event or to attend it. French sociologist Pierre Bourdieu used opera performances as an example, stating that such performances "are the occasion or pretext for social ceremonies enabling a select audience to demonstrate and experience its membership in high society in obedience to the integrating and distinguishing rhythms of a 'society' calendar."[54] Similarly, charity events provide elites and wannabe elites with such venues.

Extensive media coverage of high-priced charity parties may gain the admiration (or the disdain) of the general public. When the media record these prestigious, by-invitation-only events, they provide people in other classes glimpses of how key players in high-society social events conduct their lives. The typical tone of such reports can be seen in an article ("Hi, Society!") describing the socialite party organizer for an expensive charity event benefiting Houston's Stages Repertory Theatre:

> "Oh, you must come. You simply *must* come," Becca Cason Thrash exclaimed. [The journalist] had called her to see if he could get himself invited to the party she was throwing in April to benefit Houston's Stages Repertory Theatre. "We're calling the night 'A Celebration of American Fashion,'" she said. . . . "And I assume it's black-tie?" [the journalist] asked. "High black-tie, my dear. This party is going to be flawless, absolutely flawless, and I expect everyone to look their best."[55]

This article uses admiration framing in the introduction and follows with a personality profile of a key person involved. Eventually this article, and others like it, discuss the significance of the large sums of money raised by the event. However, most articles emphasize the elaborateness of the event itself rather than the worthiness of the cause being benefited. Based on admiration framing, the behavior of those who spend thousands of dollars on tickets and clothing to wear to the event is justified because the event raises a large sum of money for a worthy cause.

However, as some journalists point out, not all charity fund-raising is so glamorous. Some big-ticket fund-raisers benefit causes such as AIDS research, homes for abused and neglected children, or schools for the disadvantaged. In this case, high-profile organizers and donors are important for the success of the event, because they will capture more media coverage than less-well-known individuals. For example, media sources—ranging from websites to news magazines and daily papers—carry lead stories about very wealthy people and well-known people like Bill and Melinda Gates when they give away billions of dollars for such nonelite causes as bringing better health care to the world's poorest children[56] or providing better schools for the disadvantaged in the United States.[57] Rather than emphasizing opulent events, these media reports focus on the down-home nature of foundations like the one started by Gates.

According to one media report, the Gates Foundation, unlike the posh old-line charities, operates in the "bare bones" environment of a refurbished check-processing plant that abuts a working dock on Lake Union (in Seattle) and has no imposing nameplate on the building, just a street number.[58] The seemingly low-profile, "no publicity please" approach of some contemporary philanthropists may diffuse public frustration about current economic crises and the excesses of contemporary capitalism. Philanthropy, when set in an admiration frame by the media, may help soften the rough edges of the capitalist economy in much the same way that the sociologist G. William Domhoff suggests that the charitable work of privileged women volunteers helps to offset the public negative image of their elite husbands' sometimes unsavory business practices.[59]

Although the down-home nature of some philanthropists may be the focus of some media reports, many other articles and television shows highlight what the rich and famous are doing in expensive surroundings, enjoying lavish food and entertainment in the name of charity fund-raising. From Manhattan to Houston and from San Francisco to Atlanta, media descriptions of these parties typically are similar to this one about the charity parties organized by the social organizer mentioned above, Becca Cason Thrash of Houston:

> Some of Becca's parties looked like they cost a small fortune. At one Venetian-themed fete for [the] Houston Grand Opera, she had an authentic gondola shipped from St. Louis, lowered by a crane through a skylight, and placed in her swimming pool. At another party for Best Buddies, which she called "Shanghai in the Spring," she transformed her home into . . . a Far East still life filled with Asian statuary, golden parasols, and dangling lanterns.[60]

According to journalists, organizers of lavish charity events like these argue that such expenditures and visible signs of conspicuous consumption are necessary for successful major fund-raising endeavors, because they inspire rich donors to contribute to a good cause. Privileged women who frequently plan these social/charitable events for the wealthy and well connected also believe that media coverage is crucial for the success of the event.[61] Evidence of this is found in columns such as "Boldface Names" in the *New York Times,* in the lifestyle sections of local newspapers, and the "neighborhood" newspapers (such as *Park Cities People* in Dallas) available in expensive residential enclaves.

Admiration framing is also widely used by the media to describe situations in which naming rights have been purchased. The term *naming rights* describes a practice whereby universities, hospitals, and other charitable organizations offer, for a large fee, to name a building or a portion of a structure (such as the surgical wing of a hospital, a theater within an arts complex, or even a stone paver) after an individual, family, or corporation. Many examples of naming rights can be found on university campuses throughout the nation. For example, although since 1981 the University of Texas at Austin's basketball arena and special events center had borne the name "Frank C. Erwin, Jr. Special Events Center," in honor of a former regent of the UT system, the university in 2003 announced that naming rights for the newly renovated building were for sale at a cost of up to two million dollars a year.[62] Some colleges, universities, hospitals, museums, and arts venues bear the names of corporations—such as Comcast Arena (at the University of Maryland) or Value City Arena (at Ohio State University); other buildings are named for individuals or families who have made significant financial contributions. The McCombs School of Business at the University of Texas at Austin, for example, is named for Red McCombs, a major university donor who owns car dealerships and a National Football League franchise. Humor is frequently employed in media framing of stories about very wealthy philanthropists like McCombs. For example, media accounts of the McCombs naming event often mention a comment by the also-very-wealthy Southwest Airlines founder Herb Kelleher: "For $50 million, I'll change my name to Red McCombs."[63]

Not all media reports of naming events describe acknowledgments on such a grand scale as placing major donors' names on the sides of coliseums or academic buildings. Some stories relate how people who give fifty or a hundred thousand dollars in charitable donations receive little recognition other than having their name placed on a small stone paver or a donors' wall. Media reports of philanthropy at Disney Hall in Los Angeles are an example. According to one journalist, Disney Hall came in at nearly double the original projected construction budget and that consequently this project "became a rare naming opportunity, a kind of permanent billboard for wealthy people to have their names inscribed."[64] Newspaper and television accounts of this naming event showed that donors giving fifty thousand dollars were honored with stone pavers (with their names two inches tall on them) in the concert hall's terrace garden, while those contributing a hundred thousand were honored with inch-and-a-half letters on the "Donors Wall" (located in a more visible interior position). According to media reports, many people seized upon this naming opportunity and gave much more: "Every atrium, every staircase, every reception room, even every escalator in and around Disney Hall carries the name of a benefactor."[65]

Even in situations where a major naming-rights donor later is involved in a scandal or crime, media representations continue to speak about the individual with a degree of admiration. What happens when the name of a major donor who has bought naming rights later becomes tarnished? A typical example arises in the *New York Times* article, "If a Name Is Tarnished, but Carved in Stone," which describes the problem experienced by administrators and regents at the University of Michigan at Ann Arbor when A. Alfred Taubman, an extremely generous donor, was convicted of price fixing:

> Valets were parking cars and assisting patients at the A. Alfred Taubman Health Care Center here last Wednesday when a federal jury in Manhattan convicted Mr. Taubman, principal owner of Sotheby's, in a price-fixing scheme. Just down the hill, University of Michigan students were entering the A. Alfred Taubman Medical Library to study for exams. Nearby, aspiring designers were completing end-of-term projects at the A. Alfred Taubman College of Architecture and Urban Planning. . . . Mr. Taubman, who attended Michigan but left before graduating, has given more than $35 million to the university. His generosity does not stop there. His name is on institutes at Harvard and Brown, he leads a list of the most generous donors at Michigan State University, and he has given millions to Detroit area charities.[66]

In articles about the Taubman scandal and how it might affect naming-rights issues at universities and medical centers, media writers chronicled Taubman's good works and frequently concluded with statements such as this: "Mr. Taubman's philanthropy, rather than his conviction, could still prove to be his legacy."[67]

Admiration framing by the media typically includes informing ordinary people how much it costs to be considered a real philanthropist. Journalists place price tags on donations and tell what contributors received in return. Admiration framing sends a mixed message to media audiences about philanthropy. On one hand, by informing readers and viewers about the large sums of money contributed by wealthy individuals, the media suggest that the average person cannot make a difference, while on the other, editorials may urge each of us to learn from the good deeds of others and follow their example. It is at this point that admiration framing becomes blurred with emulation framing, which suggests that ordinary people should be like rich people.

EMULATION FRAMING:
THE WEALTHY PERSONIFY THE AMERICAN DREAM

The most obvious example of emulation framing of the rich and famous is often found on the editorial pages of major newspapers or in television commentaries about the charitable contributions of the very wealthy. Although news articles about philanthropists reiterate the generosity of those who give money for a good cause and typically include photographs of those individuals, editorial comments further edify readers and viewers with the *significance* of major charitable contributions and tend to suggest that ordinary people should also be philanthropists. Two editorials are instructive on this point.

The first is about the Long Center for the Performing Arts in Austin, Texas. Banker and lawyer Joe R. Long and his wife, Teresa, had given an initial gift of twenty million dollars to start the fund-raising campaign for transforming an old city auditorium (previously named for Lester E. Palmer, a former mayor) into a state-of-the art performing arts venue. Long is quoted as saying: "It gives us a great deal of satisfaction in seeing something done with our money while we're still alive. . . . [This project] could have an impact on lives in this community for the next 50 years." The editorialist's comments, "In the coming years, that kind of thinking and generosity will be important not only for maintaining, but advancing, the quality of life Austinites revere."[68] Although other wealthy donors, including Michael and Susan Dell, have reached into their pockets to give ten million dollars to help complete the project,[69] average citizens do not see themselves as in the same financial league as these individuals, and funds have been slow coming in long after the construction project should have commenced.[70]

The second editorial, from the *Dallas Morning News* and also reported on its affiliated television station, WFAA, is about philanthropist Margaret McDermott's eight-million-dollar contribution for the design of two Trinity River bridges to enhance the appearance of roadways entering the city of Dallas. The editorial quotes McDermott: "If I'm a small catalyst in bringing this goal—this dream to reality, I'm thrilled. Also, I feel it might be the most meaningful thing I have been able to do for my city." The editorial comments, "This is the kind of philanthropy that turns a good city into a great one. . . . Ms. McDermott shows us how it is done. Let's all follow her lead."[71] It is unclear in either case what the average individual might do to equal such largesse, and editorialists typically do not suggest that small contributions might be as valuable to the public well-being as multimillion-dollar gifts from the wealthy.

Individuals on the lower rungs of the class system may be able to ignore the philanthropy of the rich and famous, but it is more difficult to ignore media stories about people who move from "rags to riches" through hard work and determination. This kind of emulation framing raises the question, "If they can do it, why can't you?" It further suggests that the United States is the land of opportunity where anyone who works hard and plays by the rules can achieve the American Dream.[72] Basic tenets of this dream are the beliefs that each generation should have a higher standard of living than the previous one[73] and that all people, regardless of their race, creed, color, national origin, gender, or religion, are on a level playing field. with an equal opportunity to get ahead. According to the political scientist Jennifer Hochschild, four key beliefs are associated with the American Dream: everyone can participate equally and can always start over if they need to; it is reasonable to anticipate success; success results from individual actions and traits that are under the individual's control; and success is associated with virtue and merit, whereas failure is linked to lack of talent or will.[74] These beliefs are incorporated into emulation framing of stories about the rich, particularly those who came from working-class or poverty-level origins.

Contemporary framing of media stories about individuals from humble origins who made fortunes during their lifetimes is inspired by the old Horatio Alger rags-to-riches stories of the late nineteenth century. Horatio Alger–type stories perpetuate the American Dream by telling sagas of people who rise from poverty to wealth through hard work, individual initiative, and merit. Although belief in the American Dream may give working- and lower-class people some degree of hope for a better future, this ideology hides structural barriers to upward mobility. Ironically, some American Dream stories in the media contradict the notion that hard work and traditional values are important, because a few tell of individuals who get rich by nothing more than "good luck" in games of chance. According to recent television, Internet, and newspaper accounts, the contemporary American Dream may be achieved through winning the lottery or being chosen the winner on TV reality shows like *American Idol* or *Bachelorette*.

Looking more closely at the lottery, stories about people who win multimillion-dollar lotteries like Powerball typically include at least these three points: the humble origins of the winners, their extreme luck—which might also come to others if they purchase lottery tickets, and the hardworking nature of the winners, even after their windfall. The story "School Cooks Win over $95 million in Powerball" contains all three ingredients:

> They waited until the students got their lunch, then 15 school cooks and one janitor who each put a quarter into a lottery pool came forward Monday night as the holders of a Powerball ticket worth more than $95 million.
>
> The women started their first Monday as millionaires back on the school lunch line where they fed the students in the tiny Holdingford School District before hopping a bus to the state lottery headquarters to claim their prize.[75]

From that media report we learn of the persistence of the school workers, in that they put a quarter from each paycheck toward the purchase of four Powerball tickets for more than a decade before one of theirs became one of the two winning tickets for the $190.9 million Powerball jackpot. The women's continuing dedication to their jobs was emphasized by the journalist, who pointed out that the women did not plan to immediately give up their school lunch jobs, because, as one of the winners stated, "The kids come first."[76]

Although some rags-to-riches media stories are based on one-time windfalls like winning the lottery, other stories employing emulation framing describe how an individual rose from poverty to wealth through entrepreneurship. Media sources around the world have told the inspiring story of Oprah Winfrey, one of the world's wealthiest women, because she is seen as personifying the American Dream. Since the often-repeated theme of her television program, books, and lectures is the importance of self-empowerment, she serves as a media role model among the downtrodden for success. A typical example of media framing about her humble origins and her rise to wealth is, "Somewhere en route from dirt-poor Mississippi schoolgirl to TV news anchor to talk-show empress to award-winning actress to therapist for an anxious nation, Oprah Winfrey became a businesswoman."[77] Journalism accounts of Winfrey's success carefully regale audiences with the fortune she has amassed from *The Oprah Winfrey Show,* which has twenty-two million U.S. viewers, airs in 107 countries, and brings in about $300 million each year. This amount does not include $140 million from *O, the Oprah Magazine,* or proceeds from her extensive business empire in movie production, cable TV, and the Internet. Winfrey's message, "You are responsible for your own life," is in keeping with the ideal of the American Dream, and this makes it all the easier for journalists to frame stories about her in the emulation model.

Winfrey herself has never suggested that anyone can be "Oprah," but media accounts of her success suggest that others could do as well. According to one journalist, "By making herself and her struggles central to her message, [Winfrey] taps deeply into the American psyche and its desire for self-reliance."[78] According to "The Church of O" (an article in *Christianity Today*), Winfrey has become one of the most influential spiritual leaders in America by seeking to empower others.[79] Her gospel includes the belief that people can change and that they are responsible for their own destinies. Members of media audiences who see Winfrey as a role model may gain the unrealistic expectation that they too can become successful if they only work harder or are willing to change some negative aspect of their lives. This is a central message of emulation framing: "You too can get ahead (like this person) if you try hard enough. If you are not successful, you have no one to blame but yourself."

Emulation framing involves not only class but race and gender. As an African American woman, Winfrey becomes the model for economic, gender, and racial/ethnic empowerment. She is not alone, however, in being praised for her ability to rise about inequalities based on race and class. Another example is E. Stanley O'Neal, an African American who rose from humble origins to become chief executive of Merrill Lynch:

> The chief executive of Merrill Lynch, E. Stanley O'Neal, has never been big on clubs. To Mr. O'Neal, who grew up poor in a small Alabama town as a grandson of a slave, clubs symbolize one thing: exclusion. Last June, Mr. O'Neal became a director at the New York Stock Exchange, the oldest and most exclusive club on Wall Street. . . . "They run that place like a club, and I've never been part of that club," a Merrill Lynch executive said Mr. O'Neal told him.[80]

Emulation framing in news stories on wealthy individuals of color suggests that two barriers can be broken down relatively easily in our society: class-based inequality and historical patterns of racism. This type of framing suggests that low-income people, even those who historically have been the objects of discrimination, can rise up and achieve the American Dream of success and wealth. Given the long odds against such an outcome, emulation framing not only creates unrealistic expectations given current economic and social realities but provides an excuse for those who are better off financially to be derisive of those who are not. Emulation framing of stories about self-made millionaires and billionaires, particularly those who have demonstrated business acumen or talent as entrepreneurs, entertainers, or athletes, perpetuates the myth of the American Dream. Beyond descriptions of how the rich and famous attain the American Dream, media stories also suggest that a part of that dream is the continuous consumption of expensive goods and services in accordance with a gospel of materialism.

PRICE-TAG FRAMING:
THE WEALTHY BELIEVE IN THE GOSPEL OF MATERIALISM

The term *price-tag framing* describes the practice of making the cost of luxury items a key feature in media stories about the rich and famous. While straight news accounts typically provide information about the basic *who, what, when, where, why,* and *how,* price-tag framing focuses on *how much.* Notwithstanding the old saying, "If you have to ask how much it costs, you can't afford it," price-tag framing informs media audiences how much luxury items cost and who owns them. From the Internet and television to news-papers and magazines, price-tag framing is an extremely popular storytelling device, because it has the effect of entertaining and shocking media audiences with the costly spending habits of the very wealthy. Media descriptions of the power-lunch hamburger (stuffed with foie gras and short ribs) for twenty-nine dollars, the six-thousand-dollar shower curtain in the maid's room, or the twenty-million-dollar mansion inform audiences about how at least some of the wealthy spend their money.

However, publicizing the price tag of goods and services also sets apart the wealthy from other people and in the process establishes a barrier between the lifestyles of the rich and those of other classes. According to one journalist's account of power lunches in New York's finest restaurants, "[Prices] can act as a kind of velvet rope to keep out tourists and people paying their own way, allowing a big hitter to tuck in a napkin secure in the belief that no one who works for him can afford to walk in the door."[81] Price-tag framing provides "outsiders" with information about what luxury items cost, but it also establishes the notion that people in other classes are categorically excluded from many elite settings by their inability or unwillingness to pay such prices.

Journalists employing price-tag framing for their stories typically use the concept of *conspicuous consumption,*[82] formulated by the economist Thorstein Veblen (who wrote at the turn of the twentieth century), to describe the excessive and extravagant purchases of the wealthy. According to Veblen, conspicuous consumption is one of many signs of the superfluous lifestyle of the wealthy. However, contemporary media reports often not only condemn but glorify excessive spending on the part of the wealthy, in order to gain media audiences and advertising revenue.

If one tenet of the American Dream is that individuals can rise from humble origins to great wealth, another is that given great wealth a person can spend extravagantly and enjoy the "good life." Returning to the American Dream saga of Oprah Winfrey, for example, media reports about her not only mention stories of her childhood, youth, and rise to fame but also how much it costs to be Oprah. An example is this *Chicago* magazine article, "The Richest Chicagoans" (which was also carried by the Associated Press, CNN, and FOX News International, among others):

> If the economic downturn is worrying some, it's not stopping the world's most famous woman, who in April dropped $50 million for a 10,000-square-foot estate on 40 acres in Montecito, near Santa Barbara, California. She retains her homes in Colorado and downtown Chicago, and a farm in LaPorte, Indiana. *Forbes* estimates her wealth at around $900 million.[83]

In two brief sentences, the article makes readers aware of Winfrey's ownership of multiple residences, the latest of which cost an amount equal to what the United Nations requested in 2003 to feed two million Colombian refugees.

The cost of luxury residences and the identities of the rich and famous people who live in them underlie one of the most widely used forms of price-tag framing in the media. Another example is a recent report about the most expensive gated communities in the United States. According to *Forbes* magazine and Forbes.com,[84] one of these communities is Beverly Park (Los Angeles), California, where homes, ranging in size from eight to forty thousand square feet, sell for between $7 million and $23.5 million; current residents include media stars Denzel Washington, Sylvester Stallone, Eddie Murphy, and Paul Reiser, and such top executives as Sumner Redstone, CEO of the media giant Viacom.

Price-tag framing the homes of the wealthy is not limited to how large the residence is or where it is located; some stories emphasize intangible factors, such as how much a view costs. An example is the article "How Much Is That View in the Window?" in the *New York Times*. In the article, one of several that described fund-raising parties given in celebration of the 150th birthday of Central Park in Manhattan, the key issue was the cost of residences with the best views of the park: "'Central Park is the most expensive view,' Frederick W. Peters, the president of Ashforth Warburg Associates, said, and the most expensive views of it are from Fifth Avenue. Even in the less fashionable 90's on Fifth, a full-floor apartment with a view of the park, he said, 'will command 10 million bucks.' The same apartment on Fifth Avenue and 73rd street, he added, can run to $14 million."[85]

However, as the article notes, the price tag of the residence is based on both its view and its location: "There are limits to the power of views, however. The Manhattan skyline from New Jersey is incomparable. 'But once you go through the tunnel and cross the bridge, your real estate values drop,' said Henry Robbins, the vice president of Yale Robbins. 'Real estate is about location, location, location—and you're in New Jersey.'"[86] Price-tag framing makes readers aware that for some wealthy people residences are a statement of power and control. When owners have guests over, they insist that their guests look at the view; "their guests admire the view and [therefore] admire them."[87]

Although we might expect that celebrities who are continually in the media spotlight would be the subjects of price-tag framing, they are not the only ones who receive this kind of publicity. Articles about residences of the rich are not limited to those of the super rich living in large urban centers such as New York City, San Francisco, and Chicago. Local and regional newspapers and television stations often report on sales of top-priced luxury real estate. An article in the *Austin American-Statesman,* "Austin Mansion Sale's a Stunner," is an example:

> Radio industry millionaire Steve Hicks and his wife, designer Donna Stockton-Hicks, are buying the most expensive existing house in Austin: a 13,362-square-foot estate in the heart of Pemberton Heights, West Austin's most exclusive neighborhood. The asking price: $8.5 million, down from $10 million. . . . The estate's property tax bill last year was $138,000, not much less than the current median home price in Austin of $158,900.[88]

This article makes a point of comparing the tax bill on this luxury estate with the current median home price in the area to show how utterly unaffordable this property is for most people.

Even more elaborate descriptions of luxury residences, interior design, and other material possessions of the rich and famous are found in specialty magazines like *Millionaire, Robb Report,* and *Worth*; in business publications such as *Forbes* and *Fortune;* in regional magazines like *Texas Monthly;* and in city magazines, such as *D Magazine* (Dallas) and *Chicago*—all of which print articles and copious advertisements showcasing the luxury acquisitions of the affluent. Articles in these publications typically are available on companion websites such as Millionaire.com, and their subjects receive additional coverage from the Associated Press and other news services, bringing this information via Internet, television, or newspaper into the homes of people who do not subscribe to these high-end publications.

Luxury magazines targeting upper-middle- to upper-class readers frequently have tie-ins (whether intentional or not) between published articles and advertisements. *Texas Monthly,* which frequently publishes articles such as "Who Wants to Be a Billionaire? Ten of the Richest Texans Tell You How," carries many residential ads that sell "class" as well as a piece of real estate. A recent ad for The Woodlands, a relatively expensive residential community (prices range from four hundred thousand dollars to over two million) outside of Houston bears the headline: "Move to the Head of Your Class." A portion of the ad copy reads: "There is a class distinction that sets The Woodlands apart. An unparalleled class of living that you simply won't find anywhere else." After detailing such amenities as the six championship golf courses, the "peaceful, forested home sites," the lakefront estates, and the "unparalleled luxury and exclusivity of a private, gated community," the ad declares that the residences and the families who own them are "truly in a class of their own."[89]

As this advertisement suggests, how to live like the rich is a continuing subplot in price-tag framing by the media. Television networks such as E!, HGTV (Home and Garden Television), The Travel Channel, the Food

Network, and VH1 attempt to provide useful insights for middle- and working-class viewers into how the rich spend money. The Travel Channel, for example, offers programs such as "How the Rich Stay Young" and "Ways to Vacation Like a Millionaire," informing viewers that "when your ship does come in, you'll know where to go and escape to luxury." Suggesting that it might be possible for the ordinary viewer to live the lifestyle of the rich and famous, or to at least share a small sample of it, is a key technique in price-tag framing. Consider, for example, HGTV's program *Sensible Chic,* which features an expensive designer room that is re-created in an affordable way for the average viewer. A decorating expert first analyzes the design principles used in the expensive original, then viewers see at first hand how they too might apply those principles to produce a satisfying version that is less expensive but "sensibly chic." In programs like this viewers learn what luxury items cost and also that they can have the "look" without the price, giving them an opportunity to feel superior to people who spend excessively on material possessions.

It is not possible to provide examples of all the ways in which price-tag framing is used by the media. However, the following are frequent subjects of media price-tagging: lavish residences and residential enclaves; rare and highly valuable items such as art collections; luxury cars, yachts, and airplanes; tuition and other expenses incurred at private schools and elite universities; expensive toys for rich children and adults; membership dues in private clubs; and the cost of luxury dining, travel, and other leisure pursuits.

Of these, money spent on residences, lavish entertainment, and "toys" for the wealthy is a particular favorite for media coverage. The Neiman Marcus department store chain receives millions of dollars in free advertising each year from the media through articles and news stories about the items for sale in its annual *Christmas Book.* In 2003, the book's most expensive item was a Learjet 60, priced at more than twelve million dollars. Other "fantasy gifts" included a one-of-a-kind 44.6-karat yellow diamond for eight hundred thousand dollars and a 2004 BMW limited-edition coupe for seventy-five thousand. By informing everyday people of the prices of these luxury goods, the media make people aware of the conspicuous (or at least excessive) consumption of the wealthy and credit worthy. The department store is pleased to receive the free publicity about its merchandise, and media audiences have an inside view of how the rich might spend their money. According to a Neiman Marcus vice president of public relations, "Everybody is so jaded today, there's so little out there that makes you go, 'Oh, wow!' I like to think of the fantasy element as the equivalent of a Barbie dreamhouse for adults. There's nothing anyone really needs, but there's definitely things they can fantasize about having."[90]

Children's toys are another topic for media stories, particularly near Christmas. The old adage "The only difference between men and boys is the price of their toys" may have less meaning today than in the past, because the cost of some children's toys has skyrocketed. Manufacturers and retailers of expensive lines rely on the media to carry "news" stories about their toys, so as to fuel consumer desire for the latest playthings and gadgets for children. These "news items" typically have headlines like "Over-the-top gifts for junior? How about a $15,000 Lego life-size model of an NBA star, or a $2,500 gumball machine?"[91] Consider, for example, this item on *CNN Headline News* and CNN/Money.com:

> For parents eager to pull out all the stops for their kids' holiday gifts this year, there are a slew of hard-to-find pricey toys that run the gamut from cute and kitschy to blatantly outrageous. At Chicago-based retailer Hammacher Schlemmer, the hottest picks of unique playthings when money is no object, include a $2,500 Route 66 Gumball Machine, a human lawn-bowling game costing close to $6,000, and a $15,000 "levitating" Hover Scooter that supposedly transports the rider across the land on a cushion of air. Meanwhile, the "2003 Ultimate Toy Catalogue" from toy retailer FAO Schwarz features a holiday collection of expensive spoils such as a $15,000 Lego life-size model of NBA superstars Jason Kidd and Alan Houston and a $30,000 gasoline-powered off-roader vehicle, designed to give kids "their first driving experience." "These are lavish toys but they're also a lot of fun for both kids and adults," said Hammacher Schlemmer spokeswoman Sabrina Balthazar.[92]

Although fantasy toys such as junior-sized SUVs do not show up under the Christmas trees in most U.S. homes, journalists frequently report on the rich and famous who actually purchase such items for their children. For example, one "news" story told about actor Chris O'Donnell and NBA star Jason Kidd purchasing custom-built playhouses (with heat, insulation, and running water) for their children.[93] Based on media reports on wealthy parents' purchases for their children, some parents with average- or lower-than-average incomes feel inadequate because they cannot afford even the far-less-expensive items that they would like to buy for their own children.

Placing a price tag on exclusive residences, lavish toys, and other trappings of the rich and famous is not a recent media practice. In the 1980s, the television series *Lifestyles of the Rich and Famous* profiled the self-made members of that set, providing detailed reports on what they bought and how much it cost. Created and hosted by Robin Leach, himself a model for the American Dream who had risen from a shoe salesman to a wealthy television personality, *Lifestyles of the Rich and Famous* ran for thirteen seasons in over thirty countries and continues today in syndication and video games. Leach was the master of price-tag framing, showing viewers some of the lavish residences, luxury vehicles, and exotic travel destinations enjoyed by the world's wealthiest people.[94] At the end of each episode, Leach wished his viewers "champagne wishes and caviar dreams."

As that tag line suggests, the lifestyles of the rich and famous shown on Leach's program could be nothing more than "wishes" or "dreams" for the typical viewer. However, the series supported one of the key tenets of the gospel of materialism, namely that "greed is good," as the stockbroker Gordon Gekko (played by Michael Douglas) declared in the 1980s film *Wall Street*. The framing techniques employed in *Lifestyles of the Rich and Famous* apparently remain popular with television networks in the 2000s. For example, ABC has launched a new series, *Life of Luxury*, in which Robin Leach once again informs and entertains viewers with the luxurious possessions of such celebrities as the Hilton sisters (heiresses to the multimillion-dollar Hilton Hotel fortune), the Olson twins (actresses whose movies appeal to adolescent girls), Athena Onassis (granddaughter of the late, very wealthy shipping magnet Ari Onassis), and Tiger Woods (the professional golfer).

Price-tag framing not only tells media audiences how much the rich pay for their possessions but may suggest that ordinary people can live *like* millionaires, if on a reduced scale. An example is this promotional piece for the video game spun off from *Lifestyles of the Rich and Famous:* "You deserve to live the high life. The *Lifestyles of the Rich and Famous®* game gives you that rich feeling. . . . Limo, mansion and yacht symbols animate in amazing 3-D fashion when you land in winning combinations, adding adrenaline to the thrill of receiving a big payout. . . . With the *Lifestyles of the Rich and Famous®* game, you can get a taste of champagne wishes and caviar dreams."[95] By looking behind the scenes at how the rich live, *Lifestyles* shows and games place price tags on the lavish material possessions of the rich and famous, and offer viewers a chance either to pretend that they are part of that lifestyle or to ridicule it.

More recently, price-tag framing has been used in the story lines of many TV reality shows. Perhaps the most blatant example has been the flurry of news and entertainment stories about Paris and Nicky Hilton, the previously mentioned Hilton Hotel heiresses. VH1's *The Fabulous Life of the Hilton Sisters* is an excellent example of price-tag framing; in it the price of their various lavish possessions pops up on the TV screen (like an old-fashioned cash register) as the story of the sisters' lives unfolds. Viewers get the "inside scoop" on the costs of birthday celebrations, clothes, residences, and private jet travel. Everything from the tiny tigers the sisters own to their huge residences in the Hollywood Hills, South Hampton, and New York

City is given a price tag. The cost of the items is carefully put into perspective for middle- and lower-class viewers. For example, a one-hour shopping trip to Dior, the couture fashion designer, costs the Hilton sisters much more than the average person spends on clothing in a year.

As further evidence of the Hiltons' belief in the gospel of materialism, the sisters are shown wearing their $695 shoes or parading their Chihuahua, which is wearing a four-hundred-dollar dog sweater or a Chanel outfit that matches the sisters' clothing. As one reporter commented, "Even their dogs dress better than you do." The general consensus of reporters for celebrity publications who were interviewed for this VH1 program was that "the Hilton Sisters can have anything they want" and that "being a Hilton means that on the day you're born, you're already filthy rich." It should be noted that although this show describes the Hiltons' potential inheritance, the show also dutifully informed viewers that the Hilton sisters are out making their own fortunes through hard work, including starring in reality TV shows, modeling designer clothing, creating a line of fragrances, and designing handbags.

Media fascination with the Hilton sisters reveals the fine line between so-called reality and fiction in stories about the rich and famous. The price-tag framing found in *The Fabulous Life of the Hilton Sisters* is sharply contrasted with *The Simple Life,* another TV series about Paris Hilton, which was shown during the same TV season. *The Simple Life* tries to show that there is something money cannot buy—common sense. Episodes in this series frequently ridicule Paris Hilton (the great-granddaughter of Hilton Hotel founder Conrad Hilton) and Nicole Richie (daughter of singer Lionel Richie) as they leave behind their upper-class city lives for a rough-and-tumble existence on a working-class farm in Altus, Arkansas. The young women are expected to do farm chores and, in one episode, to work at a local Sonic Drive-In. Hilton and Richie demonstrate their ineptitude at tasks that ordinary people can easily perform. Media audiences might laugh at the "rich girls" because of their lack of savvy and their inability to live on a limited budget, but viewers may envy them anyway—because they do not *need* to know how to do these things and could live very well without ever working a day in their lives. The message is clear: these rich girls can easily get by without having to do the mundane tasks that are required of people in other classes. The fact that Hilton and Richie cannot keep a budget or buy groceries for fifty dollars may be humorous, but it also shows that money does not mean much to them. For example, in one episode, when the young women reach the grocery checkout counter and realize that they do not have enough money for their purchases, they ask the cashier to let them have the items anyway. The cashier replies, "This isn't a soup kitchen." Richie asks, "What does that mean, 'soup kitchen'?"

The issue of price-tag framing also comes into play in *The Simple Life* in regard to where people shop. Whereas Hilton and Richie come from a world of designer boutiques and luxury department stores, the Ledings, their Arkansas hosts, appear to be Wal-Mart people. Richie asks the Ledings, "Do you guys hang out at Wal-Mart? I've always heard that people hang out at Wal-Mart." Then Paris Hilton asks, "What is Wal-Mart? It is, like they sell wall stuff?"[96] After filming for the show was completed, Hilton admitted to reporters that she had heard of Wal-Mart: "I was just playing a part. If I knew what everything was, it wouldn't be funny."[97] Still, what television audiences saw was Hilton claiming never to have heard of Wal-Mart and giving the distinct impression that she is a rich kid who lives in an exclusive world of high-priced designer boutiques.

Some TV critics attribute the popularity of this show to the fact that it allows audiences to make fun of rich people and their apparent frailties. According to one critic, *The Simple Life* highlights "the tension between the rich and the poor using such extreme examples that the audience can feel superior to both."[98] As another critic stated, by showing the wealthy as having a "fish-out-of-water ineptitude," it also serves as a social leveler that gives the rich a "comeuppance."[99] We might ask, however, if viewing audiences do not also receive messages about the gospel of materialism from shows such as this, which they watch primarily to see individuals simply because they are rich. As the journalist Frank Rich suggests, *The Simple Life* is popular with some viewers because:

> money remains the last guilty pleasure in America. The obscenely rich engaging in conspicuous consumption or conspicuously idiotic behavior is the only excess that hasn't lost its power to amuse, titillate and shock. People watch Paris Hilton make a fool of herself because she's an heir to the $300 million Hilton hotel fortune, not because her wares top the thousands of competitors in the country's overstocked erotic supermarket.[100]

Apparently, there is truth to this assessment due to the popularity of a number of recent TV shows, ranging from *Born Rich, The Simple Life,* and *Rich Girls* to entertainment series like *The O.C.* and *Arrested Development,* all of which have story lines based on the rich. MTV's *Rich Girls* follows the antics of "repellent shopoholic heroines" Ally Hilfiger (daughter of Tommy Hilfiger, the clothing designer) and her wealthy friend Jamie Gleicher.[101] According to the *Rich Girls* website, the girls are "normal teenagers who enjoy doing normal teenage things like shopping, talking on the phone, and going to the prom." However, as the site notes, "There's one important difference between them and the rest of us—they're rich. Really, really, really rich."[102]

THE "TWENTY-FOUR-KARAT GOLD FRAME": EFFECTS OF FRAMING THE WEALTHY

How the media frame stories about the wealthy influences the opinions of people in other classes. Lacking personal encounters with extremely wealthy individuals, people in the middle, working, and poverty-level classes look to the media for an insider's view of how the other "half" lives. Television programs such as *E!, Entertainment Tonight, Inside Edition,* and *Access Hollywood* advertise that by watching them viewers can go behind the scenes to learn what goes on the lives of the rich and famous. Vicarious living through the media helps ordinary people feel that they know about celebrities and other wealthy individuals. Whether it is celebrity gossip ("Will Jennifer Garner and Ben Affleck get married?") or news stories about the scandals of the rich ("Can you believe that former Tyco International Chief Executive Dennis Kozlowski spent two million dollars for a week-long birthday party for his wife?"), many people talk about the good deeds and misfortunes of the wealthy as if they had personal knowledge of them. This illusion of familiarity is created over time by extensive media coverage of the rich and famous. However, it is important for us to evaluate the framing, because, like rose-colored glasses, a frame used to tell a story may distort our perceptions. As an artist once suggested, "The frame you select can completely change the look and feel of my painting. Choose your frame very carefully."

Similarly, as powerful purveyors of information and entertainment, how the media frame stories is a significant concern, because the frame constitutes a mental shortcut (schema) that we use in forming our thoughts not only about the wealthy but also about larger issues of social stratification and inequality. Media messages about the rich, such as that the wealthy are more powerful and somehow better than other people, may influence not only our views about the affluent but those about the poor and homeless.

This chapter has discussed four of the most frequently used frames for building news stories or entertainment story lines about the upper class. Consensus framing depicts the wealthy as like people in other classes and suggests that "we all put on our pants one leg at a time" regardless of our location in the class hierarchy. This framing technique ignores invidious distinctions in material possessions and life chances, distinctions brought about by vast economic differences in society. Showing the wealthy dining on meatloaf ignores larger social realities about the exploitative nature of capitalism or such pressing social problems as poverty and hunger. Left out of the picture by this frame are the vast differences between the rich and poor in regard to life expectancy, health care, police and other security protection, and many of the other factors that influence one's life chances. Consensus framing leaves media audiences with the impression that the concerns of the wealthy are the most important issues facing the nation.[103]

Admiration framing, which casts the wealthy as generous and caring people, provides media audiences with copious examples of how the rich help others. Based on the concept of *noblesse oblige* (that those who have much should give to those who are less fortunate), admiration framing highlights the contributions of the rich to prestigious institutions like universities and hospitals. A central message of admiration framing is that though the rich have so much money that they can afford to give away millions without diminishing their wealth, other people should follow their good example to whatever extent their finances allow. Admiration framing deflects criticism of the wealthy by portraying them as good citizens who put their money to work for others.

Emulation framing casts the wealthy in a very positive light. However, this type of framing goes one step beyond admiration framing by suggesting to media audiences that they should *be like* the rich, not just admire them. Based on the ideology of the American Dream, emulation framing plays on the widely held belief that anyone can become rich through hard work and determination. This type of framing offers people in other classes suggestions as to how they might emulate the lifestyle of the rich in small ways, such as by purchasing a bar of "luxury" soap or designing a room so that it will "look like a million" and thus share in the lifestyle of the rich and famous.

Emulation framing and price-tag framing are intertwined in many media stories. Cost often becomes a central issue in news or entertainment accounts about the rich and famous. For example, how much the individual spends on spa and beauty treatments and cosmetic surgery may become a major topic in a celebrity profile, overshadowing the person being interviewed. Although individuals are the topics of the news article or television story line, in actuality it is the products and services that are the stars. Audiences are left to ask, "Can you believe how much that costs?" Journalists and television writers realize that price-tag framing often produces ambivalent responses but know that it brings in viewers and readers in targeted age categories. Media audiences receive conflicting messages, one that preaches the gospel of materialism and another that disputes its worth. Preaching the gospel of materialism as practiced by the wealthy encourages some viewers to engage in excessive consumerism. Other audiences reject the idea that the measure of a person's worth is how much he or she owns. Overall, the message we may receive from price-tag framing—whether on middle- and working-class television shows like *The Price Is Right* or on upscale, celebrity programs like *Lifestyles of the Rich and Famous*—is that material possessions make some people happy and that a trip to the shopping mall can, at least temporarily, help us forget our worries.

In sum, media audiences receive mixed messages about the wealthy based on media portrayals of them. The ancient Greek philosopher Aristotle (384–322 BC) suggested that human passions (emotions) are present in antagonistic pairs: love and fear, shame and shamelessness, pity and resentment, and envy and contempt. Our beliefs about the rich and famous, as framed by media depictions, may come in pairs as well. We may simultaneously pity them ("Poor little rich girl") and resent them ("Life is unfair! Why do the rich have more than I do?"). We may not feel bad because a rich celebrity owns a particular possession (such as $250,000 sports car), but we may feel bad because we cannot afford that item ourselves. Stories about the wealthy particularly evoke contradictory emotions in audiences when the media employ two additional kinds of framing—sour grapes or wealthy scoundrel—as discussed in chapter 3.

NOTES

1. "How the Rich Kids Live," CNN.com, 2003.

2. F. Scott Fitzgerald, "The Rich Boy," in *The Short Stories of F. Scott Fitzgerald,* ed. Mathew J. Brucoli, 317–49 (New York: Scribner, 1995 [1926 in *Redbook* magazine]), 318.

3. Robert M. Entman and Andrew Rojecki, *The Black Image in the White Mind: Media and Race in America* (Chicago: University of Chicago Press, 2000).

4. Entman and Rojecki, *The Black Image in the White Mind,* 48–49.

5. Entman and Rojecki, *The Black Image in the White Mind.*

6. Dixon Wecter, *The Saga of American Society: A Record of Social Aspiration 1607–1937* (New York: Scribner, 1937), 348.

7. Mary Cable, *Top Drawer: American High Society from the Gilded Age to the Roaring Twenties* (New York: Atheneum, 1984).

8. Wecter, *The Saga of American Society,* 349.

9. Wecter, *The Saga of American Society,* 350.

10. Wecter, *The Saga of American Society.*

11. Quoted in Wecter, *The Saga of American Society,* 357.

12. Wecter, *The Saga of American Society,* 358.

13. Wecter, *The Saga of American Society,* 358.

14. Wecter, *The Saga of American Society,* 360.

15. Cable, *Top Drawer.*

16. Wecter, *The Saga of American Society.*

17. Quoted in Wecter, *The Saga of American Society,* 370.

18. Wecter, *The Saga of American Society,* 368.

19. Wecter, *The Saga of American Society.*

20. Cable, *Top Drawer*, 198.

21. Cable, *Top Drawer;* Wecter, *The Saga of American Society.*

22. Lucy Kavaler, *The Private World of High Society* (New York: David McKay, 1960), 77.

23. Kavaler, *The Private World of High Society,* 89.

24. Kavaler, *The Private World of High Society,* 92–93.

25. G. William Domhoff, "The Women's Page as a Window on the Ruling Class," in *Hearth and Home: Images of Women in the Mass Media,* ed. Gaye Tuchman, Arlene Kaplan Daniels, and James Benet, 161–75 (New York: Oxford University Press, 1978).

26. Domhoff, "The Women's Page as a Window on the Ruling Class," 175.

27. Alex Witchel, "Tacos, Stir-Fries and Cake: The Junior League at 102," *New York Times,* October 15, 2003, D1.

28. Witchel, "Tacos, Stir-Fries and Cake," D6.

29. S. Elizabeth Bird and Robert W. Dardenne, "Myth, Chronicle and Story: Exploring the Narrative Qualities of News," in *Social Meaning of News: A Text Reader,* ed. Daniel A. Berkowitz, 333–50 (Thousand Oaks, Calif.: Sage, 1997).

30. See also Linda Holtzman, *Media Messages: What Film, Television, and Popular Music Teach Us about Race, Class, Gender, and Sexual Orientation* (London: M. E. Sharpe, 2000); Gregory Mantsios, "Media Magic: Making Class Invisible," in *Privilege: A Reader,* ed. Michael S. Kimmel and Abby L. Ferber, 99–109 (Boulder, Colo.: Westview, 2003).

31. Dennis Gilbert, *The American Class Structure in an Age of Growing Inequality,* 6th ed. (Belmont, Calif.: Wadsworth, 2003).

32. Carmen DeNavas-Walt and Robert W. Cleveland, "Money Income in the United States: 2001," U.S. Census Bureau, Current Population Reports, P60-218 (Washington, D.C.: U.S. Government Printing Office, 2002).

33. David Cay Johnston, "Top 1% in '01 Lost Income, but Also Paid Lower Taxes," *New York Times,* September 27, 2003, B1, B2.

34. Gilbert, *The American Class Structure in an Age of Growing Inequality,* 101.

35. Jan Pakulski and Malcolm Waters, *The Death of Class* (Thousand Oaks, Calif.: Sage, 1996), and "The Reshaping and Dissolution of Social Class in Advanced Society," *Theory and Society* 25 (1996): 667–91.

36. Pakulski and Waters, "The Reshaping and Dissolution of Social Class in Advanced Society," 683.

37. Paul W. Kingston, *The Classless Society* (Stanford, Calif.: Stanford University Press, 2000).

38. David Croteau and William Hoynes, *Media/Society: Industries, Images, and Audiences,* 3rd ed. (Thousand Oaks, Calif.: Pine Forge, 2003); Mantsios, "Media Magic."

39. Lawrence Mishell, Jared Bernstein, and John Schmitt, *The State of Working America, 1998–99* (Ithaca, N.Y.: Cornell University Press, 1999), as cited in Croteau and Hoynes, *Media/Society,* 222.

40. Croteau and Hoynes, *Media/Society,* 222.

41. Mantsios, "Media Magic," 103.

42. Mantsios, "Media Magic," 103–4.

43. Nancy Haas, "Off and Running for the Silk Stockings," *New York Times,* October 6, 2002, ST2.

44. Haas, "Off and Running for the Silk Stockings," ST2.

45. Haas, "Off and Running for the Silk Stockings," ST2.

46. Haas, "Off and Running for the Silk Stockings," ST2.

47. Allen Salkin, "Homes, Sweet Homes: Michael Bloomberg's Real-Estate Holdings Are Fairly Modest—for a Multibillionaire," *New York Magazine,* April 15, 2002, 23.

48. Jennifer Steinhauer, "Bloomberg's Salon, Where the Powerful Mix over Meatloaf," *New York Times,* May 8, 2002, A1.

49. Steinhauer, "Bloomberg's Salon," A1.

50. Steinhauer, "Bloomberg's Salon," A1.

51. Steinhauer, "Bloomberg's Salon," A29.

52. David Carr, "Condé Nast Redesigns Its Future: Newhouse Plans a Transition but Tightens His Grip," *New York Times,* October 26, 2003, BU1.

53. See Diana Kendall, *The Power of Good Deeds: Privileged Women and the Social Reproduction of the Upper Class* (Lanham, Md.: Rowman & Littlefield, 2002).

54. Pierre Bourdieu, *Distinction: A Social Critique of the Judgement of Taste,* trans. Richard Nice (Cambridge, Mass.: Harvard University Press, 1984), 272.

55. Skip Hollingsworth, "Hi, Society!" *Texas Monthly* (September 2002): 165.

56. See Geoffrey Cowley, "They've Given Away $24 Billion. Here's Why. Bill's Biggest Bet Yet," *Newsweek,* February 4, 2002, 44–52.

57. See Karen W. Arenson, "Gates to Create 70 Schools for Disadvantaged," *New York Times,* March 19, 2002, A16.

58. Cowley, "They've Given Away $24 Billion."

59. Domhoff, "The Women's Page as a Window on the Ruling Class."

60. Hollingsworth, "Hi, Society!" 198, 200.

61. See Kendall, *The Power of Good Deeds.*

62. John Maher, "What's in a Name?" *Austin American-Statesman,* June 28, 2003, C1, C8.

63. Shonda Novak, Lori Hawkins, and Amy Schatz, "Overheard in Austin," *Austin American-Statesman,* February 22, 2002, D1.

64. Christopher Mason, "Where Everybody Has a Name," *New York Times,* October 26, 2003, ST1.

65. Mason, "Where Everybody Has a Name," ST1.

66. Micheline Maynard, "If a Name Is Tarnished, but Carved in Stone," *New York Times,* December 9, 2001, BU4.

67. Maynard, "If a Name Is Tarnished, but Carved in Stone," BU4.

68. "Philanthropy: Enriching Our Communities through Giving," *Austin American-Statesman,* January 1, 2002, A11.

69. Michael Barnes, "An Inside Look at the New Long Center," *Austin American-Statesman,* February 13, 2001, A1, A9.

70. Stephen Scheibal, "Long Center Asks City for $25 Million," *Austin American-Statesman,* February 1, 2003, A1, A10.

71. "Changing a City: Philanthropist Believes in Building Bridges," Dallas-News.com, 2003.

72. Jennifer L. Hochschild, *Facing Up to the American Dream: Race, Class, and the Soul of the Nation* (Princeton, N.J.: Princeton University Press, 1995).

73. Sheldon Danziger and Peter Gottschalk, *America Unequal* (Cambridge, Mass.: Harvard University Press, 1995).

74. Hochschild, *Facing Up to the American Dream,* 26–30.

75. "School Cooks Win over $95 Million in Powerball," *Dallas Morning News,* October 28, 2003, 5A.

76. "School Cooks Win over $95 Million in Powerball," 5A.

77. Patricia Sellers, "The Business of Being Oprah," *Fortune,* April 1, 2002, www.fortune.com (accessed March 30, 2002).

78. Sellers, "The Business of Being Oprah," 2002.

79. LaTonya Taylor, "The Church of O," *Christianity Today,* April 1, 2002, 38–45.

80. Landon Thomas, Jr., "Dismantling a Wall Street Club," *New York Times,* November 2, 2003, BU1.

81. David Carr, "The Powering Up of the Power Lunch," *New York Times,* December 10, 2003, D4.

82. Thorstein Veblen, *The Theory of the Leisure Class,* intro. Robert Lekachman (New York: Penguin, 1994 [1899]).

83. Jan Parr and Ted Shen, "The Richest Chicagoans: Who's Up, Who's Down?" *Chicago* (February 2002): 49.

84. "Most Expensive Gated Communities in America," Forbes.com, 2003.

85. Andrea Truppin, "How Much Is That View in the Window?" *New York Times,* September 18, 2003, D4.

86. Truppin, "How Much Is That View in the Window?" D4.

87. Truppin, "How Much Is That View in the Window?" D4.

88. Shonda Novak, "Austin Mansion Sale's a Stunner," *Austin American-Statesman,* September 25, 2003, A1.

89. "Move to the Head of Your Class" (advertisement), *Texas Monthly* (October 2003): 137.

90. Robert Janjigian, "A Learjet? You Shouldn't Have!" *Austin American-Statesman,* November 4, 2002, E1.

91. Parija Bhetnagar, "Over-the-Top Gifts for Junior," CNNmoney.com, money.cnn.com/2003/11/20/news/companies/expensive_toys/index.htm (accessed December 1, 2003).

92. Bhetnagar, "Over-the-Top Gifts for Junior."

93. Annelena Lobb, "Gifts for Kids Who Have It All," CNNmoney.com, 2002.

94. Barber and Associates, "Robin Leach," www.barberusa.com/pathfind/leach_robin.html (accessed November 20, 2003).

95. IGT, "Lifestyles of the Rich and Famous® Video Slots."

96. Quoted in Marc Peyser and B. J. Sigesmund, "Heir Heads," *Newsweek,* October 20, 2003, 54.

97. Michael A. Lipton and Steve Barnes, "Just How Real Was *The Simple Life? Take a Gander,*" *People,* December 15, 2003, 68.

98. James Poniewozik, "The New Class Action," *Time,* September 29, 2003, n.p.

99. Alessandra Stanley, "With a Rich Girl Here and a Rich Girl There," *New York Times,* December 2, 2003, B1.

100. Frank Rich, "When You Got It, Flaunt It," *New York Times,* November 23, 2003, AR1.

101. Alessandra Stanley, "Focusing on Residents of Gilded Cages," *New York Times,* October 27, 2003, B8.

102. Youthful viewers are encouraged to "Get a first-hand look at their super-fabulous life when MTV follows two of the wealthiest teens on the planet to see how they spend their mountains of money." After inviting teenaged girls to "get acquainted" with these very rich young women, it regales them with how much money the young women spend and encourages viewers to engage in vicarious living. Distinctions between the wealthy girls and viewers in the television audience are made readily apparent on the program's companion website in a feature titled "Reality Check: Us vs. Them," which reads:

> Rich Girls live on Park Avenue: We live in a trailer park.
> Rich Girls' dads own a clothing line: Our dads hang clothes from a line.
> Rich Girls live in penthouses: Our cousin once posed for *Penthouse.*
> Rich Girls take their dogs everywhere they go: We step in dog poo when we're on the go.
> Rich Girls enjoy filet mignon prepared by world-renowned chefs: We chow on Salisbury steak prepared by Lean Cuisine.
> Rich Girls lather themselves in riches: We steal hotel soap.

Rich Girls: Welcome to the World of Rich Girls. MTV, 2003. www.mtv.com/onair/rich_girls (accessed October 22, 2003).

103. See Mantsios, "Media Magic."

3

GILDED CAGES: MEDIA STORIES OF
HOW THE MIGHTY HAVE FALLEN

Kenneth Borovina, a 34-year-old carpenter from Dumont, N.J., has a lot to be stressed out about these days. His grandmother is in the assisted living wing of a local nursing home, and her life savings have gone from $600,000 to $250,000 in the last year, decimated by the sagging stock market. But there's one thing that cheers him: news that yet another rogue chief executive is under investigation or, better still, arrest.

"They're getting what they deserve," Mr. Borovina said. "That makes me feel great."

Mr. Borovina is indulging in what seems to be [a] favorite guilty pleasure—delighting in others' misfortune, or schadenfreude.[1]

As this news article suggests, certain types of media framing of stories about wealthy scoundrels produce *schadenfreude,* a feeling of malicious satisfaction in learning of the misfortune of others. However, the "sour-grapes" and "bad-apple" framing discussed in this chapter typically produces ambivalent feelings of both schadenfreude and a desire to know more about—and perhaps possess—the premium-price goods and services that are enjoyed by the very wealthy, even when they are in trouble with the law. Although media audiences may gain some satisfaction from learning about the problems of the rich, readers and viewers often believe that if they had as much money and all of the material possessions of the wealthy, they would do things differently: They would not be unhappy or get in trouble with the law because of excessive greed.

Recent coverage of the downfall of top corporate executives like L. Dennis Kozlowski (of Tyco) and Kenneth L. Lay (of Enron) has amply proven this point. Media reports of their legal problems have been full of stories about their residences, lavish lifestyles, and other forms of consumption in which they have engaged. These articles have been like a catalogue of conspicuous consumption, or as one journalist stated (in an article aptly titled "Lifestyles of the Rich and Red-Faced"), *mogul style* is less about conspicuous consumption than it is about *contemptuous consumption*: "It's the giddy spending of money—sometimes shareholders' money—and it results not in the pleasure of ownership or connoisseurship, but in the succulent gratification of making other moguls quake in their Gucci loafers."[2] This type of consumption, when made public by courtroom trials and the media, also influences people's perceptions about how the rich live and the emotional gratification that they too might receive from certain luxury possessions.

Sour-grapes and bad-apple framing focus on the problems of the rich as *individual* pathologies, not as structural concerns rooted in the larger economic, political, or social hierarchies of society, and these forms of framing often include detailed descriptions of the material possessions of the very wealthy. In sour-grapes framing, the rich are portrayed as frequently unhappy and dysfunctional people; in bad-apple framing, the rich have problems but still enjoy the good life. Since the focus of bad-apple framing typically is the *individual* scoundrel rather than many people or established corporate practices that may be harmful, media audiences typically view the problem as one of individual, rather than corporate, abuse. According to the media scholar Michael J. Parenti, when the wrongdoings of the rich are treated as nothing more than isolated deviations from the socially beneficial system of "responsible capitalism," the larger structural features of the system that produce these problems are overlooked.[3] When the abuses of the wealthy are portrayed in the media as isolated problems rather than as predictable and frequent outcomes of the economic and political system, readers and viewers have little reason to question the status quo. Parenti states that when we view the misconduct of the wealthy as nothing more than an occasional *individual* aberration, this viewpoint serves to legitimate, rather than challenge, existing systems of social inequality.[4]

SOUR-GRAPES FRAMING:
THE WEALTHY ARE UNHAPPY AND DYSFUNCTIONAL

One of Aesop's fables, "The Fox and the Grapes," tells the story of a fox who strolls through an orchard, finds a bunch of grapes ripening on a vine, and decides that they are "Just the thing to quench my thirst." However, after several unsuccessful attempts to run, jump, and grab the bunch, he walks away with his nose in the air, saying, "I am sure they are sour." The adage of this fable is, "It is easy to despise what you cannot get."[5] Similarly, sour-grapes framing shows media audiences the abundance of material possessions and opulent lifestyles of the rich and famous but then suggests that the "grapes," which are out of reach for the typical reader or viewer, are not worth having—that they are flawed and thus not desirable. A classic example of sour-grapes framing is the "poor little rich girl (or boy)" story. Books, television, and films have popularized stories about the problems of people who have inherited large sums of money and then lived lives of despair. Stories about such people as the Woolworth heiress Barbara Hutton[6] and the tobacco heiress Doris Duke[7] are examples, telling of unhappy childhoods, personal traumas, and misfortunes among the wealthy. From best-selling biographies to media tabloids and television entertainment shows like *E!*, *Hard Copy*, and *Entertainment Tonight*, audiences learn about the supposed problems and heartaches of the wealthy and famous.

One message contained in many of these stories is that ordinary people are better off, because the rich and famous suffer as a result of their wealth and typically do stupid things because they cannot cope with the real world. Within this frame, middle- and working-class media audiences are given a bird's-eye view into the lives of the wealthy, but they also receive a cautionary tale about the problems associated with great wealth and notoriety. However, audiences may be drawn to stories with this type of framing, which provide opportunities to feel good about themselves even though they have not achieved the American Dream of success, wealth, and perhaps fame. Readers and viewers can conclude that being rich is not all it might seem to be ("the grapes are sour") and that they should be content with their own lives. An example of this kind of thinking is seen on a website posting by "Grace" from Seattle, her review of the book *Poor Little Rich Girl: The Life and Legend of Barbara Hutton,* by C. David Heymann:

> I think I got a pretty good idea of what Ms. Hutton was about, and have a hard time sympathizing with her . . . poor little rich girl indeed! She popped into a Woolworth's *once* in her life, just to sign a few autographs. Her cheesy poetry netted her less than $200, the only money she truly earned of her own effort. Someone else handled all her financial matters (luckily for her, usually quite well), because she couldn't be bothered. . . . [S]pending money takes time, you know. She dropped husbands as soon as they no longer entertained her. Yes, she had exquisite taste in clothing and jewelry, and traveled incessantly to places I can only dream of ever seeing, but had no grasp on reality—she once sent one of her employees to the bank to change a bill because she had no change. . . . [I]t was a $10,000 bill (I didn't even know those existed!). I enjoyed this book because it took me somewhere I could never go myself. It's hard to feel sorry for her though. . . . [S]he dug her own grave!!![8]

Like many others who read biographies or watch television shows or films about the rich, Grace enjoys living vicariously and is quick to point out Barbara Hutton's "exquisite taste in clothing and jewelry" and her ability to travel incessantly "to places I can only dream of ever seeing." However, she also emphasizes the *individual* character flaws of Hutton, such as that she never worked a day in her life and spent her time and money frivolously. Comments like Grace's may be typical of media audiences who do not question the larger economic conditions that produced the Woolworth-Hutton family fortune or other macro-level concerns associated with capitalism and excessive consumerism.

Another distinct possibility, however, is that media audiences may receive the message that the wealthy do not take advantage of their opportunities and that happiness would be within their reach were it not for character flaws that keep them from finding personal satisfaction with their great wealth. From this perspective, viewers and readers can conclude that if they had that kind of money, they would know how to spend it and would be able to find happiness, unlike the maladjusted and seemingly dysfunctional individuals described in news accounts and portrayed in the story lines of entertainment programming.

Sour-grapes framing is used in newspaper articles and television entertainment programs about people who have inherited great wealth and those who are newly rich. Unlike "Old Money" families that have had vast wealth for three or more generations and are considered to be the "old guard" in their respective cities, "New Money" families have accumulated vast economic resources in the current generation and may not be considered social elites in their communities.[9] A popular form of sour-grapes framing about "Old Money" is the "cautionary tale" about heirs to great wealth. Consider the article "Suddenly Popular," in which inheritor Mark McDonough relays this story:

> So first of all . . . there's this closet called the Green Closet. It's one of the last taboos. This culture tells you, if you have more money, you'll be happier. But rich people are in this unique position to say, "You know what? More stuff *doesn't* mean more happiness." But as a rich person, you absolutely cannot tell anybody that there's anything wrong with your life because, first, everybody knows you should be really happy, and second, they say, "I should have your problems!" Then there's the shame component. With inherited wealth, there's this little logic chain: I have a lot of money, I should be really happy, but I'm not happy, so I must be really *bad*.[10]

Although it is undoubtedly true that possession of great wealth does not equal happiness, sour-grapes framing emphasizes the problems rather than the advantages of such wealth. Problems faced by some wealthy inheritors include low self-esteem and self-discipline, difficulty using power, boredom and alienation, and guilt and suspiciousness.[11] In addition, articles often point out how difficult it is for rich people to establish positive relationships with others because they never know whether someone loves them for themselves or for their money; heirs must fend off "opportunists, speculators, hustlers, and potential lovers" who only want to get their hands on their money.[12] The message that media audiences may gain from such articles is that having a large amount of money may be a problem, not something people should desire. However, some readers and viewers respond with "I should be so lucky," convinced that if they only had the money of the "poor little rich girl (or boy)," they indeed could find happiness.

Aside from suggestions that it is easier to have high self-esteem if individuals earn their own money, sour-grapes framing shows the pratfalls of the nouveau riche, particularly in television entertainment series. The story line of the rich, dysfunctional family was popularized by the long-running hit series *Dallas* (shown on CBS from 1978 until 1991 and still in worldwide syndication). This show portrayed J. R. Ewing (Larry Hagman), the leading character, as a ruthless oil tycoon worth nearly three billion dollars who is always plotting evil deeds and having bitter battles with his family and business associates. Ewing prides himself on evading federal regulators, on taking down anyone who stands in the way of Ewing Oil, and on maintaining off-the-books partnerships to boost profits and hide debt.

The legacy of J. R. Ewing as the prototype of the rich misfit continues, preserved in such tributes as his recent pseudo-biography in *Forbes*'s "Fictional Fifteen Richest Americans."[13] Continuing interest in the lifestyle of this fictitious family is evident in the fact that the Ewing family's estate, Southfork Ranch, has become a tourist attraction. Several thousand people from around the world each year visit Southfork's large white mansion, pool, barns, and other settings where *Dallas* was filmed. Tourists also visit the ranch's two retail stores, "Lincolns and Longhorns" and "Ranch Roundup," to buy souvenirs and other merchandise with the Southfork label attached. However unhappy and dysfunctional the Ewings seemed in the sour-grapes framing of this popular series, media audiences continue to show interest in their supposed material possessions and lifestyle.

In the twenty-first century, the story line of the rich, dysfunctional family remains popular in such television shows as *Arrested Development* and *The O.C.* Consider this description of the Bluth family in *Arrested Development*:

> The first episode . . . opens on a yacht, chartered for the retirement party of the family patriarch, George Bluth, founder of a louche development

company in Orange County, Calif. Michael (Jason Bateman), the one relatively normal and reliable son, is expecting to be named chief executive at long last. As the champagne begins to flow, his mother Lucille (Jessica Walter), an imperious socialite, looms in front of Michael and declares, "Look at what the homosexuals have done to me." He replies mildly, "Can't you comb it out and reset it?" Actually she was referring to chanting gay activities on a nearby boat protesting discrimination at the yacht club. The feds prove even more disruptive. Almost as soon as George announces his decision to appoint Lucille his successor, the police board the yacht and arrest George on fraud charges brought by the Securities and Exchange Commission.

As the title of this program suggests, not only is the father arrested by law enforcement officials but family members exhibit less than full maturity. Like *Dallas,* this show portrays the wealth of the Bluth family (as revealed by their clothing, yacht, and penthouse residence), but it also shows what happens when their assets are frozen after the father gets arrested for shifty accounting practices. *Arrested Development* deals with a unique, dysfunctional family and makes "sly, satisfying digs at the rich," according to one TV critic.[14] The characters are portrayed in keeping with sour-grapes framing. For example, the daughter Lindsay (Portia de Rossi) is depicted as a "spendthrift social climber who uses company money to finance her swanky fundraisers, including a black-tie party for an anti-circumcision group that earns her the ire of the Jewish Defense League."[15] Lindsay's mother is a "flamboyant, stylish and spoiled society matron who finds herself alone in her Balboa Bay Club penthouse without the financial means to maintain it."[16] Sour-grapes framing in *Arrested Development* ridicules the charitable activities of the rich, who, in the case of Lindsay, not only use company funds for lavish parties but support fringe causes.

Another FOX hit, *The O.C.,* frequently shows charity fund-raisers as places for the moneyed residents of Newport Beach to gather, make catty remarks about each other, and occasionally get into brawls. *"The O.C."* refers to Orange County, California, which has been described as "the largest suburban, affluent, Republican county between Los Angeles and San Diego."[17] Setting up a contrast—and potential conflict—between classes, *The O.C.* portrays the problems of Ryan Atwood (Benjamin McKenzie), a "smart, poor kid" from the working-class community of Chino, as he comes to live with the Cohen family in Newport Beach. After getting in trouble with the law in Chino, Ryan goes to live with Sandy Cohen (Peter Gallagher), a public defender from humble origins who now lives with his wife Kirsten (Kelly Rowan) in Newport Beach. Kirsten's father is a wealthy and sometimes unscrupulous real estate developer. Ryan is accepted by the Cohen family and his living arrangements become permanent, but television audiences receive regular reminders that Ryan comes from a lower-class, dysfunctional family; however, they are also shown that many Newport Beach residents are dysfunctional snobs who look down their noses at outsiders and have their own dirty laundry to hide. Sour-grapes framing is used in the story line to depict Newport Beach residents as unhappy, alcohol and drug dependent, or at least "nerdy," as one TV critic stated. "The dirty secret in most rich-people soaps is corruption. In *The O.C.*, it's insecurity—from the next-door neighbor, who had defrauded his investment clients to maintain his family's lifestyle, to the Cohens' charming but nerdy son Seth, who is proof that money doesn't equal social acceptance."[18]

As shown in *The O.C.*, supporting a lavish lifestyle gets people like the Cohens' next-door neighbor, Jimmy (Tate Donovan), in trouble; he defrauds his neighbors to pay for the luxury home and elegant lifestyle to which his family has become accustomed. According to sour-grapes framing, even young people are negatively affected by wealth. The Cohens' son, Seth (Adam Brody), has all of the opportunities available to an affluent young man. He attends a prestigious private school and owns all the material possessions he might desire, but he is portrayed as a social misfit (despite such redeeming qualities as humor) who can turn potential success at school or in an interpersonal relationship into instant failure. Media audiences laugh at Seth as a "nerd"; in contrast, Ryan's working-class background apparently equips him with the necessary "street smarts" to maneuver out of difficult situations even in wealthy Newport Beach.

The O.C. portrays the good life of the rich, showing multimillion-dollar mansions, luxury vehicles, and black-tie events, such as charity fundraisers at the country club or debutante balls. But there is always a dark cloud over the rosy picture. Examples are the story lines that have Marissa (Mischa Barton), who is Jimmy's daughter and Ryan's girlfriend, attempt in one episode to overdose on drugs because of her parent's pending divorce and in another episode to drink herself into a stupor. *The O.C.* incorporates a rags-to-riches story line, played out through the characters of Sandy Cohen and Ryan, but one critic suggests that the series also shows the "slippery slope of wealth" and the empty promise of trying to have it all.[19]

Recent website postings suggest that some viewers are aware of the ambivalent message that *The O.C.* sends to viewers. Consider this comment by "LASAS211":

> It's a great show. (Let me say again *show*). That's what people like to watch and if that brings in money you better bet their gunna air more and more shows like it. And no not everybody is rich, but everyone

wants to be rich and have a fun life. So what's so wrong with people liking the show and liking the story line, and liking to watch the show. Also this show is not just about spoiled rich kids, they have problems like drinking, family issues and relationships, etc. I mean have you ever watched the show or you just putting the show into a stereotype.[20]

Sour-grapes framing, whether in television entertainment series or news accounts, often brings out ambivalent feelings in media audiences. They can experience pleasure looking at expensive merchandise and luxury residences while at the same time becoming more aware of the problems associated with wealth and social prominence. Although television shows about families in various economic classes (such as *Malcolm in the Middle, According to Jim, Everybody Loves Raymond,* and *King of Queens*) often make fun of the seemingly dysfunctional American family, the rich and famous are favorite subjects of sour-grapes framing, because it may be easier to laugh at the pretentiousness and conspicuous consumption of the rich than the problems of the working class and poor.

If sour-grapes framing of media stories typically involves the "poor little rich girl/boy" scenario or cautionary tales about wealth, bad-apple framing focuses instead on the deviant and criminal behavior of the rich. However, even bad-apple framing primarily emphasizes the individual nature of these actions rather than the larger patterns of corruption that may be a part of the standard business practices of many "wealthy scoundrels."

BAD-APPLE FRAMING #1:
SOME WEALTHY PEOPLE ARE MEDIA HOGS

A relatively mild form of bad-apple framing is used by the media to report stories about wealthy individuals who are publicity hogs or have perceived personality flaws; stronger forms of bad-apple framing are utilized to describe criminal behavior. In both instances, the media provide extensive information not only about the misdeeds of the individuals but their net worth and costly possessions. According to the sociologist Gregory Mantsios, the media send several messages about the wealthy as bad apples:

> On rare occasions, the media will mock selected individuals for their personality flaws. Real estate investor Donald Trump and New York Yankees owner George Steinbrenner, for example, are admonished by the media for deliberately seeking publicity (a very un-upper class thing to do); hotel owner Leona Helmsley was caricatured for her personal cruelties; and junk bond broker Michael Milkin was condemned because he had the audacity to rob the rich.[21]

As Mantsios's statement suggests, some of the wealthy can be viewed as bad apples because they seek the media spotlight. Donald Trump, the New York real estate developer, is an example. Throughout the years, Trump has been available to the media for profiles about his empire, including his numerous high-rise buildings and development projects in New York City and his hotels and casinos in Atlantic City, New Jersey. Despite his billions, Trump recently appeared in McDonald's ads selling dollar-priced sandwiches[22] and hosts a reality show, *The Apprentice,* where sixteen candidates vie for a six-figure job as Trump's assistant. In this show Trump plays a starring role, personally firing one candidate at the end of each episode, and leaving the others to compete in the next elimination round.

According to media analysts, Trump likes the media spotlight and chooses projects that will maintain his high profile; however, in doing so he violates one of the cardinal rules of the upper class, namely (as we have seen in previous chapters) that a person's name should appear in the news only three times: when the individual is born, gets married, and dies. However, Trump describes his starring role in *The Apprentice* from a different perspective: "I think there's a whole beautiful picture to be painted about business, American business, how beautiful it is but also how vicious and tough it is. The beauty is the success, the end result. You meet some wonderful people, but you also meet some treacherous, disgusting people that are worse than any snake in the jungle."[23]

If Trump and other wealthy high-profile individuals may be framed as bad apples primarily because they are "media hogs," other rich people are the subjects of bad-apple framing because of problematic behavior suggesting that they believe their wealth can buy them anything they want.

BAD-APPLE FRAMING #2:
SOME WEALTHY PEOPLE BELIEVE THEY CAN BUY ANYTHING

Bad-apple framing has been used in news stories to show how the wealthy buy, or attempt to buy, whatever they want. Of the many examples that might be given, perhaps the one that received the most media attention in recent years was what came to be known as the "nursery school scandal" in New York City. What happens when your child is not accepted into a nursery school? For most parents, the answer would be simply to find another school. However, this was not what the twenty-million-dollar-a-year stock analyst Jack Grubman chose to do when his twin daughters were not accepted at the exclusive 92nd Street Y preschool in Manhattan. Instead, Grubman allegedly bargained with Sanford I. Weill of Citicorp (who was also an AT&T director), offering to increase his rating of AT&T stock if

Weill would make a few calls to 92nd Street Y board members to arrange admission for Grubman's toddler twins. Citicorp also pledged a million dollars to the school. According to media accounts, Grubman sent Weill an e-mail that stated, "There are no bounds for what you do for your children."[24]

This statement is the essence of this form of bad-apple framing: The rich believe that everything and everybody has a price, that all you have to do is find out what that price is and pay it. Many other wealthy parents were not surprised by this type of behavior, given the competitiveness of everything in their lives, including the nursery schools their children attend. One journalist summed up the situation as follows:

> To normal people living anywhere else, the news that someone might offer a pledge of $1 million just to get a child into the right nursery school must seem absurd. That an analyst might recommend a particular stock in order to curry favor with a powerful banker who might then help that analyst's child win a coveted spot in a nursery school seems stranger still. But on Manhattan's Upper East Side, the story that Jack Grubman, the former star telecom stock analyst for Citigroup, attempted to get his twins into the 92nd Street Y nursery school by changing his rating on AT&T stock was greeted with knowing nods rather than disbelief.[25]

Although this news account questions the priorities of Grubman, it makes clear that other affluent parents were not surprised by his conduct. As the former head of another prestigious school told reporters, "This is not a couple of bad apples. . . . This is a systemic problem. That there is corruption down to nursery school is just ghastly. Bartering children this way, and sullying a fine school. The adults have lost their way. They have forgotten that school is about children."[26]

For wealthy parents, rejection by a prestigious nursery school is seen not only as harmful for their children but also as a negative reflection on the family's social standing. As one analyst explains, "[Being rejected] is one of those crystallizing moments when the neuroses and status anxieties of upper-class Manhattanites are laid bare."[27] Also, sociological research bears out to some extent the importance of getting the "right" education, whether in nursery school, high school, or college. In a study of elite private schools, for example, the sociologists Peter W. Cookson, Jr., and Caroline Hodges Persell concluded, "To be accepted into a private school is to be accepted into a social club, or more generally speaking, a status group that is defined as a group of people who have a sense of social similarity. People sharing the same status have similar life-styles, common educational background, and pursue similar types of occupations."[28]

When a "high society" scandal like the Grubman case occurs, media coverage of the event provides audiences with more than a news account of just the facts—who, what, when, and where. The message media audiences receive is that some wealthy people believe you can buy anything and see their belief often confirmed by the way others acquiesce and do their bidding. Framing of media stories about how the rich buy what they want typically includes information for everyday readers and viewers about the competitive nature of life in the upper classes and how different the rich are from everyone else. For example, articles and info-tainment television shows and websites provide lengthy summaries of the wealth of individuals involved and the value or prestige of the things they desire in their privileged social circle.

Although the central story of the nursery school scandal was about the conduct of Grubman, Weill, and the 92nd Street Y's board, news reports included commentaries such as: "Getting a child into a Manhattan private school is like getting a box seat at the Knicks game," placed under headlines such as "First Good Preschool, Then Harvard"[29] or "No Talking Out of Preschool."[30] These articles give readers insiders' views of how the "right kind of people" live. Consider, for example, this description of the people and cars that can be seen outside this prestigious nursery school: "Sleek black town cars idled three deep outside the 92nd Street Y, their drivers ignoring the pleas of traffic officers. A mother in riding breeches and boots wrestled a stroller through the heavy brass doors, headed for the sixth-floor nursery school. Another tapped her foot impatiently, waiting for the nanny who would meet her on Lexington Avenue to take her child inside."[31] Another article, "The Baby Ivies," takes readers inside the school's opulent interior:

> To enter the 92nd Street Y Nursery School, parent and child pass through a large granite and marble lobby. Beyond the Felix M. Warburg Lounge, beneath an exquisitely stenciled ceiling, they wait in a long line behind a red velvet rope for the special elevator that carries them to the sixth floor. When the shiny brass door opens, an impressive display case filled with ribbon designs and candleholders made by the children greets them. No ordinary handprint art here.[32]

Descriptions like these are typical of the kinds of information that media audiences receive when journalists go behind closed doors and describe what money buys for the wealthy. Given this emphasis on the "good life," it is no surprise that even when the media are describing the unethical and sometimes criminal conduct of wealthy elites, some middle-, working-, and poverty-class people might believe that if they were rich, they could live happily ever after and not make the mistakes of some wealthy people.

BAD-APPLE FRAMING #3:

BAD APPLES WITH GOOD TASTE—WEALTHY WOMEN AND CRIME

Scandals involving wealthy women such as Martha Stewart, the lifestyle expert, or Diana D. Brooks, former chief executive of the famous auction house Sotheby's, are often framed in such a manner as to show that the women have impeccable taste even when they are accused of committing crimes. Despite the charges of conspiracy, obstruction of justice, and securities fraud against Martha Stewart, she remains for many people an icon of good taste and good living. Stewart successfully marketed her products and her lifestyle, referring to herself as "America's most trusted guide to stylish living" and reaching millions of people through her television shows, books, *Living* magazine, and her website.

As the business authors Michael J. Silverstein and Neil Fiske state in their recent, popular book *Trading Up,* Martha Stewart generated more than eighty-eight million consumer impressions each month through her media and retail empire, and in this way she "inspired millions of Americans to reach for a richer, more tasteful, more sophisticated lifestyle."[33] According to Silverstein and Fiske, Stewart is one of the leaders in New Luxury spending, which they define as comprising "products and services that possess higher levels of quality, taste, and aspiration than other goods in the category but are not so expensive as to be out of reach" for middle- and upper-middle-income shoppers.[34] For example, New Luxury products such as an eight-thousand-dollar Sub-Zero stainless refrigerator or a $1,199.95 KitchenAid frozen dessert maker for ice cream and frozen margaritas have lower-cost competitors, but the less-expensive products do not have as many features as, or the prestige of, the more expensive brands.[35] As a wealthy women convicted of obstruction of justice, Stewart is still seen as having good taste, and she has remained popular with many of her followers: "Even during [Martha Stewart's] difficulties . . . involving insider stock trading, her popularity and influence did not decline, although her company's share price did. As one woman said . . . 'Martha is one of the first people who said your home is important. She gives the family validity. She is a source of comfort.'"[36]

Throughout Stewart's legal ordeal—including time served in the Alderson federal prison—the media frequently reminded audiences that she was the icon of "good living" and that her motto is "It's a good thing." Journalists often borrowed her favorite expressions, as shown in one article about her criminal defense attorney, Robert Morvillo: "For Martha, [Morvillo] could be the ultimate good thing."[37] Media reports saw everything in Stewart's life as a form of consumerism, including her choice of a defense attorney: "Stewart was impressed by Morvillo, but thought hard about her choice. 'This is not like shopping for a fur coat,' she says. 'This is shopping for your life, okay?'"[38]

Even media reports that described Martha Stewart as a bad apple acknowledged that she was a major force in the *trading-up phenomenon* and is a "homemaking icon." Comedians and nighttime television hosts who made seemingly cruel jokes about Stewart's lifestyle and legal problems typically made disclaimers similar to the one made by David Letterman on his *Late Night* TV show: "Now, don't get me wrong. I like Martha Stewart; she's been on our show a number of times, and she makes some really great stuff." Or consider this introductory comment in a *New York Times* op-ed column, "In Defense of Martha" (accompanied by a cartoonlike caricature of Stewart with needle and thread nearby and some sewing pins stuck in her, much like a pattern pinned to cloth before it is cut):

> I'm no Martha Stewart fan—I rarely pronounce her name without clamping it in quotation marks, as if that proved the falsity of her whole perfect-living enterprise. And yet I find myself wanting to defend her. Or at least wondering, Why do we get so much pleasure from cutting Martha with a mandoline into paper-thin slices? True, she cashed in her ImClone stock for $227,824 one day before it took a dive, and she's close to ImClone's former chief executive, Sam Waksal, who was arrested on insider trading charges. . . . They also shared a broker, and now she is being investigated for the stock sale, making her fair game for the press. . . . [However,] the reaction is so bitter that you can't help thinking Martha Stewart is in trouble less for her investments in ImClone than for our investments in her images—and maybe her secret role in our own self-image.[39]

Although some journalists focused on the positive aspects of Stewart's good-living empire, the headlines of some newspaper and magazine articles told another story. Among these are a *Newsweek* cover story, "Martha's Mess: An Insider Trading Scandal Tarnishes the Queen of Perfection"[40] and other magazine and newspaper articles such as "Martha's Dirty Laundry,"[41] "Tarnish, Anyone?,"[42] "Martha Stewart's To-Do List May Include Image Polishing,"[43] "Canapés and Investment Tips Are Served to Well-Heeled,"[44] and "Blue Lights or Not, Martha Stewart Remains Calm,"[45] the latter referring to Stewart's contract with Kmart, the giant retailer, to sell her brand of linens and housewares. Headlines and articles used puns about housecleaning, polishing silver, serving elegant food, and similar household-related references to describe Stewart's legal problems and to predict how her business empire would do in the future. Note, for example, this journalist's aside about Stewart's supposedly snobbish taste in home decorating: "For Martha, the greatest misfortune may be that the scandal comes when her own company is thriving. Martha Stewart Living Omnimedia is performing so well, Martha's just brought out her own line of linoleum. (Who knew that Martha even *approved* of linoleum?)"[46]

Early in the twenty-first century, Stewart's reputation as "the doyenne of all things domestic" and as the "tireless dispenser of advice" continues to be highlighted in most media reports.[47] Some journalists have changed the term *schadenfreude* to read *blondenfreude,* saying that it describes "the glee that some people feel when a rich, powerful, and fair-haired business woman stumbles."[48]

Despite bad-apple framing in many stories about Martha Stewart, the photos and images accompanying the articles typically reveal a positive image of her as the guru of good taste and a wealthy businesswoman. For example, three photos accompanied an article about "image polishing": the first photo showed a smiling Stewart carefully arranging flowers in one of her custom vases; the second showed a smiling Stewart standing beside a former president of the New York Stock Exchange and a former chairman of Kmart Corporation at the Big Board's opening bell on Wall Street; and the third showed a former chairman of the Federal Reserve with his arm casually placed around Stewart at a fund-raising dinner.[49] These photos convey the message that Stewart has enjoyed great success, knows the "right people," and has good taste even with regard to ordinary activities like arranging flowers.

In addition to photographs like these, Martha Stewart's image was widely used in political cartoons to spoof her legal problems. One cartoon showed her using her own brands of designer paint and accessories to decorate her jail cell. A second cartoon, published after Kmart Corporation announced that it was filing for bankruptcy (while still owing Stewart roughly thirteen million dollars), depicted Stewart on the set of her TV show saying to her audience, "With a little paint a dumpster can make a lovely studio apartment," while offstage the cameraman says to the sound person, "It's been like this since K-Mart went bankrupt."[50] However, as the media have pointed out, Stewart may have the last laugh. Her net worth soared by about two hundred million dollars (at least on paper) while she was in prison, as Kmart staged a takeover of Sears, Roebuck and Company, expanding the potential market for Martha Stewart products.[51]

The use of "bad apple with good taste" framing is not unique, particularly in the coverage of privileged women accused of criminal activity. Another example is the framing of stories accompanying the conviction of Diana D. Brooks, the former chief executive of Sotheby's, for her admitted role in fixing commission rates with Christie's, a rival auction house. As a cooperating witness in the antitrust prosecution of her former boss, A. Alfred Taubman, Brooks received a sentence of three years' probation, a fine of

$350,000, a thousand hours of community service, and six months under house arrest. As part of the agreement, Brooks returned her Sotheby stock options, worth ten million dollars, plus the approximately $3.25 million she had received in salary after the conspiracy started.[52] Of all these penalties, which some people considered to be too lenient given the magnitude of the charges, the one that most interested journalists was the idea that she was being "punished" by house arrest—in her twelve-room, five-million-dollar co-op apartment on the Upper East Side. News stories carried headlines such as "When Home Is a Castle and the Big House, Too"[53] and "You Say House Arrest, I Say Paradise."[54]

A photo of Brooks accompanying one of the articles had the caption "Velvet Cuffs: Diana D. Brooks just before she was sentenced to home detention," suggesting that she was being treated as a privileged person by the criminal justice system. The journalist set the stage by showing how well Brooks lived:

> On August evenings, the limestone canyons of Park Avenue and the white-glove streets of the East 70's are quiet, abandoned by the well-to-do for breezier destinations. . . . But last week on East 79th Street, a solitary window emitted a hopeful rectangular glow. The window, on the 10th floor of one of Manhattan's best co-op apartment buildings, belongs to Diana D. Brooks, the former chief executive of Sotheby's, who is four months into a six-month sentence of home detention. . . . She is allowed to leave her 12-room, $5 million apartment for two hours each Friday to go grocery shopping at any store selling food or products related to food preparation. . . . Her forays have included trips to Gristede's and D'Agostino supermarkets and to a Starbucks, according to a friend of Ms. Brooks. . . . [However], Ms. Brooks is not allowed to exercise in Central Park and may not travel to her $4 million oceanfront home in Hobe Sound, Fla., but she may use her telephone and work from home, which is where she has been continuing her volunteer work for troubled girls in public schools.[55]

As this article suggests, the elegant lifestyle of Brooks, including her trips to other exclusive residences or appearances at high-society parties, was prohibited, but she was able to enjoy the luxury of her costly home, which protected her from interactions with "garden-variety criminals." Judging from several letters to the editor, newspaper readers often viewed Brooks's treatment as too lenient. As one stated:

> To the Editor:
>   I'm a 20-something working as an assistant in a financial institution. I have laundry piling up because by the time I get home, the cleaners are

closed. I don't cook because I'm too tired. Send Ms. Brooks to my house to do some community service.[56]

Or, as another reader argued:

To the Editor:
If Gerry Shanahan's article ("You Say House Arrest, I Say Paradise," May 2) on the light sentence handed to Diana Brooks, the Sotheby's executive, was meant to anger your readers, it succeeded. A member of my family was also convicted in federal court, in this case of a securities fraud that cost innocent citizens millions. She is serving 16 years for her first offense, with no parole for 14 years. An elite felon serves short time at home, while uneducated poor women receive long sentences. Both are miscarriages of justice, albeit at different ends of the spectrum.[57]

As these letters suggest, some people do not believe that the criminal justice system treats elite criminals such as Brooks like it does individuals in other classes. There may be some validity to this assertion. When rich and famous women are found guilty, they often receive seemingly lenient sentences, and media framing continues to suggest that they are "bad apples with good taste."

Wealthy women who are accused of offenses like insider trading, collusion, or even more mundane crimes such as shoplifting typically receive extensive media coverage. Two recent examples of bad-apple-with-good-taste framing for shoplifting are stories of the well-known actress Winona Ryder and the less-well-known Dallas socialite Brooke Stollenwerck Aldridge. The Winona Ryder shoplifting trial was a topic not only of newspaper and magazine accounts but also such television entertainment shows as *E!, Entertainment Tonight, Hard Copy, Inside Edition,* and *Access Hollywood.* Writers for *Saturday Night Live, The Tonight Show with Jay Leno,* and *Late Night with David Letterman* created numerous jokes about "Winona's five-finger discount" and the expensive designer clothing she wore to her trial ("No cheap orange jump suit for Winona," for example). Articles such as "For the Ryder Trial, a Hollywood Script" provided a commentary on, not just a factual description of, her trial for shoplifting $5,560 in merchandise from Saks Fifth Avenue in Beverly Hills:

Ms. Ryder, who spent her 31st birthday in court on Tuesday, has arrived each morning dressed in conservative but very chic outfits and impeccably made up. On Wednesday, she sat alone at a side table for almost half an hour before the proceedings in a black Marc Jacobs dress with peach-and-white collar trim that crisscrossed at the bosom. Her doelike eyes staring somewhat pensively into space, she occasionally stole a glance into the crowded gallery. She was conspicuously alone, that long, swan-like neck seeming to anticipate the axe.[58]

In the bad-apple-with-good-taste framing of stories about rich celebrities like Ryder, no detail is spared, particularly when it involves the individual's insatiable desire for expensive goods or the preferential treatment they receive in their everyday life:

> Probably the biggest gasp in the Winona Ryder shoplifting trial . . . came when two sales clerks in a row testified that the willowy actress had asked them to fetch her Coca-Colas from the Saks Fifth Avenue cafeteria. By the testimony, Ms. Ryder not once, but twice, asked solicitous helpers hovering outside separate dressing rooms to please bring her a Coke on the afternoon of December 12, 2002, when she was in the midst of what authorities say was a $5,560 shoplifting spree. What was unclear was the reason for the gasp. Was it that the audience in the small, crowded Beverly Hills courtroom had caught the prosecutor's intimation that Ms. Ryder had used a need for refreshment to give her more privacy for scissoring security tags from designer clothes and trinkets? Or was it the very notion that a person could actually order up a beverage while trying on clothes—that is, if one is the right sort of person?[59]

Many local examples can also be found of bad-apple-with-good-taste framing of a wealthy woman who has committed a crime. Consider, for example, these headlines regarding the shoplifting charges and conviction of the Dallas socialite Aldridge: "An Unfashionable Turn for Stylish HP Socialite,"[60] "Charity Co-Chair Steps Down over Shoplifting Charge,"[61] and "Shop Till You Get Caught."[62] In stories about the Aldridge case, journalists typically did more than simply describe the charges against this socially prominent woman, as evidenced by these introductory sentences from a *Dallas Morning News* front-page article:

> It was sure to be another triumphant evening for one of Dallas' society darlings. A good time, a good cause, a good place to see and be seen. As usual, Brooke Stollenwerck Aldridge would be a conspicuous focus of attention—this time, though, as a consummate contradiction to her lofty social status and inspired volunteer work. During the countdown to the big night, some of the city's wealthiest jaws would drop over a shoplifting scandal that shattered the flawless image of a party planner nonpareil, a chic benefactor with a happy, privileged life.[63]

According to numerous articles, Aldridge, heir to part of her mother's East Texas timber and real estate fortune, easily could have paid for the $485 pair of black designer pants, the $1,250 Hermes wallet, and the $120 Kate Spade wallet that she placed in her purse or shopping bag at the Neiman Marcus store. Most news accounts indicated Aldridge's good taste by including the brand names of the stolen merchandise.[64]

Articles and television accounts about the shoplifting convictions of Ryder and Aldridge utilized bad-apple-with-good-taste framing to show a few wealthy individuals—who can afford anything they want—who apparently have psychological problems or other complicated reasons for engaging in such deviant conduct. However, even when they get caught, privileged elites are described as displaying the most expensive merchandise, demonstrating refined taste, and having the right connections to help them out with their plight. Consider, for example, media reports about Aldridge's arrest: "[Aldridge's] $500 bond was paid in cash by her father, lawyer Henry Stollenwerck. . . . 'It's unusual to pay cash if you're poor, but not for somebody of that stature,' Sgt. Don Peritz, the Dallas County sheriff's spokesman, said of the bond. 'It's probably like walking money for them, I'm reckoning. My guess is Daddy was waiting there with his engine idling.'"

The deputy's glib characterization was not uncommon. Once news of the arrest became public within a couple of weeks, the topic leaped from lips in North Dallas social circles, Highland Park salons and far beyond. Internet sites posted her jail mug shot and salivated over a downfall among the rich. "Ms. Aldridge . . . suddenly was the subject of speculation and gossip completely counter to the publicity she'd received in high-society forums and magazines such as *Vogue*, which included her fashion views in a four-city survey last year."[65]

Accompanying the articles about Aldridge were photos that told an interesting story in themselves. Newspaper articles included not only the somber booking photo of Ms. Aldridge at the time of her arrest but photos of her being escorted down the runway at Neiman Marcus after being selected one of the 2001 Crystal Charity Ball's ten best-dressed women in Dallas and at a 2002 fashion show fund-raiser with a friend, who in the aftermath of Aldridge's arrest told reporters, "The community will stand by her no matter what."[66]

As communications scholars have suggested, photographs serve as a form of pictorial stereotyping in the media. Sometimes these representations create or maintain distorted images of individuals and contribute to bias against people based on their ethnicity, gender, age, disability, sexual orientation, or other characteristics;[67] however, in the case of wealthy women accused of a crime, the "rich and tasteful socialite" stereotype is maintained through the visual images that accompany media reports of their misconduct. By contrast, consider what kind of media coverage, if any, a working-class woman would receive for shoplifting a twenty-five-dollar pair of shoes and a forty-nine-dollar pantsuit from Wal-Mart or another discount chain. Would a photo of that woman volunteering at her church bazaar be included in news accounts of her arrest and conviction? In any case, most media coverage of the rich and famous who commit crimes focuses on the wrongdoings of elite men.

BAD-APPLE FRAMING #4:
BAD APPLES WITH MOGUL STYLE—WEALTHY MEN AND CRIME

The high status of wealthy men and the cost of their entertainment and luxury possessions are key components in media coverage about the downfall of corporate CEOs and their companies. As previously mentioned, *mogul style* refers to the idea that some rich corporate executives are less interested in conspicuous consumption for its own sake than they are in contemptuous consumption, spending money (sometimes not their own) not for the pleasure of ownership or connoisseurship but for the gratification they receive by making other moguls fearful or jealous.[68] In describing the downfall of executives at such corporations as ImClone, Enron, Tyco, WorldCom, and HealthSouth, one journalist suggested, "The gossip columns and the glossy magazines got it all wrong. For years they've been glorifying the homes and lives of the rich and famous by defining the rich and famous as movie stars, fashion designers and rap music impresarios. But it turns out that the trend they missed was Mogul Style: excessive spending on the chief executive's imperial lifestyle."[69]

Whether in the national news, business, or lifestyle sections of the local newspaper or on info-tainment TV shows like *Dateline, 20-20,* or *Sixty Minutes,* the arrests and trials of executives have garnered many headlines and given media audiences opportunities to look at the mogul style these men displayed, whether at corporate parties or in their private residences. In fact, the lifestyles of some top (and former) CEOs have been described as "more flamboyant and expensive than Hollywood Style, than anyone on *MTV Cribs* or in the pages of *In Style* magazine. . . . Whereas celebs are trying to impress their fans, moguls are trying to impress each other."[70]

Media framing using the bad-apple-with-mogul-style theme was widely employed by journalists and news correspondents in stories about the demise of Enron Corporation, at that time the country's seventh-largest company. In the Enron case, the U.S. Department of Labor filed a civil lawsuit against CEO Kenneth Lay and other former executives seeking to recover hundreds of millions of dollars in employees' lost retirement money. Criminal charges were also filed against Lay and other officers of Enron, including chief financial officer Andrew Fastow, who later pleaded guilty to two counts of wire and securities fraud and was sentenced to ten years in prison. According to one media report, "Enron hid billions of dollars in debts and operating losses inside private partnerships and dizzyingly complex accounting schemes that were intended to pump up buzz about the company and support its inflated stock price."[71] Apparently, Enron officials would not have been able to perpetrate their criminal acts had it not been for an accounting firm that looked the other way, and for the failure of the government to take action when it should have. As one journalist stated:

> It is a failure of government: having greased nearly every campaigner's palm in Washington, Enron worked overtime to keep the regulators from looking too closely at a balance sheet gone bad. And it is a failure of character, especially inside Enron, where managers who knew something was badly wrong did not say anything publicly until the subpoenas began to arrive.[72]

In worldwide media coverage of the Enron scandal and the corporation's subsequent collapse, stories about Kenneth Lay, the former CEO, were often based on bad-apple-with-mogul-style framing, regaling audiences about his broad influence in business and politics as well as the lavish lifestyle he and other top Enron executives had enjoyed. One journalist described the glory days of Enron in terms of the material possessions of its top employees: "You could always tell it was bonus time at Enron when the shiny new silver Porches began arriving in the company garage. The $100,000 sports car was the status symbol of choice among the young Masters of the Universe who worked at the global trading company."[73]

Even the death notices of Clifford Baxter (a former Enron executive who committed suicide after challenging the corporation's secret partnership agreements, and who had resigned before the scandal broke) provided a laundry list of his mogul-style material possessions, including the Mercedes-Benz S500 sedan in which he died, the seventy-two-foot yacht, *Tranquility Base,* that he used for weekend relaxation, and his family's seven-hundred-thousand-dollar residence in an exclusive Houston suburb.[74]

Initial media framing of stories about Lay typically portrayed him as a low-key, Horatio Alger–type individual who, as the son of a Baptist preacher and sometime tractor salesman, had seen lean financial conditions in his youth, such as when his family ate "cold cuts instead of roasted turkey" one Thanksgiving Day.[75] However, once the extent of Enron's spending and Lay's lavish lifestyle became known to journalists and correspondents, story framing often shifted to mogul style. Lay's vast stockholdings and real estate investments were made public at a time when many Enron employees were losing their jobs, retirement savings, and homes. The media reported stockholders losing their investments, including the oft-told story of President George W. Bush's mother-in-law losing eight thousand dollars on her Enron stock.[76]

Media stories of the collapse of Enron emphasized that "lavish excess" had been typical at corporate events and in the luxury travel and expensive restaurants enjoyed by top executives. Even when the economic tide had shifted at the corporation, officials had set aside $1.5 million for a Christmas party at Enron Field (now Minute-Maid Park) in Houston. As one news report stated, "Everything Enron did had to be better and flashier—from the new business ventures it unveiled nearly every year to the way it celebrated Secretaries' Day with gifts of Waterford crystal—and no gesture seemed too lavish, workers and competitors agree."[77] Some of the lavish spending occurred within the corporate culture, to impress employees or get word out to competitors; an example was having a live elephant make a surprise appearance at an employee meeting, spending hundreds of thousands of dollars to build a "Potemkin-village trading floor to impress equity analysts invited to a conference," or renting the eighty-five-acre Astroworld amusement park for an employees' family picnic.[78] Photos accompanying stories about the fall of Enron typically included the elephant or Enron executives, dressed in leather jackets and chaps, riding into an annual meeting on a Harley-Davidson motorcycle with the *Survivor* theme song "Eye of the Tiger" blaring in the background.[79]

Perhaps the bad-apple-with-mogul-style framing was best shown in articles that covered not only the problems of Ken Lay but delved into how his wife was dealing with what she referred to as the family's "financial ruin." From her appearance on the *Today* show to numerous newspaper and magazine interviews, Linda Lay frequently portrayed her husband as a victim of others' deceit and declared that her family was, for all intents and purposes, broke: "It's gone. There's nothing left. Everything we had mostly was in Enron stock."[80] As journalists commented, however, her words were offset by the plush surroundings of the Lays' Houston home where she was interviewed:

> Only the lush backdrop of Oriental carpets and wood paneling and an occasional verbal incongruity ("We are fighting for liquidity") clashed with Mrs. Lay's message [that] she and her husband and children were also deceived, pitiable victims of Enron's collapse. She described the family as financially ruined, and said all its property "other than the home we live in" was for sale.[81]

Of course, the claim was widely disputed by journalists who further explored the Lays' assets. The visual image of Linda Lay crying on the NBC interview and saying "We've lost everything" was shown around the world on the Internet, cable television, newspapers, and magazines. Media sources quickly pointed out that "broke" was a relative term—Ken Lay had gotten most of his money by selling Enron stock early and had reaped more than a hundred million dollars over three years, a period of time in which he had also received a salary and bonuses totaling more than seventeen million. According to one report:

> The Lays own at least 20 properties in Colorado and Texas. These include their principal home—a five-bedroom high-rise condo in Houston that's worth at least $8 million—as well as rental properties from Houston to Galveston that are worth an additional $4.5 million. The Lays are selling all their Aspen, Colo., properties, including a 4,537-sq.-ft. log cabin and a four-bedroom riverfront house, together worth about $20 million.[82]

According to one journalist, Mrs. Lay may have hoped that her television appearance, for which she was coached by a relative who works for a well-known public relations firm, would "rev up the nation's sympathy for her man."[83] Instead, what that journalist (and a number of others) concluded was that the Enron scandal and the behavior of Mrs. Lay helped to show outsiders what goes on inside some major corporations: "What we see is a world in which insiders get to play by one set of rules—entree to Enron side partnerships that could turn minimal investments into millions overnight—while the unconnected and uninitiated pick up the bill."[84]

Journalists, cartoonists, and talk show hosts had a field day stereotyping the "poor little rich girl" syndrome that they believed Linda Lay had demonstrated, while still using mogul style in describing her husband. Magazine articles showed Linda Lay selling off belongings; one account was entitled "Lay Away Plan":

> Anyone who has ever had to unload $20 million worth of residential real estate real fast can appreciate Linda Lay's dilemma: What to do with a furniture collection that includes a mahogany-and-mother-of-pearl pool table and a life-size sculpture of Eve? . . . While no one has yet coughed up the $5,000 Lay is asking for that pool table or $13,000 for the Eve sculpture, other items, including a $700 crystal Baccarat bowl and some $8 Italian tiles, are selling briskly.[85]

Similar articles, with titles such as "An Enron Yard Sale," described Mrs. Lay's secondhand shop, called Jus' Stuff, where she sold off many of her family's possessions: "Jus' Stuff is operating according to two time-honored

Houston traditions: putting the best possible face on bad news, and the belief that commerce cures all ills."[86] By contrast, media coverage of Ken Lay
continued to focus on the go-go corporate culture of Enron, including its
Darwinian nature and the acquisitive and competitive nature of some corporate officials. According to a former economist at Enron Energy Services,
"Appearances were very important. It was important for employees to believe the hype just as it was important for analysts and investors to believe
it."[87] For people to believe the hype, it was necessary for mogul style to be
displayed both inside and beyond the corporation.

Perhaps bad-apple-with-mogul-style framing was most apparent in visual depictions of the Lays in cartoons and caricatures. One political cartoon
showed Kenneth Lay standing at a podium, a spotlight shining on him, saying into a microphone, "I'm poor. My valet is poor. My chauffeur is poor.
My chef is poor. My maid is . . ."[88] A caricature titled "The New Homeless" showed Linda and Ken Lay standing on a street corner; he is holding
an empty tin cup like a beggar, and she is holding a small cardboard sign that
reads, "Fighting for Liquidity."[89] Another political cartoon was labeled "Mr.
and Mrs. Lay Start Their Four Thousand Hours of Volunteer Work." The
left panel showed Mrs. Lay holding a "whining seminar" for two of her
friends. The right panel showed "Kenny-boy" (President George W. Bush's
nickname for Ken Lay) "teaching corporate math in local schools"; he has
written "Heh + Heh = Heh-Heh" on the chalkboard while two students
dutifully take notes.[90]

Media reporting about the fall of Enron and its top corporate executives is only one of many examples of bad-apple-with-mogul-style framing
of stories. The fall of former Tyco International CEO L. Dennis Kozlowski
is another example. Kozlowski was charged with enterprise corruption and
grand larceny for allegedly stealing six hundred million dollars from Tyco.
Journalists reported in elaborate detail on the two-million-dollar week-long
party on the island of Sardinia that Kozlowski threw for the fortieth birthday of his wife, Karen Mayo. Media reports included extensive details about
the videotape of that party:

> The tape [shown to jurors in Courtroom No. 1324 at State Supreme
> Court in Manhattan] shows five young women in scanty, diaphanous
> frocks cavorting around a swimming pool, male models posing for snap-
> shots with female stars and a performance from a pop star. The jurors saw
> 21 minutes of what had been a four-hour videotape. State Supreme
> Court Justice Michael Obus ordered some segments removed, saying
> they could prejudice the jury against the defendants and were irrelevant
> to whether they had committed any crimes.

The portions removed include shots of an anatomically correct ice sculpture of Michaelangelo's "David" urinating vodka, two men dressed as ancient Romans carrying Mayo [the honoree] over their heads and a scene in which a man drops his pants for the camera.[91]

In addition to all of this, media reports told of a $250,000 payment to singer-songwriter Jimmy Buffett and his group to fly to the Mediterranean island and play at the party.[92]

According to court papers, Kozlowski also used Tyco money to pay $80,000 to American Express and $72,000 to a German yacht builder. For his residences, Tyco money paid for a $15,000 umbrella stand, a $6,000 shower curtain, and a $2,900 set of coat hangers, in addition to $5,960 for two sets of sheets.[93] In discussing these expenditures, business journalists (who ordinarily do not describe accessories of interior design) learned that bad-apple-with-mogul-style framing of stories is very popular with media audiences. Consider this excerpt from a *Wall Street Journal* article, "Newest 'Tyco Gone Wild' Video Is Out, and Jurors See $6,000 Shower Curtain":

> Now it can be told: The $6,000 shower curtain was in the maid's bathroom ... in Mr. Kozlowski's opulent, $18 million apartment on Fifth Avenue in Manhattan. The dimly lit tape [shown during trial] showcased costly china, antiques, oil paintings, and four-poster beds. Prosecutors contend most of the duplex apartment's furnishings, including a $15,000 umbrella stand, were improperly bought with Tyco assets. But it was the famous shower curtain that everyone was waiting to see. When news of the costly fabric first surfaced last year, it became a symbol of corporate excess, the butt of jokes by late-night TV comedians.[94]

The shower curtain and the umbrella stand were considered to be crucial evidence in the Kozlowski trial; however, how journalists and correspondents framed their stories served to highlight even more the excesses designed to impress other moguls, sometimes at the expense of lower-level employees and shareholders.

A third example of bad-apple-with-mogul-style framing was the media coverage of HealthSouth Corporation chief executive Richard Scrushy, who was indicted on eighty-five criminal counts, including fraud, money laundering, and other crimes in connection with an accounting fraud that inflated by $2.7 billion the earnings and assets of the health-care company he had founded. What Scrushy owned was relevant to the substance of news stories, because prosecutors were seeking millions in forfeitures from Scrushy, but it also served to capture the interest of readers and viewers: "Federal prosecutors said they would seek more than $278 million in forfeitures from Scrushy, including a plantation, a yacht, two airplanes, four luxury cars, a diamond ring, antique rugs and paintings by famous artists."[95] Some accounts were more explicit about naming the famous artists whose works he owned:

> The indictment charges Mr. Scrushy with conspiracy; mail, wire and securities fraud; false statements; false certifications; and money laundering—the latter by using fraudulently obtained money to buy and support his four homes, expensive boats and cars, wine cellars, extensive real estate holdings, and an art collection that includes paintings by Picasso, Chagall, Renoir and Miro.[96]

Still other reports noted that Mr. Scrushy's assets included "houses, aircraft, a marina, jewelry, fine art and high-end cars, including a Rolls Royce and a Lamborghini."[97] However, virtually all media accounts relied at least to some degree on bad-apple-with-mogul-style framing to tell the story of Scrushy's downfall.

Media reports of the alleged crimes of real-life individuals like Scrushy, Kozlowski, and Lay are paralleled with the occasional TV story line in crime dramas in a way that reveals for viewers the elegant lifestyles of rich bad apples. The technique also typically suggests that the rich and powerful consider themselves to be above the law or feel that at the least they should not be bothered by police officers or courts.

BAD APPLES IN TELEVISION CRIME DRAMAS: "WE'RE ABOVE THE LAW"

Bad-apple framing, of various forms, in media stories about real-life rich men and women in trouble with the law are often stranger than fiction. However, crime dramas (one of the most popular television genres) frequently use fictitious characters to reflect the bad-apple behavior of wealthy people who are victims or suspects in criminal cases. As an example, wealthy people seldom come out looking noble in the NBC crime series *Law & Order.* Over the more than fourteen seasons that *Law & Order* has been televised, it has explored numerous crimes that somehow involved wealthy and influential individuals.

In each season, the story line of at least one episode has the detectives go to the residence of a rich family, typically on the Upper East Side, to ask questions about a crime that has been committed. Detective Lennie Briscoe (Jerry Orbach) routinely makes unfavorable comments about the wealth of the person or the affluent residence as he and his partner are leaving the residence, such as "Well, I guess the maid forgot to clean up before she left." The *Law & Order* story lines involving wealthy people often portray them as above the law, as too busy and important to help the detectives, or unconcerned about whether or not justice is done. In some episodes, the rich and famous make phone calls to the higher-ups in the city's administration or the judicial system, resulting in warnings to detectives or prosecutors to be careful ("You'd better be right, or there'll be hell to pay") in their investigation or prosecution.

Three examples show how stories about wealthy characters are framed in *Law & Order.* One episode, "Family Business," focuses on the police investigation of the murder of the president of New York's most popular (and expensive) department store. Detectives are led to the feuding daughters of the store's elderly owner as possible suspects; however, the store owner seeks to outsmart the district attorney.[98] In another episode, "Entitled," the police investigate the "wayward socialite daughter of a wealthy, politically connected—and threatening—grande dame" as a possible suspect in a murder. A third episode, "For Love or Money," tells the story of detectives who investigate the murder of a rich man and come to believe that the victim's widow might have hired a hit man to kill him.

In yet another episode, "Darwinian," the detectives investigate a case in which a homeless, mentally ill person apparently has been killed in a hit-and-run accident; subsequent investigation reveals that the victim "was trapped inside the car's windshield after the accident and that the driver—a high profile publicist—left the man dying in her garage" before disposing of the body.[99] "Darwinian" has what *Law & Order* refers to as a "ripped-from-the-headlines" story line that combines two real criminal cases, one in which a woman (of more modest means than in the TV show) left a man to die on the windshield of her car after a hit-and-run accident, and a second involving well-known New York society publicist Elizabeth Grubman (not related to Jack Grubman of the nursery school scandal), who was convicted on the felony charge of leaving the scene of an accident (that injured sixteen people) and on a misdemeanor assault charge.

These charges arose from an incident in which Grubman belligerently backed her Mercedes SUV into a group of people going to a night club. Angry that she had been asked by club employees to move her vehicle out of a fire lane, Grubman addressed a security employee with an expletive and called him "white trash." As the judge in her case commented, "They were hardworking people, decent people, and you treated them in a way that might be considered arrogant and certainly rash."[100] That seems to be one of the bad-apple messages that crime shows like *Law & Order* send to viewers: Some wealthy and well-connected people treat other people like trash. Another message is that when the rich and famous do bad things, other people gain satisfaction from learning about their problems. The judge stated that the Grubman case had elements of classical tragedy, in that the audience enjoyed seeing how the mighty had fallen. "There's a certain part of human nature that seems unfortunately to delight in that," said Justice Michael F. Mullen of the State Supreme Court as he gave Grubman a sixty-day sentence.[101]

Whether in the true stories of people's lives or in the story lines produced by television scriptwriters, there are key commonalities in framing. One of those commonalities is that the rich and famous live more glamorous and exciting lives than ordinary people. Even when they are in trouble with the law, their money and positions in the community make them likely to avoid the harshest penalties the system might impose. In sum, their wealth provides them with a cushion that others simply do not have.

GILDED CAGES: EFFECTS OF SOUR-GRAPES AND BAD-APPLE FRAMING

The ways in which the media frame stories about the rich and famous influence our thinking about how people in the top economic tiers of society live. Framing is also significant in whether media audiences see larger issues of inequality in terms of *individual* conditions or larger *structural* conditions embedded in the social institutions of our nation. As contrasted with the framing approaches in chapter 2 (such as framing that suggests the rich are like everyone else, framing that assumes the wealthy should be admired for their achievements, or framing that applauds the rich for their virtues and good deeds), sour-grapes and bad-apple framing send divergent messages about wealth and how the rich conduct their lives.

Sour-grapes framing portrays the rich as often unhappy and dysfunctional people. The notion of the "poor little rich girl" may lead audiences to see the problems of the wealthy as self-inflicted and based on individual character flaws. The cautionary tales of inherited wealth or the problems of the nouveau riche suggest that there is a great deal of pain to be experienced because of one's wealth. However, sour-grapes framing also sends the contradictory message that there is much pleasure to be had from great wealth. From the biographies of the unhappy rich to television series ranging from *Dallas* to contemporary shows like *Arrested Development* and *The O.C.*, story lines of corruption and insecurity carry messages similar to the real-world stories of individuals whose riches have not brought them happiness or success to the extent that they would have liked.

As the illusion that we know the rich and famous is created over time by media coverage of their activities, the frames utilized to tell stories about the wealthy may distort our perception of reality about them. Bad-apple framing frequently includes elaborate discussions of what life is like in the rarified world of luxury estates, yachts, and private jets, and million-dollar office Christmas parties, and these discussions may render the message about the evildoing of some of these individuals secondary to the impression of the good life. The sagas of corporate wrongdoing often are told as the stories of individuals, making it appear that if one or a few bad apples could be purged from the barrel, everything would be all right and business as usual could resume unimpeded. It is only when news of a number of business crises break at once, such as the financial scandals of Ivan F. Boesky and Michael R. Milkin the 1980s or more recent crises of the twenty-first century, that a pattern of corporate malfeasance may actually be noticed in media accounts about the wrongdoings of wealthy business elites.

The milder forms of bad-apple framing portray the rich as merely seeking publicity (the media hogs) or as acting as if money can buy anything (or anyone). However, the stronger forms of bad-apple framing, such as when wealthy individuals are accused of crimes, still emphasize that material possessions are important and that the accused either have good taste in merchandise (as in the case of women shoplifters) or mogul style (as in the cases of CEOs whose expenditures were meant to impress other moguls and provide their families with the best of luxury living).

The bad attitudes of the rich as revealed in their conduct toward law enforcement officials and the court system are portrayed in a number of television crime series. Although I have focused only on the NBC series *Law & Order*, other shows carry similar messages about the elegant lifestyles and arrogant attitudes of the rich and famous. Even as some readers and viewers may experience schadenfreude, the readers may also have a desire to "trade up," to own things they really cannot afford, and to blame themselves for their failure to reach the American Dream of success and wealth.

When the wealthy commit crimes, we may believe that they should be punished, but we are not surprised to learn of their differential treatment by the criminal justice system or of what money can buy them in the process. Journalists make media audiences aware of the favorable treatment that some wealthy criminals receive. An article, "For the Elite, Easing the Way to Prison," for example, describes how A. Alfred Taubman, the (then) seventy-eight-year-old principal owner and former chairman of Sotheby's, received a year-and-a-day sentence and a $7.5 million fine for leading a six-year price-fixing scheme (the same one that brought house arrest for Diana D. Brooks). It explained how highly paid lawyers representing clients like these attempt to get their clients into the best prisons with the easiest possible sentences if it appears that jail time is inevitable:

> "In these cases, the defense attorney will act almost like an agent in Hollywood, negotiating the perp's rights, wheeling and dealing to get her into the best spot," [Bill Stanton, a security consultant and investigator] said. "He can say, 'This prison has tennis, this one has nicer rooms.'"
>
> Defense lawyers have some influence over where their clients serve time, legal experts say. . . . And in the last decade, dozens of specialists have begun marketing their services to experts in sentence mitigation. These are the lawyers, criminologists, or former corrections officials known as "postconviction specialists," who—for fees that can reach into tens of thousands of dollars—navigate and cajole the prison and judicial systems, bargaining for the chance at a light, sweet sentence. They are a grim reality in the lives of the criminally convicted elite: counselors as valued in their way as the SAT prep teachers, personal shoppers and chefs who also serve the well-to-do.[102]

Media reports also inform audiences that the rich—even those convicted of felonies—are different from ordinary people. Readers and viewers learn about what journalists refer to as "a soft landing," in which elite felons like Diana D. Brooks and A. Alfred Taubman are able to use their wealth to mitigate their problems and ease their reentry into society. One journalist contrasted the reentry of an "ordinary criminal" with that of Taubman after he had served nine-and-a-half months of his sentence and was released:

> Raymond Carter's release from prison followed a familiarly bleak script. After two years at the Wyoming Correctional Facility in upstate New York for sale of a controlled substance, he was granted his freedom on June 23, and given back his personal belongings—a Social Security card and some medication—then handed 40 bucks and a one-way bus ticket to the Port Authority Bus Terminal in Manhattan. He had a little time, so he savored a quiet meal at McDonald's. . . .
>
> A. Alfred Taubman's reintroduction to society went down a little differently. . . . Mr. Taubman . . . learned on June 13 at a halfway house in Detroit that he was a free man. Mr. Taubman's first move was to order his chauffeur to pick him up posthaste. After a quiet night at home in nearby Bloomfield Hills, Mich., with his wife, Judy, amid their collection of Jackson Pollocks and Kandinskys, Mr. Taubman boarded his Gulfsteam IV and headed straight to his sprawling oceanfront estate in the Hamptons. By evening, he was savoring a meal at Mirko's . . . at the best table in the house.[103]

From media reports like this we learn that even when the wealthy reside in "gilded cages" and experience problems, their lives still appear to have silver linings when contrasted with those of people living in poverty or in the working and middle classes.

NOTES

1. Warren St. John, "Sorrow So Sweet: A Guilty Pleasure in Another's Woe," *New York Times,* August 24, 2002, A15.

2. Alex Kuczynski, "Lifestyles of the Rich and Red-Faced," *New York Times,* September 22, 2002, ST1.

3. Michael Parenti, *Inventing Reality: The Politics of the Mass Media* (New York: St. Martin's, 1986), 109.

4. Parenti, *Inventing Reality,* 109; see also Gregory Mantsios, "Media Magic: Making Class Invisible," in *Privilege: A Reader,* ed. Michael S. Kimmel and Abby L. Ferber, 99–109 (Boulder, Colo.: Westview, 2003).

5. Aesop, "The Fox and the Grapes," www.pagebypagebooks.com/Aesop/ Aesops_Fables/The_Fox_and_the_Grapes_p1.html (accessed December 4, 2003).

6. C. David Heymann, *Poor Little Rich Girl: The Life and Legend of Barbara Hutton* (New York: Random House, 1984).

7. Pony Duke and Jason Thomas, *Too Rich: The Family Secrets of Doris Duke* (New York: HarperCollins, 1996).

8. "Customer Review of *Poor Little Rich Girl: The Life and Legend of Barbara Hutton,* by C. David Heymann," Amazon.com, 2003, www.amazon.com/exec/obidos/ search-handle-form/ref=s_sf_b_as/002-5171433-1616062 (accessed December 7, 2003).

9. See Diana Kendall, *The Power of Good Deeds: Privileged Women and the Social Reproduction of the Upper Class* (Lanham, Md.: Rowman & Littlefield, 2002).

10. Quoted in Stephen J. Dubner, "Suddenly Popular," *New York Times Magazine,* June 8, 2003, 68.

11. Dubner, "Suddenly Popular," 68.

12. Dubner, "Suddenly Popular," 68.

13. See Michael Noer and Dan Ackman, "The Forbes Fictional Fifteen," *Forbes,* September 13, 2002, www.forbes.com/2002/09/13/400fictional_10.html (accessed December 7, 2003).

14. Alessandra Stanley, "All in the (Rich, Dysfunctional) Family," *New York Times,* October 31, 2003, B33.

15. Stanley, "All in the (Rich, Dysfunctional) Family," B33.

16. "Arrested Development," FOX.com, 2003, fox.com/schedule/2003/ad.htm (accessed January 10, 2004).

17. Nancy Franklin, "Sunny Money: Fox Heads Down the Coast from 90210," *New Yorker,* August 18, 25, 2003, 144.

18. James Poniewozik, "The New Class Action," *Time,* September 29, 2003, n.p.

19. Franklin, "Sunny Money," 144.

20. "*The OC.*" Forums.about.com, 2003. forums.about.com/n/mb/message.asp? webtag=ab-tvschedules&msg=2794.15 (accessed December 8, 2003).

21. Mantsios, "Media Magic," 105.

22. "McDonald's Features Donald Trump in New Ad Campaign Launching Dollar-Priced Big N' Tasty and McChicken Sandwich," McDonalds.com, 2002, www.mcdonalds.com/countries/usa/whatsnew/pressrelease/2002/10032002_a (accessed December 16, 2003).

23. Abby Ellin, "'Survivor' Meets Millionaire, and a Show Is Born," *New York Times,* October 19, 2003, BU4.

24. Quoted in Geoffrey Nunberg, "Keeping Ahead of the Joneses," *New York Times,* November 24, 2002, WK4.

25. Clara Hemphill, "Admissions Anxiety," *New York Times,* November 17, 2002, WK11.

26. Quoted in Jane Gross, "No Talking Out of Preschool," *New York Times,* November 15, 2002, A22.

27. Michael Powell, "First Good Preschool, Then Harvard," *Austin American-Statesman,* November 24, 2002, K3.

28. Peter W. Cookson, Jr., and Caroline Hodges Persell, *Preparing for Power: America's Elite Boarding Schools* (New York: Basic Books, 1985), 22.

29. Powell, "First Good Preschool, Then Harvard," K3.

30. Gross, "No Talking Out of Preschool," A22.

31. Gross, "No Talking Out of Preschool," A22.

32. Victoria Goldman, "The Baby Ivies," *Education Life: New York Times,* January 12, 2003, 22.

33. Michael J. Silverstein and Neil Fiske (with John Butman), *Trading Up: The New American Luxury* (New York: Portfolio, 2003), 166.

34. Silverstein and Fiske, *Trading Up,* 3.

35. Alison Arnett, "Counter Culture," *Austin American-Statesman,* December 18, 2003, E1, E10.

36. Silverstein and Fiske, *Trading Up,* 41.

37. Chris Smith, "Can This Man Save Martha?" *New York Magazine,* December 15, 2003, 34.

38. Smith, "Can This Man Save Martha?" 38.

39. Leslie Savan, "In Defense of Martha," *New York Times,* June 27, 2002, A27.

40. Marc Peyser, "Martha's Mess: The Insiders," *Newsweek,* July 1, 2002, 38–43.

41. Sharyn Wizda Vane, "Martha's Dirty Laundry," *Austin American-Statesman,* April 20, 2002, D1.

42. "Tarnish, Anyone?" *People,* July 8, 2002, 44.

43. Alessandra Stanley and Constance L. Hays, "Martha Stewart's To-Do List May Include Image Polishing," *New York Times,* June 23, 2002, A1.

44. Alex Kuczynski and Andrew Ross Sorkin, "Canapés and Investment Tips Are Served to Well-Heeled," *New York Times,* July 1, 2002, A1, A17.

45. Leslie Kaufman and Constance L. Hays, "Blue Lights or Not, Martha Stewart Remains Calm," *New York Times,* January 26, 2002, B1.

46. Peyser, "Martha's Mess," 43.

47. "Tarnish, Anyone?" *People,* 44–45.

48. Stanley and Hays, "Martha Stewart's To-Do List May Include Image Polishing," A1.

49. See Stanley and Hays, "Martha Stewart's To-Do List May Include Image Polishing," A24.

50. "Perspectives," *Newsweek,* February 4, 2002, 17.

51. Pam Lambert, Alicia C. Shepard, and Sharon Cotliar, "Making Herself at Home: Even behind Bars, Martha Stewart Shows That Living Well May Be the Best Revenge," *People,* December 13, 2004.

52. Ralph Blumenthal and Carol Vogel, "Ex-Chief of Sotheby's Gets 3-Year Probation and Fine," *New York Times,* April 30, 2002, A27.

53. Alex Kuczynski, "When Home Is a Castle and the Big House, Too," *New York Times,* August 18, 2002, ST1, ST7.

54. Gerry Shanahan, "You Say House Arrest, I Say Paradise," *New York Times,* May 2, 2002, F1.

55. Kuczynski, "When Home Is a Castle and the Big House, Too," ST1, ST7.

56. "Letters to the Editor," *New York Times,* May 23, 2002, F10.

57. "Letters to the Editor," *New York Times,* May 23, 2002, F10.

58. Rick Lyman, "For the Ryder Trial, a Hollywood Script," *New York Times,* November 3, 2002, ST8.

59. Lyman, "For the Ryder Trial, a Hollywood Script," ST1.

60. Mark Wrolstad, "An Unfashionable Turn for Stylish HP Socialite," *Dallas Morning News,* October 25, 2003, 1A, 10A–11A.

61. Alan Peppard, "Charity Co-Chair Steps Down over Shoplifting Charge," www.dallasnews.com (accessed September 29, 2003).

62. "Shop Till You Get Caught," *D Magazine,* November, 2003, 20.

63. Wrolstad, "An Unfashionable Turn for Stylish HP Socialite," 1A.

64. See Peppard, "Charity Co-Chair Steps Down Over Shoplifting Charge."

65. Wrolstad, "An Unfashionable Turn for Stylish HP Socialite," 10A.

66. Wrolstad, "An Unfashionable Turn for Stylish HP Socialite," 11A.

67. See Paul Martin Lester, ed., *Images That Injure: Pictorial Stereotypes in the Media* (Westport, Conn.: Praeger, 1996).

68. Kuczynski, "Lifestyles of the Rich and Red-Faced."

69. Kuczynski, "Lifestyles of the Rich and Red-Faced," ST1.

70. Kuczynski, "Lifestyles of the Rich and Red-Faced," ST8.

71. Michael Duffy, "What Did They Know and When Did They Know It?" *Time,* January 28, 2002, 17.

72. Duffy, "What Did They Know and When Did They Know It?" 50.

73. Evan Thomas and Andrew Murr, "The Gambler Who Blew It All," *Newsweek,* February 4, 2002, 19.

74. Anne Belli Gesalman, "Cliff Was Climbing the Walls," *Newsweek,* February 4, 2002, 24; Margot Habiby and Jim Kennett, "Ex-Enron Executive Killed Self, Police Say," *Austin American-Statesman,* January 26, 2002, A1, A4; Cathy Booth Thomas, "Enron Takes a Life," *Time,* February 4, 2002, 20–21.

75. Thomas and Murr, "The Gambler Who Blew It All," 20.

76. Michael Duffy and John F. Dickerson, "Enron Spoils the Party," *Time,* February 4, 2002, 19–25; Frank Rich, "State of the Enron," *New York Times,* February 2, 2002, A29; Alessandra Stanley and Jim Yardley, "Lay's Family Is Financially Ruined, His Wife Says," *New York Times,* January 29, 2002, C1, C6.

77. Neela Banerjee, David Barboza, and Audrey Warren, "At Enron, Lavish Excess Often Came before Success," *New York Times,* February 26, 2001, C1.

78. Banerjee, Barboza, and Warren, "At Enron, Lavish Excess Often Came before Success," C6.

79. Banerjee, Barboza, and Warren, "At Enron, Lavish Excess Often Came before Success," C6.

80. Quoted in Stanley and Yardley, "Lay's Family Is Financially Ruined, His Wife Says," C1.

81. Quoted in Stanley and Yardley, "Lay's Family Is Financially Ruined, His Wife Says," C1.

82. Daniel Eisenberg, "Ignorant & Poor?" *Time,* February 11, 2002, 38.

83. Rich, "State of the Enron," A29.

84. Rich, "State of the Enron," A29.

85. "Lay Away Plan," *People,* June 10, 2002, 76.

86. Mimi Swartz, "An Enron Yard Sale," *New Yorker,* May 6, 2002, 50.

87. Quoted in Banerjee, Barboza, and Warren, "At Enron, Lavish Excess Often Came before Success," C6.

88. "A New Kind of Poverty," *Newsweek,* November 22, 2003, www.msnbc .msn.com/id/3540672 (accessed April 2, 2004), 103.

89. "Notebook: The New Homeless," *Time,* February 11, 2002, 15.

90. Jeff Danziger, "Mr. and Mrs. Lay Start Their Four Thousand Hours of Volunteer Work," *New York Times,* February 3, 2002, WK5.

91. Samuel Mauli, "Jurors in Tyco Case See Edited Tape of Lavish Party," *Austin American-Statesman,* October 29, 2003, C1.

92. Mauli, "Jurors in Tyco Case See Edited Tape of Lavish Party"; Andrew Ross Sorkin, "Birthday Party Video Takes Center Stage at Kozlowski Trial," *New York Times,* October 29, 2003, C4.

93. "Put It on My Tab," *Austin American-Statesman,* September 22, 2002, H1.

94. Colleen DeBaise, "Newest 'Tyco Gone Wild' Video Is Out, and Jurors See $6,000 Shower Curtain," *Wall Street Journal,* November 26, 2003, C1, C7.

95. James Vicini and Verna Gates, "HealthSouth's Founder Hit with Criminal Charges," Reuters News, 2003. aolscv.news.aol/news/article.adp?id= 20031105051809990002 (accessed November 5, 2003).

96. Milt Freudenheim and Eric Lichtblau, "Former HealthSouth Chief Indicted by U.S," *New York Times,* November 5, 2003, C8.

97. Marilyn Geewax, "HealthSouth Founder Is Indicted in Fraud Case," *Austin American-Statesman,* November 5, 2003, D6.

98. *Law & Order,* NBC.com, 2003, www.nbc.com/Law_&_Order/about/index.html (accessed December 22, 2003).

99. *Law & Order,* NBC.com, 2003.

100. Quoted in Elissa Gootman, "Publicist Gets Jail Sentence and Scolding," *New York Times,* October 24, 2002, A28.

101. Quoted in Gootman, "Publicist Gets Jail Sentence and Scolding," A28.

102. Alex Kuczynski, "For the Elite, Easing the Way to Prison," *New York Times,* December 9, 2001, ST1, ST2.

103. Warren St. John, "Advice from Ex-Cons to a Jet-Set Jailbird: Best Walk on Eggs," *New York Times,* July 13, 2003, ST1.

4

FRAGILE FRAMES:
THE POOR AND HOMELESS

New York Times, January 30, 1870:

Down in the squalid environs of ——— street this woman lives, whose story we shall tell, having been sought out in the crusade of a *Times* reporter among the haunts of a starving and in the main, ill-used class. Through a foul alley, reeking with noisome odors, lay the approach to a den of a room—odorous of pestilence, one might suppose, intuitively desiring to keep one's mouth shut while waiting. . . . The dingiest of dingy old women threw out a tub of suds as we approached, then conveyed us to the room. A young child was there, begrimed and sooty. These and the mother of the latter were the occupants, and it is of this mother that we shall principally speak. Young she was, and pretty but for the pinched and perished look one sees so often, it is grievous to say, among this class of laborers. . . .

[The mother] was out of work now. Her last situation had paid her $5 per week.

"And you lost it—how?" we asked.

"I will tell you," was the reply. "I was to have reached the place by 7 o'clock in the morning. I told them I would; but as it happened, one or two mornings there was no one to be with my little child, and I was behind time; it might have been forty minutes, at most, but hardly more than half an hour, I think. . . . Next day I was discharged, and here I am—nothing to help myself with, only because I wanted to do a mother's part by my little one. I have sometimes heard of mothers drowning themselves and their children in straits like mine. I couldn't do that, but I oftentimes think could that be much worse than to live as we live."[1]

In this early article about poverty in New York City, the reporter frames the story to show that the poor are to be pitied, particularly if they are willing to work. More than 130 years later, journalists still employ a sympathetic frame in some articles about the poor and homeless, but most articles and stories about people on the bottom rungs of society either treat them as mere statistics or have a critical edge, portraying the poor as losers, welfare dependents, mentally ill persons, or criminals.

This is quite different from the frames that are used in articles and story lines about the rich and famous. As discussed in previous chapters, the upper class is typically presented in frames that encourage us to believe that what is good for the wealthy and famous is good for everyone else (consensus framing) or that we should admire or emulate the upper class, even if there are a few bad apples in the bunch.

Articles and stories about the upper classes appear frequently in newspapers and on television, but the poor are invisible, except when they are presented as faceless statistics or when they are shown to be "problems" to be dealt with in a community. In this chapter, I show how the poor have generally been ignored by the media, and that when they do appear in what we read and watch, how they are portrayed often in a negative light that ignores larger community and societal conditions that may have contributed to or exacerbated their current condition.

MEDIA FRAMING OF STORIES ABOUT THE POOR AND HOMELESS

The relative invisibility of the poor in media reporting has been referred to as a case of "benign neglect"[2] that hides the realities of poverty from middle- and upper-class readers and viewers. This neglect may be intentional, because media audiences do not want to have the poor in their faces:

> Fear of poverty rests at the very core of the American culture—the "American dream" is precisely the hope of rising from rags to riches. . . . The media offer those who are not poor, especially Whites, little guidance in reconciling the conflicting emotions toward poverty embedded within American culture, with its simultaneously sympathetic and impatient assumption that America offers the promise of escape from poverty to all who work hard.[3]

By providing only a few stories about the poor, journalists do not have to deal often with middle- and upper-class fears about poverty or with the conflicting emotions that might be generated by a greater awareness of poverty, hunger, and homelessness in a nation that is referred to as the land of opportunity.

How are *poor* and *poverty* used in the media? There is no standard usage. Some journalists use the terms loosely to refer to people on the bottom rungs of the nation's economic ladder, whereas others use the official *poverty line* that the Social Security Administration creates to represent the minimum amount of money required for living at a subsistence level in any particular year. The poverty line is computed by determining the cost of a minimally nutritious diet (a low-cost food budget on which a family could survive nutritionally on a short-term, emergency basis) and multiplying this figure by three to allow for nonfood costs. Based on this method of calculation, about thirty-one million people (more than 11 percent of the U.S. population) lived below the official government poverty level of $18,660 for a family of four in 2003.

According to critics, however, measuring poverty in terms of cash income and household size does not take into account the increased cost of other basic needs, such as housing, health care, and child care.[4] When the formula for the official poverty line was created, low-income families spent about one-third of their income on food; food today constitutes about one-fifth of low-income budgets, and housing costs have sharply increased to about 30 percent. The poverty line also employs a one-size-fits-all logic, operating on the assumption that the same standards for poverty can be applied in New York City as in rural communities of the South.[5]

The framing of news stories based on statistics and trends is often referred to as *thematic framing,* which in this case means that journalists primarily write about such facts as changes in the poverty rate, how the government defines poverty, and which states have the largest increases in poverty or hunger.[6] In these stories, the object of the coverage is abstract and impersonal,[7] sending a message to media audiences that "the poor are faceless."[8] According to some analysts, thematic framing of poverty is dehumanizing, in that it "ignores the human tragedy of poverty—the suffering, indignities, and misery endured by millions of children and adults."[9]

By contrast, *episodic framing* reveals poverty "in terms of personal experience: the viewer is provided with a particular [episode] of an individual or family living under economic duress."[10] This type of framing provides a human face for poverty, but it often ignores the larger structural factors (such as high rates of unemployment) that affect the problem of poverty, or it portrays the poor in negative images based on the actions of the few individuals featured in the article. For example, episodic framing of some stories may suggest that most of the poor are undeserving because they are welfare cheats, drug addicts, or greedy panhandlers.[11] Episodic framing may cause audiences to conclude that the poor have only themselves to blame, because of their bad attitudes and behavior.[12] As communications scholars Robert

M. Entman and Andrew Rojecki state, media audiences may infer that "inexplicably, some people choose to live in deteriorating neighborhoods where they frequently commit or become victims of crime, or have trouble receiving health care and finding adequate schools."[13]

Episodic framing of stories about the poor suggests that the poor are an eyesore on the landscape of daily life.[14] Stories about panhandlers disturbing people on city streets or about individuals standing in line outside homeless shelters portray the poor as part of the urban blight, particularly when viewed through the eyes of middle-class observers interviewed by journalists because of their concerns about the placement of a homeless shelter or having been accosted on the street by panhandlers. Typically, the voices heard in this type of reporting are not those of the poor but of the middle class expressing disdain for the poor.[15]

Perhaps the most benevolent message that episodic framing conveys about poverty is that the poor are down on their luck.[16] This type of framing is especially popular in news stories published near holidays like Thanksgiving or Christmas, asking readers to help meet temporarily some of the needs of the poor. However, most newspaper coverage of the poor over the past 150 years seems to have been more intent on selling newspapers to middle- and upper-class readers than on assisting persons in poverty.

HISTORICAL FRAMING:
THE POOR YOU WILL HAVE WITH YOU ALWAYS

Framing of early newspaper articles about the poor used vivid terminology to portray their plight, including descriptions such as "squalid environs," a "foul alley reeking with noisome odors," and "begrimed and sooty."[17] Today, the language of newspaper reporting has changed somewhat, but the format for describing the poor has not been significantly modified to examine the larger structural issues that perpetuate poverty, such as growing rates of economic inequality, a decline in the number of available jobs, continuing racial and gender discrimination, and other social and technological changes that reduce opportunity.

A systematic examination of the *New York Times* archives between September 1851 and December 1995 reveals 4,126 articles having the word "poverty" in the headline. Many of the early articles linked poverty to other social problems, such as suicide and murder. "Distressing Case of Poverty and Suicide," for example, described the suicide of John Murphy, a forty-five-year-old Irish immigrant tailor and the father of five who had lost his job. According to the article, Murphy's unemployment had produced mental illness and ultimately led to his suicide: "Finding his family in a starving condition, it affected him so at times he was out of his mind."[18] In the end, "the deceased . . . came to his death by cutting his throat with a razor, while laboring under a temporary derangement of mind, consequent upon his destitute condition."[19]

This article is typical of a number of nineteenth-century articles that blamed the suicides of indigent people on derangement resulting from their destitute condition. Other examples include "Melancholy Case of Suicide: Pride and Poverty the Cause"[20] and "A Sad Case of Poverty: A Woman Commits Suicide, Her Husband at the Point of Death,"[21] both of which told of residents in tenement houses who had taken their lives when they could no longer stand their impoverished condition. People who had once been more affluent and ended up in poverty were believed to be prime candidates for suicide, as in "A Sad Life Story: Reduced from Wealth to Poverty and Dying Almost without Friends,"[22] which described the death of a "remarkable septuagenarian lady, Mary Jane Marquis," who had ended her own life after being reduced to poverty.

The framing of nineteenth-century articles about the relationship between poverty and suicide was in keeping with the common sociological thought of the day, as found in the works of the French sociologist Emile Durkheim. According to Durkheim, *fatalistic suicide* is likely to occur among "persons with futures pitilessly blocked and passions violently choked by oppressive discipline."[23] Many reports in the *New York Times* told of people overcome by such fatalism, including poor women with children to feed, recent immigrants who were lonely and had no home, merchants whose businesses had failed, and the elderly.[24]

Just as suicide and poverty were often linked in early media reports, so too were crime and poverty. "Down among the Lowly: The Sights That One Sees in the Fourth Ward" described the "intense, and perhaps undeserved suffering" in the Fourth Ward of New York City, where "coarselooking men and slovenly women stand listlessly in the doorways of the huge tenement houses, or gaze stupidly out of the windows."[25] The reporter focused his article on the relationship between poverty and crime:

> The reputation of the Fourth Ward for crimes of every nature has created a general distrust toward all of its inhabitants, which has prevented or neutralized many efforts for their improvement. Dismal tales of foul outrage and drunken brutality, combined with the loathsome appearance of the place, have given to it a far worse name than it deserves, for Police records will show that though there are none that can equal it in misery, there are several wards in this City that surpass it in criminality.

Indeed, almost all of the crimes committed there can be traced directly or indirectly to the common curse of poverty, which has blighted the hopes and aspirations of its inhabitants.[26]

However, of all the possible poverty-and-crime stories, journalists were most interested in cases in which parents killed their children. An example is "Terrible Tragedy: An Insane Mother Kills Her Daughter,"[27] which described how the Elliott family's poverty brought about the insanity of the mother, who murdered her seventeen-year-old daughter. Like most of the poor in news stories of that day, the Elliott family lived in a tenement house; the father had been unemployed for some time, thus reducing the family to almost abject poverty. Worse yet, according to the journalist, Mr. Elliott had become "addicted to the use of intoxicating liquor, and for the last three weeks he had been on a continual spree." When he left the house one day, Mrs. Elliott strangled their daughter, laid her body out on the bed, and calmly informed her husband when he returned home that the girl was dead.[28] Headlines for articles about parents in poverty who killed their children frequently summarized the entire story, as in this example: "A Father's Awful Crime: Shooting His Three Little Girls. Why John Remmler . . . Killed His Children—Poverty and a Fear for Their Future His Reasons."[29]

Linkages between poverty, region, and race were quite evident in the framing of stories about the poor in the South. Northeastern newspapers like the *New York Times* periodically published articles informing urban dwellers how bad off the poor were in the South, particularly in the former slave states,[30] and many contemporary stereotypes of "poor," "black" African Americans can also be found in nineteenth-century news reporting.

From the 1850s to the present, many stories about the poor have been embedded in articles about how charitable the wealthy are. An 1870 *New York Times* article, "Poverty and Charity," states that "all God's poor" will be taken care of by acts of public and private charity, particularly by the wealthy:

In no other country of the world is public charity dispensed more lavishly or with so tender a regard to the feelings of those whom vice or misfortune [has] compelled to solicit our bounty. . . . And [the poor] do move us, as a community, to deeds of disinterested endeavor and practical succor that should put all other countries under heaven to the blush. In this way, better than any other, is the humanizing influence of our republican form of government made apparent. Here the brotherhood of man is fully recognized. . . . Our rich men may be self-seeking, and even avaricious—they may be worldly and even irreligious—but they are not uncharitable. They pity poverty and are always ready and willing to relieve it.[31]

This article is framed more to praise the generosity of the rich than to explore the condition of the poor. Similarly, "Feeding the City's Poor: Giving Bountiful Dinners to Children and Poverty-Stricken People" tells how the "city's poor, its prisoners, and its other charges had their share yesterday of the good things that are distributed on Thanksgiving" when about "11,000 mouths" were fed at "the various hospitals, prisons, and asylums."[32]

Journalists in the 1800s also reported on the problem of the homeless; the framing of these articles focused on the destitute situation of homeless children. One article, "Walks among the New York Poor: Homeless Children," for example, described children whose most frequent statement was that they "don't live nowheres!"[33] Another article, "Homeless Children," emphasized how difficult it was at Christmastime for the more affluent to walk by and see "the number of wretched little children in our streets who have no homes to go to, nor any parents or guardians to provide them."[34] Reporters also praised charitable groups that provided residences for homeless children. "Lodging-House for Homeless Girls a New Project of the Children's Aid Society" described the "Girl's Lodging-House" as "a place which is intended to invite to a decent bed and satisfactory meal, she of the unsuccessful search after a situation, or the little pilgrim through the busy streets, attracting purchasers for her basket variety of temptingly arranged wares."[35] Similarly, News Boy's Lodging-House, a residence for homeless boys and young men, was opened "in view of the terrible destitution and homelessness of the poor this Winter."[36]

CONTEMPORARY FRAMING OF STORIES ABOUT THE POOR AND HOMELESS

The media serve as important sources of information about the extent and distribution of hardship in the contemporary United States.[37] Some media reports provide causal analysis that demonstrates how political leaders and governmental agencies contribute to, or seek to reduce, poverty, hunger, or homelessness, whereas other news items focus on the lives of the poor, sometimes portraying them as partly responsible for their own plight due to certain actions (such as dropping out of school or taking illegal drugs) or failure to act (such as not looking for a job or being unwilling to utilize the services of a homeless shelter).

When poverty is framed in news stories as primarily an *individual problem,* responsibility is assigned to those who are poor. This individualistic perspective makes it possible to blame the poor for their plight and hold them responsible for numerous other community problems. Suggestions that homeless people create disorder on the streets, are bad for business because they discourage shoppers, and are a drain on taxpayers because of the added expense of maintaining law and order are only a few of the examples of how homeless people might be blamed for other problems. By contrast, when journalists frame stories in a manner that portrays poverty as a *general outcome*—meaning a systemic perspective that places responsibility on communities and the nation—they characterize poverty, hunger, and homelessness from a structural approach focusing on such factors as how local and national economic and housing conditions produce homelessness.[38]

As mentioned previously in this chapter, news reports and articles about poverty and homelessness in the United States use two general categories of framing devices: thematic framing, which places events in broad context and provides details about trends; and episodic framing, which puts a human face on poverty by telling true stories about people who are poor and homeless. Episodic framing of poverty has four major subcategories: sympathetic framing, negative-image framing, exceptionalism framing, and charitable framing. Before turning to these forms of episodic framing, let us examine thematic framing in greater detail.

THEMATIC FRAMING:
THE POOR AS STATISTICS, NOT REAL PEOPLE

In a newspaper headline or the title of a television news segment about poverty or homelessness, words relating to numbers can be a good indicator of thematic framing in the accompanying story. For example, the headlines "Census Shows Ranks of Poor Rose by 1.3 Million"[39] and "New Poverty Guidelines Unveiled"[40] both refer to numbers—the number of people below the poverty line and the number of dollars that determine that line, respectively. The article about new poverty guidelines began as follows, reflecting the tendency of thematically framed articles to treat the poor as statistics rather than as real people:

> Who counts as poor? The government has just released the 2004 federal poverty guidelines in today's issue of the Federal Register. The poverty guidelines are sometimes loosely referred to as the "federal poverty level." It defines who is officially considered poor. In 2004, a single adult earning $9,310 or less every year is now at the poverty level. For a family of two, that figure is $12,490 or less per year. While for a family of three it's $15,670 or less. Each year, the poverty level is adjusted to account for inflation. State and federal agencies use the numbers to determine who is eligible for a range of programs, including the National School Lunch Program and Food Stamps.[41]

On television, a story like this may be accompanied by video footage of a poor African American man shuffling despondently down a city street. Newscasters typically report this information in a detached manner, as if there is much more important news to cover—such as war, crime, missing children, and current market reports.[42]

Stories about poverty have similar formats on television and in the newspapers, and they offer virtually identical information, frequently prepackaged by the Associated Press or other news organizations that provide news, photographs, and audio and video feeds to 1,700 U.S. newspapers and more than five thousand radio and television outlets in the United States.

Thematic framing not only provides data about poverty guidelines but emphasizes the number of Americans living in poverty and whether this number has increased or decreased over the previous year. An example is the following:

> The number of Americans living below the poverty line increased by more than 1.3 million last year, even though the economy technically edged out of recession during the same period, a [2003] Census Bureau report shows. The spike in economic hardship hit individuals and families alike. The report indicated that the total percentage of people in poverty increased to 12.4 percent from 12.1 percent in 2001 and totaled 34.8 million. At the same time, the number of families living in poverty went up by more than 300,000 in 2002 to 7 million from 6.6 million in 2001.[43]

The format of this article is typical in that it begins with data from the Census Bureau and then provides a quote from a spokesperson about the data, often followed by statements from economists who hold differing views as to what the figures mean. Later in the article quoted above, for example, economist Stuart Butler of the Heritage Foundation, a conservative Washington policy institute, stated that the increase in people living in poverty was "a fairly predictable product of the slowing economy." Then Butler shifted his focus to the relationship between poverty and welfare reform: "The issue is, what do you do to continue to strengthen the economy? You take the necessary steps to encourage people to move back into the work force, plus making sure we don't do anything to weaken the welfare reforms put in place some years ago."

The clear message is that poverty is related to the unwillingness of some workers to "move back into the work force," regardless of the availability of jobs in various regions of the country. After Butler's remarks, the article provided a counterpoint statement by Robert Greenstein, executive director of the Center on Budget and Policy Priorities: "Some people had drawn a Pollyanna-ish conclusion that somehow changes in the welfare system would insulate children from increases in poverty during economic slumps. These new data show that that assumption is flatly incorrect. It also underscores the mistake in federal tax policies that exclude the very families who are hurting the most." The inclusion of statements by Butler and Greenstein in the article, without additional explanation, assumes that readers are aware of current social policy debates pertaining to poverty rather than exploring the issues they raise.

When journalists report on statistical data issued by government agencies, their articles sometimes reveal political controversies about how the data are gathered, computed, and interpreted. These are often contentious topics among politicians, and journalists quickly pick up on these issues as being newsworthy. Many of the topics remain in the news year after year, as an examination of the *New York Times* archives shows.

Two recurring issues raised in thematic framing about poverty are who the poor *are* and *how many* people in the United States should be considered poor. The dividing line for identifying the poor is a contested terrain, because many analysts believe that the government's definition of poverty is out of date. Headlines in the 1990s reflected articles about these statistics: "In Rising Debate on Poverty, the Question: Who Is Poor?,"[44] "Poverty Rate Is the Highest in 16 Years, a Report Says,"[45] and "A Proposed Definition of Poverty May Raise Number of U.S. Poor."[46] However, these issues were not resolved in the 1990s, and headlines continue to identify the same issues and ask similar questions: "One Number Can't Measure Poverty"[47] and "Who's Poor? Don't Ask the Census Bureau."[48] Here is one article's description of the problem in determining the poverty line:

> As soon as the government announced the second straight yearly increase in the nation's poverty rate [in 2003], politicians and special-interest groups began tossing around the numbers like the political football the poor have become. But researchers say the government is not very good at keeping score. There is a near-unanimous agreement among experts and politicians that the method used to measure poverty—based on the spending habits of the 1950s—is flawed and outdated. The current measure of poverty, which takes into account household size and income, underestimates the number of poor by as much as 50 percent, some experts contend.[49]

Why is the government unable to update its method of identifying the poor? According to some media reports, changing the method of determining who is poor would have unpopular political ramifications. If the poor were more accurately counted, millions of people would be added to the eligibility rolls of anti-poverty programs, a process that would dramatically increase the national debt and further sink states into budget deficits.[50]

As debates rage on in the political arena and in newspapers and television news reports about the minute details of poverty statistics, larger societal issues about the root causes of poverty and homelessness are ignored. Controversy sells newspapers and brings in larger viewing audiences for television news programs, and the media are likely to focus on issues that bring in revenues.

Like news reports about poverty, thematic framing is frequently used in stories about hunger. "Hungry Families in U.S. on the Rise"[51] is a typical headline for an article about the growing problem of American families that cannot afford to buy adequate food (now more than twelve million). Hunger is most often the subject of news stories shortly before holidays, such as Thanksgiving and Christmas, and at times when new statistical data on the problem are released. On the basis of data from the U.S. Department of Agriculture (USDA) and the Census Bureau, recent media reports have described an increase in the number of hungry people in the United States, indicating that in 32 percent of all U.S. families, someone went hungry at one time or another during the previous year. Thematic framing of stories about the USDA's categories of hunger, such as "food insecure" and "food insecure, with hunger," convey to audiences the message that hunger (among the poor) is a messy topic that is not the problem of middle- and upper-income readers and viewers. Articles like "Of Fuzzy Math and 'Food Security'"[52] describe the extent to which tabulating hunger "is an inexact science and a political test" rather than a cause for concern about the number of hungry people in this country.

Media reporting about hunger often increases when data are released about changes in the number of hungry people in this country. After the U.S. Conference of Mayors (an organization that includes the mayors of 1,183 cities with populations of thirty thousand or more) reported a 17 percent increase in the demand for emergency food during 2003, headlines like "Homelessness, Hunger Worsen" in the *Boston Globe* and "Survey Indicates More Go Hungry, Homeless" in the *Washington Post* reported the story.[53]

Thematic framing that focuses on statistics and emphasizes increases or decreases in hunger may deflect people's attention from more pressing issues about the causes and consequences of hunger, particularly for children. "Are some groups exaggerating the numbers of people who are hungry?" is a far different question from "What can be done about the problem of hunger?" When the news media carry articles about the "numbers" debate, hunger appears to be a numbers game and of little consequence. Consider, for example, one journalist's comment about the likelihood of service providers, such as soup kitchen operators and food bank administrators, exaggerating in order to sustain contributions to their organizations:

> So what's the real story? Social ills like hunger and need for food assistance are notoriously difficult to measure. In a flagging economy, or even in boom times, those on the front lines—soup kitchen operators and food bank administrators, who must rely on donations and government subsidies—are always in the shadow of a shortfall. So it is not surprising that the mayors' survey, which relies primarily on the collected impressions (and varied record keeping) of these agencies, would consistently report an increase in demand.[54]

The visual images that accompany articles and television news accounts about hunger typically show political leaders like the president helping out at a Washington food bank or the mayor of a major city serving lunch at a homeless shelter on Thanksgiving Day. In this way, the seemingly dry statistics related to poverty and hunger are imbued with empathy and a humanitarian façade. Important officials are portrayed as caring individuals who feed the hungry rather than as merely vote-seeking politicians who show up for the occasional photo-op with those who are less fortunate.

Framing of stories about the homeless, like those about poverty and hunger, often describe how counting the homeless is problematic. Since statistics on homelessness are not available from the Census Bureau or other federal agencies, news organizations rely on data gathered by the U.S. Conference of Mayors and the National Coalition for the Homeless. According to the latter, there is no easy answer to the question of how many people in the United States are homeless: "In most cases, homelessness is a temporary circumstance—not a permanent condition. A more appropriate measure of the magnitude of homelessness is therefore the number of people who experience homelessness over time, not the number of 'homeless people.'"[55] According to some media reports, the homeless are seriously undercounted, because most studies count only those who are on the street on a specific date or live in shelters. Many homeless people stay with relatives and friends in crowded, temporary arrangements and are not counted if they are not visibly homeless when the data are gathered.[56]

Over the past two decades, media reports about the homeless—often carrying headlines such as "The Real Face of Homelessness"[57] or "Homelessness Grows as More Live Check-to-Check"[58]— have outnumbered those on poverty or hunger. According to the legal scholar Gary Blasi, *homelessness* won out over *poverty* in media accounts because both politicians and the general public reacted more favorably to the homeless.[59] Turning poverty and homelessness into separate issues shifted the focus of media coverage and public policy: "The homeless" came to be viewed more favorably, at least temporarily, than "the poor," even when the terms were used to describe the same individuals, perhaps because media audiences and the general public could more easily empathize with the homeless. Moreover, homelessness appeared to have an easier short-term solution than poverty. Homelessness could be declared an "emergency situation" that could be resolved by providing individuals with temporary shelter so that they would not freeze to death on a park bench, whereas poverty is a more complex problem. As Blasi states, "We may not be willing to support the kind of massive restructuring that would end poverty, but surely we could provide the homeless poor the same kind of shelter we provide to victims of natural disasters."[60]

Recent media coverage about homeless statistics, however, has shown the short-sighted nature of this solution to the problem. Framing in media stories about homeless shelters often refers to these establishments as revolving doors: "You don't see homeless people as much as you did in the '80s because the one great policy initiative of the past 20 years has been to move them from grates into the newest form of the poorhouse, the shelter. Even though cities are building shelters as fast as they can, the homeless are pouring out of them again, returning to the grates."[61] Television news reports have particularly focused on homeless individuals who have given up on homeless shelters, providing local data on the number of beds available in such shelters, the overcrowded conditions that occur in winter, and individuals who choose not to stay inside regardless of conditions outside.

As we have seen, thematic framing in news reporting emphasizes data and how they are gathered. Although the occasional "human face" of the poor may be shown to media audiences, the larger issues associated with poverty, hunger, and homelessness are easily lost in debates over how government statistics are generated, interpreted, disseminated, and employed in social policy decisions. The concern expressed by Greg Mantsios remains valid: The poor are rendered "faceless" by the manner in which the media frame many stories about poverty.[62] They are rendered faceless also by the lack of media attention generally given to this problem. A study by the Project for Excellence in Journalism that examined local television news coverage since the terrorist attacks of September 11, 2001, concluded that local television news provided relatively little reporting on topics like welfare and poverty. Of the 7,423 news stories examined in 2002, researchers found that only thirteen stories were about poverty and welfare, and only nine were about aging and Social Security—topics directly related to the life chances and opportunities of people in the lowest income categories.[63]

Because local television news reporting is often organized around assigned beats, such as medicine/health, crime/police, consumer news, and government/politics, the problem of poverty does not surface unless it arises in regard to one of these areas, like a report on infant mortality rates and poverty on the "health beat."[64] As media analysts have pointed out, the tacit rule "If it bleeds, it leads" prevails in most television newsrooms, where stories of crime, disaster, and war predominate while topics like poverty receive about 1.8 percent of air time.[65] Even when social issues such as poverty or hunger are briefly presented, the context is usually absent, and attention is focused on a tragic event (such as the death of a homeless person) rather than on what might have caused the event to occur.

Episodic framing of newspaper and television stories about poverty may provide more insight than does thematic framing regarding what it means to be poor, hungry, and homeless in an affluent society like the United States. By examining the individual's personal experience, reporters provide their audiences specific examples of individuals or families living under economic duress.[66] The four forms of episodic framing—sympathetic, negative-image, exceptionalism, and charitable—will each be discussed in this chapter.

SYMPATHETIC FRAMING: CHILDREN, THE ELDERLY, AND THE ILL

Episodic framing of media stories about the poor uses the personal experiences of individuals living in poverty as examples of a larger category of people who are under extreme economic duress.[67] The people living in poverty who are most likely to be portrayed in a sympathetic manner by the media are children, the elderly, and the chronically ill.

"Locked Out at a Young Age," the headline of journalist Bob Herbert's op-ed piece on how poorly some children in low-income Chicago families fare, is an example of sympathetic framing that does not point a disapproving finger at the poor. According to Herbert, the U.S. involvement in the war in Iraq has drawn attention away from "millions of young people in America's urban centers," who are "drifting aimlessly from one day to the next. They're out of school, out of work, and . . . all but out of hope."[68] The data discussed in Herbert's article were from Chicago, where about 22 percent of all residents between the ages of sixteen and twenty-four were neither in school nor employed at the time of the report. Ridiculing the popular sound bite *disconnected youth,* which has been widely employed to describe the situation of young people like those in Chicago, Herbert argued that the difficulties these young people face will become, in one way or another, "difficulties to be faced by the society as a whole."[69]

A child's death typically produces sympathetic portrayals of the plight of the poor. However, the judgment of a parent is often brought into question in news reports about a child's death. An example is the *New York Times* article "Daily Choice Turned Deadly: Children Left on Their Own," which described the loss of two children in a residential fire that allegedly was deliberately set. The journalist painted the scenario as follows:

> Last Sunday, as her night shift neared, Kim Brathwaite faced a hard choice. Her baby sitter had not shown up, and to miss work might end her new position as assistant manager at a McDonald's in downtown Brooklyn. So she left her two children, 9 and 1, alone, trying to stay in touch by phone. It turned out to be a disastrous decision. Someone, it seems, deliberately set fire to her apartment. Her children died. And within hours, Ms. Brathwaite was under arrest, charged with recklessly endangering her children.[70]

Although the children's mother was not a suspect in the arson case that destroyed their residence, law enforcement officials held her responsible for leaving the children unattended—a decision that, according to the journalist, "experts suggest, cuts uncomfortably close to some choices made every day by American families."[71] This news report and others like it across the nation briefly call attention to the fact that more than three million children under age thirteen, including some as young as five years, are left alone at least a few hours a week on a regular basis.

The headline "Daily Choice Turned Deadly" is clearly an effort to portray the Brathwaite family in a sympathetic manner. Accompanying the article were photos of the two smiling children whose lives were to be cut short by the fire. The journalist asked, "What age is old enough to be left alone? The law rarely specifies." Like many other stories that might be told about the working poor, Ms. Brathwaite was in a Catch-22 situation: If she did not go to work, she could not support the children, but if she went to work, she had no one to care for the children, and her low-wage job at McDonald's made it impossible to afford reliable child care. According to Brathwaite's lawyer, "She is guilty of nothing more than being a single mom working a 12-hour shift."[72]

Sympathetic framing regarding children in poverty is found in some newspaper columns authored by political and social analysts affiliated with think tanks like the Brookings Institution. An example is "Handing Out Hardship" by E. J. Dionne, Jr., a senior fellow at Brookings and a *Washington Post* columnist. In this article, Dionne chastises the Bush administration for wanting eighty-seven billion dollars in new spending for Iraq while proposing cutbacks on child care for mothers trying to leave welfare. Using a satirical approach, Dionne wrote:

> Not to worry. It may be good for those poor working mothers not to have the child-care money. Warning against the idea of child care as an entitlement, Sen. Rick Santorum, a Pennsylvania Republican, reassured us: "Making people struggle a little bit is not necessarily the worst thing."
>
> You should be inspired by those words the next time you see a mother working behind the counter at an ice cream place or a Burger King with her kids in tow. Just tell her having the kids around is good for family values. Struggle will build character. The kids can always do their homework in the corner.[73]

Like stories about children living in poverty, media reports about the elderly poor often employ sympathetic framing that focuses on the problems of individuals deemed representative of a larger category of people. One article, "Golden Years, on $678 a Month," tells the story of Anna Berroa, who is sixty-eight and poor:

> She trudged languorously along the thrumming streets of Elmhurst, Queens, lost in her early evening thoughts. . . . Walking consumes time, and in the awkward caution of her life it drains her of troubled memories. She does this loop from her apartment every day. She derives comfort from one of the few things she can do that carry no price tag. . . . This is a doleful life that Anna Berroa never anticipated. It seems to catch her unawares. One moment she was middle class, envisioning a placid old age, and then a series of untoward events ambushed her. . . . Poverty is particularly frightful from the lens of old age, when there are few, if any, opportunities to enhance one's prospects and the only escape hatch seems to be death.[74]

Tracing the steps in Berroa's life, from Havana, Cuba, to New York, and the road that took her from a relatively comfortable economic status to poverty, the journalist shows the austerity of Berroa's current condition. For example, she spent her sixty-eighth birthday alone in her room; a friend had asked her to dinner, but "she felt funny because she knew she couldn't reciprocate, so she declined."[75]

Most of this article focused on the experiences of Anna Berroa. The framing of her story was sympathetic, and the journalist sought to show that Berroa's situation was not unique among the elderly living in large cities like New York. However, poverty among older people is often invisible; because others assume that the elderly can take care of themselves.

Unlike the generally sympathetic framing employed by the journalist in the Berroa article, many news reporters tend to juxtapose the needs of the elderly poor with those of young people and communities' budgets. "An Aging Population, a Looming Crisis," for example, discussed the problems of older people in upstate New York and quoted officials who stated that the bill for caring for the poorest of the state's elderly was beginning to strangle communities and would only get worse in the future:

> "We are dealing with seniors burning through their financial resources and having to go on Medicaid," County Executive [Mark] Thomas, a Democrat, said in an interview at his office in Mayville, the county seat. "And because of the way the system is financed in New York, their overwhelming health care needs become a burden to the rest of us. These expenses dwarf everything else."[76]

According to this article, the aging population in Chautauqua County and other areas of upstate New York is potentially a great burden on younger residents of the area, particularly when the older people have limited economic resources. As young residents have relocated to other communities for better jobs, they have left behind the senior members of their families, whose "needs are often overwhelming: the county helps many people pay their heating bills, build wheelchair ramps outside houses, clean up after themselves, get to doctors' appointments and get food."[77] Although this article described the problems of the elderly poor in somewhat sympathetic terms, it is clear from its framing that this story considers these individuals in terms of the potential burden on other people and on the budgets of their counties that they represent.

Many other articles have been written, with somewhat sympathetic framing, about the health concerns of people of all ages living in poverty. The cover of a *New York Times Magazine* greets readers with a sepia-toned photo of a hazy city in the background and a shirtless African American man walking barefoot, head down, in the foreground. The caption reads: "There's a killer haunting America's inner cities. Not drugs. Not handguns. But . . . stress?" The accompanying article (titled "Enough to Make You Sick?") describes "America's rundown urban neighborhoods" and explains how the "diseases associated with the old are afflicting the young."[78] Beginning with the lived experiences of a woman who resided in a housing project in southwest Yonkers, the article describes her many medical problems, including asthma, diabetes, high blood pressure, rheumatoid arthritis, gout, an enlarged heart, and blood with a dangerous tendency to clot spontaneously. The journalist partly attributed the woman's problems, like those of many other inner-city residents, to the fact they live in "poor urban minority neighborhoods [that] seem to be especially unhealthy."[79]

The stress of living in poverty in these neighborhoods was described as producing "weathering, a condition not unlike the effect of exposure to wind and rain on houses."[80] The description of this neighborhood can evoke in readers either a sympathetic or a negative ("Thank God, I don't have to live there") response:

> The neighborhoods where Beverly, Monica, Ebony, Dominique and Jo-Scama live look like poor urban areas all across the country, with bricked-up abandoned buildings, vacant storefronts, broken sidewalks and empty lots with mangy grass overgrowing the ruins of old cars, machine parts and heaps of garbage. Young men in black nylon skullcaps lurk around the payphones on street corners. These neighborhoods are as segregated from the more affluent, white sections of metropolitan New York as any township in South Africa under apartheid. Living in such neighborhoods . . . is assumed to predispose the poor to a number of social ills, including drug abuse, truancy and the persistent joblessness that draws young people into a long cycle of crime and incarceration. Now it turns out these neighborhoods could be destroying people's health as well.[81]

In this article, the journalist Helen Epstein provides a candid portrait of the poor and their health problems, emphasizing that those who are able to move away from their troubled neighborhoods feel much better, that their health improves away from the stress brought about by living in deprived conditions. According to Epstein, stress is related not only to the objective condition of poverty but also to the subjective condition of hopelessness, which is associated with such factors as rising rates of unemployment, an increase in job loss in many occupational sectors, a sharp rise in the number of people being added to the ranks of the poor, and the lack of effective governmental action to reduce these problems. For Epstein, all of these factors produce a psychological miasma that damages people living in poverty and generates many of the stress-related illnesses that afflict the poor.

Like newspaper accounts, television news reports on poverty often focus on interviews that can be turned into brief sound-bites to be aired along with an accompanying story. Coverage of the poor often involves cut-and-paste interviews with public officials, providers of services (such as the director of a food bank or soup kitchen), and a few poor individuals who derive benefits from these services. When there is a threat of funding cuts, the poor who are interviewed typically state that they do not know what they would do without the food, clothing, shelter, or other services that have been provided for them by the organization facing budget cuts.

Sympathetic framing regarding the homeless is found in the story lines of some television entertainment shows, particularly those with a "moral" tone, such as CBS's *Joan of Arcadia*. This series is about a family with a supposedly average teenage daughter, Joan (Amber Tamblyn), who has conversations with God as relayed through other human beings. In the "Double Dutch" episode, God tells Joan to leave her clean suburban community and visit an inner-city area, which viewers can easily identify as poor and rough by the garbage strewn around, graffiti written on the walls, and homeless people wandering around aimlessly or hanging out on discarded furniture. As implausible as it might seem, God's mission for Joan is to jump rope with a teenage girl at a concrete playground. After Joan meets Casper (Erica Hubbard), a homeless African American teenager, the other teenagers make fun of Joan when she falls while trying to jump rope. However, when Joan senses that Casper does not have anywhere to eat, she invites Casper to her house for dinner. At Joan's house, Casper leaves before dinner when she learns Joan's father is a police officer; the next day Joan confronts Casper about her quick exit. Casper asks, "You think I'm frontin'? Okay, Princess, why don't you come to my house for dinner?" and pulls out a laminated card that she shows to Joan, who asks, "A shelter?" Casper replies: "Yeah. . . . I sleep there every night. Me and my fifty crazy-ass homies." Joan persuades Casper to enroll in her school, but turmoil ensues, and Casper leaves, apparently for good. God sends another messenger, who tells Joan, "You did what you were supposed to do" by befriending Casper when she needed it most.[82]

Episodes like "Double Dutch," focusing on the problems of a single character like Casper, use episodic framing to show young television viewers that hunger and poverty exist in inner-city, predominantly minority, neighborhoods. However, negative racial and class-based stereotypes also may be reproduced through the portrayal of characters (exaggerating "ghetto" language, for example) and the setting in which the action takes place (homeless people of color lounging around menacingly). By contrast, Joan, a white middle-class character, is shown as having great courage for going into the inner-city neighborhood and jumping rope. The relationship with Casper continually gives Joan the upper hand, because Joan has a home, food, and a good school to attend, whereas all Casper has is an elaborate rope-jumping routine.

When homeless characters are portrayed on television entertainment shows like *Joan of Arcadia,* the goal typically is to show them in a sympathetic light and to provide the main characters on the series opportunities to "shine"; however, there can also be a downside to the messages sent to media audiences, particularly children and adolescents. This is even more of a concern when the framing of story lines is judgmental, sending the message that poor people are responsible for their own condition.

NEGATIVE-IMAGE FRAMING: DEPENDENCY AND DEVIANCE

Negative-image framing in stories about poverty is often subtle and thus open to a variety of interpretations by readers. Two topics that are frequently the subject of such framing are welfare programs and homelessness. Although readers might expect that partisan publications, produced by politicians, public interest groups, or conservative think tanks, would take moral stands on these issues, media audiences might assume that newspaper and television news reports are more balanced and less judgmental; however, this is not always the case.

The issue of welfare is an example of media framing that sometimes conveys a negative image. Research that examined media depictions of welfare in 252 magazine articles published between 1929 through 1996 identified four recurring (but contradictory) themes: that welfare helps the needy, provides family support, creates dependency, and undermines families.[83] Although the prevalence of each of these themes shifted over time, each of them could be identified in magazine articles throughout the twentieth century. The idea that welfare results in dependency and undermines families was most widely found in articles in the 1960s and 1970s, but this theme remains popular in newspaper and television news today.

A key-word search for "welfare dependency" produced numerous newspaper articles and television news reports on welfare reform in the 1990s and 2000s. When President Bill Clinton signed the Personal Responsibility and Work Opportunity Reconciliation Act of 1996 into law, he stated his hope that this legislation would end "welfare as we know it" and bring a new day of hope for former recipients. The new law replaced Aid to Families with Dependent Children—a program that had provided both short-term and long-term cash assistance to poor families since 1950—with Temporary Assistance for Needy Families. Now the assistance was to be temporary, and women would be required to participate in job training programs or meet work requirements that eventually would get them off welfare altogether. Some analysts assert that the overhaul of welfare is a success, citing data showing that hundreds of thousands have moved from welfare to work and that many have higher incomes. Other analysts attribute a rise in marriage and a decline in the teenage pregnancy rate to changes in welfare laws.[84] However, media representations can obscure the problems of people who have fallen through the cracks, some of whom ultimately may be judged to have done so because of their own moral failings.

By using framing that focuses on the lives of individuals, these reports may cast a spotlight on the negative attributes of poor people who are believed to be welfare dependent. Consider, for example, a news article about a foundation offering help to the working poor. The headline was "Foundation Offers Help to Working Poor: Organizers Say Many Need Mentoring to Quit Welfare Dependency."[85] The subheading of this story may predispose some readers to think of the issue primarily in terms of "welfare dependency" and the necessity of having middle-class mentors teach the poor "life, job-hunting and career-management skills" so that they can overcome their problems. As is typical of much episodic framing, this article begins with a story about one woman's efforts to improve her life.

Readers may conclude from the introduction that the life of Shelly Vaughan, like others on various forms of welfare, is not as stable as individuals in the middle class might believe it should be. The excerpts set forth below describe the positive work of the organization but use Vaughan's life as an example:

> Survival keeps getting in the way of Shelly Vaughan's attempts to improve her life. The Garland resident earned an associate's degree in junior college, but it wasn't enough to begin a career in her chosen field. So she ended up working minimum-wage jobs in retail and manufacturing. Later, she studied to become a medical assistant and then missed taking the certification test because she became pregnant. Now, the 38-year-old single mother of two, including one with special needs, has a full-time job and help from relatives, but has trouble making ends meet. She recently separated from her children's father and started receiving housing assistance. But she said she wouldn't consider relying only on welfare to get by. "I'm raising two boys. I don't want them to grow up thinking this is how it should be," she said.[86]

In this description of Vaughan we learn not only that she is optimistic about the foundation helping her through the welfare-to-work process but that her attempts at education have been fragmented, that pregnancy derailed one of her attempts at a career, that although she holds a full-time job she cannot make ends meet, and that she is no longer living with the father of her two sons. Single parenthood, whether through out-of-wedlock births or divorce, is one of the key factors raised by critics of welfare programs, who argue that some women seemingly enjoy welfare dependency. By contrast, the journalist quotes Vaughan as saying that she does not want to become dependent on welfare, nor does she want her to sons to think "this is how it should be." Although the foundation described in this article appears to have the potential to make a positive contribution for the working poor, the article supports the idea that welfare dependency is often a long-term proposition:

> According to LifeMentors data, 29 percent of working U.S. families with one to three children under age 12 can't afford necessities. The foundation says that the longer they're poor, the more they depend on welfare, food stamps, subsidized housing and other programs paid with tax dollars. And experts say that dependence often passes from generation to generation.[87]

Consequently, the purpose of LifeMentors is to break the cycle of welfare dependency by providing weekly coaching, intensive instruction, and internships. According to an official with Dallas County Health and Human Services, "[LifeMentors] is an important program because it helps people get out of the emotional and psychological cycle that can be created by welfare programs. When you're working so much, yet still can't pay the bills or put enough food on your table, sometimes it's easier just to go back to welfare programs."[88]

How poor people perpetuate the cycle of poverty and welfare dependency is one of the subtle judgments sometimes found in articles about welfare. For example, an article entitled "Millions Have Left Welfare, but Are They Better Off? Yes, No and Maybe"[89] provides a generally sympathetic frame in reporting on recent studies about the overhaul of welfare but concludes with the example of one woman whose situation shows how difficult the cycle is to break. After comparing the arguments of those authorities who believe that welfare reform is a success with recent studies by the "left-leaning" Urban Institute, the journalist concludes that some former welfare recipients are better off, others are worse off, and still others fall somewhere in between. Families that were off welfare but unemployed were among the hardest hit, particularly when no one had been employed for three years or more. Cynthia Brown was used as an example of people in this category:

> Cynthia Brown of New Haven is feeling that pinch. Ms. Brown, 31, who says she is healthy, has spent most of her life on welfare. "I just came from that," she said with a shrug.
>
> In 2001, Connecticut denied her benefits, saying she had already hit her lifetime limit. Ms. Brown and her three children did not cope well. They lived with an aunt in public housing until she made them leave,

fearing the overcrowding would cause her to lose her lease. They lived in a park for a week and then in a homeless shelter for three months, until Ms. Brown obtained subsidized housing and a year's extension on welfare, the last reprieve she will get under state law.

Two months before the extension will expire, Ms. Brown says she is earnestly looking for work but has not found any. She was briefly employed at Yale as a cook, but says she lost the job after her cutting skills were found wanting. Now, she says, her only chance is that something in her life will go so wrong that she will be exempted from the state's rules. "I am hoping for a disaster," she said.[90]

Although the plight of Brown is described in generally sympathetic tones, readers may interpret this piece in a judgmental manner based on the snippets of Brown's life that are presented. Here, it would seem, is a "healthy" woman who "came from welfare" and thus expects others to take care of her and her children. Moreover, she cannot keep a job doing something as simple as cutting up the ingredients for meals.

Like coverage of welfare and laws to reform it, media representations of hunger describe the concern of some politicians that low-income families will become dependent on food stamps and subsidized school lunches. Recent media reports described, for example, how advocates of revamping these programs argue that too many people who do not need the help are being served, and that even those who do need help can become dependent on food stamps. According to a Heritage Foundation spokesperson quoted in "Welfare Wars: Are the Poor Suffering from Hunger Anymore?," "Food stamps and cash welfare are two halves of a whole. All the things about cash welfare that discouraged work and marriage, and encouraged long-term dependence, apply identically to food stamps."[91] The issue of food stamps is politically charged and provides a hot topic for media coverage, because any family with an income that falls below 130 percent of the poverty line is eligible for food stamps.

By telling the stories of individuals who have recently experienced hunger but are considered by medical standards to be obese, journalists frame stories to suggest that there is a linkage between food handouts by the government and the growing weight problem in the United States. "Welfare Wars: Are the Poor Suffering?" quotes a spokesperson for the conservative American Enterprise Institute's Project on Social and Individual Responsibility in this regard: "We are feeding the poor as if they are starving, when anyone can see that the real problem for them, like other Americans, is expanding girth."[92] Advocates for the poor deny any causal relationship between food stamps and increasing obesity among low-income individuals but also acknowledge that the nature of hunger has changed in recent decades because although the "food insecure" may occasionally miss meals and feel hungry, hunger is not an epidemic. Media framing of stories about hunger often end with statements like this: "No longer are advocates for the poor discussing 'hunger,' with its dire implications, but 'insecurity,' a more nuanced, less compelling justification for help. If conservatives have got food advocates to concede this much, perhaps they have already won Round 1 of the battle."[93]

Just as negative-image framing is often used in articles about poverty and hunger, much contemporary media framing of stories about homelessness either directly or indirectly relates to the problem of deviancy. In *Reading the Homeless: The Media's Image of Homeless Culture*, Eungjun Min argues that media images of the homeless show them as "drunk, stoned, crazy, sick, and drug abusers."[94] Although he acknowledges that these images may be true as to some people, he points out that the images create obstacles that limit other people's understanding of the homeless and the issues surrounding the larger problem of homelessness. According to Min, the media frame homeless issues in a manner that presents the homeless as being socially dysfunctional rather than providing homeless individuals with the chance to "describe their conditions in their own discourses to provide a more accurate and balanced depiction of the homeless."[95] In Min's view, "media narrative and image blur and distort the distinction between fact and fiction and between information and entertainment."[96]

Nowhere is the problem described by Min more evident than on some Internet postings about the homeless. "Down and Out in Santa Monica," an Internet article by Eric Olsen, shows a concern for both dependency and deviance on the part of homeless individuals: "The problem with the homeless is the problem with social welfare policies in general: we want to provide for the individual, legitimately needy, but we don't want to encourage dependence upon such help, to foster a 'culture of dependency.'"[97] After describing Santa Monica, California, as being very liberal until it was "inundated with the homeless, who like all other organisms are drawn to where the living is easiest: it's just gravity," Olsen argues that the homeless have unfairly taken advantage of local residents and that the homeless largely are to blame for their own problems:

> Not all homeless people have themselves to blame for their homelessness, especially in hard economic times, but many, if not most, do. Besides those legitimately down on their luck and temporarily unable to house themselves—for whom we must do all we can to keep them invested in society—the homeless also consist of alcoholics, drug addicts, the mentally ill (these three categories often blend together), general

misfits . . . sluggards, and miscellany others. Please do not accuse me of lumping them all together because every homeless person has his/her own story to tell, but collectively, past a certain level of density and visibility, the homeless are a blight on a community for all of the obvious reasons: sanitation, petty crime, eyesore, annoyance, all of which lead to downward pressure on property values, and downward pressure on one's beach side property is the fastest way to turn a liberal into a conservative.

Although the presence of large numbers of homeless individuals clearly placed a burden on Santa Monica, causing the city to crack down on the problem, the vitriolic language of Olsen's blog calls attention to the judgmental attitudes often expressed about the homeless. The Internet now makes it possible for people to express their opinions to much larger audiences than they could sitting in the local coffee shop expounding their beliefs.

Just as Olsen's blog points out negative attributes of the homeless, stories about the homeless in mainstream newspapers and television news shows typically focus on what the homeless have done wrong. This negative-image framing is often found in articles describing tragedies or crimes for which homeless individuals are believed to be at least partly responsible. An example is the Associated Press article "Homeless Couple Charged in Firefighter Deaths," describing the deaths of six firefighters in Worcester, Massachusetts. According to the article, a homeless couple "allegedly knocked over a candle during an argument" on the second floor of an abandoned warehouse where they had lived for several months and, after trying unsuccessfully to extinguish the fire, fled without attempting to report the fire. The blaze grew rapidly, and when firefighters arrived, two went into the building to rescue the "squatters who had been living there." Lost in the thick smoke, the firefighters called for help, and four others entered the structure. All six firefighters died in the blaze, and the homeless couple was charged with involuntary manslaughter.

Some articles about homeless individuals make them look irresponsible and willing to lie about their actions. Others make them appear to be desperate or mentally deranged. "Homeless Woman Arrested for Threatening Postal Worker," for example, was the lead story on a San Diego County television station. The homeless woman, who allegedly put a thirteen-inch knife to a postal worker's side and threatened him as he was sorting mail, said that all she wanted was to secure shelter in jail because she had nowhere else to stay. According to media reports, she was rewarded for her efforts by being jailed on suspicion of kidnapping and attempted carjacking.[98]

Just as this woman's behavior received widespread media attention, stealing shopping carts has also received much coverage. A Dallas city ordinance makes it illegal to possess a shopping cart off the premises of the business that owns it. One article—"Losing Their Cart Blanche: Police Say Basket Ban Is about 'Safety And Crime,' Not Targeting Homeless"—about this ordinance begins with episodic framing, telling the story of one homeless person with a shopping cart:

> Darryl Johnson is homeless and doesn't have a car. So he uses an abandoned shopping cart he found near a creek to move around his blankets, clothes and other belongings. Because of a new city ordinance that police will start enforcing today, Mr. Johnson may want to ditch the cart— or face jail or a fine. . . . Police and city officials announced the law in November as part of a crime-fighting initiative. But Mr. Johnson, other homeless people and their advocates say the ordinance unfairly targets the homeless. "We have no place to stay, and we have to move our stuff when they run us off," said Mr. Johnson, 38, who's been homeless for several years and sleeps near downtown Dallas. "It's not hurting anybody."[99]

According to the article, the main purpose of the shopping-cart ordinance is to cut property losses: "Taking a shopping cart from the owner is theft," police officials stated.[100] The article suggests that the homeless are the main people who steal shopping carts, and that they do so to store their possessions in them on the streets. A homeless-rights advocate quoted in the article asserts that the shopping-cart ordinance punishes and criminalizes the homeless: "The focus is taken off the more underlying and serious problem of homelessness."[101] However, the article concludes with this statement from Mr. Johnson: "All these people are running around robbing, killing and raping, and they focus on the homeless. That's not right. We're just trying to survive."

Descriptions of the actions and appearance of homeless people, even when objectively stated, may imply a negative judgment when interpreted from a middle-class perspective. A news report on CNN from Phoenix, Arizona, "Treating the Homeless Where They Live," is an example. The report begins with this description:

> Blood was oozing from Joel Holder's scalp and from Shelly Holder's face one recent morning as nurse Kay Jarrell and case manager John Gallagher walked into their trash-strewn campsite near 35th Avenue and the Salt River bed. Jarrell and Gallagher were making their daily rounds on behalf of Healthcare for the Homeless, a program of the Maricopa County Department of Public Health. Shelly sobbed as Jarrell daubed her face. Joel sat in a chair, smiled and drank from a can of Natural Ice. Two other residents of the campsite also downed beer. "We've been

drinking pretty steady for two days now, and I'm afraid we had a little violence a few hours ago," Joel said, smiling with as many teeth as he could muster.[102]

The report then describes how another homeless camper became angry and punched Shelly in the face and whacked Joel over the head with a baseball bat. The focus of this report actually was Healthcare for the Homeless, a program that helps homeless individuals with their medical needs; however, the framing that highlighted the problems of the Holders portrayed a less than sympathetic tone, which was followed up by interviews with Gallagher and Jarrell, the health professionals, who stated:

> "Most of the people we see don't want to live in a shelter and feel safe in their own little camp. . . . Most have drug and alcohol problems." Such people need more than just a few weeks of drying out, [Gallaher] said. . . . "They get sober and remember that they spent 10 years being sexually abused by Dad," Jarrell said. "All they want is to forget their pain. Drugs and alcohol are their way of doing that."[103]

Alcohol and drug dependency are recurring themes in stories about the homeless, and these problems are made more vivid by framing that tells the stories of particular individuals and how they were unable to change their lives. Also apparent in many articles is the fact that a number of homeless individuals dislike shelters so much that they are willing to risk living outdoors or in other undesirable settings to avoid the problems that they believe exist in them.

Since the writers of many television legal and crime shows take a "ripped from the headlines" approach for developing story lines, the portrayal of the homeless in series like *NYPD Blue* and *Law & Order* often conveys a negative message similar to that found in newspaper articles and Internet postings. The relationship between homelessness and mental illness is an especially popular topic on *Law & Order*, where numerous story lines have included characters like the "homeless schizophrenic allegedly killed by a car" (in an episode entitled "Darwinian"), the "delusional homeless man" ("Asylum") accused of stabbing a man to death in front of a coffee shop, and the "bloodied and bruised homeless man" ("Volunteers") accused of murder by a neighborhood-watch group that wanted the transient off their street.

Homeless characters on *ER* are brought into the hospital because of drug overdoses, fights, and other injury-causing behavior, and when they have exhibited raving, psychotic behavior. One episode featuring Sally

Field, playing intern Abbie's homeless mother, was particularly frustrating to a homeless advocate who posted this summary online:

> This is the show I most often slap my forehead about for its stereotypical and reductive portrayals of homeless characters. On *ER* those characters are always crazy or chronic public inebriates. They're usually violent (e.g., the mad genius student who stabbed Dr. Carter and Lucy the intern) or smelly. . . . Playing intern Abbie's mother, Field arrived at the ER unexpectedly last fall, having been evicted from her apartment and burnt the bridge of connection to her son. Although she charms the other residents, it doesn't take long to figure out she has bipolar disorder. We watch helplessly, as Abbie does, while Field goes through her cycles. Abbie is alternately seduced and frustrated by her mother's energy, and finally says, " I just can't do this any more," refusing to let her continue staying at her apartment. Then Abbie relents, and we watch her hold her sobbing mother at an El station. Next episode we hear the mom has had a brainstorm and returned to Florida.[104]

A number of television series have homeless persons as witnesses to crimes, and in this context they are often shown as incapable of providing good eyewitness accounts of what happened at the crime scene. Despite the fact that many eyewitnesses—regardless of class—cannot provide investigating officers with accurate information about what happened or a good description of the perpetrator, homeless individuals are particularly portrayed as incompetent and "off the wall" in their remarks to law enforcement officials. An episode of ABC's *The Practice* is a classic example of this problem. In "Trees in the Forest," a homeless pedestrian is killed in a hit-and-run accident to which the only witness is another homeless man. Mr. Snow, the witness, is able to describe the driver of the Mercedes as the one who committed the crime, but his statements are dismissed as flippant or bizarre in the courtroom. When assistant district attorney Helen Gamble asks Snow if he knew the victim, he replies, "Nope, he's a homeless man, bigger bum than me." Gamble becomes frustrated with every homeless person she sees, including a "squeegee man" who cleans her windshield at a stoplight. However, when Gamble learns that Snow has led a hard life, including having had his throat slit in a fight with another homeless man, she shows empathy in her closing argument to the jury:

> If a man dies in a forest and nobody hears him cry . . . then he doesn't make a sound, does he? The other day I was stopped at a traffic light and some bum came up asking to wash my windshield. I couldn't tell you what he looked like 'cause I never looked at him. I never look at 'em. Do you? Easier not to. But when you run one of these bums over . . .

maybe we should stop the car. Take a look. I guess that's the question for you to go back and decide . . . is there any intrinsic value to human life? Or does he have to be somebody? I don't know. It's your call."[105]

After the wealthy Mercedes driver is acquitted, the final scene shows Gamble going home alone, passing homeless men huddled around burn barrels on Boston street corners.

Burn barrels are a central prop in crime dramas that involve homeless characters. Whether in Las Vegas, New York, Boston, or other major cities around the nation, the television depiction of homelessness usually includes burn barrels. A typical scenario is described in this Internet summary of "The Hunger Artist," an episode on *C.S.I.*:

> We're . . . at a highway underpass outside Vegas; the sight of a man huddled over a burning trash can provides the visual indication that this is where Las Vegas's homeless population lives. We see Brass and Gil meet by a shopping cart; they're hemmed in by a perimeter of yellow police tape marking off the area surrounding the cart. Brass . . . tells Gil that the body hasn't been ID'd. The body in question is a woman, blonde, wrapped in a blanket and stuffed into a shopping cart.[106]

In this brief description, we have many of the key ingredients for story lines involving homeless individuals: the highway underpass, the burning trash can, and the shopping cart. As a result, media audiences may come to see the homeless not only as omnipresent on the streets, warming their hands over barrels, but also as unreliable witnesses because they are deviants—dirty, surly, alcoholic or drug dependent, and often visibly mentally ill.

Television news and entertainment programming, like newspaper articles about the poor and homeless, has the potential to make viewers and readers more aware of those who have serious, sustained problems in our society. However, there is a fine line between a sympathetic portrayal of such individuals and a judgmental approach that perpetuates old stereotypes and introduces new ones as times change.

EXCEPTIONALISM FRAMING: "IF THIS PERSON CAN ESCAPE POVERTY . . ."

Some media stories about poverty focus on people who have risen from poverty or left lives of homelessness. These inspirational stories show the importance of the human spirit in rising above adversity; however, they also suggest that others might be able to do likewise if they set their minds to it.

"Bronx Girl Follows Vision: A Future Far from Home" begins with a description of Faile Street in the Hunts Point section of the Bronx: "Its painted women sell themselves at the bodega on the corner. Its ragged men sell bags of dope from cars along the curb. It passes underneath the ruckus of the elevated highway and then dead-ends in the stench of a sewage treatment plant. Faile Street is poor. It is loud. It is often dangerous. Often, it smells."[107] From these humble origins comes Jenise Harrell, who gets good grades at a private school, where she serves on the student council, participates in many other activities, and hopes to attend a prestigious university like Harvard. According to the journalist, "She is trying to escape. 'I know I have it in me to get out,' [Jenise] says. 'I have to get out. There's nothing for me here.'"[108] After describing the problems in Jenise's life and her hopes for the future, the journalist concludes: "It is nonetheless understood that Jenise's life will not be like her mother's. 'I love my mother . . . but she grew up in Hunts Point and she's still in Hunts Point. I don't want to be like that.'"[109]

While it remains to be seen if Jenise Harrell will be able to fulfill her dream of rising above poverty and the problems in her neighborhood, the television movie *Homeless to Harvard: The Liz Murray Story* convinced media audiences that just such a move is possible. Based on the true story of a young girl who spent her early years worrying whether her parents were going out to "score" drugs and when she would eat her next meal, Liz Murray survived by sleeping on subway cars and eating from dumpsters. Despite these obstacles, Murray continued to pursue an education, graduated from high school, and won a scholarship to Harvard University.

Similar success stories are sprinkled through newspaper accounts and "happy talk" news stories typically shown on evening television news programs. Another example is the story of Richie Spagnole, who rose from poverty and homelessness to a life of respectability with a job and an apartment of his own. "Amid Manhattan's Wealthiest, a Beggar Found Open Hearts" describes how, after ten years on the streets of the Upper East Side of Manhattan, Spagnole succeeded in his quest for a decent life:

> To many New Yorkers, the Upper East Side is a clubby, outsiders-beware territory, where immaculately uniformed doormen and snotty co-op boards guard the gates for billionaires and their personal trainers; a sometimes heartless province where poodles get manicures but maids get minimum wages. But for Richie Spagnole, who lived for a decade on the streets of the city's richest neighborhood, the Upper East Side was a place of astonishing generosity.[110]

According to the article, merchants give Spagnole food; residents provided him with contributions of as much as fifty dollars at a time; he slept in the boiler rooms of tenement buildings on cold nights. Growing tired of crack cocaine and being homeless, Spagnole decided to turn his life around when he was offered a job as a delivery person for Rosedale Fish Market. Attributes of Spagnole that the journalist states helped him to get off the streets include having "an infectious smile and a rat-a-tat-tat speaking style," being a "man of energy and humor," originally "coming from a good family," being "a special homeless guy . . . who wasn't dirty or smelly, and he was helpful," being "clean" and always caring about people. According to the article:

> Being helpful was part of Mr. Spagnole's come-on [when he was homeless]. He told restaurant owners that he would not beg in front of their places during the day and would keep an eye out for thieves at night if they would just donate left-over food. He also did favors like clearing snowy sidewalks with shovels "borrowed" from local buildings. For the employees of one restaurant he was the lookout, watching for the police while they gambled inside.[111]

Eventually, Mr. Spagnole was reunited with a daughter whom he had not seem for a number of years, and the "lived happily ever after" ending seems to be apparent in the conclusion of this Valentine's Day news article.

Media reports about the success of poor and homeless individuals who have overcome their problems provide heartwarming stories. This is exceptionalism framing: singling out individuals who have overcome obstacles, praising their accomplishments—such as leaving the streets, finding a job, and graduating from high school or college—and giving the impression that anyone in a similar situation could do the same thing. "Man Overcomes Homelessness, Will Graduate from ASU" is an example: Chris Newton, who learned that "shaking the image of [being] a homeless kid" was almost as hard as being homeless, completed his college education and received a degree from Arizona State University.[112] The article points out that, by taking charge of his life at an early age and never giving up, Newton provided a better life for himself and his son: "When things are bad, you maintain an image. You keep the rest inside," Newton stated to the reporter.[113]

Individuals like Newton, who improve their living conditions, overcome hardships and addiction, and find happier lives clearly are examples of "pulling yourself up by your own bootstraps," but exceptionalism framing ignores the more typical experiences of the poor and homeless and leaves media audiences with an individualistic look at poverty and homelessness that does not focus on the larger societal issues associated with poverty. The individualistic approach to framing of news reports is particularly prevalent in fund-raising appeals on television and in "neediest cases" articles in newspapers.

CHARITABLE FRAMING: HOLIDAYS AND DISASTERS

Although sympathetic framing of media stories about the poor typically shows empathy for those who are down on their luck, it does not suggest that readers or viewers should take action on behalf of those in need. By contrast, the purpose of charitable framing is to highlight individuals and families who are in need of financial assistance and to motivate audiences to contribute money or goods (such as "Coats for Kids," or "Toys for Tots") for the poor.

Research shows that most forms of media give minimal coverage to the poor and homeless throughout the year but begin a gradual increase in reporting in the fall that peaks during the Christmas holiday season and the cold-weather months and then drops sharply through late winter to early spring.[114] During the peak period of these human-interest stories, members of the press barrage service providers at soup kitchens and homeless shelters for interviews, and volunteers are shown serving turkey dinners to the poor at Thanksgiving and preparing baskets of food for indigent families at Christmas. Cartoonist Gary Trudeau captured the essence of media reporting about holiday assistance to the poor by showing how out of place some reporters are when they try to impose their own thinking on the homeless people they are interviewing. In one *Doonesbury* comic strip, for example, a homeless man is standing in line waiting for his free meal on Thanksgiving Day. A journalist talks to the homeless man: "You're getting a free meal today ... but afterwards ... what do you hope for?" The homeless man replies, "Seconds." The journalist counters: "No, no ... I mean in the long term." The homeless man replies, "Dessert ... definitely dessert." As this cartoon shows, the homeless man and the journalist are operating under different assumptions about life and what the future should hold for people.

Holiday coverage of the poor and a call for donations appears in reports across the nation; one of the longest-running series is "The Neediest Cases," published in the *New York Times*. Persons seeking assistance range from families who need medical care or a place to live to individuals who have recently arrived in the United States with no money and no way to escape a life of poverty. Each article tells the human-interest story of a person or family seeking financial assistance; each employs charitable framing. A representative example is "Offering a Hand, and Hope, in a Year of Record Homelessness in New York," which describes the problems of Gloria Hernandez, who was among the more than thirty-eight thousand homeless people residing in New York in November 2003:

> Gloria Hernandez tries to be strong for her five children, but strength, like privacy or full stomachs, does not come easily when you and your

family live in a shelter for the homeless. "The children say, 'Mommy, when are we going to get out of here?'" Ms. Hernandez, 40, said softly, her eyes downcast. "You see it in their faces: they don't speak, but they show it. They say it's your fault."[115]

A new landlord who purchased the apartment building where Hernandez had been living for ten years told her and her children to move out, claiming that he needed the space for himself and that she had too many people living in her unit. The photo accompanying the article shows Hernandez, looking depressed, standing with her nine-year-old son, whose arm is protectively wrapped around her neck. The article also carries the story of several other families and explains how the Neediest Cases Fund provides temporary assistance for "the homeless, the gravely ill and the down and out."[116]

According to the *New York Times,* publication of stories like the one about Hernandez has been an annual occurrence since Adolph S. Ochs, publisher of the paper from 1896 to 1935, came across a "shabbily dressed beggar" on Christmas Day 1911, leading Ochs to publish stories about the poor in the hope that readers would show compassion toward them. The Neediest Cases in the *New York Times* is replicated in newspapers and television news programs across the country; journalists and anchors appeal to audiences to send money, toys, food, and clothing to help the less fortunate in their communities. Programs like "Toys for Tots" at Christmas and "Coats for Kids" during the cold winter months have been a big success at many television stations, as the media work cooperatively with local community service organizations to provide at least a minimal level of assistance to those in poverty.

In the past, researchers have found that charity fund-raising activities publicized in the media typically show more minority group members, particularly African Americans and Latinos/Latinas, than white (Euro) Americans. According to these analysts, even though charity fund-raising through the media is for a worthy cause, the manner in which persons in need are portrayed might firmly establish the notion in readers' and viewers' minds that poverty and minority status are synonymous. A 1990s study of news magazines and television news found, for example, that African Americans were featured in stories about poverty between 62 and 65 percent of the time, though only 29 percent of poor Americans are black. Based on a systematic examination of *Time, Newsweek,* and *U.S. News and World Report,* political scientist Martin Gilens concluded that news magazines exaggerated the number of African Americans who are poor, with African Americans shown 62 percent of the time in stories about poverty. In weeknight news shows broadcast by ABC, CBS, and NBC, a similar pattern was identified: African Americans represented the poor 65 percent of the time.

According to Gilens, those media stories that were framed to show the negative aspects of the underclass, such as welfare dependency or drug abuse, typically presented African Americans, whereas those showing the poor in a more sympathetic manner, such as articles about the elderly poor or poverty-level workers in job training programs, were more likely to feature white Americans. Gilens argues that overrepresentation of African Americans in stories about poverty perpetuates stereotypes about race and provides white Americans with more reason to express discontent regarding social welfare programs.[117]

In addition to raising much-needed money for charitable organizations and bringing in toys or clothing for children, charitable framing provides media audiences with a way to feel good about themselves. After one series, "Season for Caring," the *Austin American-Statesman,* for example, printed a follow-up about the families who had benefited from readers' contributions. One article, "Thanks, Austin!" described the gratitude of Clydia Jones who "doesn't know where to begin thanking people. 'It's been a blessing. Just a blessing,' she says." According to the article, Jones's eleven-year-old disabled granddaughter had received an electric wheelchair donated through the Season for Caring campaign.[118]

Although such campaigns perform a valuable service for a few of the poor, Greg Mantsios suspects that "these 'Yule time' stories are as much about the affluent as they are about the poor: they tell us that the affluent in our society are a kind, understanding, giving people—which we are not."[119] The seasonal nature of charitable framing in the media has also been criticized because the problems of the poor exist throughout the year and not just during holidays, as one *Los Angeles Times* editorial acknowledged: "The charity of the holiday season is traditional—and welcome. The problem is that so much is seasonal. . . . Come January, when people go back to their normal routines, the hunger and homelessness recognized in the holiday season will remain. It would be nice if most of the spirit of giving remained, too."[120]

Like news stories, charitable framing of the poor in the story lines of television "family" entertainment shows is also seasonal. A representative example is "Here Comes Santa Claus," an episode of WB's *Seventh Heaven;* it takes place during the Christmas season, when the Reverend Eric Camden (Stephen Collins) encourages his oldest children to do charity work for the community. Mary Camden (Jessia Biel), one of the daughters, is working in a soup kitchen feeding the homeless when her father comes in to volunteer. Reverend Camden sees that his daughter is unusually happy to be doing the charity work that she initially did not want to do, but then he realizes she is flirting with Carlos, a client at the soup kitchen. When she tells her father about Carlos, she states, "That is Carlos. He got hit by a bus. Isn't he cute?" She also tells her father that Carlos is homeless and that she would like for him to stay at the Camden residence for the holidays. Other than Mary's description of Carlos as being homeless, viewers would have little indication of his status based on his appearance, described by one reviewer in this way: "How stupid is Mary to invite a homeless man she barely knows to stay at her house? It's a good thing he's a sanitized, *7th Heaven* version of a homeless guy, with his healthy complexion, perfectly kept hair, sparkling white teeth, and rugged good looks, and not, like, a more realistic depiction of a homeless person."[121] By the end of the episode, viewers learn that Carlos is not really homeless after all.

Like media representations of the poor and homeless that focus on the need for a helping hand during holidays, similar stories focus on the effects of disasters on the poor. A typical example is the article "At River's Edge, Left with an 'Empty Feeling,'" which describes the devastating effects of a flood on a formerly homeless person:

> Things were looking up for Robert Gray. After three months in a homeless shelter in Calvert County, he landed a job paying $10 an hour doing ironwork, found a home in the Hallowing Point trailer park along the Patuxent River, and filled it with enough furniture so that he could live comfortably. But in the time it took for the rising flood waters of Hurricane Isabel to crash through the glass storm door, burst through his closet wall and fill his home with three feet of water, Gray was down again.
>
> "I lost everything," said Gray, who returned Tuesday to sift through his mud-filled quarters for anything salvageable. "I came here with nothing and I pieced it all together, and now it's like, damn, I have to start over."[122]

Although disasters such as floods typically harm people across all socioeconomic categories and racial and ethnic categories, the poor often are left in greater peril, because they lack insurance and do not have the money to purchase replacement items. Describing the differential effects of a 2003 hurricane, one journalist stated:

> Hurricane Isabel was an equal-opportunity destroyer, flooding the houses, snapping the trees and cutting the power of rich and poor alike. But the lingering hardships imposed by the storm are not likely to be so democratic, officials from across the region say. People with low or fixed

incomes, the elderly and the unemployed are struggling harder to re-build, the officials say. Many had little or no insurance; many lost every-thing they owned.[123]

Unlike the widespread media appeals for the poor at the holidays, dis-aster relief draws only a brief span of media coverage, often describing how government agencies and volunteer organizations like the Red Cross are helping the victims. Overall, the recurring framing of the coverage focuses on how neither the poor nor the wealthy are spared from natural disasters. This point is emphasized in headlines like "A Great Equalizer: Isabel Was Her Name,"[124] although the poor are harmed more significantly by even moderate losses than are the more affluent in our society.

Acknowledgment that homelessness itself is an ongoing disaster that continually affects the lives of many people can be seen in some recent re-ality television entertainment shows. In 2004, A&E Television Network staged a reality show, *House of Dreams,* in which sixteen would-be home-owners who had never built a house came together for thirteen weeks to build one; one would ultimately win the house. Some of the contestants wanted to win the house for other, less fortunate individuals; for example, a real estate broker wanted to win the house for a family she hoped to rescue from poverty, and a former investment banker wanted to win for an at-risk high-school student he was counseling. However, another of the contestants was Tony, an out-of-work landscaper who—with tears in his eyes—told his competitors in the first episode that, if they did not win the house, they could go back home, but that he and his family had no home to return to, only a homeless shelter.[125]

EFFECTS OF MEDIA COVERAGE
OF POVERTY AND HOMELESSNESS

How do media representations of poverty affect viewers and readers? Clearly, the poor and homeless are portrayed in a manner that sends a different mes-sage than do depictions of the rich and famous. Whereas the upper classes are represented by framing based on consensus, admiration, emulation, and the price tag, the poor are—at best—accorded sympathy and applauded when they are able to escape poverty. At worst, the poor are shown through the-matic framing as "faceless" statistics or, in episodic framing, as invisible except at holidays or following natural disasters. For the most part, some degree of blame is placed on the poor, providing media audiences with the opportunity to participate in blaming the victims if they choose to do so.

Over the past 150 years, a poor person has not only been considered the *outsider* or *the Other* but has been portrayed as an *object* to be observed, commented on, and derided. The poor have sometimes been represented as neediest cases or as the beneficiaries of elaborate charity fund-raising events attended by wealthy patrons who dress up in their finery to eat and dance the night away while patting themselves on the back for raising money for organizations that benefit the poor.

An examination of thematic framing in the media shows the extent to which newspaper and television news reports about poverty, hunger, and homelessness provide audiences with statistics and trends while ignoring the untold stories of millions of people living in poverty in the United States. Reporting of increases and decreases in the poverty rate or in the number of hungry or homelessness people provides a relatively sterile perspective for media audiences on a major social problem that has many systemic causes and large-scale social consequences for everyone in the nation; the media, however, largely ignore macro-level concerns.

By contrast, episodic framing too often turns exclusively to discussions of *individuals* and what may appear to audiences to be their *personal troubles*. When the media frame stories in such a way that the shortcomings of the poor or homeless are emphasized, those who are better off may conclude that the poor have created their own problems. The exception, perhaps, is the category known as the working poor, people who typically work long hours for low wages, as discussed in the next chapter. Otherwise, the poor are usually portrayed as violating middle-class values (including those of cleanliness, hard work, and moral behavior) and as committing crimes that are far less interesting than those of wealthy elites, who engage in stock fraud or other clean, white-collar offenses. As noted in chapter 3, even when the rich are convicted of major crimes, they may be admired and praised for their good taste and expensive material possessions.

Throughout my research, I was surprised by the consistency of media coverage linking poverty and deviance. Although most people living in poverty do not commit suicide, homicide, or other crimes, articles over the past 150 years usually have focused on how *different* the poor are from other people and how less interesting their lives are compared to those of the middle and upper classes. Whether the poor steal food to eat or remove shopping carts from stores so that they can stow their few worldly goods, the deviant behavior of poor individuals is more pronounced in media representations than their "normal" behavior.

Those most likely to receive sympathy in the framing of media stories about the poor are children, the elderly, and the ill. However, in the latter category, the illness typically is defined as a physical health problem or a physical disability. Sympathetic framing often does not extend to individuals who are thought to be mentally ill, particularly if it includes frightening or threatening behavior. Subtle derision of the mentally ill homeless in television crime shows, for example, may convey the message to viewers that all homeless people are dangerous and should be feared, when for many the central problem is one of economic hardship and deprivation.

When the media need heartwarming or "feel good" stories, particularly during holidays and disasters, the poor are good subjects for articles, because they are easily accessible to reporters. Of course, some holiday and disaster coverage of the poor comes as a result of the efforts of nonprofit agencies and poverty advocates to gain media coverage for their cause so that money can be raised to help affected individuals and families.

One of the major problems that my research identifies in regard to media representations of the poor is that the larger structural nature of the issues associated with poverty, hunger, and homelessness has been shifted into a softer, more humanitarian, type of coverage that provides media audiences with only isolated examples that show the problem's immediate effects on individuals at the personal level. I agree with other scholars' assessments of how television news reports, as well as the "professional" behavior of news anchors, influence audiences' perceptions on homelessness:

> The anchor's gaze functions as an ultimate window through which . . . all other views of the world must be relayed, including the public's view of itself. Due to this authoritative, omnipotent and reliable quality of the anchor's position, he is able to comfort the viewer and relieve the tensions accumulated throughout the narrative [about poverty]. His concluding remarks sound as if he were saying to us, "We have some problems out there. But don't worry. I'll take care of them. Everything will be fine. You have a good night."[126]

Perhaps it is this feeling that comes to viewers when they reach the end of other news reports or entertainment shows where the lead character has spent several hours serving the poor in a soup kitchen or has taken clothing to a homeless shelter. We can easily believe that someone else is looking after the problems of the poor, that we have no need to worry about it or to demand political and economic changes to reduce the gravity of this problem. Perhaps it is for this reason that some poverty advocates are creating their own media resources, through grassroots efforts and extensive use of the Internet, to get the message out to others about poverty and homelessness as they seek to provide audiences with the "real" story of the poor rather than the packaged, sanitized sound bites and video clips in news reports or the occasional subplot in an entertainment show.[127] However, the extent to which media audiences actually want to know about poverty, hunger, and homelessness has been questioned by a number of media analysts, including *Wall Street Journal* reporter Jonathan Kaufman:

> Coverage of race or poverty has begun to mirror the intractability of these problems. I sometimes worry we have succeeded too well in communicating the bleak prospects of the inner-city underclass. . . . Have [these stories] had the unintended consequence of making these problems seem beyond solution or hope? Faced with bleak statistics of poverty, single-parent families, dropout rates, and incarceration, most readers throw up their hands. They read these stories the way many of us read about tragedies in distant lands. . . . It's a shame, but it doesn't really affect us and, therefore, it is not news to which we find connections.[128]

Thus, the question remains: Have U.S. media audiences seen too much, or too little, of the true nature of poverty? Regardless of the answer to this question, one fact remains undisputed—that how the media cover the poor is far different from how they cover the upper and middle classes, which are used as the norm for how things ought to be in this country. The effects of classism in media coverage deserve far more attention and systematic research in the future than they have received in the past.

NOTES

1. "Walks among the Poor," *New York Times,* January 30, 1870, 6.

2. Robert M. Entman and Andrew Rojecki. *The Black Image in the White Mind: Media and Race in America.* Chicago: University of Chicago Press, 2000.

3. Entman and Rojecki, *The Black Image in the White Mind,* 94.

4. Jeff Kunerth, "One Number Can't Measure Poverty," *Austin American-Statesman,* October 5, 2003, E4.

5. Kunerth, "One Number Can't Measure Poverty,"

6. Shanto Iyengar, "Framing Responsibility for Political Issues: The Case of Poverty," *Political Behavior* 12 (March 1990): 19–40, and *Is Anyone Responsible? How Television Frames Political Issues* (Chicago: University of Chicago Press, 1991, 1994).

7. Iyengar, "Framing Responsibility for Political Issues," 19–40.

8. Gregory Mantsios, "Media Magic: Making Class Invisible," in *Privilege: A Reader,* ed. Michael S. Kimmel and Abby L. Ferber, 99–109 (Boulder, Colo.: Westview, 2003), 101.

9. Mantsios, "Media Magic," 101.

10. Iyengar, *Is Anyone Responsible?* 22.

11. Mantsios, "Media Magic."

12. Mantsios, "Media Magic."
13. Entman and Rojecki, *The Black Image in the White Mind,* 97.
14. Mantsios, "Media Magic."
15. Mantsios, "Media Magic."
16. Mantsios, "Media Magic," 102.
17. "Walks among the Poor," *New York Times,* January 30, 1870, 6.
18. "Distressing Case of Poverty and Suicide," *New York Times,* January 1, 1855, 4.
19. "Distressing Case of Poverty and Suicide," 4.
20. "Melancholy Case of Suicide: Pride and Poverty the Cause," *New York Times,* March 20, 1873, 1.
21. "A Sad Case of Poverty: A Woman Commits Suicide, Her Husband at the Point of Death," *New York Times,* July 13, 1874, 5.
22. "Poverty Leading to Suicide: Another Body of a Woman Found at New Haven," *New York Times,* September 3, 1881, 5.
23. Emile Durkheim, *Suicide* (New York: Free Press, 1951 [1897]), 276.
24. See for examples "Poverty Leading to Suicide"; "Cause of Mr. Hilsen's Suicide: His Capital Exhausted and Poverty Staring Him in the Face," January 25, 1883, 8; "Driven to Suicide by Poverty," February 25, 1884, 8; "Unable to Endure Poverty," June 2, 1884, 2; and "A Violinist in Despair: Domenico Mariani on the Verge of Suicide, Seized as He Was about to Jump from a Hoboken Dock—Poverty in His Old Age Unbearable," August 30, 1885, 12 (all *New York Times*).
25. "Down among the Lowly: The Sights That One Sees in the Fourth Ward," *New York Times,* May 7, 1871, 8.
26. "Down among the Lowly," 8.
27. "Terrible Tragedy: An Insane Mother Kills Her Daughter," *New York Times,* July 6, 1872, 2.
28. "Terrible Tragedy," 2.
29. "A Father's Awful Crime: Shooting His Three Little Girls. Why John Remmler, of Holyoke, Killed His Children—Poverty and a Fear for Their Future His Reasons," *New York Times,* June 22, 1879, 7.
30. Headlines such as "Alabama: Mobile a Prostrate City, Alarming Decline in the Value of Real Estate, Two Hundred and Fifty Stores without Occupants. Poverty and Depression Some of the Causes" (*New York Times,* October 21, 1874) and "Destitution in New Orleans: The Existing Poverty and Its Causes: Lotteries and Beer Shops . . ." (*New York Times,* May 7, 1875) emblazoned stories about poverty in the South. Written by "Occasional Correspondent," who reported on the "decay and dilapidation which everywhere prevails," these articles were framed in such a manner as to suggest that depressed economic conditions were not the only causes of poverty in the South but that they were exacerbated by the presence of lotteries, beer shops, and other attractions that usurped money from the poor. In the 1870s, the category of "poor whites" was popularized by the media, as evidenced in headlines such as "Poor Whites in the South: Their Poverty and Principles" (*New York Times,* May 13, 1877). The headnote of the article shows the contempt "Occasional

Correspondent" held for people in this category: "The most degraded, ignorant, and hopeless class in the South—the poorest of the poor whites—how they live in the mountains—loose notions of morality and utter ignorance their chief characteristics." Although the article is framed in a seemingly sympathetic manner, explaining that poor whites were to be pitied because they had been barred from commerce and other success by the "monopoly of money and power in the planter," the journalist also emphasized that their plight might not have been so dire if they had developed a sense of discipline and subscribed to the work ethic.

31. "Poverty and Charity," *New York Times,* November 8, 1870, 2.

32. "Feeding the City's Poor: Giving Bountiful Dinners to Children and Poverty-Stricken People," *New York Times,* November 28, 1884, 3.

33. Walks among the New York Poor: Homeless Children," *New York Times,* May 4, 1854, 6.

34. "Homeless Children," *New York Times,* December 22, 1856, 4.

35. "Lodging-House for Homeless Girls a New Project of the Children's Aid Society. *New York Times,* May 25, 1862, 3.

36. "A Lodging-House for the Homeless in the Thirteenth Ward," *New York Times,* February 21, 1868, 5.

37. Oscar H. Gandy, Jr., Katharina Kopp, Tanya Hands, Karen Frazer, and David Phillips, "Race and Risk: Factors Affecting the Framing of Stories about Inequality, Discrimination, and Just Plain Bad Luck," *Public Opinion Quarterly* 61 (Spring 1997): 158–82.

38. Iyengar, "Framing Responsibility for Political Issues," and *Is Anyone Responsible? How Television Frames Political Issues.*

39. Lynette Clemetson, "Census Shows Ranks of Poor Rose by 1.3 Million," *New York Times,* September 3, 2003, A1.

40. Associated Press, "New Poverty Guidelines Unveiled," KATU News, Portland, Oregon, February 13, 2004, www.katu.com/news/story.asp?ID=64558 (accessed February 29, 2004).

41. Associated Press, "New Poverty Guidelines Unveiled."

42. See Wally Dean and Lee Ann Brady, "Local TV News Project—2002: After 9/11, Has Anything Changed?" Journalism.org, 2004 (accessed February 29, 2004).

43. Clemetson, "Census Shows Ranks of Poor Rose by 1.3 Million," A1.

44. Jason DeParle, "In Rising Debate on Poverty, the Question: Who Is Poor?" *New York Times,* September 3, 1990, A1.

45. Kimberly J. McLarin, "Poverty Rate Is the Highest in 16 Years, a Report Says," *New York Times,* July 14, 1995, B3.

46. Robert Pear, "A Proposed Definition of Poverty May Raise Number of U.S. Poor," *New York Times,* April 30, 1995, A1.

47. Kunerth, "One Number Can't Measure Poverty," E4.

48. Jared Bernstein, "Who's Poor? Don't Ask the Census Bureau," *New York Times,* September 26, 2003, A25.

49. Kunerth, "One Number Can't Measure Poverty," E4.

50. Kunerth, "One Number Can't Measure Poverty,"

51. "Hungry Families in U.S. on the Rise," MSNBC.com, 2003, www.msnbc .msn.com/id/3341630/ (accessed February 10, 2004).

52. Tom Zeller, "Of Fuzzy Math and 'Food Security,'" *New York Times,* January 11, 2004, WK16.

53. Zeller, "Of Fuzzy Math and 'Food Security.'"

54. Zeller, "Of Fuzzy Math and 'Food Security.'"

55. National Coalition for the Homeless, "How Many People Experience Homelessness?" NCH Fact Sheet 2, 2002, www.nationalhomeless.org/numbers .html (accessed February 14, 2004).

56. National Coalition for the Homeless, "How Many People Experience Homelessness?"

57. Joel Stein, "The Real Face of Homelessness," CNN.com, January 13, 2003, www.cnn.com/2003/ALLPOLITICS/01/13/timep.homelessness.tm/index.html (accessed February 11, 2004).

58. Stephanie Armour, "Homelessness Grows as More Live Check-to-Check," *USA Today,* August 12, 2003, A1.

59. Gary Blasi, "And We Are Not Seen: Ideological and Political Barriers to Understanding Homelessness," *American Behavioral Scientist* (February 1994): 563–87.

60. Blasi, "And We Are Not Seen."

61. Stein, "The Real Face of Homelessness."

62. Mantsios, "Media Magic."

63. Dean and Brady, "Local TV News Project—2002."

64. Dean and Brady, "Local TV News Project—2002."

65. Jeff Cohen and Norman Solomon, "On Local TV News, If It Bleeds It (Still) Leads," *Media Beat,* December 13, 1995, www.fair.org/media-beat/951213.html (accessed February 29, 2004).

66. Iyengar, "Framing Responsibility for Political Issues," and *Is Anyone Responsible?*

67. Iyengar, *Is Anyone Responsible?*

68. Bob Herbert, "Locked Out at a Young Age," *New York Times,* October 20, 2003, A19.

69. Herbert, "Locked Out at a Young Age," A19.

70. Bernstein, "Who's Poor?" A25.

71. Bernstein, "Who's Poor?" A25.

72. Quoted in Bernstein, "Who's Poor?" A25.

73. E. J. Dionne, Jr., "Handing Out Hardship," *Washington Post,* September 16, 2003, A19.

74. N. R. Kleinfield, "Golden Years, on $678 a Month," *New York Times,* September 3, 2003, B1.

75. Kleinfield, "Golden Years, on $678 a Month," B1.

76. Lydia Polgreen, "An Aging Population, a Looming Crisis," *New York Times,* November 4, 2003, A25.

77. Polgreen, "An Aging Population, a Looming Crisis," A25.

78. Helen Epstein, "Enough to Make You Sick?" *New York Times Magazine,* October 12, 2003, 75.

79. Epstein, "Enough to Make You Sick?" 77.

80. Epstein, "Enough to Make You Sick?" 76.

81. Epstein, "Enough to Make You Sick?" 76.

82. Television without Pity, "Here Comes Santa Claus," televisionwithoutpity .com/story.cgi?show=&&story=5940&page=5 (accessed February 28, 2004); "Double Dutch," *Joan of Arcadia*. TV Tome, 2004, www.tvtome.com/tvtome/servlet/Episode ReviewPage/showid-17466/epid-282012/bl (accessed February 29, 2004).

83. Joya Misra, Stephanie Moller, and Marina Karides, "Envisioning Dependency: Changing Media Depictions of Welfare in the 20th Century," *Social Problems* 50 (2003): 482–504.

84. Leslie Kaufman, "Millions Have Left Welfare, but Are They Better Off? Yes, No and Maybe," *New York Times,* October 20, 2003, A16.

85. Kristine Hughes, "Foundation Offers Help to Working Poor: Organizers Say Many Need Mentoring to Quit Welfare Dependency," *Dallas Morning News,* July 3, 2003, 1S.

86. Hughes, "Foundation Offers Help to Working Poor," 1S.

87. Hughes, "Foundation Offers Help to Working Poor," 1S.

88. Hughes, "Foundation Offers Help to Working Poor," 1S.

89. Kaufman, "Millions Have Left Welfare, but Are They Better Off?"A16.

90. Kaufman, "Millions Have Left Welfare, but Are They Better Off?"A16.

91. Leslie Kaufman, "Welfare Wars: Are the Poor Suffering from Hunger Anymore?" *New York Times,* February 23, 2003, WK4.

92. Kaufman, "Welfare Wars," WK4.

93. Kaufman, "Welfare Wars," WK4.

94. Eungjun Min, ed., *Reading the Homeless: The Media's Image of Homeless Culture* (Westport, Conn.: Praeger, 1999), ix.

95. Min, ed., *Reading the Homeless,* ix.

96. Min, ed., *Reading the Homeless,* x.

97. Eric Olsen, "Down and Out in Santa Monica," Blogcritics.org, 2003, www .blogcritics.org/archives/2003/01/06/200033.php (accessed February 22, 2004).

98. "Homeless Woman Arrested for Threatening Postal Worker," KFMB.com, January 16, 2003, www.kfmb.com (accessed February 2, 2004).

99. Kim Horner, "Losing Their Cart Blanche," *Dallas Morning News,* January 14, 2004, 1B.

100. Horner, "Losing Their Cart Blanche," 1B.

101. Horner, "Losing Their Cart Blanche," 1B.

102. William Hermann, "Treating the Homeless Where They Live," August 9, 2000, www.cnn.com/2000/LOCAL/pacific/08/09/azc.homeless.medical/index .html (accessed February 8, 2004).

103. Hermann, "Treating the Homeless Where They Live."

104. Michele Marchand, "On the Air and Outside: Homelessness on TV," www.anitra.net/books/activist/mm_on_the_air.html (accessed February 28, 2004).

105. Quoted in Marchand, "On the Air and Outside: Homelessness on TV."

106. Television without Pity, "The Hunger Artist," televisionwithoutpity.com/ story.cgi?show=15&story=3487&page=2 (accessed February 28, 2004).

107. Alan Feuer, "Bronx Girl Follows Vision: A Future Far from Home," *New York Times,* October 4, 2003, A1.

108. Feuer, "Bronx Girl Follows Vision," A1.

109. Feuer, "Bronx Girl Follows Vision," A14.

110. Leslie Kaufman, "Amid Manhattan's Wealthiest, a Beggar Found Open Hearts," *New York Times,* February 14, 2004, A1.

111. Kaufman, "Amid Manhattan's Wealthiest, a Beggar Found Open Hearts," A14.

112. Pat Kossan, "Man Overcomes Homelessness, Will Graduate from ASU," *Arizona Republic,* May 2, 2003, www.azcentral.com (accessed February 28, 2004).

113. Kossan, "Man Overcomes Homelessness, Will Graduate from ASU."

114. David A. Snow and Leon Anderson, *Down on Their Luck: A Case Study of Homeless Street People* (Berkeley: University of California Press, 1993); William K. Bunis, Angela Yancik, and David Snow, "The Cultural Patterning of Sympathy toward the Homeless and Other Victims of Misfortune," *Social Problems* (November 1996): 387–402.

115. Arthur Bovino, "Offering a Hand, and Hope, in a Year of Record Homelessness in New York," *New York Times,* November 2, 2003, A25.

116. Bovino, "Offering a Hand, and Hope, in a Year of Record Homelessness in New York," A25.

117. Martin Gilens, *Why Americans Hate Welfare: Race, Media, and the Politics of Antipoverty Policy* (Chicago: University of Chicago Press, 1999).

118. Ricardo Gándara, "Thanks, Austin!" *Austin American-Statesman,* February 1, 2004, K1, K12.

119. Mantsios, "Media Magic," 102.

120. "If Only the Spirit of Giving Could Continue" (editorial), *Los Angeles Times,* December 25, 1988, 16.

121. Television without Pity, "Here Comes Santa Claus."

122. Joshua Partlow, "At River's Edge, Left With an 'Empty Feeling,'" *Washington Post,* September 25, 2003, SM3.

123. James Dao, "Hardships and Damage Linger after Hurricane," *New York Times,* October 2, 2003, A18.

124. David Stout, "A Great Equalizer: Isabel Was Her Name," *New York Times,* September 26, 2003, A17.

125. Pam Harbaugh, "Dreamers Battle for Home in Harmony," *Florida Today,* January 4, 2004, www.floridatoday.com/!NEWSROOM/peoplestoryP0105 DREAM.htm (accessed February 2, 2004).

126. Insung Whang and Eungjun Min, "Blaming the Homeless: The Populist Aspect of Network TV News," in *Reading the Homeless: The Media's Image of Homeless Culture,* ed. Eungjun Min (Westport, Conn.: Praeger, 1999), 131.

127. Miranda Spencer, "Making the Invisible Visible," *Extra!* (January–February 2003), www.fair.org/extra/0301/poverty.html (accessed February 29, 2004).

128. Jonathan Kaufman, "Covering Race, Poverty and Class in the New Gilded Age," *Nieman Reports* (Spring 2001): 25.

5

TARNISHED METAL FRAMES:
THE WORKING CLASS
AND THE WORKING POOR

C hicago, Illinois:

Something stinks, and it's not the [Chicago] Cubs. Garbage is piling up across the city as a national television audience focuses on the historically woeful Cubs and their run in baseball's playoffs. The refuse spills from alleys behind grocery stores and businesses as well as suburban trash cans as a strike by independent garbage haulers enters its seventh day. The 3,300 Teamsters who collect garbage at apartment buildings, restaurants and shopping centers rejected management's proposed 24% pay increase over five years. The union wants 30% over three years. Both sides are expected to resume talks today with a federal mediator. While they negotiate, up to 15,000 tons of garbage is accumulating daily, said Matt Smith, a spokesman for the city Department of Streets and Sanitation. "We know there are serious labor issues on the table, and we're trying to stay out of that, but to be absolutely frank, our patience is wearing very thin," Smith said. "Every day garbage is not collected increases the threat to the health and safety of people in Chicago."[1]

The framing of this article about a strike by unionized sanitation workers in Chicago suggests that what stinks is not only the piled-up garbage but the greed of unionized haulers who are demanding a significant pay increase, inconveniencing ordinary people, and causing significant health risks. Although it might appear that these unionized workers, earning from ten to twenty-one dollars an hour, have little in common with Caroline Payne, a convenience store clerk who earns eight to twelve thousand dollars a year, both categories of workers typically are lumped into a generic *working class* category by the media, and their stories are typically framed differently from those about the classes above them.

Muncie, Indiana:

> Caroline Payne embraces the ethics of America. She works hard and has
> no patience with those who don't. She has owned a house, pursued an
> education and deferred to the needs of her child. Yet she can barely pay
> her bills. Her earnings have hovered in a twilight between poverty and
> minimal comfort. . . . She is the invisible American, unnoticed because
> she blends in. Like millions at the bottom of the labor force who con-
> tribute to the country's prosperity, Caroline's diligence is a camouflage.
> At the convenience store where she works, customers do not see that she
> struggles against destitution.[2]

As is typical of many media stories about the working class, the
episodic framing used in this article provides a description of Caroline
Payne's economic condition and establishes that she is representative of millions of other people who are among the working poor, earning less than a
living wage and remaining largely invisible as they "sew clothes, clean of-
fices, harvest fruit, serve Big Macs and stack merchandise at Wal-Mart."[3]
Like most of the working poor, Payne has an income above the official
poverty line, but she cannot afford many basic necessities.[4] In media framing of news articles and entertainment story lines, Payne is representative of
the working poor, whereas labor unions are representative of the entire
working class—despite the fact that most individuals in this socioeconomic
category are not union members.

THE WORKING CLASS AND WORKING
POOR IN SOCIOLOGY AND THE MEDIA

Media framing generally represents members of the *working* class as just
that—primarily as workers, laborers, or, in Marxian terminology, the proletariat. Like stories about the poor and homeless, news reports about the
working class usually employ episodic framing that provides little information about people in this socioeconomic category beyond a "human interest" angle. As Michael Zweig suggests, "Workers are seen, when they are seen
at all, as faces in a crowd or in sound bites, rarely as people with thoughtful
things to say about their condition and their country. In the media, the working class is truly the silenced majority."[5] Human-interest stories about the
working class are usually based on economics or politics. Examples include
workers being laid off at a local factory and activists or politicians speaking
out on behalf of residents of a working-class neighborhood who feel threatened by economic development, such as the construction of a Wal-Mart su-

percenter (a type of retail outlet known in media and commercial parlance as a "big box"). As is true of other forms of episodic framing, many of these media representations do not look at the larger structural issues that produce such problems; their primary focus is on the outrage of the unemployed or people displaced by gentrification. By contrast, business articles in major newspapers often refer to the working class as "organized labor," whereas reporters on the political beat describe them as "blue-collar workers" who live in "working-class neighborhoods." Similarly, television shows that focus on the home life of the working class emphasize the workers' humble origins, lack of taste, proletarian lifestyle, and disgust with their work. The characters are often made the object of jokes and portrayed as buffoons who are sloppy in appearance, ignorant, and sometimes racist.

One of the major problems in media representations of the working class is that there is no clear definition of what constitutes the working class, a fact that makes it easier for journalists and television writers to place the working class "comfortably" in the lower tier of the middle class. For example, a *New York Times* editorial describing a strike by grocery workers in southern California stated that these workers "are the front line in a battle to prevent middle-class service jobs from turning into poverty-level ones."[6] If "Wal-Martization"—as the *Times* calls this process—indeed occurs in southern California and other grocery stores start to match Wal-Mart's wages, workers' salaries will drop from about eighteen to fourteen thousand dollars per year, an amount below the $15,060 official poverty line for a family of three. From a sociological perspective, it is questionable whether workers earning eighteen thousand dollars a year, particularly in high cost-of-living states like California, should be considered "middle class." However, many media reports place working-class people in a large, undefined middle class where "everybody" belongs.

Sociologists identify the working class by occupation (such as manual, supervised, or unskilled or semiskilled workers), by how people are compensated for their work and how much they are paid, and by the level of education typically required. The "old" working class, primarily made up of semiskilled blue-collar workers in construction and manufacturing, has been shrinking since the 1950s. By contrast, the working class of the twenty-first century also includes people who are employed in routine white-collar jobs (such as bank clerks, cashiers, and retail sales workers) and in the rapidly growing service sector (for instance, home health care workers and employees in fast-food restaurants). According to stratification scholars, the primary characteristics of the working class are that its members "do not have much control or authority over the pace or the content of [their] work and they're not a supervisor and they're not the boss."[7] Some analysts believe that about 62 percent of the U.S. labor force should be classified as working class.[8]

In the past, another defining characteristic of the working class was union membership, particularly in the era when goods-producing jobs were a major source of employment in the United States. However, as goods-producing jobs have decreased, union membership has dropped to a small fraction of the labor force.[9] Consequently, the power of the working class to influence economic and political decisions has diminished; today the working class is frequently characterized by the media as low in political participation.

Some scholars believe that the working poor should be a category separate from the working class, but my examination of media coverage suggests that the "working class" and the "working poor" are often discussed somewhat interchangeably, particularly as more working-class employees are "only a step—or a second family income—away from poverty."[10] As a result, societal lines, like media distinctions, between the working class and the working poor have become increasingly blurred. Global shifts in the labor force through outsourcing, downsizing, and plant closings have created more fluidity between the working class and the working poor.

Even under the best of circumstances, the working poor hold low-wage positions with little job security, few employee benefits, and no chance to save money. Their work conditions are frequently unpleasant and sometimes dangerous.[11] Some of the working poor are illegal immigrants (known as "undocumented workers"), who worry that they will be incarcerated or deported if they complain to employers about their wages or safety. Women make up a large segment of the working poor: females constitute about 60 percent of the low-wage workforce and 70 percent of the part-time labor force in the United States.[12]

Examining how the working class is portrayed in the media is challenging, because, as the economist Michael Zweig argues, this class typically is invisible in the media.[13] Sociologist Greg Mantsios agrees that the media portray the working class as "irrelevant, outmoded, and a dying breed." According to Mantsios, the media suggest that "the hardships faced by blue collar workers are inevitable (due to progress), a result of bad luck (chance circumstances in a particular industry), or a product of their own doing (they priced themselves out of a job)."[14] An analysis of the historical framing of the working class provides insights on contemporary media framing of this class.

HISTORICAL FRAMING:
THE WORKING CLASS AS LUMPS OF LABOR

Although nineteenth-century newspaper articles typically did not use the term *working class,* articles from the 1800s dealing with the laboring classes and with the working poor can be found in the archives of the *New York Times* and other urban newspapers. Framing typically focused on how laborers organized to demand better working conditions and wages and on the problems that emerged as a result of strikes. With the introduction of Labor Day as a federal holiday in the 1880s, parades and other celebrations attracted media attention and positive coverage of the so-called working man for that one day a year. During the rest of the year, however, articles focused more on workers and their union leaders as greedy and sometimes "criminal elements" meriting prosecution. One 1806 article, for example, told of the conviction on charges of criminal conspiracy of members of the Philadelphia Journeymen Cordwainers who had gone on strike demanding higher wages. For a number of years thereafter, newspapers reminded readers that this case had set a precedent by which the U.S. government fought unions for many years.

The most common framing of early stories about the working class highlighted laborers' demands for a shorter workday. Typical news reports described the demands of Boston carpenters for a ten-hour workday in 1825 and of children employed in the Paterson, New Jersey, silk mills for an eleven-hour day and a six-day workweek in 1835. By the 1850s, however, the tone of many articles had grown increasingly antagonistic toward organized labor and more positive toward workers who opposed unions. An example of the latter was a *New York Times* article, "Meeting of Front Bricklayers: A Union of Capital and Labor Advocated," that praised nonunion bricklayers for their opposition to the Bricklayers Protective Union.[15] Not long thereafter, editorials and news articles reviled labor organizers for demanding strikes, creating conflict, and inconveniencing the general public. An example is an 1868 article arguing for the "principle of harmony" in labor relations rather than confrontation:

> We submit this consideration to those cooperative associations which are now striving to upset and revolutionize all the laws of political economy which experience has taught us. These societies do not simply ask Government to regulate the hours of labor. They have ulterior aims. They propose to distract the political parties from the issues which divide them by bringing into prominence the vexed questions between the capitalist and the laborer.[16]

Acknowledging that workers' organizations had evolved into a full-fledged social movement, this journalist questioned what the future of such a movement might be: "Indeed, how far the movement may go, it is impossible to foresee. But it is plain enough to all intelligent observers that the schemes proposed can be productive of mischief only. The operations of political economy will take care of themselves without the help of these cooperative associations or of Labor Union Conventions."[17]

As newspapers began to question the ulterior motives of unions and their organizers, some reporters argued that the government should not intervene in disputes between workers and owners or managers. Here is an example from 1868: "Government has just as much right to establish religions as it has to regulate the laws which shall obtain between the capitalist and the laborer."[18] Citing the lack of progress made by bricklayers in bringing about changes through their tactics, this article warned other groups that their efforts would also fail:

> The recent strike of the bricklayers has fully exposed the futility of the attempt of workmen to regulate by associated effort either their hours of labor or their wages. The employers, upon whom these bricklayers attempted to impose the most arbitrary conditions, have held their ground, and they are now masters of the situation. And why? Because they knew that the exactions imposed were arbitrary and unreasonable, and that they defied all the laws of political economy.[19]

In keeping with the Adam Smith philosophy that what is good for the economy is good for everyone, some newspaper reporters became advocates of the "laws of the political economy," which typically benefited members of the capitalist class at the expense of the workers. Some articles in the 1860s even suggested that the best role for the trade unions was to send the working poor to the western United States rather than demanding higher wages for them in the Northeast. According to "Help for the Working Poor," if the "trades' unions would contribute money to send their poor to the West, instead of supporting them in idleness here, they would render a better and more lasting service."[20] In other words, there were too many working poor people sitting idle and trade unions could reduce the problem not by making demands on employers in the Northeast but by helping relocate the working poor to "the fields of the West, free for them and aching to be cultivated."[21]

For many years, the working poor and the activities of labor unions have been seen as problematic by media reporters, resulting in what some scholars suggest is an anti-labor bias deeply embedded in media culture. In his study of media portrayals of unions, the labor scholar William J. Puette concludes that the media's anti-labor bias is "heavy-handed and deliberate."[22] According to Puette, many newspaper publishers and editors are employers who must negotiate with unionized workers, and these media elites are therefore less willing to report fairly on workers' issues. On rare occasions, newspapers have carried reports about alleged media bias against workers and organized labor, as in this exchange between Senator Henry William Blair of the U.S. Senate Committee on Education and Labor and

President John Jarrett of the Amalgamated Association of Iron and Steel Workers:

> Mr. Jarrett—There is an impression among the working classes that the press ought to be the mouthpiece of the sentiments of the people in general. There is also an impression that the press is subsidized by capital.
>
> Senator Blair—You will observe, however, that in the press your statement will be suppressed—unless this remark of mine leads to its publication.
>
> Mr. Jarrett—Well, there is certainly a general impression among our working people that a large portion of the press is subsidized by certain large corporations. There are a few papers, to be sure, where the working men can have their interests and views fairly presented, but that is not the case with the majority of papers.[23]

Not all newspaper articles in the late nineteenth and early twentieth centuries were negative about the working class. Some were nothing more than brief items about union meetings or about workers' grievances, such as those of Bakers' Union members who were required to work a fifteen-to-eighteen-hour day, including Sundays;[24] the "sewing women" who earned twenty-five cents per dozen shirts they made, leaving them continually impoverished despite working until 2:00 A.M. most nights;[25] and labor leaders who opposed the hiring of convict labor, in the belief that "convicts should not be allowed to compete with skilled workmen [but should be] restricted to work of a menial kind."[26] However, the framing of newspaper articles about the working class at the end of the nineteenth century typically did not tell the stories of individual workers or give voice to their concerns but rather focused on "organized labor," leaving the workers as faceless employees controlled by their bosses and union leaders.

Labor Day was not officially designated as a holiday until 1884, but the first celebration took place on September 5, 1882, in New York City, when the Central Labor Union organized about ten thousand men to participate in a parade that was "conducted in an orderly and pleasant manner."[27] The headline of a *New York Times* article about that city's celebration of this holiday in 1902 was typical of media coverage at the time: "Big Labor Day Parade: Thirty Building Trade Unions to be Represented. Forty Bands to Play in the Procession—Preparations to Handle Holiday Crowds."[28]

However, not all workers were equally celebrated. Media conveyed the message that U.S. workers should fear "immigrant, foreign labor" as a threat to their livelihood and a menace to public safety.[29] The *San Francisco Chronicle*, for example, carried lengthy articles in 1904 explaining how Japanese laborers were taking jobs away from U.S. workers, reflecting a pattern of media reporting regarding the immigrant labor problem, which continues to be a topic in the twenty-first century.

Some articles in the 1890s and early 1900s portrayed the laboring classes as greedy, dangerous, and causing grave inconvenience for people in other classes. The violence connected with some labor strikes was a recurring theme, such as during the 1890 Homestead Strike, when eighteen people were killed as Pinkerton guards attempted to help scabs break picket lines at the Carnegie Steel mill, and the bloodshed and looting during a strike against the Pullman Palace Car Company in 1893. During the 1920s and 1930s, media representations of workers and the labor movement grew more negative; not only was the violence continuing but (in the latter decade) political leaders placed blame for the nation's industrial depression and high rates of unemployment on organized labor and its leaders.[30] An example is the article, "Blames Union Labor for Work Shortage," which quoted from a speech by Senator Knute Nelson of Minnesota:

> I am getting tired of these strike threats. I do not know but that it would be a good thing for the country if these railroad men should start a strike. Let the people of this country understand once for all what these men mean by their striking. Let the people realize that they will be deprived of their food supply, their fuel and everything else. If the employees ever embark on such a strike, leading to such results, I venture the prediction that the American people will rise in their might and wipe them from the face of the earth.[31]

The tone of Nelson's statement and the news article that contained it show the negative image that workers were getting because of their demands for change. The focus had shifted from workers' issues and why they were threatening to strike to how workers' actions inconvenienced and harmed other people.

Congressional investigations, governmental actions, and violence during labor strikes provided reporters with fodder for numerous articles on the working class and its problems; however, the focus of many stories was primarily on labor organizers and what Puette refers to as a "cartoon image" of labor unions—one that portrayed the "worthless, unproductive, overpaid blue-collar work force, which is considered the unhappy but inevitable result of unionization."[32] In articles ranging from coverage of the 1920 Palmer Raids (in which federal agents arrested more than five thousand people to break a nationwide strike)[33] to news reports about passage of the Taft-Hartley Labor Act in 1947 (which curbed union strikes),[34] reporters had ample opportunity to inform their readers about key issues facing workers. They typically chose instead to use only a few, narrow frames that often told the story from the perspective of politicians and business leaders.

By the 1950s and 1960s, both newspaper and television coverage of the working class focused almost exclusively on walkouts and strikes, the threat of them, and the alleged criminality of some union leaders. Several reporters covering the labor beat sought to expose the involvement of organized crime in labor unions and the large, direct contributions of unions to candidates for federal office. One example is Victor Riesel, a well-known New York newspaper columnist and radio commentator whose reports on organized crime and its infiltration of labor unions hit so close to home that Riesel was attacked in 1956; a mob threw acid in his face, blinding him for life. However, according to his obituary, he "never stopped inveighing against gangster infiltration and other corruption in labor unions that had stirred his emotions since his youth."[35]

Some scholars argue that media reporting on organized labor has shifted over time "from incendiary to invisible."[36] However, others, including Puette,[37] hold that blatant discrimination against unions and their members still exists in the media but has become more subtle:

> The image of labor has not been reduced to invisibility so much as it has been refocused and filtered into more subtle, indirect projections than before. . . . Television portrayals tend to emphasize the pettiness or foolishness of union bargaining goals and take the cinematic portrayals a step further by portraying good unionists out of power and generally suppressed by their local or national leaders, whose power is considered excessive, out of touch, and corrupt. Television and print news share a preference for using employers as sources, which causes them to adopt the employer's perception of the issues as the basic premise of their reports.

Based on an examination of television news programs like *60 Minutes* in the 1970s and 1980s, Puette concluded that the media's portrayal of unions typically was unsympathetic and tended to label union concerns as nothing more than special interests that might be the undoing of the country. Similarly, Puette concluded that in television dramas depicting the working class and labor unions, labor terminology is frequently abused and unrealistic situations are often dramatized "without respect for realism or the true plight of the union or nonunion labor depicted."[38] According to Puette, basic "lenses" color and distort media portrayals of organized labor and its leaders. Among these media images are stereotypes that labor unions protect unproductive, lazy, and insubordinate workers; that unions undermine the ability of the United States to compete internationally because they have forced employers to pay exorbitant wages; that unions do not represent the best interests of the working class; that union leaders are not from the educated/cultured (privileged) classes and thus are more likely to be corrupted by power than are business or political leaders; that unions are no longer necessary; and that unions create conflict rather than resolving it.[39] If Puette's lenses are accurate representations of how the media portray workers and labor unions, these depictions no doubt have contributed to what he describes as a "systematic and relentless disparagement of the most visible effort at collective empowerment by working Americans."[40]

How much of this past framing is still reflected in contemporary media representations of the U.S. working class? In the following sections, I discuss five frames I identified in my research on media representations of the working class:

- Shady Framing: Greedy Workers, Unions, and Organized Crime
- Heroic Framing: Working-Class Heroes and Victims
- Caricature Framing #1: White-Trashing the Working Class
- Caricature Framing #2: TV's Buffoons, Bigots, and Slobs
- Fading Blue-Collar Framing: Out of Work or Unhappy at Work

SHADY FRAMING: GREEDY WORKERS, UNIONS, AND ORGANIZED CRIME

The media today continue to frame the working class primarily as a *laboring class*. Reports often fail to look at the wide diversity of individuals who might be classified as working class, focusing instead on labor unions, their members, and their activities. Despite the fact that fewer than one in six American workers are union members, news reports about the working class typically emphasize the problematic aspects of labor unions. These stories employ several recurring themes, including the portrayal of unionized workers as greedy individuals who engage in behavior (such as work stoppages and strikes) that harm others, and representations implying that most—if not all—unions have linkages to organized crime.

Negotiations between unions and management are a frequent topic in business reporting, where "news analysis" framing provides an opportunity for journalists to take a side in the controversy. In "Auto Deal or Bust: Was Anyone Taken for a Ride in the U.A.W.–Big 3 Contract Talks?" the journalist Danny Hakim describes a meeting of union leaders and representatives of the "Big Three" U.S. automobile manufacturers (General Motors, Ford, and DaimlerChrysler): "Last week the United Automobile Workers offered more concessions to the Big Three than it has in the last two decades of contract talks. Then again, concessions have not really been a feature of the last two decades of contract talks in the American auto industry."[41] Drawing attention to problems the Big Three face with global competition, it portrays the automobile workers as greedy because they want far more than the typical American worker has in wages and benefits:

> Of course, many white-collar workers would love [concessions gained by the U.A.W.]—paying $10 for brand name drugs—or salaries. The average Ford assembly worker made $70,206 in 2002, and the average skilled worker made more than $80,000. Such high labor costs have been a chief contributor to an exodus of 2.7 million manufacturing jobs over the last three years.[42]

Statements like this hold up blue-collar workers against white-collar employees, making the working class appear greedy, as seeking higher wages and better benefits than most middle-class workers enjoy. Portraying unionized workers as having a most-money-for-the-least-work attitude has been a recurring theme in media reports over the past century.

When workers consider strikes to gain concessions from management, media coverage about the workers and their leadership often becomes more visible and more negative. In a study of *New York Times* coverage of strikes and nonstrike wage settlements between 1949 and 1991, management scholars Christopher L. Erickson and Daniel J. B. Mitchell have found that among the factors that determine the extent of news coverage about labor are the "occurrence of a strike, strike duration, number of workers involved, occurrence of federal intervention, key industry status (that is, whether the affected industry was among those industries identified as exceptionally important for wage-setting), and proximity to New York City."[43] The presence of one or more of these factors increases the likelihood of extensive news coverage of labor activities. Erickson and Mitchell note the irony of this finding: "The fact that strikes are a key attraction for coverage . . . poses a dilemma for unions, since it implies that perhaps the surest way to claim attention in the papers is to be involved in bad news."[44] Also, as other media and labor analysts have demonstrated, public approval of unions decreases as strike-related coverage increases in the media.[45]

Media coverage of the working class suggests by focusing on *problems* brought about by union actions that union members are not only greedy but harm others. Two recent examples include reports on the 2003 Chicago trash haulers' strike and the 2004 California supermarket strike. News reports of the Chicago strike emphasized how much garbage was piling up and the ways in which residents and business owners were being inconvenienced by the striking workers.[46] For example, although some news reports suggested that the entire city of Chicago was rapidly becoming one big garbage dump, the strike was against private haulers and primarily affected commercial areas, apartment buildings, and suburban neighborhoods, not city neighborhoods with single-family residences, which were served by public garbage crews. According to one article published shortly after the trash haulers rejected a settlement offer from management, "A group of private waste haulers and striking workers failed to agree Sunday on a new contract, *assuring millions of Chicagoans and suburbanites that they would have to endure a fifth day of mounting heaps of refuse and the stench from overstuffed trash bins.*"[47] As this statement suggests, ordinary people were having to "endure" problems such as "mounting heaps of refuse" and "the stench" because the workers could not reach a settlement. Little attention was paid to the striking workers' grievances or the conditions under which they were expected to work. According to spokespersons for the trash haulers, their concerns pertained not only to wages but to the increasing (and from their perspective, unreasonable) demands that were being routinely placed on them to haul off large items such as sofas and king-sized mattresses.[48]

Media framing of articles about the trash haulers' strike is not unique in its emphasis on the problems caused by striking workers. When members of the United Food and Commercial Workers union (made up of stock clerks, cashiers, and other grocery workers) walked off their jobs in southern California in 2004 and set up picket lines in front of hundreds of supermarkets, their reason—to protest plans by various supermarket chains to reduce health care benefits and to require that workers pay a greater proportion of their insurance costs—was a secondary issue in news reports, which emphasized the disruptive effects of strike supporters' behavior:

> A hundred union supporters shut down a Safeway in Santa Cruz for an hour and a half recently, dancing and chanting in a conga line through the store. Others disrupted a golf tournament in Pebble Beach on Friday, shouting slogans at two supermarket board members who were about to tee off. Labor leaders are threatening to harass supermarket executives wherever they vacation, be it on beaches or ski slopes.[49]

As is typical of reports on labor issues, the longer the strike continued, the more negative media coverage became. By the fourth month of the strike, news articles routinely focused on problems that the strike was causing for ordinary people. For example, "Grocery Strike Wearing on Customers, Workers" begins with a narrative about a shopper who was inconvenienced by the work stoppage:

> Encinitas, Calif.—Linda Cugno avoided shopping at her neighborhood Albertson's store for the first month in support of striking grocery work-

ers. She tried to stay away in the second month of the strike, and the third. But as the grocery workers' strike in Southern California enters its fourth month with no end in sight, she can no longer justify driving out of her way to other stores. "I literally live right up the hill," she said, gesturing while loading groceries in an Albertson's parking lot in this San Diego suburb. "I feel bad (for the strikers) . . . but this has been going on long enough." That's what everybody—shoppers, picketers, grocers—seems to be saying about the work stoppage that has dragged on since October 11, affecting 70,000 workers and 860 stores in Southern California and everybody here who needs milk, eggs, and toilet paper.[50]

Clearly, work stoppages and strikes do inconvenience people; however, the media may now give more coverage to this issue than to investigative, behind-the-scenes analysis of what causes strikes in the first place, how they might be resolved, or what the broader implications are. In the case of the supermarket strike, for example, the grocery workers' union offered to participate in federal mediation, but supermarket officials were unwilling to pursue this route, thereby playing a largely unacknowledged part in prolonging the work stoppage. By the time the picket lines had ended, supermarket officials had largely defeated the workers' demands. Media attention was predominantly given grocery store executives who believed that cost cuts were necessary to keep the stores open and fight off competition from Wal-Mart, a nonunionized superstore.[51] After the strike, media headlines like "Grocery Workers Relieved, if Not Happy, at Strike's End" framed the work stoppage as having been a hardship on everyone, including the employees: "For many workers the dispute meant weeks of misery. No longer able to afford child care, many said they left their children alone when they served their four hours on the picket line for $25 a day."[52]

In some news reports about this strike, journalists looked narrowly at how this situation affected people in southern California. Others, however, briefly explored the broader implications of the work stoppage: "Although the labor dispute is local, the strike has nationwide implications because it centers on the companies' desire to reduce health care costs by eliminating some benefits and requiring workers to pick up a greater share of the cost."[53]

Media framing of articles about labor unions focuses not only on workers' alleged greed but on labor racketeering. According to the Federal Bureau of Investigation, *labor racketeering* is "the domination, manipulation, and control of a labor movement which affects related businesses and industries."[54] As a result of racketeering, workers' rights are often denied and great economic losses are suffered by businesses, insurers, and consumers. Media have reported on how the FBI uncovered the involvement of La

Cosa Nostra, the so-called Gambino family, and other crime syndicates in unions, which they ran for their own profit, national power, and influence.[55]

Newspaper headlines and television news "leading stories" like "Union Boss Indicted" reinforce the connection between unions and crime in the thinking of media audiences having little actual knowledge of union labor. In the late 1990s, union corruption was a key topic in news reports as government officials investigated corruption within the leadership of unions. Pointing out clear class distinctions between the union leaders and the rank-and-file workers was a key theme in many reports on these scandals, as shown in the opening statement of one article:

> The scandal that swept the president of New York City's janitors' local *from his union penthouse* earlier this month was the latest in a series of stinging labor setbacks, stemming from an unusual combination of forces, that have made the city the national capital of union excess and corruption. Other cities are well known for union corruption, of course, among them Chicago, Boston, Providence, R.I., and several New Jersey locales. But labor investigators and experts say no other city today comes close to New York in the number of officials under investigation or the dozens of union locals under trusteeship. "I don't think there's any question that New York, because of some historical reasons and some unfortunate traditions, has the unfortunate rank as the No. 1 labor racketeering city in the nation," said Michael Cherkasy, a former prosecutor who is chief operating officer of Kroll Associates, the investigative firm.[56]

According to the article, the head of the janitors' union received a $450,000 salary, lived in an extravagant penthouse, and received $1.5 million in severance pay while supposedly representing janitors and other custodial workers, who were in the bottom tier of the working class. The journalist who wrote the article concluded that several factors resulted in New York City's unions being more prone to corruption, including the entrenched Mafia presence, the city's many construction projects, the availability of large numbers of immigrant workers, and the juxtaposition of large, powerful unions to small, vulnerable businesses.[57]

Media reports regarding union corruption have highlighted the FBI's efforts to enforce the Racketeer Influenced and Corrupt Organizations Act (RICO) since the 1970s and bring an end to labor racketeering. According to the FBI, some unions, including the International Brotherhood of Teamsters and the International Longshoremen's Association, have in the past been "completely dominated by men who either have strong ties to or are members of the organized crime syndicate."[58]

Even with extensive media reports of the FBI's successes in curtailing organized crime's involvement in unions, criminal connections between some unions and the crime mobs persist in the twenty-first century. A 2002 *New York Times* article, "U.S. Indicts Gottis, Saying They Operated Dock Rackets," describes how the Gotti crime family took over the New York waterfront by gaining control over the appointment of officials in the International Longshoremen's Association, forcing dock workers to pay for their jobs, and reaping highly profitable kickbacks from the union's prescription drug plan:

> The indictment charges that the defendants used "threats of force, violence and fear" to control the docks in Brooklyn and Staten Island, where it says they rigged union elections. They were also able to secure the award of a prescription contract for GPP/VIP, a company controlled by one of the defendants, Vincent Nasso, earning themselves a $400,000 payment, the indictment said.[59]

The framing of articles about the working class that have almost exclusively focused on corrupt labor leaders and less-than-honorable workers has neither provided media audiences with a balanced picture of life in the working class nor provided useful information about the needs and concerns of people in this socioeconomic category. Moreover, media emphasis on labor corruption has ignored the efforts of many hard workers and legitimate unions that seek to better workers' conditions. This harms organized labor in general: "The high-profile episodes of corruption and skulduggery in New York and elsewhere are unquestionably hurting efforts to revive the labor movement," according to Nelson Lichtenstein, a University of Virginia labor historian.[60] Whereas the labor movement in the past brought about positive gains for the working class, including the eight-hour workday, safety nets such as unemployment compensation and pension plans, and safer workplaces in heavy industry and mining,[61] contemporary labor unions have a bad reputation based on the real-life actions of their leaders and fictionalized portrayals in television and film of mob-infiltrated unions.

One of the most widely watched and discussed examples of fictionalized portrayals of mob life and its connection with labor is shown weekly on HBO's popular series *The Sopranos*. Although the socioeconomic status of Tony Soprano (James Gandolfini) appears at first to be middle to upper-middle class, based on such visible cues as his luxurious residence in an affluent New Jersey suburb and the cars his family drives, Tony is portrayed as a slob who fits media stereotypes of the working class. He displays stereo-typic working-class attributes in how he dresses (ambling down his drive-way in a bathrobe and floppy slippers to get the morning paper), speaks (a pronounced ethnic accent with poor grammar and limited communication skills), eats (a napkin tucked into his collar as he gorges on huge piles of pasta and talks to his cronies with his mouth full of food), and amuses him-self (with mistresses or by watching strippers at his club, the Bada Bing).

Some *Sopranos* story lines touch on the relationship between organized crime and labor. One episode, "Do Not Resuscitate," involved a picket line set up by African American jointfitters, led by the Rev. Herman James, Jr., who supposedly wanted jobs at the Massarone Brothers construction site. The owner, Jack Massarone, asks Tony to "fix" the problem, not knowing that Tony had a "business arrangement" with Reverend James. As the episode ends, James acknowledges that he is in cahoots with Tony: "I'm lin-ing my pockets with [the picketing jointfitters'] blood."[62] With Tony's en-couragement, Massarone agrees to put five no-shows on his payroll; how-ever, unbeknownst to Massarone, Tony collects the proceeds and divides them with Reverend James.

Although the intersection of crime and labor is not a constant theme in *The Sopranos,* this connection is shown often enough in the story lines to keep viewers associating labor with corruption and with other mob activities, such as drug dealing, loan sharking, gambling, and hijacking. Control of even small-time work is portrayed as an obsession with mob leaders in this program. One episode showed the attempts of Feech LaManna, a recently paroled "wiseguy" who was sent to prison during the 1980s crackdown on organized crime, to take over running the yard maintenance business in certain neighborhoods to grab back his old turf.[63] Although *The Sopranos,* like the entire genre of or-ganized-crime dramas on television and in film, is described by many people as nothing more than entertainment, its portrayals of the working class as cor-rupt cast a negative light on millions of hard-working Americans on the lower socioeconomic rungs of society. (In addition, *The Sopranos* has been the subject of much criticism from members of Italian-American organizations, who be-lieve that this show perpetuates Cosa Nostra stereotypes.[64])

As discussed earlier in this chapter, the media generally have either per-petuated stereotypes or ignored the working class except when labor issues were involved. According to the media analyst Phil Primack, newspaper and television newsrooms that adhere to such an approach never report many important working-class stories:

> Most of the few labor reporters left today, like most of the new breed of
> workplace writers, are assigned to their papers' business sections, where

space is tight and the investigative approach is not commonly encouraged. If the workplace were treated more as a hard news beat, and if reporters felt that their pieces could more easily make it to page one, coverage might quickly improve. . . . Stories about factory dangers or worker hassles require getting into factories and talking to workers. This means good old-fashioned beat development and reporting, whether it is called labor or workplace or something else. Meanwhile, the nation's workplaces remain a largely untapped gold mine of stories.[65]

Primack asserts that the lack of media coverage about working-class issues and labor is less a "press conspiracy to ignore workers" than a lapse brought about by a "combination of laziness, questionable priorities, and a growing socioeconomic gap between journalists and blue-collar readers and viewers."[66] According to a *Los Angeles Times* labor reporter, "You get the impression sometimes that [working-class] people just do not count except when they shoot someone."[67] One exception to this general rule is media framing of stories about labor in the aftermath of a major crisis or a natural disaster, of which a classic example is the "working-class hero" depicted in the aftermath of the terrorist attacks on the United States in 2001.

HEROIC FRAMING:
WORKING-CLASS HEROES AND VICTIMS

No recent event in United States history did more to popularize the images of working-class heroes and victims than the terrorist attacks of September 11, 2001, and their aftermath. According to media reports issued during the weeks following those attacks, more than one thousand of the victims had belonged to labor unions. Some were praised for their work as firefighters, police officers, and emergency medical technicians who lost their lives in the effort to rescue thousands of other people; others were union members who lost their lives as they went about their daily jobs in the twin towers of the World Trade Center complex. According to one media account published in *The Village Voice* shortly after the attack:

> Union members . . . worked throughout the towers. At Windows on the World, the swank restaurant atop One World Trade Center, as many as 79 members of Local 100 of the Hotel Employees and Restaurant Employees International Union perished. Twenty floors below them, at least 39 members of the Public Employees Federation, most of them workers at the Department of Taxation and Finance on the 86th and 87th floors of the south tower, are missing. Some 27 maintenance workers,

members of Local 32B-J of the Service Employees International Union are missing, according to union spokesman Bill Meyerson. "They were window cleaners, security officers, elevator starters," said Meyerson. In addition, at least 50 members of the building trades were killed, union officials estimate. About 17 of them were carpenters assembling office partitions, another 15 were electricians, five were painters, and four were laborers. . . . In a harbinger of the rescue efforts their fellow members would make later that day, union officials believe some tradesmen died trying to help after the attack.[68]

As later news accounts confirmed, many of those described as missing in this report were confirmed to be among the dead.

Media framing of articles about the working class in this case was extremely positive, emphasizing the heroism not only of police officers, firefighters, and other emergency personnel but of union members across New York who rushed to the World Trade Center site to help in the wake of the attack. At the carpenters union headquarters, for example, more than three hundred members arrived early in the morning on September 12 to volunteer their services: "We unloaded every pair of gloves we had, gave them goggles, hard hats, whatever we could find. Then they marched straight down to the site. Their pass was their union card and their hard hat; they didn't take 'no' for an answer," according to Steve McInnis of the New York District Council of Carpenters.[69] Furthermore, union rules about trade demarcation (e.g., steamfitters are not supposed to drive nails, carpenters do not touch wiring) were ignored during the gritty excavation work.[70] The heroism of these union workers was celebrated by a journalist who wrote that whatever message the terrorists tried to send by this horrendous act was "effectively refuted with every shovelful lifted from the pile"—much of it, in this case, by union workers who (as discussed earlier in this chapter) often are the objects of media criticism rather than praise.

Media framing of articles about the victims of the terrorist attacks told the stories of people in all classes who lost their lives on September 11, but for the six months following this crisis the working class received some of the most positive news coverage it had garnered in many decades. Shortly after 9/11, Mayor Rudolph W. Giuliani declared to the New York City firefighters, police officers, and other public servants, "You're all my heroes," a sound bite and headline that was used in the framing of many stories about the role the working class played in the aftermath of this tragedy.[71] Framing of the stories typically focused on remarks by Mayor Giuliani, President George W. Bush, and others that the "toll would have been even higher were it not for the extraordinary valor of firefighters, police officers and emergency service workers who ran to the disaster scene to help."[72] Journalists also reported on religious leaders, such as Cardinal Edward M. Egan of New York, who publicly declared that the "fallen firefighters, police and other emergency workers" were indeed heroes.[73] Even schoolchildren became part of the media's story on the heroic efforts of public servants, as evidenced by articles about notes posted near the collapse site: "'Dear Mr. or Mrs. Fireman,' begins one note posted in St. Joseph's Chapel, and from a novice speller, 'Dear Mr. Frieman.' They call the rescue workers heroes, thank them, and encourage them to get home safely."[74]

As these examples show, members of the print media clearly empathized with members of the working class and their efforts to help others during this national crisis. Television and Internet journalists expressed similar sentiments toward both those who had been killed and those who valiantly worked to help others. For example, in a September 21, 2001 special called "America: A Tribute to Heroes," all networks and some cable television channels carried a salute to the victims of September 11, including photographs and commentaries on police, fire, and other emergency workers.

Little is written or broadcast, however, about the everyday activities of members of the working class, their small acts of kindness or bravery, such as firefighters putting out a residential fire, construction workers digging a ditch in the street without bursting a water main or gas pipe, or an aide helping an elderly person get comfortable in a nursing home bed. There are, of course, exceptions on local television news programs and in human-interest stories on national network news. However, media reports of this kind typically are triggered by some organization giving an award or recognition to some individual or group, not by journalists seeking out members of the working class to praise for their energy and efforts. An example of local news coverage precipitated by an award was the story "Everyday Heroes: Firefighters," broadcast by an ABC television affiliate in Saginaw, Michigan: "Every year the American Red Cross recognizes those who show courage, kindness and character. All this week on ABC12 news at 5, 6, and 11 we'll introduce you to some of these 'Everyday Heroes.' That includes four firefighters from Thomas and Saginaw Townships who risked their lives to pull a woman from a burning building."[75] The news anchor then described the courageous rescue of this woman by the firefighters and noted that the firefighters had stressed that "it's teamwork making a rescue like this possible. After pulling her out, it really took all four of us to get her out of the house. Teamwork's a very big thing," said Josh, one of the rescuers.[76]

Crises and tragedies bring to the media foreground *individual workers* rather than images of the *organized labor* that many in the media have found to be either unnewsworthy or blameworthy. Stories of trapped miners, for example, highlight the role that teamwork plays in saving lives. Articles about miners in such situations are often framed to emphasize their heroism, as was true in a Brookwood, Alabama, disaster that was one of the nation's worst mining calamities in recent decades. Journalists described how some coal miners who initially escaped the cave-in that followed the initial explosion at the mine did not flee but courageously raced to aid their fallen comrades and became victims themselves when they were caught in a second explosion forty-five minutes later.[77] Even more media coverage occurs when there are happy endings, as in a mining accident at the Quecreek Mine in Pennsylvania in 2002, when all nine of the trapped miners escaped without serious harm and were soon able to appear on television entertainment shows like the *Late Show with David Letterman*. Letterman introduced the miners and interviewed one of them, Blaine Mayhugh, who described the despair that he and the other eight miners felt when they were trapped for three and a half days in a four-foot-high tunnel with water up to their chins. Seeking a moment of levity, Letterman asked Mayhugh if anything was said or done to break the tension while the men were trapped. According to Mayhugh, one of the trapped miners said, "We'll be getting a lot of overtime for this."[78]

By the time the Letterman show had been broadcast, hero/victim framing of the working class had reached its peak with news, entertainment shows, and advertisements that focused on the heroic status of blue-collar workers, as one advertising analyst noted:

> The media and advertisers have responded to Americans' post–September 11 need for heroes by elevating firemen and police officers to mythical status and saturating every conceivable communications vehicle with their images. Last month's trapped miners saga was no different: suffocating coverage and a celebration of heroic efforts to liberate the workers. . . . People who get sweaty rather than wear suits (or pantsuits) to work have become the ultimate content marketing ploy. News, entertainment, advertising, whatever. Just trot 'em out and watch 'em grab eyeballs and sell stuff.[79]

Although there may be an occasional "overload" of working-class portrayals in the media, actual heroic framing of news stories about this class appears to be situational and to occur primarily when a tragedy of major proportions has taken place.

In sharp contrast to the positive framing of the working class that typically focuses on those persons who risk their lives for others, media framing of news articles and television entertainment story lines more often employs caricatures that depict working-class women and men in a less favorable manner than people in the middle and upper classes.

CARICATURE FRAMING #1:
WHITE-TRASHING THE WORKING CLASS

Although the middle and upper classes may be the objects of caricatures in some media representations, people in the working class are particularly vulnerable to media framing that emphasizes or misrepresents their appearance or behavior in such a manner as to produce an exaggerated or comic effect and turn them into objects of ridicule. One way this occurs is when the media represent members of the working class as inferior to those in the upper classes, by branding members of the working class with derogatory labels like "white trash."

Early usage of the term *white trash* typically referred to low-income individuals who were judged by the more privileged members of society to be tasteless, uneducated, lazy, and otherwise inferior. As cultural studies scholars Matt Wray and Annalee Newitz have suggested, "White trash is 'good to think with' when it comes to issues of race and class in the U.S. because the term foregrounds whiteness and working-class or underclass poverty, two social attributes that usually stand far apart in the minds of many Americans."[80] According to Wray and Newitz, many people think of "whiteness" as being associated with the middle and upper classes, not realizing that it exists across class lines. In regard to the poverty class, classic films like *Gone with the Wind* popularized the phrase "po' white trash"; more recently the white-trash caricature has been employed by the media to portray blue-collar and lower-income white-collar families.

The term has also been bantered about in television situation comedies like the now-syndicated show *Roseanne,* which featured a working-class family that prided itself on its "trashy" origins and behavior. An episode titled "White Trash Christmas" revolved around a story line in which Roseanne Conner, a blue-collar working mother, and her husband Dan (John Goodman) snub their neighbors by putting up gaudy Christmas decorations outside their house. In another episode Roseanne is sitting in the garage on a favorite sofa the family discarded when they purchased a new one. Roseanne is laughing at an old episode of the *Beverly Hillbillies,* a "white-trash-made-good" show, which she is watching on the family's old, discarded TV set. As Dan and Roseanne talk nostalgically about their old furniture, Roseanne jokingly reveals how she sees their family's class location: "We're white trash and we'll stay white trash until they haul us out to the curb."

Airing from 1988 through 1997 on network television and still showing in global syndication, *Roseanne* no doubt has influenced viewers' ideas about what it means to be "white trash" and has portrayed the working-class lifestyle as a mixture of tasteless behavior and the genuine love and respect that members of the Conner family show toward each other. Over the nine years the show ran, Roseanne held several working-class jobs, including factory worker, hair washer at a beauty salon, magazine telemarketer, and waitress at the local mall. The family's acceptance of its "white trash" status was made clear to television audiences through comments the Conners made to each other as well as a website (Roseanneworld.com), which pictures a small metal house trailer with the door wide open, chairs and flowers out front, and the general impression that visitors are welcome. In this symbolic gesture, Roseanne aligns herself with not only the concept of "white trash" but that of "trailer park trash."

As used by the media, the terms "white trash" and "trailer park trash" often have similar meanings, whether or not the individuals in question actually live in trailers. Late 1990s media coverage of the Paula Jones sexual harassment lawsuit against President Bill Clinton was a good example of how one comment about a person being "trailer park trash" can produce a media wildfire that rages out of control for months. Briefly stated, Paula Jones alleged that in 1991, when she was a low-wage, hourly employee in an Arkansas state office, she was propositioned by Governor Clinton. However, her allegations were not made public until Clinton was elected president of the United States and became embroiled in a sex scandal involving Monica S. Lewinsky, the White House intern who publicly admitted that she had had sexual relations with the president. When Jones's claims were made public in the media, commentators widely discussed a statement by James Carville, a former Clinton campaign adviser and an ardent defender of the president, who accused Jones of being "trailer park trash" in an effort to discredit her claims. According to various media sources, Carville made this statement in explaining why he thought Jones had come forward with her allegations: "Drag a hundred-dollar bill through a trailer park and you never know what you'll find."[81]

By using the term *trailer park,* Carville implied that Jones's testimony against the president had been bought and that her humble origins should discredit her testimony.[82] According to one journalist who followed the case closely:

> Carville didn't rely on the well-worn femme cliches of sexual opportunist, hysterical harpy or angry woman spurned when he went after Jones. He fingered a crevice of the American psyche that promised to spurt forth all that and more. She was white trash, part of a subset blamed for everything from garishly bad taste in dress, America's obesity problem and Elvis adulation to incest, child abuse, alcoholism, spouse beat-

ings, the fracturing of the family and out-of-wedlock motherhood, not to mention Roseanne and Tom Arnold. So powerful are those words that the media took up the smear campaign unquestioningly, for a time.[83]

Although Carville later claimed that he never called Jones "white trash," he did concede that he had used similar language in reference to Gennifer Flowers, another woman who claimed that she had had a long-standing affair with Clinton.[84] Regardless of the intended victim of this class-based attack by Carville, all media outlets, including television, radio, Internet, newspapers, and magazines, regaled audiences with "play by play" coverage of the battle of words that ensued.

By publicizing Carville's use of the white-trash caricature, the media kept the stereotype before people much longer than it might otherwise have existed. An article from the *Washington Post* asking "Should James Carville apologize for humiliating millions of decent Americans by demeaning Paula Jones as 'trailer park trash'?" is an example.[85] This article stated that members of the Arundel Mobile Homeowners' Association believed that Carville should apologize: "We have become the innocent victims of a personal problem between President Clinton and Paula Jones. All hard-working, responsible mobile-home owners have been needlessly insulted by the careless handling of this incident."[86] In response to criticisms like this, Carville replied, "The people I was talking about were the whole gallery of folks who come up with these stories about the president. You give them enough money and they'll say anything. . . . Hey, my sister married someone who lived in a mobile home, so it can't be all that bad."[87] Other journalists have argued that the national media treated Paula Jones differently, highlighting comments like "white trash" because of Jones's working-class origins, particularly as compared with better-educated women like Anita Hill, who accused Clarence Thomas, now a Supreme Court justice, of sexual harassment.[88] For example, Jones was portrayed as a woman "with big hair coming out of the trailer parks" and as a woman from Lonoke, Arkansas, a "land of big hair and tight jeans and girls whose dreams soar no further than a stint at hairdressers' school, an early marriage and a baby named Brittany or Tiffany or Brooke."[89]

Just as news stories in the mainstream media may amplify negative images of the working class, another genre, referred to as "white trash culture" by one scholar,[90] also represents working-class whites in a derogatory fashion. White-trash culture refers to media forms such as tabloids (e.g., the *National Inquirer*), low-brow television talk shows (such as *The Jerry Springer Show*), and cable networks showing "prole sports" (demolition derbies, tractor pulls, and female mud wrestling). According to the sociologist Laura Grind-staff's recent study of "trashy" television talk shows, "The issue here is not the race or income level of guests per se but the relation of class and trash. ('They're white trash, black trash, Hispanic—any kind of, like, low-caliber people.')"[91] In Grindstaff's interviews, one producer described typical "guests" on this kind of talk show as follows:

> The trailer-park joke is not far from the truth. . . . Not that they neces-sarily live in trailer parks, but a lot of these people lead very transient lives. I would say their education level is high school for the most part, people who are semiskilled. It's the crowd that would have been on an assembly line in a major manufacturing plant before all those jobs disap-peared. It's a particular type because it satisfies—because we watch these things and it's almost like, "Gee, at least I'm not that bad off."[92]

The extent to which television talk shows banter around terms like "white trash" was further demonstrated by Bill Maher, the host of *Politically Incorrect,* a late-night television show featuring a celebrity panel talking about "current events." On one program, panelists were discussing the shooting death of former *Jerry Springer Show* guest Nancy Campbell Panitz, who had been killed by her ex-husband shortly after she, her ex-husband, and his new wife appeared on a 2000 *Springer* episode. One of Maher's pan-elists described the kind of people who appear on shows like *Jerry Springer* as white trash and joked that such shows serve as a safety valve for lower-class "guests." Maher responded, "So you're saying Jerry Springer is doing a service to America by having white trash kill each other?"[93]

Although excused by many as "just joking," use of "white trash" to re-fer to people by class would not be permitted if the individuals being de-scribed were racial or ethnic minorities. Moreover, media portrayals of working-class people as white trash are further reinforced by television en-tertainment shows featuring working-class characters as buffoons or bigots.

CARICATURE FRAMING #2:
TV'S BUFFOONS, BIGOTS, AND SLOBS

In one well-known study of prime-time television, the media scholar Richard Butsch argues that media depictions of the working class are either absent or biased:

> The working class is not only underrepresented; the few men who are portrayed are buffoons. They are dumb, immature, irresponsible or lack-

ing in common sense. This is the character of the husbands in almost every sitcom depicting a blue-collar (white) male head of house. *The Honeymooners, The Flintstones, All in the Family* and *The Simpsons* being the most famous examples. He is typically well-intentioned, even lovable, but no one to respect or emulate. These men are played against more mature, sensible wives, such as Ralph against Alice in the *Honeymooners*.[94]

The sitcoms mentioned by Butsch feature male characters in blue-collar jobs, such as bus driver Ralph Kramden in *The Honeymooners;* rock-quarry "crane" operator Fred Flintstone, dockworker Archie Bunker, and low-level nuclear power plant technician Homer Simpson. These characters are typically portrayed as inept bumblers who cannot achieve success because they do not have the necessary drive or intelligence. Working-class wives in these shows are typically portrayed as more intelligent, level-headed, and in control than their husbands. According to Butsch, "Situation comedy is built around a humorous 'situation' which is resolved during the half hour. In working-class series the character typically caught in the situation, usually of his own making, was the man. Usually his wife had to help him out of the situation."[95] Unlike some middle-class sitcoms where the "man of the house" is portrayed as wise, cooperative, sensible, and mature, working-class sitcoms invert gender status and devalue male characters. Such media portrayals of working-class men preserve the status quo by reinforcing the notion that the male proletariat needs direct supervision at work and at home.

Early representations of the working class in television situation comedies were based on both class location and ethnicity. In NBC's *The Life of Riley,* Chester A. Riley (played in 1949–1950 by Jackie Gleason and from 1953 to 1958 by William Bendix) was an Irish American airplane riveter who lived in suburban Los Angeles with his nuclear family. Although each episode took place in the family's residence, Riley's job at the factory was a topic of frequent conversation, particularly in regard to his frustration with his boss and his animosity toward the upper classes, with their "pretentious nature."[96] The stereotype of the working-class buffoon was central to the story line of each episode, as described in one review:

> Each week, Riley first became flustered, then overwhelmed by seemingly minor problems concerning his job, his family, or his neighbors. These small matters—once Riley became involved—escalated to the verge of disaster. Riley's catch phrase—"What a revoltin' development this is!"—expressed his frustration and became part of the national idiom. His patient wife, Peg . . . managed to keep the family in order despite her husband's calamitous blunders.[97]

Following a similar format, CBS's *The Honeymooners* featured Ralph Kramden (Jackie Gleason) as a New York City bus driver who lived in a rundown Brooklyn apartment with his wife, Alice. In most episodes, Kramden was the object of ridicule and tongue-lashings by Alice, who frequently said, " I told you so." Although Ralph expressed ambivalence toward affluent people, he was not above trying one "get rich quick" scheme after another, such as investing in no-calorie pizza and marketing what he thought was Alice's homemade sauce (only to learn that it was dog food).[98] Ralph's working-class background was often shown by comments he made to Alice, including "Just you wait Alice, one of these days, pow, right in the kisser,"[99] alluding to domestic violence, which audiences supposedly knew would not actually happen in the Kramden household. Airing between 1952 and 1970 as *The Honeymooners* or as *The Jackie Gleason Show,* this situation comedy is still available on the TVLand network and on DVD.

Buffoonery in the working class is also evident in animated comedy series like *The Flintstones* and the more contemporary FOX show, *The Simpsons.* In each of these series, the leading male character appears to be inspired by the characters of Chester Riley and Ralph Kramden. Like Chester and Ralph, Fred Flintstone and Homer Simpson are loudmouths who often talk before they think. Like the earlier working-class sitcom wives, Peg Riley and Alice Kramden, the animated wives, Wilma Flintstone and Marge Simpson, are depicted as smarter than their husbands and often getting the men out of self-inflicted jams. In most episodes of *The Simpsons,* Homer does something at home or work that creates a crisis that others have to resolve. Homer often concocts harebrained get-rich-quick schemes that backfire, and his work ethic is lacking both at the nuclear power plant and at home, where he is largely useless in matters of house maintenance and family life. Although kindhearted, Homer is generally a negative role model for his children, watching television constantly, eating junk food from the refrigerator or a sack, drinking beer and throwing the empties on the floor, belching loudly, talking in blue-collar speech patterns, and hanging out at Moe's, the local blue-collar bar. Like Riley's daughter Babs, Homer's daughter Lisa is studious, talented, and well organized. In *The Simpsons,* Lisa, although only a second-grader, beats Homer at Scrabble while Bart, the son, beats dad in a video boxing game.[100]

In *The Life of Riley, The Honeymooners,* and *The Simpsons,* traditional gender roles are reinforced: The father earns the family's income while the wife maintains the household. Although the creators of *The Simpsons* might argue that their show is nothing more than a parody of earlier sitcoms like *Riley, Honeymooners,* and *Flintstones,* the roles of the leading characters, including the flustered husband, rock-solid wife, and children who are smarter

or more conniving than their father have been reinforced for new generations of television audiences.

Framing of situation comedy story lines not only creates and reinforces
the image of the working-class buffoon but portrays some members of this
class as bigots. Archie Bunker (Carroll O'Connor) of *All in the Family* has
been referred to as the "quintessential, all-American bigot . . . who was part
of the old guard who failed to recognize the melting pot mentality of the
modern world."[101] Indeed, Bunker's character was a bigoted, opinionated,
and uneducated blue-collar dock foreman who drove a taxi on the side to
earn extra money. Eventually, Archie bought a bar and renamed it Archie
Bunker's Place, but Bunker himself remained a bigoted proletarian throughout the show's nine seasons. Even though Archie was sometimes kindhearted when dealing with his wife, Edith (Jean Stapleton), or his daughter,
Gloria (Sally Struthers), he used working-class, sexist remarks, such as referring to Edith as "Dingbat" and speaking to her demeaningly. Edith was portrayed as ditzy and subservient but kind to other people, a perfect balance
for the harsh character of Archie.[102]

Much of Bunker's racism was brought out through conversations with
his son-in-law, Mike Stivic (Rob Reiner), and through verbal battles with
his African American neighbor, George Jefferson (Sherman Hemsley). The
Jeffersons' son, Lionel (Mike Evans), shared Mike's liberal views, and bitter
debates took place with Archie on one side and Mike and Lionel on the
other.

George Jefferson's character was as bigoted as Archie's, but Jefferson
was portrayed as a wealthier, opinionated African American, as contrasted
with Archie's role as a white, working-class bigot. In early seasons of *All in
the Family*, Archie's racism was apparent in such episodes as one where he
refused to donate blood because he did not want his blood to be mixed with
that of a black person. In another episode, "Lionel Moves into the Neighborhood," Archie tried to prevent a black family from buying the house
next door, not realizing that the potential buyers, the Jeffersons, were Lionel's parents. Since Lionel had been a frequent visitor at the Bunkers'
house in the past, Archie's opposition created embarrassment for the Bunker
family, but it was soon overshadowed by the barbs exchanged by Archie and
George.[103] George Jefferson became the lead character in a spin-off series,
The Jeffersons, after George became wealthy and moved from Archie's neighborhood to Manhattan's affluent Upper East Side.

By the ninth (and final) season of *All in the Family*, another black family had moved into the Bunkers' neighborhood, but Archie maintained his
racist attitude. When Edith prepares sandwiches to welcome the new neighbors, Archie loudly rails at her for her desire to befriend them. Showing

how deeply ingrained his attitudes are, Archie tells Edith, "You know damn well there's certain things about me I ain't never gonna change. But you keep asking me to make out like I'm gonna," to which Edith replies, after a lengthy pause, "That's right."[104] With this conclusion to the show, Archie, the working-class buffoon and bigot, showed that he was either unable or unwilling to change.

Norman Lear, creator and producer of *All in the Family,* has argued that Archie's attitudes throughout the series were nothing more than a reflection of how life really is in the United States: "If a couple thousand years of Judeo–Christian ethic have not solved the problems of bigotry and narrow-mindedness, I'd be a fool to think a little half-hour situation comedy is gonna do the trick."[105] Some media scholars have argued, however, that por-trayals of working-class characters as "lovable bigots" may be used as "proof that racism really isn't a dangerous thing. It might be embarrassing, or un-settling, but never dangerous."[106] As one analyst stated after Carroll O'Con-nor's death in 2001:

> Archie Bunker never led a lynch mob, but the "Bunkerish" attitude al-lows for modern lynch mobs that target Blacks, whether in police de-partments, courts or social service agencies. . . . Images do matter. They help to legitimize, uplift and protect or dehumanize, violate and make expendable. So the world may miss Mr. O'Connor, but don't grieve for Archie Bunker, he's alive and well.[107]

Working-class women are less likely to be portrayed as buffoons or bigots, but they are depicted in some situation comedies as lacking in class, particularly when compared with their middle- and upper-middle-class counterparts. The character of Roseanne Conner is perhaps the closest fe-male equivalent of an Archie Bunker. According to one media scholar, the sitcom *Roseanne* contributed to the "Roseannification" of working-class women in the media by showing these women as violating the "codes of bourgeois respectability and the codes of femininity."[108]

Recent working-class situation comedies have been more subtle in their portrayals; however, earlier stereotypes are reinforced by the characters' behavior, the sets on which the episodes are staged, and other tell-tale signs of the characters' proletariat status. Consider, for example, the popular CBS series *The King of Queens,* a situation comedy set in the working-class New York City borough of Queens. The show revolves around Doug Heffernan (Kevin James), a delivery man for a UPS-type company, and his wife Car-rie (Leah Remini), who holds down various jobs over the course of the se-ries. Like most other working-class families on television, Carrie is more ambitious than Doug, and her desire to shop far exceeds the family's budget. Consequently, the Heffernans have numerous financial crises that are intensified by events such as mold damage to their house and Carrie's being laid off. To make matters worse, Carrie's obstinate, opinionated father, Arthur Spooner (Jerry Stiller), lives in the Heffernans' basement, which previously had been Doug's recreation room, where he and his pals watched a large-screen television. Spooner is often the brunt of working-class jokes, as when friends of the Heffernans reluctantly took him to a Mexican food restaurant and let him eat the hot sauce.

As in earlier working-class sitcoms, Doug is portrayed as a kindhearted bumbler with a "slob factor" that is evidenced by extensive discussions about his weight and his fixation on food. Like his sitcom predecessors, Doug is also a slob when it comes to doing tasks around the house; in one case he cannot even find the scissors and tape to finish a project, and Carrie has to come to his rescue. The slob factor intensifies when Doug hangs out with his friends, Deacon and Spence, and his cousin, all of whom experience male bonding and share "guy" humor. In "Wild Cards," for example, Doug and Deacon (who is also his coworker) are returning from a delivery in Philadelphia when they decide to go to Atlantic City for an evening of gambling. Since Doug had promised Carrie that they would see a Broadway play that night, he tells her that he cannot go because he has to make an unexpected night delivery. Doug loses all his money and gets into a dispute with Deacon; Carrie catches him in the lie and chastises him about his "boys' night out."[109]

The working-class slob stereotype is reinforced by the setting of *King of Queens.* Like the set of *Roseanne,* the Heffernans' living room has an over-sized sofa with a shawl draped across the back. In the cluttered kitchen, there is a small wooden table and chairs and a refrigerator covered with magnets and pictures. Other than his delivery uniform, Doug usually wears a "Jets" T-shirt or similar attire, while Carrie, who has a "shopping problem," sometimes buys expensive clothes at department stores and boutiques and returns them. If portrayals on television of working-class families like the Heffernans have grown somewhat more sophisticated, many of the recurring themes and characterizations of earlier shows can still be identified in contemporary situation comedies where the working class typically does not fare as well as the upper classes.

Although sitcoms reinforce the idea that the working class still exists in the United States, some media framing has focused on just the opposite conclusion, namely, that the kinds of work that have typically been considered working class in this country are vanishing.

FADING BLUE-COLLAR FRAMING:
OUT OF WORK OR UNHAPPY AT WORK

Media representations of the working class early in the twenty-first century have described the diminished political and economic clout of the laboring class as compared to the heyday when unionized blue-collar workers earned relatively high wages and had good benefits and job stability. The focus of news reports is now on the "fading" of blue-collar work due to job loss, the threat of cheap immigrant labor, the downgrading of blue-collar work generally, and the number of working-class families that are joining the ranks of the working poor. A recent political cartoon summed up the problems of the formerly well-paid union factory worker by showing a man wearing a hard hat and work shirt sitting across a desk from a young woman at a computer. Behind them is a sign that reads, "U.S. Job Placement Agency." The man says, "I'm an experienced factory worker." The woman replies, "What's a factory?"

In this visual image, the cartoonist Signe Wilkinson captures a major problem facing the working class: Blue-collar workers are becoming dinosaurs as their jobs continue to vanish. For example, an article ("The Last Grain Falls at a Sugar Factory") about the closing of a sugar factory tells the story of a worker who had been employed for twenty-eight years at the Domino Sugar plant in Brooklyn, which had been in continuous operation since the 1880s and had provided work for thousands of people. However, as Richard Rednour, the laid-off worker, lamented, "I learned this past week that I'm a dinosaur. . . . Having a job for a long time in one place is not necessarily a good thing. It used to mean I was reliable."[110] According to media reports, Rednour's situation is not an isolated one, as manufacturing jobs in Brooklyn have shrunk from more than 222,000 in 1958 to about 34,000 jobs in 2003.[111]

Framing of articles about plant closings often focuses on the effects of globalization on the U.S. working class. One recurring theme in some news reports pits native-born American workers against workers in other countries. Another theme highlights the potentially negative impact of immigrant labor on the U.S. working class. In the first of these, the job losses that American workers experience when plants are closed are juxtaposed against the gains of workers in other countries who are hired in similar positions—for much lower wages and fewer benefits—when the factories relocate. An example of this framing is found in articles about the closing of the Levi Strauss plant in San Antonio, when frustrated former employees realized "their" work was being exported to Mexico. Newspaper headlines like "As Levi's Work Is Exported, Stress Stays Home"[112] tell this story in few words. When factories are closed as work is exported to other countries, former employees bear the brunt of the problems, including the stress triggered by being out of work and without a paycheck.

In factories across America, employees have arrived at work one day expecting to do their job and instead have learned that the factory is closing soon and that they will unemployed. According to one longtime Levi Strauss employee, "There still probably is an American dream [for workers in other countries]. But what about us? What happens to our American dream?"[113] The photos accompanying such articles typically show longtime employees dejectedly leaving the factory after learning of its closing and their unemployment. Accompanying an article describing the closing of the Syracuse, New York, Carrier plant is a photo of a twenty-five-year-employee who has his back to the camera so that the writing on his T-shirt is visible: "UTC Carrier: The Un-American Dream."[114] The linkage between working-class job loss and the decline of the American Dream is a key framing device in many media accounts of plant closings.

Framing of articles and news reports about the "Americano Dream" pits indigenous U.S. workers not only against workers in other countries but against immigrant labor coming into the United States as so-called cheap labor.[115] Media sound bites that are used to describe the tension between indigenous labor and other workers include not only "cheap labor" but also terms such as "illegal aliens," "illegal workers," and "undocumented workers." Frequently, this terminology is employed when a major corporation is accused of labor violations, as was the case when Wal-Mart, the nation's largest private employer (with 1.1 million U.S. workers), was accused of using undocumented workers to clean its megastores. Although earlier media coverage of the Wal-Mart chain had primarily praised this corporation's economic success and applauded the ingenuity of the company's founder, Sam Walton, and other members of his family after his death, recent news reports have focused on questionable labor practices, such as the use of undocumented workers.[116] According to Wal-Mart officials, the company hired subcontractors to do the janitorial work without knowing that the labor contractors hired illegal immigrants:

> After federal agents raided 60 Wal-Mart stores in October and found more than 200 illegal immigrants in the cleaning crews, the world's largest retailer was quick to defend itself from this enormous embarrassment. Wal-Mart's officers said they had no idea those workers were illegal, insisting they knew next to nothing about the workers from Mexico, Mongolia, Russia and elsewhere because they were employed by contractors. Nor did Wal-Mart know, its spokesmen said, that the contractors were cutting corners by not paying overtime or Social Security taxes or by flouting other labor laws, as the investigators claimed.[117]

In news stories like this, journalists tend to focus on two sides of the same issue. On the one hand, subcontractors help keep corporate costs down and profitability up; on the other hand, some of the workers are in this country illegally, and such labor practices tend to suppress wages for native-born workers. Terms like "cheap labor" are bantered around by the media as reporters describe the immigrant workers—documented or not— as a potential threat to the indigenous working class. As cheap labor, undocumented workers lack access to many legitimate jobs, and they are vulnerable to exploitation by labor contractors, unscrupulous immigration officials, and others who prey on their "illegal immigrant" status.

Media framing of articles about undocumented workers not only questions the legality of such hiring practices but raises the issue of whether these workers take jobs away from U.S. citizens and suppress the wages of the working class in this country. These issues arise, according to some analysts, because Wal-Mart's labor contractors serve as middlemen in the low-wage economy, hiring undocumented workers who are paid less than what Wal-Mart would be required to pay to people on corporate payrolls.

Because the U.S. labor market has lost more than 1.2 million jobs in recent years, many news reports have focused on where the jobs have gone and who is benefiting from the jobs that do exist. Some journalists have publicized data suggesting that immigrants have fared better in the job market in recent years than natives have.[118] Even union officials representing organized labor have realized that immigrant workers are not going away, and organizations like the AFL-CIO, which represents thirteen million American workers, have developed an "immigration-friendly stance" as union leaders continue their efforts to organize these workers.[119] As a spokesperson for one Latino advocate group stated, "The old way of thinking was immigrants are the enemy of the American worker; the new way of thinking is immigrants *are* the American worker."[120]

According to many news accounts, it is highly unlikely that immigrant workers will stop coming to the United States even if officials continue to try to close the border: These workers would earn only sixty or seventy dollars for a forty-eight-hour work week at the Mexican maquiladora factories if they were fortunate enough to find jobs at all in their country of origin. If for no other reason, illegal migration is worth the risks in the minds of some undocumented workers because of the money that they can send to family members in other countries. For example, the article "U.S. Payday Is Something to Write Home About" describes how immigrants working low-paying jobs send more than a billion dollars a month to families living in Mexico:

Inside his little Western wear store [in Austin, Texas] . . . Francisco Javier Aceves can't help but feel a kinship with the angular young men who come in to buy jeans, cowboy boots, phone cards and cell phones. As sure as a regular payday, they come in also to wire money to their families back home in Mexico, in places such as Veracruz, Tabasco, Chiapas and Oaxaca. "Sometimes they come three or four in a car," Aceves said about his customers. "Sometimes they just start lining up to wire money."[121]

The men described by this shop owner earn between two and four hundred dollars a week and may send a hundred to three hundred dollars to family members in Mexico. To put this figure in perspective, journalists estimate that immigrant workers send more money back to Mexico annually than that country earns from tourism or foreign investment.[122] As a result, guest worker programs—such as the one proposed by the Bush administration in 2004 that would provide more than seven million undocumented immigrants with special work visas for up to six years and increase their chances of becoming naturalized citizens—are a hot topic in media coverage of working-class labor issues of the twenty-first century.[123] Some analysts argue that high levels of immigration, legal and illegal, are putting fiscal strains on state and local governments, depressing wages for low-income workers, widening the U.S. income gap, and displacing Americans in the job market.[124] By contrast, other analysts assert that foreign workers are revitalizing cities that would otherwise have lost population, paying taxes to prop up Social Security and the federal budget, fueling growth, and bolstering wages at the other end of the income scale.[125] For newspaper and television reporters, illegal workers and proposals about the guest worker program produce heated debates that generate a larger audience share than do less controversial topics.

Media reports have also shown that the nature of blue-collar jobs may be changing for the worse. Stories about the fading of blue-collar positions describe not only the shift from a heavy concentration in manufacturing toward positions in services, utilities, and other sectors but how more blue-collar positions are becoming "dead end" jobs. As one article suggests, many jobs available today to the working class are in the low-wage, service sector:

According to forecasts issued last month by the Bureau of Labor Statistics, 7 of the 10 occupations with the greatest growth through 2012 will be in low-wage, service fields requiring little education: retail salesperson, customer service representative, food-service worker, cashier, janitor, waiter and nursing aide and hospital orderly. Many of these jobs pay less than $18,000 a year.[126]

As this statement emphasizes, the future of the working class may not be very bright because many jobs provide only low wages, offer few opportunities for advancement, and are closely controlled by employers. Recent media coverage of Wal-Mart's labor practices, for example, has brought the issue of control over workers to public attention. A 2004 *New York Times* article, "Workers Assail Night Lock-Ins by Wal-Mart," described how some Wal-Mart stores lock in late-shift workers restocking shelves after the store has closed for the day. (Wal-Mart executives claim that this practice has occurred only on a store-by-store basis in an effort to prevent theft and to protect workers from intruders.)[127]

This practice was not called to public attention by the media until a locked-in worker, Michael Rodriguez, needed medical attention after his ankle was shattered by heavy machinery; he could not find a manager with a key to let him out of the store so that he could go to the hospital. According to media reports, Rodriguez feared that he would be fired if he used the emergency door. Lock-ins at other Wal-Mart stores also had allegedly harmed workers, including an employee who suffered a heart attack, Florida workers who could not get out of the building when a hurricane hit, and male employees who could not leave when their wives went into labor.[128] Although many businesses employing working-class people no doubt employ questionable labor practices, many journalists focus on Wal-Mart because of its strength as a retail giant and the perceived problem of the "Wal-Martization of America," a term that, among other things, refers to the corporation's use of nonunion, low-wage employees to cut operating expenses, maximize profits, and drive numerous competitors out of business.

The final theme in fading blue-collar framing is the increasing impoverishment of the working class as more people join the ranks of the working poor. Like many other topics of media interest, the issue of the working poor has been analyzed by journalists and academics in the framework of the lives of people who are employed full-time but cannot make ends meet. The publication of a best-selling or scholarly book often generates reviews and articles in the print media and heated debates on television "news" programs. Three books have served as the catalyst for recent stories about the fading nature of blue-collar work and increases in the working poor: *Nickel and Dimed: On (Not) Getting By in America,* by Barbara Ehrenreich;[129] *The Working Poor: Invisible in America,* by David K. Shipler;[130] and *The Betrayal of Work: How Low-Wage Jobs Fail 30 Million Americans and Their Families,* by Beth Shulman.[131]

Shipler's and Shulman's books were based on interviews with low-wage workers; Ehrenreich took a series of low-wage jobs herself as waitress, hotel maid, cleaning woman, nursing-home aide, and Wal-Mart sales clerk to see if she could make ends meet on the meager wages she earned. The "play" that the media gave these books through reviews, reprints of excerpts, author interviews, and other commentaries turned the subject of the working poor, at least temporarily, into a hot topic. Journalists made changes to the phrase "take this job and . . ." for headlines that proclaimed the bad fortune of the working poor: "Take This Job and Starve" was the banner of a *Time* magazine review;[132] a *New York Times* book review declared, "Take This Job and Be Thankful (for $6.80 an Hour)."[133] According to the *Time* review, the fading of the working class into the ranks of the working poor is partly, but not entirely, the fault of society:

> Shipler doesn't place all the blame on society. The people he meets often lack the soft skills that employers require, like showing up on time, following directions, even knowing how to comb their hair. To be sure, they need better schools and reliable medical insurance, but they also need to know better than to use their precious tax-refund checks to get tattoos. Sometimes they clip coupons and turn up faithfully at job training. Sometimes they get drunk and disorderly. They go in for ill-advised sex and foolish spending sprees. In other words, the working poor are not so different from Paris Hilton, except that they have less money. And that makes all the difference. When they stumble, low-wage earners have nothing to fall back on.[134]

Although the author of *The Working Poor* is credited with "exposing the wretched conditions of these invisible Americans" and thus performing a "noble and badly needed service,"[135] media framing of articles about the working poor based on popular books tends to shape the discussion within the initial framework established by the book's author, an approach that typically does not bring in diverse viewpoints on the same issue. For example, Shipler's book tends to blame women who are single heads of household for their low-income status, as when he writes, "Married, Ann was in the middle-class. . . . Divorced, she sank rapidly."[136] By contrast, Barbara Ehrenreich's *Nickel and Dimed* provides more anecdotal evidence, based on her personal journey as a low-wage worker, to suggest that corporate greed and other societal factors, rather than the behavior of the working poor, should be blamed for their economic condition. In fact, her approach is closer to the headline—"Can't Win for Losing"—of a notice in the *New York Times Book Reviews* of Shipler's book.[137]

Were it not for books like Ehrenreich's, Shipler's, and Shulman's, the mainstream media might not have published articles and aired television news reports about the growing problems of the working poor and how more blue-collar workers are sliding into this category. Even business-oriented

Fortune magazine was intrigued by Shulman's book and interviewed her for an article titled "The Question Authority: Exploding Myths about the Poor," in which Shulman (a lawyer and former vice president of the United Food and Commercial Workers Union) stated that low-wage jobs—more than lack of education or globalization—are the major problem that makes it difficult for the working class to stay afloat and dashes hopes of upward mobility.[138] Similarly, a *Newsweek* article, "A New Kind of Poverty," informed millions of readers and Internet users visiting the MSNBC website that, according to Shulman, "even in the go-go '90s one out of every four American workers made less than $8.70 an hour, an income equal to the government's poverty level for a family of four. Many, if not most, of these workers have no health care, sick pay or retirement provisions."[139] These thirty million people, or one in every four workers, perform valuable services for society:

> They don't exist at the margins of our economy, but in the mainstream; they are the nursing home staff, poultry processors, pharmacy attendants, call-center workers, janitors, child care workers, and guest room attendants that make the economy tick but are largely invisible. Most are women. Many are minorities or immigrants. And low wages are just the beginning of their problems. Their jobs are the least likely to offer health and retirement benefits, child-care, or sick leave; and are the most likely to be part time, inflexible, and dangerous.[140]

Through articles like these describing the fading nature of blue-collar jobs and the growth of the working poor as a category within the larger class system, journalists provide media audiences with information and explode myths that have perpetuated and exacerbated economic and social inequalities in this country for many years. In regard to this myth, *Newsweek* states:

> America is a country that now sits atop the precarious latticework of myth. It is the myth that work provides rewards, that working people can support their families. It's a myth that has become so divorced from reality that it might as well begin with the words "Once upon a time. . . ." The American Dream for the well-to-do grows from the bowed backs of the working poor, who too often have to choose between groceries and rent.[141]

Here, we return to where this chapter began, with the individuals who are largely invisible because they blend in or work without having much voice in what they do, particularly in light of the diminished power of labor unions and other workers' advocate groups. Perhaps these people find their primary "voice" in the work of analysts who write about their dilemmas and the reports of journalists and television reporters who pick up on their stories, for "human interest" filler if nothing else.

EFFECTS OF MEDIA FRAMING OF THE WORKING CLASS

The media typically focus on minute details about how the rich and famous live, including how many parties Martha Stewart attended immediately prior to the 2004 hearing at which she was sentenced to prison for lying to investigators, but the working class simply does not have the same appeal to most journalists and television entertainment writers. Whereas the upper and upper-middle classes are showcased for their conspicuous consumerism and lavish leisure pursuits, the working class—which produces many of the goods and provides most of the services enjoyed by the leisure classes—is largely invisible in the media.[142] Frequently, this invisibility results from journalists' absorbing members of the working class into an all-inclusive "middle class majority," creating an inaccurate assessment of the actual resources and social status of the working class. Thus (mis)placing working-class people in the middle class helps to perpetuate the idea of the American Dream, as the communications scholar Linda Holtzman states: "The working-class characters [in television shows] do little to challenge the dominant ideology and the myth of the American Dream."[143]

When the working class is represented in the media, some stories focus on the greed of workers (for better wages, working conditions, and benefits) but say nothing about "greedy" owners, managers, and shareholders, whose wealth can partly be attributed to the work of those below them in the class structure. At best, working-class union members are portrayed as greedy; at worst they are represented as shysters or criminals. Even nonunion members of the working class are suspect when it comes to honesty and integrity on the job. This stereotype is played for "humor" in television comedies like WB's *The Help,* one episode of which was based on possible theft by the hired help. The "rich lady of the house," Arlene Ridgeway (played by Brenda Strong), accused her maid, cook, nanny, chauffeur, personal trainer, and dog walker of stealing a thousand dollars from her purse. At the end of the episode, viewers learn that Ridgeway had misplaced the money herself but, in the meantime, "the help" had scrounged to come up with money so that she would not fire them. Although sitcoms like this are supposed to poke fun at class warfare, these shows also reinforce negative stereotypes of the working class as untrustworthy. Even when the joke behind the stereotype is known, such representations may make the middle and upper classes feel that they are better than the working class. As the "rich woman" in *The Help* derisively declares, "*I* wouldn't want to be a maid."

Derogatory depictions of the working class are not limited to issues of trustworthiness and reliability. Stereotypes also highlight the supposed lack of values, taste, and good manners among people in this class. As contrasted with the media's emphasis on the middle class as the backbone of the nation and the standard bearer with respect to values, the working class is sometimes portrayed as white trash, buffoons, bigots, and slobs. These depictions raise important questions: Are middle- and upper-class audiences laughing *with* the working-class characters, or are they laughing *at* them? Do working-class people identify with these negative images and see themselves as lacking in values, taste, and refinement? Is the embracing of a "proletariat" identity by some members of the working class a genuine affirmation of who they believe they are, or is it a reflection of the way in which the media have popularized and commercialized negative images of the working class so that a T-shirt emblazoned with "Trailer Park Trash" is thought of as humorous or stylish?

Perhaps it is in faded blue-collar framing that the media come closest to providing an accurate representation of the working class and of the issues that affect people in this segment of the class structure. By showing real issues that are of importance to members of the working class, including job loss, an increase in immigrant workers who might threaten their jobs, the changing nature of available jobs, and dramatic increases in the number of working poor, the media sometimes raise important questions. Perhaps the media should reassess the importance of the working class and view its members as the proverbial "canaries in the coal mine." In that light, as the gap between the wealthy and the poor continues to grow wider, the problems of working-class people should be taken as a warning that many people—even on other rungs of the class ladder—will be negatively affected by current trends. If the media continue to ignore the concerns of "the Silenced Majority," they will ignore pressing issues faced by all of us.

Although the working class and the working poor often serve as little more than political props for politicians in election years and receive media coverage in that connection, a few journalists see the crucial links that exist between the working class and the middle and upper-middle classes. One is Bob Herbert:

> It's like running on a treadmill that keeps increasing in speed. You have to go faster and faster just to stay in place. Or, as a factory worker said many years ago, "You can work 'til you drop dead, but you won't get ahead." American workers have been remarkably productive in recent

years, but they are getting fewer and fewer of the benefits of this increased productivity. While the economy, as measured by the gross domestic product, has been strong for some time now, ordinary workers have gotten little more than the back of the hand from employers who have pocketed an unprecedented share of the cash from this burst of economic growth.[144]

Though the media focus on consumption over production and on owners and shareholders more than on everyday workers, there is hope that more journalists and entertainment writers will include the working class in their framing of articles and stories, and not only on Labor Day or when members of the working class have helped pull a community or the nation through a major disaster.

Currently, the predominant messages we receive from the media regarding the working class are that this class does not exist at all or that it comprises people who are uninteresting other than as sources of labor. Working-class people are not treated as thoughtful individuals who might have important things to say. Instead, the media tend to view the opinions of the middle and upper classes as more important and more relevant to the interests of audiences. Perhaps the tarnished metal frames (metaphorically speaking) that have been employed by the media in portraying the working class should be rethought and polished to allow more accurate representations of the working class, including the opinions of its members, how they live their everyday lives, and the positive contributions that they make at home, work, and in the community. Most important, perhaps, would be a more accurate assessment of the class-related issues and realities of social inequality that affect people in this class; their problems should be of greater concern to everyone, rich and poor alike, if "As the working class goes, so goes the nation" is accurate. If some analysts are correct that the working class actually constitutes the majority in this nation, it may indeed be an accurate assessment of where we (and the media) should be looking to see the future of the United States.

NOTES

1. Debbie Howlett, "Stay Upwind in Windy City: Foul-Smelling Trash Keeps Piling Up as Hauler's Strike Enters Day 7," *USA Today*, October 7, 2003, A3.

2. David K. Shipler, "A Poor Cousin of the Middle Class," *New York Times Magazine*, January 18, 2004, 22.

3. Shipler, "A Poor Cousin of the Middle Class," 22.

4. See Barbara Ehrenreich, *Nickel and Dimed: On (Not) Getting By in America* (New York: Metropolitan, 2001); John E. Schwarz and Thomas J. Volgy, *The Forgotten Americans* (New York: Norton, 1992); Shipler, "A Poor Cousin of the Middle Class" and *The Working Poor: Invisible in America* (New York: Knopf, 2004); Beth Shulman, *The Betrayal of Work: How Low-Wage Jobs Fail 30 Million Americans and Their Families* (New York: New Press, 2003).

5. Michael Zweig, *The Working Class Majority: America's Best Kept Secret* (Ithaca, N.Y.: Cornell University Press, 2001), 57.

6. "The Wal-Martization of America," *New York Times,* November 15, 2003, A26.

7. Zweig, *The Working Class Majority.*

8. Felicia R. Lee, "Q&A: Welcome to the Working Class!" *New York Times,* July 13, 2003, A15.

9. Dennis Gilbert, *The American Class Structure in an Age of Growing Inequality,* 6th ed. (Belmont, Calif.: Wadsworth, 2003).

10. "The Wal-Martization of America."

11. Gilbert, *The American Class Structure in an Age of Growing Inequality.*

12. Shulman, *The Betrayal of Work.*

13. Zweig, *The Working Class Majority.*

14. Gregory Mantsios, "Media Magic: Making Class Invisible," in *Privilege: A Reader,* ed. Michael S. Kimmel and Abby L. Ferber, 99–109 (Boulder, Colo.: Westview, 2003), 106.

15. "Meeting of Front Bricklayers: A Union of Capital and Labor Advocated," *New York Times,* August 30, 1860, 8.

16. "Labor Unions," *New York Times,* August 26, 1868, 4.

17. "Labor Unions," 4.

18. "Labor Unions," 4.

19. "Meeting of Front Bricklayers," 4.

20. "Help for the Working Poor," *New York Times,* April 22, 1869, 4.

21. "Help for the Working Poor," 4.

22. William J. Puette, *Through Jaundiced Eyes: How the Media View Organized Labor* (Ithaca, N.Y.: ILR, 1992).

23. "The Working Men's Views: President Jarrett before the Senate Committee," *New York Times,* September 8, 1883, 8.

24. "Managing Labor Interests: Harmonizing Rival Unions and Concluding to Do without Prayers," *New York Times,* June 11, 1883, 8.

25. "Not Able to Earn a Living: The Letter of a Sewing Woman to the Central Labor Union," *New York Times,* February 16, 1885, 5.

26. "The Working Men's Views."

27. "Working Men on Parade: An Orderly Labor Demonstration—Ten Thousand Men in Line," *New York Times,* September 6, 1882, 8.

28. "Big Labor Day Parade: Thirty Building Trades Unions to Be Represented. Forty Bands to Play in the Procession—Preparations to Handle Holiday Crowds," *New York Times,* August 31, 1902, 24.

29. Puette, *Through Jaundiced Eyes*.

30. "Blames Union Labor for Work Shortage," *New York Times*, October 2, 1921, 1.

31. "Blames Union Labor for Work Shortage," 1.

32. Puette, *Through Jaundiced Eyes*, 154.

33. "Reds Plotted Country Wide Strike. Arrests Exceeded 5,000, 2,635 Held; 3 Transports Ready for Them," *New York Times*, January 4, 1920, 1.

34. "Senate Vote Voided Veto of Labor Bill," *New York Times*, June 24, 1947, 1.

35. Pete Hamill, "In Defense of Honest Labor," *New York Times*, December 31, 1995, SM18.

36. Maureen Williams, "From Incendiary to Invisible: A Print-News Content Analysis of the Labor Movement," *Labor Center Review* 10 (1988): 23–27, quoted in Puette, *Through Jaundiced Eyes*, 153.

37. Puette, *Through Jaundiced Eyes*, 153.

38. Puette, *Through Jaundiced Eyes*, 58.

39. Puette, *Through Jaundiced Eyes*, 154–55.

40. David Croteau and William Hoynes, *Media/Society: Industries, Images, and Audiences*, 3rd ed. (Thousand Oaks, Calif.: Pine Forge, 2003), 222.

41. Danny Hakim, "Auto Deal or Bust: Was Anyone Taken for a Ride in the U.A.W.–Big 3 Contract Talks?" *New York Times*, September 23, 2003, C2.

42. Hakim, "Auto Deal or Bust," C2.

43. Christopher L. Erickson and Daniel J. B. Mitchell, "Information on Strikes and Union Settlements: Patterns of Coverage in a 'Newspaper of Record,'" *Industrial and Labor Relations Review* (April 1996): 395.

44. Erickson and Mitchell, "Information on Strikes and Union Settlements," 406.

45. Diane E. Schmidt, "Public Opinion and Media Coverage of Labor Unions," *Journal of Labor Research* 15 (Spring 1993): 151–64, cited in Erickson and Mitchell, "Information on Strikes and Union Settlements," 406.

46. Howlett, "Stay Upwind in Windy City," A3.

47. Jo Napolitano, "As Garbage, and Smell, Rise in Chicago, Striking Trash Haulers Reject a Raise Offer," *New York Times*, October 6, 2003, A9 [emphasis added].

48. Jo Napolitano, "Chicago Strike Leaves Garbage Piling Up," *New York Times*, October 3, 2003, A18.

49. Steven Greenhouse, "Labor Raises Pressure on California Supermarkets," *New York Times*, February 10, 2004, A12.

50. Bob Keefe, "Grocery Strike Wearing on Customers, Workers," *Austin American-Statesman*, February 6, 2004, C1.

51. Steven Greenhouse and Charlie LeDuff, "Grocery Workers Relieved, if Not Happy, at Strike's End," *New York Times*, February 28, 2004, A8.

52. Greenhouse and LeDuff, "Grocery Workers Relieved, if Not Happy, at Strike's End," A8.

53. John M. Broder, "California Supermarket Strike Deters Shoppers," *New York Times*, October 14, 2003, A12.

54. Federal Bureau of Investigation, "Organized Crime Section: Labor Racketeering," www.fbi.gov/hq/cid/orgcrime/lcn/laborrack.htm (accessed March 22, 2004).

55. "Organized Crime and the Labor Unions," AmericanMafia.com, 2004, www.americanmafia.com/Crime_and_Labor.html (accessed March 22, 2004); Federal Bureau of Investigation, "Organized Crime Section."

56. Steven Greenhouse, "Scandals Affirm New York as Union Corruption Capital," *New York Times,* February 15, 1999, B1 [emphasis added].

57. Greenhouse, "Scandals Affirm New York as Union Corruption Capital," B1.

58. Federal Bureau of Investigation, "Organized Crime Section."

59. William K. Rashbaum, "U.S. Indicts Gottis, Saying They Operated Dock Rackets," *New York Times,* June 5, 2002, B1.

60. Quoted in Greenhouse, "Scandals Affirm New York as Union Corruption Capital," B1.

61. See James T. Bennett and Jason E. Taylor, "Unions Work Selves Out of Job," *USA Today,* August 28, 2003, A13.

62. Allen Rucker, *The Sopranos: A Family History* (New York: New American Library, 2001).

63. Alessandra Stanley, "TV Weekend—Bullies, Bears and Bullets: It's Round 5," *New York Times,* March 5, 2004, E1.

64. Stanley, "TV Weekend."

65. Phil Primack, "We All Work, Don't We?" *Columbia Journalism Review* (September–October 1992): 56.

66. Primack, "We All Work, Don't We?"

67. Quoted in Primack, "We All Work, Don't We?" 56.

68. Tom Robbins, "Working-Class Heroes: Towering Losses, Towering Deeds." *Village Voice* (September 26–October 2, 2001), www.villagevoice.com/issues/0139/robbins.php (accessed March 4, 2004).

69. Quoted in Robbins, "Working-Class Heroes."

70. Robbins, "Working-Class Heroes."

71. "The Mayor's Remarks: 'You're All My Heroes,'" *New York Times,* September 17, 2001, A7.

72. "Heroes amid the Horror," *New York Times,* September 15, 2001, A22.

73. Randal C. Archibold, "A Nation Challenged: St. Patrick's: City Celebrates Its Heroes and Grieves Over Their Loss," *New York Times,* September 18, 2001, B8.

74. Amy Waldman, "A Nation Challenged: Reporters Notebook—'Dear Mr. or Mrs. Fireman,'" *New York Times,* September 18, 2001, B8.

75. Larry Elliott, "Everyday Heroes: Firefighters," abc12.com, May 5, 2003, abclocal.go.com/wjrt/news/050503_NW_r2_heroes_firefighters.html (accessed March 13, 2004).

76. Elliott, "Everyday Heroes."

77. David Firestone, "4 Dead and 9 Missing in a Pair of Alabama Mine Blasts," *New York Times,* September 25, 2001, A14.

78. Michael Z. McIntee, "The Wahoo Gazette: Wednesday, July 31, 2002—Show #1852," 2002, www.cbs.com/latenight/lateshow/exclusives/wahoo/archive/2002/07/archive31.shtml (accessed March 13, 2003).

79. Jack Feuer, "Miner Chord: Is a Working-Class Hero Still Something to Be?" *ADWEEK Southwest,* August 5, 2002, 9.

80. Matt Wray and Annalee Newitz, eds., *White Trash: Race and Class in America* (New York: Routledge, 1997), 4.

81. Quoted in Susan Eastman, "White Trash: America's Dirty Little Secret," *Ace Magazine,* 1998, www.aceweekly.com/acemag/backissues/980916/cb2_980916.thml (accessed March 14, 2004).

82. Melinda Henneberger, "Testing of a President: The Accuser; The World of Paula Jones: A Lonely Pace Amid Clamor," *New York Times,* March 12, 1998, A1.

83. Eastman, "White Trash."

84. Henneberger, "Testing of a President."

85. Annie Groer and Ann Gerhart, "The Reliable Source," *Washington Post,* June 2, 1997, D3.

86. Quoted in Groer and Gerhart, "The Reliable Source."

87. Quoted in Groer and Gerhart, "The Reliable Source."

88. See Richard Harwood, "Are Journalists 'E-l-i-t-i-s-t'?" *American Journalism Review* (June 1995): 26–30.

89. Quoted in Harwood, "Are Journalists 'E-l-i-t-i-s-t'?"

90. Gael Sweeney, "The King of White Trash Culture: Elvis Presley and the Aesthetics of Excess," in *White Trash,* ed. Wray and Newitz.

91. Laura Grindstaff, *The Money Shot: Trash, Class, and the Making of TV Talk Shows* (Chicago: University of Chicago Press, 2002), 145.

92. Grindstaff, *The Money Shot,* 145–46.

93. Quoted in Larry Elder, "'White Trash' Is Politically Correct," 2000, www.townhall.com/columnists/larryelder/le200084.shtml (accessed March 14, 2004).

94. Richard Butsch, "Ralph, Fred, Archie and Homer: Why Television Keeps Recreating the White Male Working-Class Buffoon," in *Gender, Race and Class in Media,* ed. Gale Dines and Jean M. Humez, 403–12 (Thousand Oaks, Calif.: Sage, 1995), 404.

95. Richard Butsch, "A Half Century of Class and Gender in American TV Domestic Sitcoms," *Cercles* 8 (2003): 16–34, www.cercles.com/pasteach.html (accessed March 20, 2004), 20–21.

96. "The Life of Riley: U.S. Situation Comedy," Museum.tv.com, 2004, www.museum.tv/archives/etv/L/htmlL/lifeofriley/lifeofriley.htm (accessed March 13, 2004).

97. "The Life of Riley."

98. Butsch, "A Half Century of Class and Gender in American TV Domestic Sitcoms"; "The Honeymooners," TVLand.com, 2004, www.tvland.com/shows/honeymooners (accessed March 20, 2004).

99. Butsch, "A Half Century of Class and Gender in American TV Domestic Sitcoms," 22.

100. Butsch, "A Half Century of Class and Gender in American TV Domestic Sitcoms."

101. "All in the Family," TVLand.com, 2004, www.tvland.com/shows/aitf (accessed March 21, 2004).

102. "All in the Family," TVLand.com.

103. "All in the Family," Classicsitcoms.com, 2004, classicsitcoms.com/shows/family.html (accessed March 21, 2004).

104. "All in the Family," Classicsitcoms.com.

105. Quoted in "All in the Family," Classicsitcoms.com.

106. Richard Muhammad, "Archie Bunker Lives!" 2001, www.blinks.net/magazine/channels/issues/doc_page5.html (accessed March 14, 2003).

107. Muhammad, "Archie Bunker Lives!"

108. Grindstaff, *The Money Shot*.

109. "The King of Queens: Wild Cards," TV Tome, 2004, www.tvtome.com/tvtome/servlet/GuidePageServlet/showid-239/epid-1637 (accessed April 18, 2004).

110. Quoted in William Yardley, "The Last Grain Falls at a Sugar Factory," *New York Times,* January 31, 2004, A13.

111. Yardley, "The Last Grain Falls at a Sugar Factory."

112. Ralph Blumenthal, "As Levi's Work Is Exported, Stress Stays Home," *New York Times,* October 19, 2003, A14.

113. Quoted in Blumenthal, "As Levi's Work Is Exported, Stress Stays Home," A14.

114. Lydia Polgreen, "As Jobs Vanish, the Sweet Talk Could Turn Tough," *New York Times,* October 12, 2003, A26.

115. David Brooks, "The Americano Dream," *New York Times,* February 24, 2004, A27.

116. Lorrie Grant, "Retail Giant Wal-Mart Faces Challenges on Many Fronts: Protests, Allegations Are Price of Success, CEO Says," *USA Today,* November 11, 2003, B1; Amy Tsao, "The Two Faces of Wal-Mart," *Business Week,* January 28, 2004, www.businessweek.com/bwdaily/dnflash/jan2004/nf20040128_6990_db014.html (accessed February 2, 2004).

117. Steven Greenhouse, "Middlemen in the Low-Wage Economy," *New York Times,* December 28, 2003, WK10.

118. Eduardo Porter, "What Unions Can Gain from Immigration," *New York Times,* March 28, 2004, BU3.

119. Porter, "What Unions Can Gain from Immigration," BU3.

120. Quoted in Porter, "What Unions Can Gain from Immigration," BU3.

121. Juan Castillo, "U.S. Payday Is Something to Write Home About," *Austin American-Statesman,* December 14, 2003, J1.

122. Castillo, "U.S. Payday Is Something to Write Home About."

123. Deboray Sharp, Paul Davidson, and Tom Kenworthy, "Employers Praise Bush's 'Guest Worker' Plan: They See Lots of Cheap Labor; Migrant Advocates Skeptical," *USA Today,* January 8, 2004, A3.

124. Sue Kirchhoff and Barbara Hagenbaugh, "Immigration: A Fiscal Boon or Financial Strain? Debate Heats Up over Impact on Economy," *USA Today,* January 22, 2004, B1.

125. Kirchhoff and Hagenbaugh, "Immigration," B1.

126. Steven Greenhouse, "If You're a Waiter, the Future Is Rosy," *New York Times,* March 7, 2004, WK5.

127. Steven Greenhouse, "Workers Assail Night Lock-Ins by Wal-Mart," *New York Times,* January 18, 2004, A1.

128. Greenhouse, "Workers Assail Night Lock-Ins by Wal-Mart."

129. Ehrenreich, *Nickel and Dimed.*

130. Shipler, *The Working Poor.*

131. Shulman, *The Betrayal of Work.*

132. Richard Lacayo, "Take This Job and Starve," *Time,* February 16, 2004, 76.

133. Michael Massing, "Take This Job and Be Thankful (for $6.80 an Hour)," *New York Times,* February 18, 2004, B8.

134. Lacayo, "Take This Job and Starve," 77.

135. Massing, "Take This Job and Be Thankful (for $6.80 an Hour)," B8.

136. Quoted in Massing, "Take This Job and Be Thankful (for $6.80 an Hour)," B8.

137. Ron Suskind, "Can't Win for Losing," *New York Times Book Review,* February 15, 2004, 7.

138. Nicholas Stein, "The Question Authority: Exploding Myths about the Poor," *Fortune,* September 16, 2003, www.fortune.com/fortune/0,15935,487013,00.html (accessed September 29, 2003).

139. "A New Kind of Poverty," *Newsweek,* November 22, 2003, www.msnbc.msn.com/id/3540672 (accessed April 2, 2004).

140. Brooks, "The Americano Dream."

141. "A New Kind of Poverty."

142. Barbara Ehrenreich, "The Silenced Majority: Why the Average Working Person Has Disappeared from American Media and Culture," in *Gender, Race and Class in Media,* ed. Dines and Humez; Mantsios, "Media Magic."

143. Linda Holtzman, *Media Messages: What Film, Television, and Popular Music Teach Us about Race, Class, Gender, and Sexual Orientation* (London: M. E. Sharpe, 2000), 129.

144. Bob Herbert, "We're More Productive. Who Gets the Money?" *New York Times,* April 5, 2004, A25.

6

SPLINTERED WOODEN FRAMES:
THE MIDDLE CLASS

Millions of middle-class families can no longer afford to live on two incomes. A generation ago, a typical American middle-class family lived on the income of a single breadwinner. In recent years it has taken two working spouses to live the modern middle-class dream. Now, it seems even that is not enough to survive the skyrocketing cost of housing, health care and college while saving for retirement and shouldering growing debt loads.

—from a 2003 *USA Today* article,
"Middle Class Barely Treads Water"

The last time Kevin Thornton had health insurance was three years ago, which was not much of a problem until he began having trouble swallowing. . . . Mr. Thornton, 41, left a stable job with good health coverage in 1998 for a higher salary at a dot-com company that went bust a few months later. Since then, he has worked on contract for various companies, including one that provided insurance until the project ended in 2000. . . . The majority of the uninsured are neither poor by official standards nor unemployed. . . . "After paying for health insurance, you take home less than minimum wage," says a poster in New York City subways. . . . "Welcome to middle-class poverty."

—from a 2003 *New York Times* article,
"For Middle Class, Health Insurance Becomes a Luxury"

These two examples are typical not only of how the media frame news stories about the U.S. middle class today but also of how those stories have been framed for more than one hundred years: The middle class may be the backbone of the nation, holding together the best aspects of this country and its democratic ideals, but it is in peril. According to three scholars who analyzed bankruptcy filings in recent years, it is "the fragile middle class."[1] Before proceeding further, however, we need to look at exactly what category of people the media include within the definition of middle class and how accurate that categorization is.

THE MIDDLE CLASS:
AN AMBIGUOUS BUT POPULAR TERM

In his 1830s work *Democracy in America,* Alexis de Tocqueville stated that the United States had a condition of equality. For Tocqueville, the ideal of democracy was linked with equality, and he asserted that the United States appeared to have melded into one class: the middle class.[2] Yet the exact meaning of "middle class" with regard to this country—whether in the nineteenth century or today—is unclear. To some people, being middle-class means having an income of at least three times the poverty rate or being within some range of the median household income in any given year.[3] However, neither of these is an accurate method of delineating the U.S. middle class, as journalist Louis Uchitelle explains:

> The middle class of political exhortation and national myth isn't the same as the statistical middle of the wage scale. . . . Half of the so-called middle class tax cuts enacted [in 1997] went to people earning more than $93,000. And while the median household earns about $40,000 a year, the median individual wage is much lower: $11.13 an hour [in 1998], or about $23,000 a year for a 40-hour work week.[4]

According to Uchitelle, it is difficult to determine what dollar figures serve as the upper and lower cutoff points for the middle class; however, this does not keep politicians from proposing election-year plans to help the so-called middle class. When reporting on political campaigns, journalists follow suit and use "middle class" terminology as well. Journalist Tom Zeller explains why the middle class is so popular with politicians:

> Courting the middle class, as presidential candidates are wont to do, requires no great political calculus: most Americans—nearly 70 percent by one count—reckon that the siren song is directed at them. And while it's true that some wealthier folk are comfortable with the label of upper-middle class, and a good quarter of industrious citizens will tag themselves working class, stark categories like "upper class" and "lower class" remain unpopular.[5]

In fact, by the middle of the twentieth century, most people who responded to opinion polls referred to themselves as in the middle class, whether or not this was their actual income category,[6] and this tendency to consider oneself middle-class remains true today. Of the 1,216 adults who participated in a 2000 Gallup/CNN/*USA Today* poll, 69 percent identified themselves as in the middle or upper-middle class, whereas 24 percent placed themselves in the working class, and only 6 percent selected the upper or lower classes (the other 1 percent expressed no opinion).[7] Obviously, the mathematical middle has room for only 20 percent of all U.S. households, not 70 percent.

Even sociologists who have spent years studying the U.S. class structure do not agree on what constitutes the middle class or whether such a class actually exists (some assert that there are only two classes: the upper class and the working class). Social analyst Barbara Ehrenreich expresses the problem well when she states that "class is a notion that is inherently fuzzy at the edges";[8] however, it is her belief that the middle class, defined somewhat abstractly, is made up of people whose economic and social status is based on education rather than their ownership of capital or property.

Some sociologists use occupational categories to identify social classes. One widely used model divides the middle class into two categories: the middle class itself, consisting of persons who have some college education and significant skills and work under loose supervision, and the upper-middle class, consisting of highly educated professionals and corporate managers.[9] Some analysts identify a third middle-class category: the lower-middle class. The dividing line between the middle-middle class and the lower-middle class is very blurred, particularly with regard to the exact point where the middle class ends and the working class begins. Increasingly, sociologists do not distinguish between the lower-middle class and the working class, seeing them as one and the same, this category being made up of semiskilled workers, many of whom are employed in factories or in the service sector (as clerks and sales associates, for instance), where their responsibilities involve routine, mechanized tasks requiring little skill beyond basic literacy and a brief period of on-the-job training.[10]

Members of the upper-middle class are often thought to have achieved the American Dream, but—unlike many in the upper class—most members of the upper-middle class must work for a living. Early in the twenty-first century, two best-selling books offered new concepts about the upper-middle class. In *Bobos in Paradise,* David Brooks suggested that many people in the upper-middle class are now "the new upper class," a well-educated elite that he refers to as "Bobos" (bourgeois bohemians).[11] Based in part on information in the *New York Times* wedding section about brides, grooms, and their families, Brooks argued that the "white-shoed, Whartonized, Episcopalian establishmentarians with protruding jaws" are long gone from the ranks of the privileged upper class, having been replaced by "mountaineering-booted overachievers with excellent orthodontia and impressive GRE scores."[12] However, Brooks's description of the future prospects of the so-called Bobos gives them the appearance of being upper-middle class at best:

> But members of today's educated class can never be secure about their own future. A career crash could be just around the corner. In the educated class even social life is a series of aptitude tests; we all must perpetually perform in accordance with the shift in norms of propriety, ever advancing signals of cultivation. . . . And more important, members of the educated class can never be secure about their children's future. The kids have some domestic and educational advantages—all those tutors and developmental toys—but they still have to work through school and ace the SATs just to achieve the same social rank as their parents. Compared to past elites, little is guaranteed.[13]

In the other best-selling book on this subject, *The Rise of the Creative Class,* Richard Florida asserts that the United States has a *creative* class, composed of two major occupational categories: the *super-creative core,* which consists of occupations in computer sciences, mathematics, architecture, engineering, life, physical and social sciences, education, the arts, and the media; and the *creative professions,* which are occupations in management, business, finance, law, health care, and high-end sales. In Florida's view, these creative occupations stand in sharp contrast to working-class, service-class, and agricultural occupations. About 30 percent of the U.S. workforce would fit into Florida's creative class and thus would be the dominant economic group in society.

Books such as these influenced media framing of stories about the upper-middle class and produced cartoons such as one in the *New Yorker* showing a man and woman sitting in a restaurant booth and holding hands, the woman saying, "It would never work out between us, Tom—we're from two totally different tiers of the upper middle class."[14]

As compared with the upper-middle class, people in the middle-middle class are characterized as possessing a two-year or four-year college degree, having more supervision at work, and experiencing less job stability than those in the upper-middle class. Those in the "solid" middle class are typically characterized as most likely to feel the squeeze of layoffs at work, escalating housing prices, lack of affordable health insurance, and economic problems that contribute to overuse of credit cards.

FORMS OF MEDIA FRAMING OF THE MIDDLE CLASS

The media send a variety of messages to readers and television audiences about the middle class based on how the articles and story lines are framed.

Sociologist Gregory Mantsios has identified three key messages that he believes the media convey about the middle class. According to Mantsios, the first message is that "the middle class is us," meaning that the news media create a universal middle class in which everyone is portrayed as having similar problems, such as high taxes, lack of job security, and fear of crime, while sharing a feeling of intellectual and moral superiority over those in the working and poverty classes. In a nation that has embraced the "mythology of classlessness,"[15] thinking of oneself as middle class creates a mental comfort zone, where the individual is in neither the "snobbish" upper class nor the "inferior" lower classes.

The second message that Mantsios believes the media send is that the middle class is a victim. If the middle class is doing so well, as suggested by the myth that everyone is middle class, how can people in this category to be considered victims? According to Mantsios, the media frequently portray the middle class as being victimized by the wealthy (who control prices and get tax breaks), by the working class (who are greedy, demand higher wages, and drive up prices), and by the poor (who, because of their own shortcomings, run up welfare costs and stretch other governmental programs to their limits).

The third message that Mantsios believes the media project is that the middle class is not a working class. According to Mantsios, media stories typically make clear distinctions between the middle class and individuals in the blue-collar, working-class sector. In some television shows, for example, working-class people and the poor are portrayed as lacking manners, middle-class values, and social respectability.

Somewhat along these lines, I have identified three major frames that are used in stories pertaining to the middle class in newspaper and magazine articles, on websites, and in television news and entertainment story lines. These three frames are *middle-class values framing, squeeze framing,* and *victimization framing.* Middle-class values framing emphasizes that the core values held by people in the middle class should be the model for this country and that these values remain largely intact despite economic, political, and cultural changes. By contrast, squeeze framing indicates that the middle class is perilously caught between the cost of a middle-class lifestyle and the ability to pay for that lifestyle, and victimization framing suggests that many of the problems that the middle class faces are the results of actions by or on behalf of those above and below it in the social class hierarchy.

Ironically, media framing of stories about the middle class, while suggesting that nearly everyone is middle class, often assert that the middle class is rapidly shrinking and perhaps in danger of soon disappearing altogether. These seemingly contradictory messages are not recent in their origin. As far back as the 1860s, newspaper articles portrayed middle-class existence as problematic, and some of the issues raised more than a century ago are still raised as concerns by the media today.

THE PAST STILL PRESENT: HISTORICAL FRAMING OF THE MIDDLE CLASS

The major U.S. newspapers of the 1900s had barely "discovered" the middle class before journalists began using the three forms of framing described above in their discussions regarding that class. An examination of headlines in the *New York Times* archives from as early as 1851 shows the popularity of such framing. The middle class, although it was seen as the backbone of the nation, was being squeezed by its rampant spending habits and lack of savings, and it was being victimized by the capitalist and working classes.

Numerous newspaper articles descried how people in the middle class were overspending. Even in an era when major daily newspapers provided glowing details about the lavish spending and opulent lifestyles of the rich and famous on the society and women's pages (see chapter 2), these same newspapers were admonishing the middle class to be more frugal. For example, an 1868 *New York Times* article, "Economy among the Middle Classes," described the middle class as being able to make money easily but as spending it too readily: "The greatest of all obstacles to saving is, of course, the scale of living of our middle classes. People live here in a style entirely out of proportion to income. . . . Our middle classes will never accumulate property til they learn to content themselves with more simple furniture, smaller houses, and less display."[16] The negative tone of the article quoted above suggests to readers that people in the middle class (defined at the time as earning $2,500 to $6,000 annually) were acting irresponsibly by spending all of their income and not saving money. The article concluded by noting that lack of savings is a problem for the middle class because its "children are not trained to labor, and their habits will be expensive."[17] In this statement, a distinction is made between middle-class children and their working-class counterparts, who presumably are trained to work with their hands and have less-expensive habits than children raised in middle-class families.

Squeeze and victimization framing appeared not only in newspaper articles but also in book reviews, as reflected in a 1905 *New York Times* review of Walter G. Cooper's book *The Consumers: Fate of the Middle Classes*. The book equated being in the middle class with being a consumer who is ground between an upper and lower millstone—capital (the upper classes) on the top and labor (the working class) on the bottom:

Combinations of labor and capital are . . . to be feared [since] they can fix a price which the consumer must pay—a price that [should] yield a living wage and a fair return to capital. Having done this, [labor unions and capitalists] become masters of the situation, and all they have to do is raise profits and wages at the consumer's expense. Thus [the consumer] is, as Mr. Cooper said in the beginning [of the book], ground beneath the upper and nether millstone.[18]

Most readers seem to have agreed with the media about the plight of the middle class, as reflected in published letters to the editor such as this one sent to the *New York Times* by "Another Middle Classer": "While the price of houseroom, food, and clothing rises steadily every year, the large army of [people in the middle class] struggle along with no increase of wages. They have no organized unions or sympathetic strikes. If they do not like their pittances, out they go. There is a horde of waiting hungry ones to take their places."[19]

Affordable housing was a major middle-class concern in the first half of the twentieth century. A 1929 *New York Times* article, for example, described how the middle class was losing its housing to the wealthy in Manhattan: The scarcity of affordable housing was intensified by the demolition of old tenements and private residences, many of which were replaced with exclusive new apartment buildings on the Upper East Side.[20] Now known as co-ops, many of these buildings serve as homes for New York's wealthiest citizens today. As older housing was demolished, middle-class residents were forced to find new homes, and many learned that the only housing they could afford would require a commute to the city from the Bronx or Queens.

Unlike accounts suggesting that middle-income people sought housing in the suburbs because the suburbs would be more agreeable to family life, some of these articles suggest the contrary, that the urban middle class, particularly in cities such as New York, was pushed out of its original residences and replaced by wealthier occupants. According to the 1929 *New York Times* article, upper-middle-class professionals, such as lawyers, doctors, and businessmen, found that they could no longer afford to live on the Upper East Side of Manhattan. The plight of the middle class is readily apparent in this article: "The rich and the poor are being provided for, the former in the Yorkville and the Fifth Avenue sections and the latter in the lower east side, where model tenements are projected. The middle class, however, is fast being excluded from the Manhattan homes of the kind that were abundant a decade ago."[21] In other words, the middle class was being forced out of its homes by members of the upper class, who solved their own housing problems by constructing new residences that only they could afford. Meanwhile, the middle class was being victimized by those serving the interests of the poor, who would have "model tenements" in which to reside.

Almost seventy years later, journalists for the *New York Times* were still writing articles using squeeze and victimization framing to describe middle-class housing problems. Consider, for example, a 1998 article entitled "For Middle Class, New York Shrinks as Home Prices Soar," which begins:

> Todd Neuhaus, an advertising executive, and his wife, Christina, didn't want much. They wanted to rent a Manhattan apartment for less than $3,000 with a bedroom for themselves and one for their two boys. They wanted it to be near good public schools, because private school was beyond their means. [However, the couple eventually quit looking for a two bedroom apartment because nothing they liked was available in a price range they could afford.] It is one of the crueler paradoxes of the city's economic boom and bright new image [that,] even as middle-income families tend to earn more, they are finding themselves priced out of dozens of neighborhoods in and around Manhattan, say real-estate brokers and legions of frustrated apartment seekers.[22]

Reminiscent of the 1929 *New York Times* article, the 1998 *New York Times* article offers this explanation of why the middle-class housing shortage will continue in the twenty-first century:

> Housing experts say the present squeeze reflects a deeper problem [because] builders are creating new housing only for the city's wealthiest residents and, using government subsidies, for a comparatively small number of its poorest.... [F]or various reasons—chiefly the high cost of land and construction—the housing supply is not growing and, in fact, may be shrinking, for those in the middle. They are the city's teachers, nurses, civil servants, small-business owners, even mid-level executives, who want basic, affordable housing near their jobs.[23]

Over the years, stories in the media have noted other middle-class aspirations in addition to appropriate residences. A 1935 *New York Times* book review entitled "What Is the Middle Class and What Does It Want?" sets forth the reviewer's belief that the United States is a "middle-class nation in outlook and aspiration," but it continues:

> Exactly what that means you may not be sure, but you are safe in believing that it includes a desire that children shall go to college, that a new automobile be parked in front of the house, that homes be furnished in the approved fashion, that clothes, whatever else they are, shall be in style. More fundamental perhaps are the emotional urges of home

and church and country, to which must be added a profound distrust of anything intellectual.[24]

The 1935 book review saw the middle class as "smug in its values" and "unlikely to revolt" against the capitalist class: "'Trim front yards,' [the book's author] suggests, 'petty snobbery, gossip and *The Saturday Evening Post* may be discouraging soil for revolutionary doctrines, but the radicals would have done better not to ignore [the middle class].'"[25] Here again, the middle class is characterized as wanting nice homes with "trim front yards" but also as engaging in "petty snobbery" and "gossip," and having a fondness for *The Saturday Evening Post,* a magazine known for its middle-class values and portrayal of an idyllic lifestyle. That lifestyle was shown in the nostalgic cover art by Norman Rockwell, which often featured happy, middle-class American families where children were taught respect for parents, God, and country.

Despite admonitions to members of the middle class that they should be frugal, popular magazines such as *Saturday Evening Post, American Magazine, The Delineator, Ladies' Home Journal, Cosmopolitan, Munsey's,* and *McClure's* in the early- to mid-1900s featured articles about middle-class families and encouraged consumerism, particularly of goods and services that would make homes more pleasant, children more healthy, and the family's life more "modern." Magazines targeted the "common man" and the "housewife," not only as readers but as consumers. As one analyst suggested, "At this point . . . the role of the publisher changed from being a seller of [the magazine] to consumers to being a gatherer of consumers for the advertisers."[26]

Class distinctions often were obvious in how ads were framed, and the middle class was typically portrayed as being "in the know," while those in the lower classes were not. A 1910 Quaker Oats cereal ad with the headline "The Homes That Never Serve Oatmeal" is an example. Showing the slum section of a major city, with tenement houses in the background, the subcaption for the ad reads, "In the lowliest sections of our largest cities not one home in twelve serves oats. Among the highest types we breed, seven-eighths are oatmeal homes." The ad asks, "What Does This Mean?" and replies:

This doesn't mean that some can afford oats and others cannot. Quaker Oats—the finest oatmeal produced—costs but one-half cent per dish. And a pound of Quaker Oats supplies the nutrition of six loaves of bread. . . . It means that some know, and others don't know, the food needs of a child. Some know, and some don't know, what the food of youth means in a child's career. . . . Some know, and some don't know, that the highest authorities on foods for the young give the first rank to oatmeal.[27]

This is middle-class values framing, the other general category of middle-class framing: The middle class is the backbone of the nation, and its values should be encouraged and supported. It is clear from the ad that people in the middle class should know about good nutrition and desire to provide only the best for their families. According to the ad, when the Quaker Oats interviewers "canvassed hundreds of homes of the educated, the prosperous, the competent—the homes of the leaders in every walk in life . . . we find that oatmeal is a regular diet in seven out of eight . . . four-fifths of all college students come from these oatmeal homes."[28] The ad suggests that, by contrast, working-class families lack the knowledge and sophistication to feed themselves and their children properly.

Food advertisements particularly bound the middle-class woman to particular brands of products based on images that manufacturers conveyed to potential consumers. The image of the ideal middle-class family enjoying a meal together was portrayed in ads for products such as Betty Crocker pie and cake mixes. Betty Crocker, a fictitious middle-class woman, was the model of the ideal homemaker, even if her store-bought mixes might not be as tasty as the made-from-scratch variety. The image of Betty Crocker personified hearth and home, suggesting the importance of family values and supporting the positive role of the homemaker who performed kitchen magic for the benefit of her family.

Over the years, the media generally have supported the American Dream and encouraged their audiences to view themselves as upwardly mobile. In the 1935 book review in the *New York Times* quoted above, for example, the reviewer described what he believed to be the ultimate aspiration of members of the U.S. middle class:

> In the United States there is an individualist tradition, a belief in progress, which has made most men unwilling to accept the label of "worker" for more than a short time. One does not need to be a sociologist to know that Americans as a lot live in hope of a lucky break which will place them or their children on Park Avenue. With such sentiments still widely prevalent, it is wasted breath to talk about the "revolutionary working class."[29]

Politicians have long been aware of the tendency of people in the United States to view themselves as members of the middle class and have therefore lavished praise on that class while promising to do more for it than their opponents would do. The media have framed their reporting on politics in similar terms. A 1937 *New York Times* article about Congressman Bruce Barton's first speech to the House of Representatives in Washington, D.C., for example, highlighted his frequent references to the middle class as the backbone of the nation, long-suffering and slow to anger, but it also noted his belief that the middle class was beginning to "stir," particularly as it was caught in a squeeze produced by an increase in living costs.[30]

Defining the middle class as "professional men and women, small business men and shopkeepers, white-collar workers and the thrifty who have saved a few hundred dollars by their toil and invested it in the shares of American industries," Barton is quoted as saying, "Time was when these people were regarded highly; they were referred to as the backbone of the nation. But unorganized, with no lobby, incapable of political pressure, they are currently treated as of little consequence. The idea seems to be that the nation has lost its backbone or needs no backbone."[31] By quoting both the section of Barton's speech that referred to the middle class as the backbone of the country and the portion asserting that the middle class is "treated as of little consequence," this article uses both middle-class-values and victimization framing: The middle class holds the country together, but it is in peril, a peril not of its own making. Subsequent articles, such as one covering Congressman Barton's 1938 address to the New England Young Republicans, used similar framing, describing the middle class as "bruised and bleeding" and trapped between the "millstones of bad business and high taxes."[32]

Speeches by politicians have provided journalists since the early 1900s with many opportunities to write about the problems of the middle class. Headlines such as "Says Middle Class Needs Salvation: Martin Asks National Support of Republican Drive to Avert Its 'Ruin' by New Deal" (1939) and "Save Middle Class, Congress Is Urged" (1942)[33] are indicative of persistent media framing that emphasized the potential downfall of this class. Threatened by the New Deal and by higher taxes (victimization framing), the middle class often was described as being in need of salvation. The article on saving the middle class quotes Congressman August Herman Andresen of Minnesota as saying: "When the middle class is liquidated, American democracy is destroyed" and as referring to the middle class as the "backbone of the nation."[34]

During World War II, media framing of stories about the middle class typically was more optimistic than it had been in the past. Articles often focused on positive comments by politicians and other spokespersons. Consider, for example, a 1943 article with the headline "Wallace Sees All in a Middle Class: Picturing Future, He Asserts the 'Horatio Alger' Spirit Will Never Die Here," which article focused on Vice President Henry A. Wallace's forecast for the postwar United States and his vision of "an America where all can become members of the middle class—where all can share in the benefits which that class has enjoyed in the past."[35] The article presented a very positive view of the middle class, highlighting what many Americans wanted to believe at the time—that this class represented the American Dream, which would exist forever.

Although there is less political talk about Horatio Alger in the twenty-first century, politicians continue to focus on the middle class and insist they can do more for that class than their opponents during almost every election. The 2000 and 2004 presidential campaigns were no exception. Battling headlines in the *New York Times* served as the lead-in for articles discussing how the 2000 presidential candidates, Al Gore and George W. Bush, sought to garner middle-class votes: "Bush Says Rival's Tax-Cut Plan Fails Middle Class," "Gore Offers Vision of Better Times for Middle Class," and "Bush Campaign Turns Attention to the Middle Class"[36] being only a few of thousands of examples.

Rhetoric about the needs of the middle class continued in speeches and stories of the 2004 presidential election. An example is media coverage of a speech given by Senator John Kerry of Massachusetts, the Democratic candidate for president, who criticized President Bush's administration for favoring wealthy special-interest groups. Kerry spoke out against a system he believed to be "stacked against" the middle-class family, stating:

> I'm running for President because the American people are calling 911 for help. I think the American people are tired of watching corporate executives on Friday afternoons pile into their airplanes paid for by their corporations . . . going to homes paid for by the corporations, playing golf on the weekend in memberships paid for by the corporations, going to shows on Broadway paid for by the corporations, all of which is subsidized by the American taxpayer while the American taxpayer is struggling to get along.
>
> Middle-class families have an agenda, too. . . . And it's about time someone in the White House held a special meeting for them.[37]

Underlying all of these articles, from the mid-1800s through today, are the three framing devices that I have identified in stories about the middle class: the middle class and its values constitute the backbone of the nation; that class and those values are being caught in a squeeze between aspiration and anxiety; and that at least part of the problems encountered by the middle class are the result of the middle class's victimization by others. These devices will now be examined in greater detail, starting with the most positive of the three: *middle-class values framing.*

MIDDLE-CLASS VALUES FRAMING: THE BACKBONE OF THE NATION

In *Fear of Falling: The Inner Life of the Middle Class,* the social analyst Barbara Ehrenreich offered the following comments on the pervasive nature of middle-class values and their significance even to people who do not think of themselves as being in this class: "[Middle-class] ideas and assumptions are everywhere, and not least in our own minds. Even those of us who come from very different social settings often find it hard to distinguish middle-class views from what we think we *ought* to think."[38] According to Ehrenreich, "traits the middle class [likes] to ascribe to itself [include] self-discipline, a strong super-ego, [and] an ability to plan ahead to meet self-imposed goals."[39] These traits, she asserts, are used by people in the middle class to evaluate not only others in their class but those below them in the class structure, making the poor especially vulnerable to criticism. Other analysts have identified other traits or values they believe are associated with the middle class, such as "punctuality, a certain minimum of reliability and accountability (if not responsibility), as well as a minimum of orderliness [and] a certain amount of postponement of instant gratification."[40]

One of the most comprehensive lists of so-called American values was developed by the sociologist Robin M. Williams, Jr., who identified ten core values that he believed constituted the bedrock of the U.S. value system.[41] Four of these values are often associated with the middle class: individualism, achievement and success, progress and material comfort, and freedom and liberty. The value of *individualism* is based on the belief that people are responsible for their own success or failure and that individual ability and hard work are the keys to success. A belief in individualism makes it possible for middle-class people to praise those who do well while at the same time identifying the shortcomings (such as laziness or lack of intelligence) of nonachievers. The value of individualism is associated with another core value, *achievement (success),* which is based on a person's ability to compete effectively with others. One of the rewards for success, both individually and collectively as a society, is that *progress and material comfort* often follow. Individuals and nations that succeed have far more than the basic necessities required for survival, and people can enjoy a wider variety of consumer goods and services. As a core value, *freedom and liberty* is highly valued by most people, but particularly those in the middle and upper classes, who believe that among their freedoms are the right to own property and to expect the government to protect them and the "American way of life" that they enjoy. These core values are embedded in the media framing of many articles and story lines about the middle class. Even when the term "middle class" is not specifically used, there is often an assumption that these virtues are primarily shared by those in this portion of the U.S. class structure.

MIDDLE-CLASS VALUES FRAMING IN NEWS STORIES

One of the most frequent examples of middle-class values framing in reporting is found in stories about "middle-class" neighborhoods and communities. In publications ranging from *USA Today* and the *Detroit News* to CNN and CNN.com, communities that uphold certain values have received widespread publicity. A CNN cable television news report and companion statement on CNN.com regarding the high-tech boom of the late twentieth century, for example, described the Midwest as providing the "right kind" of communities for the families of information technology professionals:

> Family values, a strong work ethic and friendly folk are all things you think about when someone mentions the Midwest. But one phrase people don't always associate with the region is "high technology." Des Moines, Iowa, and Omaha are welcoming a growing population of information technology professionals as people seek an area where they can not only hone their technical skills, but can also experience an environment conducive to raising a family.[42]

Framing of this article, which was about high-tech job opportunities available at that time, also carries a message to viewers and readers about what the journalist referred to as "American dreamin'." This message was conveyed through interviews with information technology workers such as the one who stated, "The No. 1 draw for a person with a family is that the school systems are wonderful, and the general ethics and morals of the community and area in itself." Another worker told the reporter, "People believe in a fair day's labor, a fair day's wage. I think the work culture is one that is a participatory culture. They will pitch in to get the job done."[43] Although these statements are based on people's perceptions about their own community, the comments also suggest that individuals living there share good middle-class moral values and a belief in the work ethic.

National and regional news reports about the values of a community are not unique. Like the report carried by CNN, local newspapers such as the *Detroit News* extol the virtues of the middle class. Consider, for example, editorial writer George Cantor's article entitled "Middle-Class Livonia Turns into Wayne County Power":

> Livonia is a seething hotbed of middle-class values. It has an almost invisible crime rate. Neat residential streets, many of them looking as if they had been time-warped from 1956 Detroit. . . . But it is Livonia's sheer lack of drama that is its charm. "The American dream writ large,"

approvingly says an attorney friend of mine who specializes in munici-
pal finance. Because middle-class values do matter. They supply the essential balance of any community. A sense of restraint. Of responsibility.
Of work ethic. If someone asked me to pinpoint exactly when Detroit
hit the wall, it would be when the city's political leadership dismissed
middle-class values.

Whether in Des Moines (Iowa), Livonia (Michigan), or Franklin (Tennessee), journalists tend to be nostalgic for the "good old days" when, supposedly, middle-class values prevailed, family life was stable, and there was
less tension and discord. In a series of articles, *USA Today* examined the "values gap" that was believed to divide Americans during the 2000 presidential election and that, its writers believed, was shaping the 2004 campaign.
Franklin, Tennessee, became the prototype for a community with middle-
class values. The community was described as "a sprawling Sun Belt suburb
with a distinct Bible Belt flavor" where "horse and dairy farms are giving
way to subdivisions and strip malls, but its values remain rooted in tradi-
tion."[44] The article quotes the president of the Gospel Music Association as
saying, "The lifestyle is at that stage where it's still idyllic. There's a small-
town feel. It's almost a return to the social and civic values of life in the
'50s." The *USA Today* journalist who wrote the article described the small-
town, middle-class-values feel of Franklin as follows:

> Franklin's hallmark is a veneer of Southern graciousness. Much is left un-
> said, and privacy is prized. Families stick close to home in neighborhoods
> they compare to movie fantasies, complete with horse fences and soda
> shops. The line between personal and public life is clearly drawn. It's a
> town where gays remain in the closet, race relations go largely undis-
> cussed and a PTA president declines to be interviewed about her
> school.[45]

The core middle-class values of places such as Livonia and Franklin have
been visibly dramatized for many years in the television situation comedies
(sitcoms) that first entered the American living room in the 1950s.

MIDDLE-CLASS VALUES FRAMING IN SITCOM STORY LINES

The middle class and its values were most favorably represented in situation
comedies in the post–World War II era, the 1950s and 1960s. According to
the media scholar David Marc, when television emerged as the new entertainment medium it gave credibility to "suburbia as democracy's utopia realized, a place where the white middling classes could live in racial serenity,

raising children in an engineered environment that contained and regulated the twin dangers of culture and nature."[46] This engineered environment was apparent in the settings and story lines of television shows such as *The Adventures of Ozzie and Harriet* (1952–66), *Father Knows Best* (1954–63), and *Leave It to Beaver* (1957–63), in which middle-class values were acted out in idealized nuclear families composed of happily married couples and their heartwarming children. With the exception of a few shows like *My Three Sons*, where the story line revolved around Steve Douglas (Fred MacMurray), an aeronautical engineer and widower raising his three sons, most sitcoms employed the tried-and-true format of the traditional nuclear family with the occasional addition of an extra family member who visited or lived with the family on a temporary basis. Common themes in these shows were the presumed middle-class values of honesty, integrity, and hard work, all of which were believed to enable people to get ahead in life and solve problems as they arose. However, the problems these families typically confronted were minor, as reflected in an *Ozzie and Harriet* episode where the crisis of the day was having to deal with a mistaken delivery of two chairs to the Nelson family. Similarly, shows such as *Father Knows Best* often showed brief children's arguments that were easily overcome by Dad's wise counsel, and easy resolutions were reached within one episode.

White Middle-Class Family Values

Middle-class situation comedies such as these were the pictures of civility. According to the media scholar Hal Himmelstein, members of the suburban middle class in early sitcoms were almost universally portrayed as being "upscale, socially conservative, politically inactive, and essentially kind to one another and their neighbors."[47] Usually the middle-class father, such as Jim Anderson (Robert Young) in *Father Knows Best,* demonstrated wisdom and good judgment, never losing his patience with his family or raising his voice when correcting the children. Middle-class status was clearly established through dialogue that made viewers aware of the father's professional position (Anderson was manager of an insurance company) or visual cues such as clothing (Anderson wore a suit to work each day and replaced his suit coat with a pull-over sweater when he came home in the evening). In many sitcoms, the residence in which the family lived and the clothing worn by the characters came to signify more than just the setting in which the story line unfolded; visual cues such as these transmitted ideological codes about the middle-class lifestyle as well. The fact that middle-class children in early sitcoms showed respect for their parents and teachers, remorse for wrongdoings, and willingness to "shake hands and make up" was not only a part of the story line and a significant proportion of the characters' dialogue but a bearer of an ideological code about middle-class values. As some analysts have noted, the middle class was portrayed as "principled and benign" and therefore deserving of the advantages that middle-class family life typically brings with it.[48]

Framing of story lines about middle-class families entertained viewers and attracted consumers for the advertisers' products but also contributed to an unrealistic view of the middle class. According to media scholars David Croteau and William Hoynes:

> Network television presented the suburban family as the core of the modern, postscarcity society, a kind of suburban utopia where social problems were easily solved (or nonexistent), consensus ruled, and signs of racial, ethnic, or class differences or conflict were difficult to find. . . . [T]his image of the postwar family—and the not-so-subtle suggestion that this was what a "normal" family looked like—was a particular story masked as a universal one. Certainly, these families were not typical American families, no matter how often they were served up as such.[49]

For whatever reason, domestic comedies prevailed in network scheduling and in popularity with viewers, and these sitcoms offered many representations of the middle-class family and of the rights and responsibilities of its members. As one media scholar notes with regard to the middle-class wife-mother role on sitcoms such as *Ozzie and Harriet:*

> [These wife-mothers] understand the cultural and personal significance of the family and work to maintain family stability. Moreover, their failings are not individual failings but family failings; the wife-mother fails intellectually without her husband, the sons fail academically without their father, and the father fails socially and personally without his wife and children. The lesson, here, is that family is fundamental and needs all of its parts to function effectively so that a wife-mother's place *and* a husband-father's place is in the home.[50]

This functionalist statement suggests the importance of the ideology of "family values" in framing entertainment shows. Family values framing stresses that the middle-class family is the backbone of the country and that certain values must be upheld and certain "rules" adhered to if these families, and society as a whole, were to function properly. Among the strongest of family values is the belief that there is only one appropriate way to establish and maintain a family—that young people should marry by a certain age (which varies over time and place), have children only after an appropriate amount of time has elapsed after the wedding, be actively involved parents, and demonstrate a high level of commitment to work, the community, and doing what's right even when tempted to do otherwise. However, Betty Friedan and other feminist analysts have argued that middle-class family values framing imposes a limited role—that of housewife-mother—on women, thus transforming motherhood from an option to a mandate. As media analyst William Douglas explains, "That is, the role of women not only was essentially domestic and defined, in the most fundamental way, by motherhood but was articulated by a more elaborate relational code that relegated women to a dependent and, so, subservient status."[51]

However, many sitcoms transcended this simple formula, showing women as willing under some circumstances to violate the family-values code. *I Love Lucy* (Lucille Ball) was a classic example of a show that sought to depict women's tension when they were torn between being a housewife and having a career. In numerous episodes, Lucy Ricardo attempted to break into show business while her husband Ricky (Desi Arnaz), a Cuban American bandleader, attempted to keep her at home, a story line that became the show's staple plot.[52] As the series progressed, the Ricardos not only had a child but became upwardly mobile, transforming themselves from a struggling, lower-middle-class family in a New York City apartment to a solid (although slightly inane) suburban family that lived in a well-appointed country home in Connecticut.

The story lines in *I Love Lucy* frequently involved issues such as home economy, childrearing, and postdating checks; however, the undercurrent of activity often questioned what constituted family values and a woman's "appropriate" role in the family. In one episode Ricky states his desire to have "a wife who's just a wife," telling Lucy, "All you have to do is clean the house for me, bring me my slippers when I come home at night, cook for me, and be the mother of my children."[53] Ultimately, Ricky does not win; the episode ends with Lucy accepting a role in a television show. Media messages about middle-class values, family life, and gender issues contained in this show are not entirely lost on contemporary audiences. In the twenty-first century (more than fifty years after it first aired in 1951), *I Love Lucy* continues to be shown on the U.S. cable network TVLand and in syndication in countries worldwide, bringing new generations of viewers the same story lines that in the past both supported and questioned middle-class family values.

The framing of some current sitcom story lines continues to reinforce the importance of family life and middle-class values. Examples include ABC's *According to Jim,* a show that is billed as a "traditional family comedy" and features Jim (Jim Belushi), his wife, Cheryl (Courtney Thorne-Smith), and their family. Jim is a contractor in a design firm with his architect brother-in-law, while Cheryl is a stay-at-home mom who keeps the three kids on the right track when Jim is at work. Two episodes serve as examples of framing in story lines where middle-class values, such as honesty and integrity, are violated and then restored through Jim's actions. In "We Have a Bingo," Jim cheats at the church fund-raising bingo game by stealing the winning bingo card from an elderly woman who has fallen asleep. Jim has to deal with his conscience for being dishonest and winning the waterbed that actually had been won by Mrs. Meyer. The minister helps Jim confront his problem, and after several more scrapes with dishonestly Jim finally comes clean with everyone. In another episode, "The Lemonade Stand," Jim tells his two daughters that they should earn their own money (the work ethic) to buy the new scooters they want (consumerism). When the daughters set up a lemonade stand to make money, they get into avid competition with the neighbor's son, and Jim has to deal with his own competitive feelings toward the boy and his father. Plots such as these include messages about family values ("In our family, we don't do that") and reinforcement of such values as honesty and being kind to others, even those whom we do not like.

Some situation comedies bring the issue of middle-class family values to light by depicting characters who oppose, rather than support, those values. Women who stray from customary family values are popular themes in the framing of such story lines. Perhaps the earliest example that garnered national media coverage was the long-running (1988–98) series *Murphy Brown* (the title role played by Candice Bergen). Episodes relating to the decision of Brown (a star television reporter on a Washington, D.C., news magazine show) to bear a child without being married generated extensive controversy among some conservative political leaders and newspaper columnists. Vice President Dan Quayle led the criticism of this character's actions, stating that such shows contribute to the moral decline of the nation.

African American Middle-Class Family Values

Family values in sitcoms were originally associated with middle-class white families, because these families were the only ones shown on network shows. The few African American characters present in early shows were "presented not only in service to middle-class, White families, but, at the same time, absent from any apparent personal family relations."[54] The African American characters typically were "comforting domestics" or "uneducated handymen [who] provided menial aid to White employers rather than love and support to families of their own."[55]

For a number of years, network television had difficulty producing shows that portrayed intact African American families that were comparable to the white (Euro-American) families being regularly featured in situation comedies. *Julia* (Diahann Carroll) portrayed a *widowed* African American nurse who took care of her daughter. Early episodes of *Good Times* featured an intact African American family, but even this family eventually became parentless; the characters who played the father and mother left the series, and the teenage son became the head of the family. Rather than supporting family values like their white counterparts, situation comedies like *Good Times* that featured African American families relied on characters and interactions that were comfortable to white viewers.[56]

The first significant shift in sitcoms featuring predominantly African American characters came with the introduction of *The Cosby Show* (1984–92), where the upper-middle-class family and its values were clearly proclaimed. This highly successful series focused on the everyday adventures of an African American family consisting of the father (a respected gynecologist), the mother (a successful attorney), and their children. As researchers have noted, in shows such as this "both husband and wife [are] present; [the] spouses interact frequently, equally, and lovingly with each other; and children are treated with respect and taught achievement-oriented values."[57] It is those achievement-oriented values that support a belief in the middle-class way of life and in the importance of family values fostering harmony and stability. When African American male characters are presented as middle class in situation comedies, they therefore are shown to be "competent, successful, and able to provide comfortably for their families."[58] In this way, programs seeking to incorporate more African Americans into mainstream television also communicate middle-class values, because, like their working-class white counterparts, blue-collar African American males are generally presented as "inept, stupid, emotional, and so on."[59]

Although *The Cosby Show* was extremely popular with viewers, scholars who have examined the representations of African Americans and other people of color in television typically have concluded that this show helped cultivate an impression that racism was no longer a problem and that people of color who had not achieved upward mobility had no one to blame but themselves.[60] According to one study, portrayals in *The Cosby Show* incorporated myths about both race and class:

> Television, in the United States, combines an implicit endorsement of
> certain middle class life-styles with a squeamish refusal to confront class

realities or class issues. This is neither inevitable nor natural. Nothing about being working or lower middle class prevents someone from being funny, proud, dignified, entertaining, or worthy of admiration and respect, even if the social setting of most TV programs would encourage you to believe otherwise.[61]

Despite such criticisms, however, many situation comedies today feature upper-middle-class African American families if they include any African Americans at all. Programs such as ABC's *My Wife and Kids* have replaced *The Cosby Show* in portraying successful African American parents who live in fashionable residences, wear nice clothing, and teach their children solid middle-class values. Michael Kyle (Damon Wayans) of *My Wife and Kids* is described as "a loving husband and modern-day patriarch who rules his household with a unique and distinct parenting style. As he teaches his three children some of life's lessons, he does so with his own brand of wisdom, discipline and humor."[62]

Changing Values in Middle-Class Sitcoms

The story lines in some recent situation comedies are framed differently from those discussed above; they may either overtly or subtly ridicule the middle-class values and lifestyle portrayed in other shows. FOX Network's *Malcolm in the Middle* is an example. The story lines in this show revolve around a middle-class family comprising "four squabbling brothers and their parents who are just trying to 'hold on until the last one turns eighteen.'"[63] The story is told through the eyes of Malcolm (Frankie Muniz), who scores very high on an IQ test and is placed in a gifted-children program in school. Rather than his parents being the voice of reason in this show, Malcolm plays the role of "parent," serving as the family's peacemaker and stabilizer on some occasions.

Frequently used plots of past sitcoms regarding family values and the possibility of striking it rich through good fortune or inheritance are regularly ridiculed in *Malcolm in the Middle*. Consider this story line from the "Family Reunion" episode, as recorded in Malcolm's journal:

> All right, so we've never been close with Dad's side of the family. There's a couple of reasons: First, Dad can't stand them. Second, they all hate Mom. It sucks though because Grandpa is totally rich and if we play our cards right, big inheritance coming our way . . . a boy can dream can't he?
>
> Anyway, it's Grandpa's birthday and we got the call to join the family at his place for a reunion of sorts. Reese [Malcolm's brother] immediately

went into "Milk Grandpa for all he's worth" strategic planning mode. Can't say I blame him, I mean, Grandpa's really rich.

[After they arrive at the party] . . . Grandpa is great. He's always laughing, joking, life of the party. He even took me to see all his Civil War Memorabilia, which is cool, but I think I feigned more interest in hope of that inheritance money. Shameless, I know. I will say this though, no money is worth me having to dress in Civil War fatigues and reenact battles with the man. Give me some credit, my hypocrisy has limits.[64]

This episode's story line is typical of the plots of many contemporary television situation comedies about middle-class families, members of which are often depicted as desiring to have upper-class wealth but as ultimately being unwilling to "sell out." The "Family Reunion" episode and Malcolm's fictitious accounting of it in his journal (as posted on the FOX website) convey the message to viewers that although a big inheritance might be desirable, there are far more important things to take into account. The episode ends with Malcolm's immediate family making his grandfather and other members of the extended family extremely unhappy. Malcolm's mother locks herself in the bathroom and starts crying upon learning that she had been intentionally excluded from the family photo; Malcolm and his siblings decide to ruin the party by driving a golf cart through the party table, trampling the birthday cake, and launching the golf cart into the swimming pool. In supposedly middle-class fashion, Malcolm concludes, "So much for that inheritance, but at least we took care of our own, which may come back to us with Mom being a little nicer . . . wait, who am I kidding?"[65]

The father in the *Malcolm* series, Hal Wilkerson (Bryan Cranston), has been described as "the antithesis of the traditional sitcom dad, bonding with his sons in wonderfully unwholesome ways and in effect becoming one of them instead of maintaining the paternal distance and the platitudes typical of the rest of TV's patriarchs."[66] However, as one television critic suggests, the framing of family values in shows such as *Malcolm in the Middle* may be much more realistic than sitcom families portrayed in the past:

Back when his star was ascendent, Newt Gingrich [then Speaker of the House of Representatives] once called for the nation's families to return to the values embodied by the Nelsons of *Ozzie and Harriet*, seemingly unaware that the family in question was actually quite dysfunctional in real life, unable to live up to its own fiction. The irony of Gingrich's pronouncement was—and remains—that America *has* been trying to live up to the ideal of TV family life and it is, to a certain degree, our failure to meet these impossible standards that has led to disillusionment. *Mal-*

colm in the Middle is very much the product of this disillusionment—Art that imitates Life's inability to imitate art—a candid Polaroid of an only slightly exaggerated family rather than the usual Olan Mills glossy of the sitcom family in its perpetual Sunday best.[67]

In addition to changing roles and values, greater diversity is evident in today's situation comedy families. Earlier shows were based almost exclusively on families that were "predominantly while, middle class, happy, and secure,"[68] but more recent shows have portrayed intergroup conflict, greater diversity in the composition of the households, and some increase in the racial and ethnic diversity of characters. For example, greater diversity in household composition is evident in sitcoms such as *It's All Relative,* where two gay dads raise a straight daughter, or in shows where members of the extended family live (or practically live) with the nuclear family, as is the case in CBS's *Everybody Loves Raymond* and ABC's *Married to the Kellys* and *Hope and Faith.* ABC's *Eight Simple Rules for Dating My Teenage Daughter,* which originally was based on a story line about a traditional nuclear family, shifted to an extended family that lives together after the death of actor John Ritter (who had played the lead role of father-figure and successful writer Paul Hennessy), at which time the cast was expanded to include Paul's father-in-law, Jim (James Garner), who moved in with the family to help his daughter, Cate Hennessy (Katey Sagal), raise three teenagers.

Throughout the history of situation comedies, the framing of the story line and the depiction of characters have inaccurately reflected the class composition of the United States. In fact, these shows do not accurately reflect even the middle class, which they claim to portray. According to one study involving 262 domestic situation comedies that aired between 1946 and 1990, most (slightly more than 70 percent) featured middle-class families, a far greater percentage than existed in the general population during that period of time.[69] Moreover, the incomes and lifestyles of the families depicted were not representative of the typical middle-income family. Nearly half of the comedy series studied had a professional, such as a physician, lawyer, or college professor, as head of the household, whereas professionals actually made up about 15 percent of U.S. workforce at the time.[70] Despite the lack of realism in situation comedies, portrayal of the middle class may help to define how some viewers interpret media messages about what it means to be middle class and what values are embraced as valid by individuals considered to be in this class.

Although television entertainment shows typically assume the stability and ongoing integrity of the middle class, the framing of many articles in newspapers and on websites typically focuses on the problems of this class and the perils it faces, particularly of being squeezed or victimized. We now turn to how stories are framed to emphasize the vise that has caught the middle class and the ways in which individuals in this class are being victimized.

SQUEEZE FRAMING: CAUGHT
BETWEEN ASPIRATION AND ANXIETY

The idea that the middle class is in peril is a key framing device for news stories about politics and the economy. Headlines like "The Middle Class: Winning in Politics, Losing in Life"[71] are not unusual. The statements made in the article accompanying that particular headline are not unusual either:

> The great American middle class. Politicians on the left and right court it. Policies, liberal and conservative, are proclaimed on its behalf. Health care reform was to have eased its cares. Tuition subsidies educate its children. . . . Most voters see themselves as members of the middle class. . . . But for all its mythic power, the middle class is finishing last in the race for improvement in the current economic boom.[72]

As this article indicates, people in the middle class, whether in times of economic boom or bust, are often seen as "losing ground to their upper- and lower-earning fellow citizens."[73]

What is the cause of the peril faced by the middle class? Newspaper articles suggest that a central problem faced by members of the middle class is that they are being squeezed between their income and what it costs to provide for their families. According to some media reports, middle-class consumers are their own worst enemy, as they engage in excessive spending, but other articles suggest that the middle class is heavily targeted by corporate advertisers seeking to expand their market for goods and services and it is this that causes excessive consumerism. For example, a *Fortune* magazine article entitled "Getting Malled" reveals the extent to which retailers compete for middle-class shoppers: "Big retailers are locked in a bloody battle for the shrinking middle-class pocketbook."[74]

Although the framing of some stories focuses on excessive middle-class consumerism, others argue that the problem is the "shrinking middle-class pocketbook," the result of a continuing decline in the median household income. According to one article, "Shaking the House of Cards," some people formerly in the middle class are now entering the ranks of the poor, at a time when top political leaders are insensitive to this problem.[75] Columnist Bob Herbert of the *New York Times* is one of the few journalists who consistently focus on the problems of the middle class in the framing of his articles; in "Caught in the Credit Card Vise," "Caught in the Squeeze," and "Living on Borrowed Money,"[76] he demonstrates how deep the financial problems of middle-class families really are. Consider, for example, his article about the "credit-card vise" squeezing the middle class. The article begins with this statement by Julie Pickett, a middle-class homemaker who quit the full-time workforce when her twins were born, "I'm still paying for groceries I bought for my family years ago." To which Herbert adds, "She meant it literally. Mrs. Pickett and her husband, Jerry, of Middletown, Ohio, are trapped in the iron grasp of credit card debt. Except for the fact that no one is threatening to damage their kneecaps, they're in the same dismal position as the classic victim of loan-sharking."[77]

According to Herbert's article, buying on credit helps the middle-class family stay afloat at least temporarily, but in the long run that family actually sinks "deeper and deeper into debt, in large part because of the overuse of credit cards."[78] Citing a report, "Borrowing to Make Ends Meet" (compiled by a nonpartisan public-policy group), Herbert states that "more and more Americans are using credit cards to bridge the difficult gap between household earnings and the cost of essential goods and services."[79] Heightening this predicament are structural problems in the U.S. economy, such as widespread job displacement, declining real wages, and rising housing and health-care costs. As a result, many in the middle class rely on credit cards as "a way of warding off complete disaster,"[80] yet the middle-class existence is threatened thereby: "It has become increasingly difficult to get into—or stay in—the middle class."[81]

A number of articles, including Herbert's, about the middle-class squeeze are framed to reflect recently published government reports or well-received books that highlight "gloom and doom" of the middle class. An example was the media coverage given in 2003 to *The Two-Income Trap: Why Middle Class Mothers and Fathers Are Going Broke,* by Elizabeth Warren and Amelia Warren Tyagi. The book has many useful "sound bites" that can be easily used by commentators and digested by media audiences, adding to the book's popularity. For example, Herbert used information from the book to inform his readers that home mortgage costs between 1970 and 2000 rose seventy times faster than the average male head-of-household's income during that same period and that two-income families are not faring well in today's economy.[82] As Herbert states, "So you end up with two parents working like crazy just to keep the family economically afloat."[83] *The Two-Income Trap* also highlights the lack of savings by middle-class families—unlike middle-class families in the past whose members saved up to

11 percent of their income, most families today save virtually nothing and continue to pile up consumer debt. Based on this book and an application of the ideology of the American Dream, journalist Herbert states, "The American Dream has morphed into a treacherous survival regimen in which the good life—a life that includes a home, family vacations, adequate health coverage, money to provide the kids with a solid education, and a comfortable retirement—is increasingly elusive."[84]

In the twenty-first century, economic peril is the most prevalent framing device found in news stories about the middle class. Journalists and television commentators lament that the "Middle Class Barely Treads Water"[85] and that "Middle Class Mothers and Fathers Are Going Broke."[86] Newspaper, magazine, Internet, and television news reports about the middle-class squeeze typically feature college-educated parents who have purchased a home and then experienced an economic catastrophe, such as a job loss due to an illness or disability that makes it difficult for them to work, that depletes any savings they had accrued. According to one news account, "the dance of financial ruin starts slowly but picks up speed rapidly, exhausting the dancers before it ends."[87] However, individuals in "financial ruin" are not those whom most people might expect to be in bankruptcy:

> They are not the very young, tempted by the freedom of their first credit cards. They are not the elderly, trapped by failing bodies and declining savings accounts. And they are not a random assortment of Americans who lack the self-control to keep their spending in check. Rather, the people who consistently rank in the worst financial trouble are united by one surprising characteristic. They are parents with children at home. Having a child is now the single best predictor that a woman will end up in financial collapse.[88]

Based on *The Two-Income Trap*, reporters on NBC's *Today* show and the website MSNBC.com framed a number of their stories by using terms such as "middle-class problems," "financial meltdown," "living from paycheck-to-paycheck," and "pressing families against the wall."[89] The sound bite "the two income trap" was widely adapted by journalists to describe the problems that middle-class families experience when both parents are employed outside the household but the family cannot make ends meet financially.

Often implicit in the framing of stories about the middle-class squeeze is the assumption of "whiteness," meaning that middle-class problems typically are associated in the minds of journalists and media audiences with the white (non-Hispanic) population. However, this is not the case in the real world, as middle-class families across racial and ethnic categories experience economic problems. A few articles, such as "Blacks Lose Better Jobs Faster as Middle-Class Work Drops," have addressed this issue. Written by the journalist Louis Uchitelle, this article originally was published in the *New York Times* but was subsequently reported on CNN TV and CNN.com.[90] Uchitelle's article reports on recent government data showing that African Americans are "hit disproportionately harder than whites" by job loss in the United States. William Lucy, president of the Coalition of Black Trade Unionists, is quoted as saying that "the number of jobs and the types of jobs that have been lost have severely diminished the standing of many blacks in the middle class."[91] Although some sociologists might argue that union jobs paying twelve to thirteen dollars an hour are properly classified as "working class," journalists typically use the term "middle class" to describe this type of work, based on the widely held myth that most workers are in the vast middle class.

As ironic as it might seem, regardless of race or ethnicity, the middle class, even with its financial woes, is consistently described in the media as the best hope for the U.S. economy. Consider, for example, the article "The Middle Class Spends Its Way to Recovery":

> Whether the object of desire was a new car, a new coat or a new indulgence, American consumers opened their wallets wide in the third quarter—helping the economy expand at the fastest rate since 1984, according to the government. But after enduring three years of a sluggish economy, what, exactly, were people rushing out to buy? In large part, people were not buying tickets to Paris. Instead, people seemed to be letting loose but in a practical, deliberate way. They were buying necessities: cars, refrigerators, clothing. And this being the American consumer, there was a frivolous little thing (or two or three) thrown in. . . . "The rich don't have to put off their purchases," said W. Michael Cox, senior vice president and chief economist of the Federal Reserve Bank in Dallas. "This is the consumption of the masses driving the economy."[92]

As this quotation suggests, the rich can afford to indulge in immediate gratification of their consumer desires, purchasing what they want on the spot and having no fears about paying for it. By contrast, the middle class must either defer its gratification until later (or perhaps never), or its members must go deeper into debt to have what they need or want.

No topic has received greater media attention regarding the middle-class squeeze than the issue of rising health insurance costs. A typical headline framing such a story is "For Middle Class, Health Insurance Becomes a Luxury."[93] Although being uninsured or underinsured is a major problem for the forty-three million people in the United States who lack health insurance, the focus of many articles on this "health crisis" is how the problem affects the middle class. There is an implicit assumption in the articles that the poor are taken care of by the charity of public hospitals or by government-funded programs. As one article states, "The majority of the uninsured are neither poor by official standards nor unemployed. They are accountants, employees of small businesses, civil servants, single working mothers and those working part time or on contract."[94] The middle-class nature of this problem is emphasized by the sources the journalist interviewed. For example, the article quoted above includes an interview with R. King Hillier, director of legislative relations for Harris County, Texas (which includes the city of Houston), who states, "Now [being uninsured] is hitting people who look like you and me, dress like you and me, drive nice cars and live in nice houses but can't afford $1,000 a month for health insurance for their families."[95] Although articles such as this do not completely exclude the working class and poor, they are framed in such a way as to suggest that the cost of health insurance is primarily a middle-class concern.

As we have seen, squeeze framing emphasizes the economic woes of the middle class and points out the danger this produces not only for individuals in this class but for the American way of life. The "Middle Class Squeeze," as shown on PBS's *Now with Bill Moyers,* summed up this problem as follows: "Some say the broadly middle class society we used to take for granted has unraveled—unraveled to the point where America is no longer the land of widespread economic and social opportunity we believe it to be."[96] That probably is an overstatement; as discussed earlier in this chapter, news stories for more than 150 years have framed articles in terms of how the middle class is getting squeezed out of existence, and yet it still exists— in fact, most people still think of themselves as being members of the middle class. However, victimization framing in news articles, which will be discussed next, points a finger at some of the potential culprits who contribute to the problems that members of the middle class believe they face.

VICTIMIZATION FRAMING:
FEAR FACTOR AND THE MIDDLE CLASS

Victimization framing identifies specific villains or perpetrators—ranging from national political leaders and top corporate executives to individuals designated as "ordinary street criminal"—whose actions allegedly threaten the middle class (although possibly threatening members of other classes, as well). One form of victimization framing suggests that the problems of the middle class were created and are now perpetuated by those who occupy top economic and political leadership positions in the nation, pitting the interests of the middle class against those of the wealthy and powerful. The other form of victimization framing suggests that the middle class is being victimized by the working class and the poor, pitting the interests of the middle class against those of persons below them in the social class hierarchy.

VICTIMIZATION BY THE RICH AND POWERFUL

Two recurring themes in the first of these forms of victimization framing are how the rich benefit—at the expense of the middle and lower classes—from changes in the tax laws and from the greed of corporate CEOs and wealthy shareholders. A typical headline about recent changes in U.S. tax laws demonstrates the first of these themes: "Plan Gives Most Benefits to Wealthy and Families."[97] The accompanying story discusses how changes in the tax law during the George W. Bush administration affected households in various income ranges. The article asserted that nearly half of the benefits in that administration's tax cut program would flow to the wealthiest 10 percent of taxpayers. To show that many middle-class people believed that they had been left out in the cold when the tax cuts were enacted, the reporter included an interview with Robert and Bee Moorhead of Austin, Texas. The article informed readers that the Moorheads were both employed and had a combined income of about eighty-eight thousand dollars but were still unable to accumulate any substantial savings. Mr. Moorhead shows typical middle-class disbelief regarding the proposed change: "They're trying to sell this once again as trickle-down economics. I have my doubts."[98] Framing of the story was facilitated by a photo of the Moorhead family sitting on their porch and looking like what most people expect members of the middle class to look like.

The general framing of the article focused on the greater benefit that would be received by wealthy families, as compared with middle-class families like the Moorheads, even though the journalist acknowledged that "President Bush's mammoth tax plan would give something to almost everybody."[99] Another article, "Caught in the Squeeze," states "Only the rich have reason to cheer" about the 2003 tax cut President Bush signed into law,[100] while another bore the headline "Tax Analysis Says the Rich Still Win."[101]

Visual framing in the form of political cartoons is also used to inform media audiences that the rich are the primary beneficiaries of new tax laws. In 2003, political cartoons throughout the nation showed how the rich benefited from the bill that cut taxes for the wealthy and increased the federal debt limit by nearly a trillion dollars. Syndicated cartoonist Ben Sargent portrayed a very obese, wealthy man in a full-length coat wiping tears from his eyes with a large handkerchief while standing in front of a house where two seemingly middle-class parents sit on the front porch staring at a photograph of their son, in uniform and evidently serving in the U.S. armed forces in Iraq. The wealthy man says to the parents, "Oh, yeah? Well, now they're talking about cutting my next massive tax cut in half! Don't talk t'me about sacrifice!"[102] Another Sargent cartoon depicts a wealthy, well-dressed (but extremely overweight) man and woman talking with a mother who has her child in a stroller. The wealthy man is holding out a sucker on a stick, offering it to the child. The wealthy man's wife says to the child's mother, "Don't mind Howard . . . He's just determined to thank the future generations who'll be paying for our lovely tax cut."[103] These cartoons reflect the visual form of victimization framing which suggests to media audiences that the middle class is harmed by many actions that benefit the rich.

The other primary theme of victimization-by-the-wealthy framing is corporate greed. "They're Getting Richer!" heralded a *Time* magazine article that described how several major corporations, including Viacom, Citigroup, and Goldman Sachs, had dramatically boosted the stock dividends paid to their top executives and shareholders after the 2003 tax cut went into effect.[104] According to this article, "Dividends are a clean way for many CEOs to give themselves a big raise—and you have to figure that they will."[105]

Victimization framing of stories about the middle class not only informs media audiences of how this class is harmed by the decisions not only of political leaders but of corporate elites. In the midst of corporate downsizing, layoffs, and offshoring of middle- and working-class jobs, one political cartoonist captured the essence of this form of victimization by portraying a baldheaded CEO, who is wearing a nice suit and tie, shopping at "The Corporate Card Shoppe." The CEO is filling his basket with cards from various sections of a rack that is labeled with greetings such as "CONGRATULATIONS! You've been downsized," "GOOD-BYE! We're moving offshore," "SORRY ABOUT YOUR PENSION," and "I'M IN RECOVERY . . . Too bad your job isn't."[106] A *New Yorker* cartoon conveyed a similar idea: A judge is shown sitting in his courtroom listening to a well-dressed attorney, who stands before the judge with his affluent client by his side. The attorney states, "Your Honor, my client would like to be tried offshore."[107]

Articles such as "Bracing for the Blow"[108] and "The White-Collar Blues"[109] ask the question "Who's next out the exit door?" as corporations continue sending jobs offshore. Although the manufacturing sector and many so-called blue-collar workers previously had been hard hit by the practice of shipping thousands of jobs to lower-paid workers in other nations, even high-paying, middle-class, white-collar positions have not been immune to the problem. In "Education Is No Protection," the journalist Bob Herbert describes a New York conference on "Offshore Outsourcing: Making the Journey Work for Your Corporation," which was being offered to executives to help them make decisions about "the shipment of higher-paying white-collar jobs to countries with eager, well-educated and much lower-paid workers."[110] As the headline of this article suggests, the education that middle-class individuals so highly value is not adequate protection against offshoring of jobs; many middle- and upper-middle-class positions formerly located in the United States can be performed less expensively by well-educated, white-collar workers in other countries.

There was extensive media coverage when IBM, once considered to be a mainstay of the American economy, announced that it was offshoring well-paid jobs such as those of computer technicians. IBM uses the term "global sourcing" for sending jobs to workers in other countries; white-collar workers in the United States see this practice as a further erosion of their way of life, as middle-class jobs become increasingly difficult to find and those that are available do not pay as well as in the past.[111]

A news report entitled "Guess Which Jobs Are Going Abroad" that was broadcast on CNN and posted in the CNN/Money website contained the following statement: "If a tax preparer gets you an unexpected refund this year, you may have an accountant in India to thank. That's because accounting firms are joining the outsourcing trend established years ago by cost-conscious American manufacturers."[112] Articles such as this send a message that middle-class employees are being victimized by corporations as those corporations move jobs, including scientific laboratory analysis and medical billing, to other nations, leaving U.S. workers in the lurch. Corporations and their profit margins are pitted against middle-class workers in the framing of these stories. Herbert quotes Thea Lee, an economist with the AFL-CIO, as saying, "If you take [offshoring of jobs] to its logical extreme, the implications for the entire middle-class wage structure in the United States are terrifying."[113] The description of these problems resonates with media audiences who see their own lives reflected in the stories. For example, in a letter to the editor of the *New York Times,* Mary E. Tyler wrote: "The offshoring of all kinds of jobs is killing our way of life. I wonder what these companies will do when there is no one left here who can afford their products. I managed to fall from the middle class to the working class during the course of my lifetime. I tremble that my children might not even do that well."[114] Obviously, the problems of this writer and many others like her are not shared by the CEOs of many large corporations or their major shareholders, who typically benefit from cost-cutting measures such as downsizing, layoffs, and offshoring of jobs.

In newspapers and television news reports across the nation, regardless of the size of the city, the loss of white-collar jobs has caught the attention of journalists, who frame their stories to show the effects such job loss will have on the local economy. For example, in "White-Collar Jobs, Too," John Young, opinion page editor for the *Waco (Texas) Herald-Tribune,* began one article with a story about how a local technical college that educated computer technicians might be affected if the jobs of server-testing support technicians were sent to workers in other countries. Young blamed the loss of 2.3 million U.S. jobs between 2000 and 2004 not only on the post-9/11 business climate and the bursting of the dot-com bubble but on those corporations and politicians who he believed had been "looking the other way as these jobs leave" and even "abetting the quest to export jobs and to hide wealth."[115] Like a number of other journalists, Young framed this article to highlight his belief that political leaders and corporate officials do not have middle-class workers in mind when they make decisions that benefit their own interests.

VICTIMIZATION BY THE POOR AND HOMELESS

Although some forms of victimization framing emphasize the role of the wealthy and powerful in subordinating the middle class, this form of framing is also used to show readers and viewers that the middle class is being victimized by those beneath it in the social class hierarchy. The theme of victimization of the middle class by the poor and homeless typically is found in articles about middle-class housing and shelters for homeless persons. Both of these residential settings are evaluated in terms of the widely held belief that the middle class is entitled to privacy, safety, maintenance of property values, and a feeling of community.

Pride of home ownership is a key ingredient in the American Dream, and many in the middle class have found the actualization of this dream in residential settings that provide physical and psychological distance from lower-income people and the poor. According to many urban scholars, the need for this social distance was a contributing factor in the growth of suburbs in the past and to the popularity of exurbia and gated communities (residential areas surrounded by walls or fences, with a secured entrance).[116] Recent news articles and television news reports discussing gated communities and reviewing popular books on the topic, such as *Fortress America: Gated Communities in the United States*[117] and *Behind the Gates: Life, Security, and the Pursuit of Happiness in Fortress America,*[118] typically have informed media audiences that these communities are becoming more popular with middle-class residents, who increasingly fear for their safety and have a desire to keep out the *others* who might victimize them. Framing of stories in this manner suggests that the gated community is not only an extension of the middle-class American Dream but symbolic of the middle-class fear of victimization:

> It transforms Americans' dilemma of how to protect themselves and their children from danger, crime, and unknown others while still perpetuating open, friendly neighborhoods and comfortable, safe homes. It reinforces the norms of a middle-class lifestyle in a historical period in which everyday events and news media exacerbate fears of violence and terrorism. Thus, residents cite their "need" for gated communities to provide a safe and secure home in the face of a lack of other societal alternatives.[119]

Some journalists note that middle-class residents seek gated communities to find safe places for their children to play, for adults to arrive at home at all hours of the day or night and not feel threatened, and in order to live near those who share similar values. According to a *USA Today* article, "What [residents of gated communities] are looking for is not so terribly different than other suburban residents. It's a sense of community, which is like American pie. It has a lot to do with nostalgia, the '50s suburbs, the image of the small town."[120] In other words, some middle-class people are attempting to relive the so-called happy days of the sitcom world of *Leave It to Beaver* and *Ozzie and Harriet*.

Extensive media coverage of middle-class gated communities and books such as *Behind the Gates* convey the message that the middle class is not only emulating the upper class in its desire for safe and exclusive residences but participating in a new phase of residential development that will have a long-term effect on other urban problems such as city planning, fighting crime, and public education. As the columnist Jonathan Yardley of the *Washington Post* explained:

> People living in urban high-rises with security systems and doormen have done that for generations, of course, but the suburban walled community is a recent phenomenon and is not, in fact, a suburb as the term has been understood until now. This is "a new phase of residential development," in which "architectural and planning parameters are redefining neighborhoods physically and socially by using walls and guards—not just distance, street patterns, and middle-class norms and mores."[121]

A number of journalists used the titles of books such as *Fortress America* and *Behind the Gates* as sound bites in their discussions of urban problems, gated communities, and middle-class fears of victimization. However, as the anthropologist Setha Low, author of *Behind the Gates*, states, the middle class may be putting too much hope in these communities:

> Architectural symbols such as gates and walls also provide a rationale for the moral inconsistencies of everyday life. For instance, many residents want to feel safe in their homes and argue that walls and gates help keep out criminals, but gated communities are not safer than nongated suburban neighborhoods, where crime rates are already low. Instead, the logic of the symbolism satisfies conventional middle-class understandings of the nature of criminal activity—"it makes it harder for them to get in"— and justifies the choice to live in a gated community in terms of its moral and physical consequences—"look at my friends who were randomly robbed living in a nongated development."[122]

Just as the gated community serves as a source of reassurance for middle-class residents, many people who do not live in such communities obtain security devices to prevent unauthorized intrusions of every type in their homes. According to the article "Fortress Home: Welcome Mat Bites," the annual International Builders Show in Las Vegas featured "all manner of newfangled security devices" ranging from security cameras that can be manipulated from anywhere in the world to protect a home's perimeter to deadbolt locks twenty-eight inches long. According to the article, consumers—many of them middle class—fall into three groups: "the anxious, those whose peers are also arming themselves with alarms and deadbolts and those who have experienced some kind of violence or violation."[123] Although the middle class is not the only socioeconomic category of people whose concerns about safety and security have been heightened in the aftermath of September 11 and media reports about crimes like sniper shootings, members of this class have the economic resources to invest in security systems and fortress-building devices for their homes, as the wealthy have done for many years.

It may initially appear to be a wide jump from a discussion of how the media frame articles about gated communities, security systems, and middle-class fear of victimization to how the media frame articles about homeless shelters, but victimization of the middle class is a recurring theme in both types of stories. Articles about the seeming infringement of the poor and homeless on the private and public spaces that members of the middle class feel entitled to call their own gain salience with media audiences because of some people's fear that they too might "fall" and end up living in a shelter themselves. Media framing contributes to this fear with headlines such as "From Middle Class to the Shelter Door: In a Trend, New Yorkers

Face Poverty after Last Unemployment Check"[124] and "From Wall Street to Mean Street."[125] In articles like these, the people who are interviewed have either lost their jobs and their unemployment benefits or they have experienced personal problems that left them destitute. Unemployment benefits have "traditionally been a safety net of the middle class, as public assistance has been for the poor," and there is now a widespread fear that this safety net is not secure enough to keep people in the middle class.[126]

The physical proximity of the poor and homeless to the daily paths of those who consider themselves to be in the middle or upper-middle class is another recurring frame. Although many examples could be given, an article entitled "Anywhere but Here: Library Tells Homeless to Move Along" is typical. According to this article, as many as five thousand people in Dallas, Texas, are homeless, and hundreds of them congregate near the City Hall, the public library, and a street where a number of shelters and soup kitchens are located. However, the library strictly enforces rules about them because of complaints from middle-class citizens about how the homeless infringe on the rights of library patrons, as this article states: "The recent crackdown is the latest in response to long-standing complaints about homeless people bathing in library restrooms, muttering obscenities, panhandling outside, littering and forming a gauntlet that makes some patrons uncomfortable. But many see it as another round in an endless cycle of dealing unsuccessfully with homelessness."[127] For middle-class patrons such as Carol Orr, the article states, going to the library is no longer an option because of the large numbers of homeless men out front: "It's like going through a gauntlet," she said. Other library users are more understanding, such as Gerome Stell, an accountant, who stated, "I'm very passionate about the homeless because I feel like that could be me. Life did them a bad hand. A lot of them are educated. They've been to high school and have college educations."[128]

Encounters between the middle class and the homeless contribute to the middle-class fear of victimization. An analysis of headlines across the nation regarding the homeless shows that numerous newspapers choose or frame stories in a way that engenders hostility from the middle and working classes toward the homeless.[129] According to one media analyst, newspaper articles about the homeless in San Francisco followed a standard frame:

> Dirty, smelly homeless people are ruining the enjoyment of facility X (in this case, a youth hostel) by upstanding group Y (tourists). City department Z (the Office of Homelessness), while trying to do its best, is just too overwhelmed to make anyone happy. Middle- or working-class citizens are interviewed about the latest dilemma, and lo and behold, out

of their mouths pop prejudice and stereotypes about the homeless. A reaction quote from advocates for the homeless rounds out the picture.[130]

The location of homeless shelters within any particular community is
often the subject of media framing which asserts that a particular location is
a potential treat to the middle class and informs media audiences of the negative responses of members of the middle class to these facilities. Examples
include articles from the *San Francisco Chronicle*, "Homeless Shelter Plan Attacked, Potrero Hill Neighbors Worry about Property Values"[131] and the
San Francisco Examiner, "Showdown over Shelter: A Gritty Little Neighborhood Fights S.F. Plan for Homeless,"[132] both of which use NIMBY ("not in
my back yard") framing and carry the underlying theme of middle-class victimization.

This approach to the framing of stories about how homeless shelters
might affect the middle class is not unique. "Chicago Looks for Home for
Shelter for Homeless" describes Pacific Garden Mission, a shelter in
Chicago that was in need of a new location because the city wanted the
property to build a new gymnasium and library for a high school. As more
middle- to upper-middle-class neighbors moved into the expensive condo-
miniums and town houses that were built as the area went through the
process of gentrification, the shelter—which at one time had been considered to be on "Skid Row," in "an undesirable neighborhood that people
would rather avoid than come to"—was now considered an eyesore and
threat to middle-class residents who lived and worked nearby.[133]

Consider one final example of the pitting of the middle class against
the homeless when it comes to shelter. Articles and letters to the editor published in the *Free Lance-Star* of Fredericksburg, Virginia, informed readers
that middle-class residents were concerned about their safety and that of
their children because there were plans to move the Thurman Bisben
Homeless Shelter to their neighborhood. "Shelter's Plan Not a Popular
Move" prominently featured a photo of Theresa Lewis, a twenty-seven-
year-old mother of four, expressing her opposition to the shelter at a local
civic association meeting. According to the article, Lewis did not want to
the shelter in her back yard: "I feel badly for the families, but I have to think
of my children. How can you guarantee their safety from these strange people?" she asked the approximately fifty people gathered for the civil association meeting.[134] In the days immediately prior to and after that news report, sharply contrasting letters were sent to the newspaper's editor: "Shelter
will bring only crime"[135] and "Please don't let the shelter ruin our neighborhood"[136] stated the middle-class victimization side of the argument, said
some; "There's no reason to fear the poor residents of a shelter"[137] and "L.A.

Confidential: A Well-Run Shelter Suppresses Crime"[138] stated the other side of the debate.

Overall, media framing of articles about homeless shelters and their effect on the middle class may contribute to a feeling on the part of members of the middle class that they are increasingly victimized not only by those above them in the class structure but also by those living in poverty and experiencing homelessness. Although a variety of social problems do harm individuals in the middle class, these problems also are harmful to people in other social classes as well. For this reason, media framing of stories suggesting that middle-class concerns are more important than those of other people is in itself an important issue to evaluate when considering the effects that media representations regarding the various social classes may have on readers and viewers.

EFFECTS OF MEDIA FRAMING ABOUT THE MIDDLE CLASS

When I began my research on how the media frame news articles and television story lines about the middle class, I assumed that I would primarily find data to support a representation of the middle class as being "us"—the vast category into which almost everyone in the United States is assumed to fit. I also expected that the media would focus on positive attributes of the middle class, such as people's values and lifestyles. Based on the popularity of books such as Brooks's *Bobos in Paradise* and Florida's *The Creative Class,* I anticipated that the middle class would be shown as "in charge" and upwardly mobile. What I found instead was that although some journalists and television writers extol the virtues of the middle class, many others focus on the constant peril of the middle class, and have for more than 150 years.

Media framing of the middle class as the backbone of the nation supports the notion that this class holds the rest of the country together and that middle-class values are the core values of the United States. Family-values framing was widely used in news reports and television situation comedies of the past, but much of this framing has given way to a portrayal of the middle class as deeply conflicted, fragmented, and fragile. This coverage is further reflected in news articles suggesting that the middle class is in peril—its existence perhaps even jeopardized.

The fragility of the middle class is a recurring theme in media framing. Many articles and news stories depict the middle class as caught in an economic squeeze. If readers and viewers accept the premise behind squeeze framing, they may see the middle class as continually caught between aspiration and anxiety. As rampant consumerism is fueled by a proliferation of products and services, coupled with "easy" credit, the middle class can be either praised or blamed for its consumer habits.

How people think about the middle class and its habits is at least partly shaped by how the news media frame stories. For example, when the media present the problems of the middle class as overspending by particular individuals, squeeze framing assigns responsibility to those individuals and their families. However, if the media present the problems of the middle class as a form of victimization, the blame shifts to corporations and government officials. Even the poor and homeless may be portrayed as infringing on the rights and property of the middle class. As the political scientist Shanto Iyengar states with regard to media framing of poverty, "While there is as yet no well-developed theory of framing effects, it seems quite likely that these effects occur because the terms or 'frames' embodied by a stimulus subtly direct attention to particular reference points or considerations."[139] Similarly, media framing of stories about the middle class also directs readers' and viewers' attention to particular reference points and considerations.

Representing the middle class as victimized by the wealthy can either produce middle-class animosity toward the rich or can bring about greater resolve to earn more money (or strike it rich playing the lottery) and join the ranks of the rich, thereby gaining their tax breaks and lifestyle advantages. It is hard to explain the public's fascination with the rich and famous if some part of us does not aspire to, or have at least a deep-seated interest in, how the wealthy are able to live "above" everyone else. Rather than systematically opposing laws and policies that benefit the rich, some in the middle classes are content to live vicariously, watching reality shows where people get rich because of their talent (FOX's *American Idol*), giving the right answer to a number of questions (ABC's *Who Wants to Be a Millionaire?*), choosing a marriage partner (ABC's *Bachelor* and *Bachelorette*), or successfully competing against others (CBS's *Survivor* and NBC's *The Apprentice* and *Fear Factor*).

By contrast, the more that media coverage of the middle class shows people in this category as victimized by the poor and homeless, the more likely it is that some in the middle class will have a greater desire to segregate themselves and their families from individuals in other classes who might do them harm. Media coverage may also encourage people to oppose national, state, or local decisions that bring low-income and homeless individuals into closer proximity with middle-class families. "Not in my backyard" and "I don't want them to take away what I've worked so hard to get" tend to be common reactions to situations such as the building of new homeless shelters.

Just as fear of others was probably one of many factors contributing to the growth of suburbs in the past, the proliferation of exurbs and gated communities in the twenty-first century may be partly due to the idea that fear sells, as well as the fact that the middle class is one of the prime targets for enhancing sales of security systems and other protection devices. For many years, the upper class fortified itself against encroachment by the poor (and even by the middle class) with its urban high-security, high-rise residences, its fenced estates and guard dogs. Now the middle class has joined its ranks, seeking fortification of its residences, children's schools, and even public spaces such as streets and city libraries against those who might harm them. As Edward J. Blakely and Mary Gail Snyder note at the conclusion of *Fortress America: Gated Communities in America,* community building has greatly diminished in the United States and the emphasis has shifted, at least among those with the ability to pay, toward "privatization, increasing atomization, and increasing localism."[140] These authors question whether democracy can long endure under these conditions, and perhaps the more that media coverage encourages the middle class to "duck and cover," the less focus there will be on community building in this country. According to Blakely and Snyder:

> When privatization and exclusion become dominant, and neighborhood connectedness and mutual support structures disappear, we must question whether an American democracy founded on citizenship and community remains possible. . . . All of the walls of prejudice, ignorance, and economic and social inequality must come down before we can rendezvous with our democratic ideals. The walls of the mind must open to accept and cherish a more diverse nation. Then the walls that separate our communities, block social contact, and weaken the social contract will also come down.[141]

Certainly, members of the middle class are not the only ones contributing to the building of the walls of separation in the United States. However, if media representations of this class over the past 150 years are any indication, much of the news reporting and many of the entertainment shows have contributed to a view of the middle class not as the great uniter in society but as part of the great divide, squeezed by economic conditions, victimized by the wealthy and the poor, and generally in fear of its future. Sociologist Barry Glassner, author of *The Culture of Fear: Why Americans Are Afraid of the Wrong Things,* argues that the news media stoke fears of many unlikely dangers, such as road rage, cyber-predators, and terrorists, while ignoring crises such as health care, education, and malnourished children.[142] According to Glassner, although people in the United States live in one of the safest times in human history, members of the media and politics "make lots of money and lots of good careers off of tapping into Americans' moral insecurities."[143] Media framing of news reports and entertainment story lines about the middle class may find a vast well of insecurities—economic, political, and social, as well as moral—upon which to prey in the presentation of the U.S. middle class.

NOTES

Epigraphs. The first epigraph to this chapter is drawn from Christine Dugas, "Middle Class Barely Treads Water," *USA Today*, September 14, 2003, www.usatoday .com/money/perfi/general/2003-09-14-middle-cover_x.htm (accessed December 31, 2003). The second epigraph to this chapter is drawn from Stephanie Strom, "For Middle Class, Health Insurance Becomes a Luxury," *New York Times*, November 16, 2003, A25.

1. Teresa A. Sullivan, Elizabeth Warren, and Jay Lawrence Westbrook, *The Fragile Middle Class: Americans in Debt* (New Haven, Conn.: Yale University Press, 2000).

2. Harold R. Kerbo, *Social Stratification and Inequality,* 5th ed. (Boston: McGraw-Hill, 2003).

3. Tom Zeller, "The Nation: Calculating One Kind of Middle Class," *New York Times,* October 29, 2000, WR5.

4. Louis Uchitelle, "Bottom's Up: The Middle Class—Winning in Politics, Losing in Life," *New York Times,* July 19, 1998, WR1.

5. Zeller, "The Nation," WR5.

6. Zeller, "The Nation," WR5.

7. Zeller, "The Nation," WR5.

8. Barbara Ehrenreich, *Fear of Falling: The Inner Life of the Middle Class* (New York: HarperPerennial, 1990), 13.

9. Dennis Gilbert, *The American Class Structure in an Age of Growing Inequality,* 6th ed. (Belmont, Calif.: Wadsworth, 2003).

10. Gilbert, *The American Class Structure in an Age of Growing Inequality.*

11. David Brooks, *Bobos in Paradise: The New Upper Class and How They Got There* (New York: Simon and Schuster, 2000).

12. E. J. Graff, "Bobos in Paradise: The New Upper Class and How They Got There," *American Prospect,* May 22, 2000, 52, quoting Brooks.

13. Brooks, *Bobos in Paradise,* 52.

14. "It would never work out . . . ," cartoon, *New Yorker,* March 25, 2002, 75.

15. Benjamin DeMott, *The Imperial Middle: Why Americans Can't Think Straight about Class* (New York: William Morrow, 1990).

16. "Economy among the Middle Classes," *New York Times,* November 9, 1868, 4.

17. "Economy among the Middle Classes," 4.

18. "*The Consumers: Fate of the Middle Classes.* By Walter G. Cooper," *New York Times,* November 18, 1905, BR774.

19. "Letter to the Editor: Tribulations of the Middle Class," *New York Times,* November 20, 1906, 8.

20. "Middle Class Finds Homes in Suburbs: Demolition of Private Dwellings in the City Drives Residences to Other Localities," *New York Times,* September 1, 1929, RE2.

21. "Middle Class Finds Homes in Suburbs," RE2.

22. Randy Kennedy, "For Middle Class, New York Shrinks as Home Prices Soar," *New York Times,* April 1, 1998, A1.

23. Kennedy, "For Middle Class, New York Shrinks as Home Prices Soar," A1.

24. Francis Brown, "What Is the Middle Class and What Does It Want?" *New York Times,* December 22, 1935, BR6.

25. Quoted in Brown, "What Is the Middle Class and What Does It Want?" BR6.

26. Charles Goodrum and Helen Dalrymple, *Advertising in America: The First 200 Years* (New York: Harry N. Abrams, 1990), 31.

27. Quoted in Goodrum and Dalrymple, *Advertising in America,* 148.

28. Quoted in Goodrum and Dalrymple, *Advertising in America,* 148.

29. Brown, "What Is the Middle Class and What Does It Want?" BR6.

30. "Living Costs Disturb Middle Class, Barton Cautions House in Speech: Warning Crop Plan Means Higher Food and Clothing Prices, He Asserts New Yorkers Ask: 'Why Do We Always Foot the Bill?'" *New York Times,* December 4, 1937, 7.

31. "Living Costs Disturb Middle Class, Barton Cautions House in Speech," 7.

32. "Barton Sees Crisis for Middle Class," *New York Times,* June 26, 1938, 3.

33. "Says Middle Class Needs Salvation: Martin Asks National Support of Republican Drive to Avert Its 'Ruin' by New Deal," *New York Times,* August 27, 1939, 5; "Save Middle Class, Congress Is Urged," *New York Times,* October 21, 1942, 1.

34. "Save Middle Class, Congress Is Urged," 1.

35. "Wallace Sees All in a Middle Class: Picturing Future, He Asserts the 'Horatio Alger' Spirit Will Never Die Here," *New York Times,* January 25, 1943, 1.

36. Frank Bruni, "Bush Campaign Turns Attention to Middle Class," *New York Times,* September 18, 2000, A1, and "Bush Says Rival's Tax-Cut Plan Fails Middle Class," *New York Times,* August 25, 2000, A22; Katharine Q. Seelye, "Gore Offers Vision of Better Times for Middle Class," *New York Times,* September 7, 2000, A1.

37. Quoted in Edward Wyatt and David M. Halbfinger, "Clark and Kerry Offering Plans to Help Middle Class," *New York Times,* January 6, 2004, A17.

38. Ehrenreich, *Fear of Falling,* 5.

39. Ehrenreich, *Fear of Falling,* 51.

40. Ben J. Ard, Jr., "Are All Middle Class Values Bad?" *Family Coordinator* 21 (1972): 223.

41. Robin M. Williams, Jr., *American Society: A Sociological Interpretation,* 3rd ed. (New York: Knopf, 1970).

42. Kim Fulcher Linkins, "Midwest Lures Family-Based IT," CNN.com, 1999, www.cnn.com/TECH/computing/9906/11/midwest.idg/index.html (accessed February 17, 2004).

43. Quoted in Linkins, "Midwest Lures Family-Based IT."

44. Jill Lawrence, "Values, Votes, Points of View Separate Towns—and Nation," *USA Today,* February 18, 2002, A10.

45. Lawrence, "Values, Votes, Points of View Separate Towns," A10.

46. David Marc, *Comic Visions: Television Comedy and American Culture,* 2nd ed. (Malden, Mass.: Blackwell, 1997), 42.

47. Hal Himmelstein, *Television Myth and the American Mind* (Westport, Conn.: Praeger, 1994), 122.

48. William Douglas, *Television Families: Is Something Wrong in Suburbia?* (Mahwah, N.J.: Lawrence Erlbaum, 2003); Nina C. Leibman, *Living Room Lectures: The Fifties Families in Film and Television* (Austin: University of Texas Press, 1995).

49. David Croteau and William Hoynes, *Media/Society: Industries, Images, and Audiences,* 3rd ed. (Thousand Oaks, Calif.: Pine Forge, 2003), 179.

50. Douglas, *Television Families,* 86.

51. Douglas, *Television Families,* 73–74.

52. Jon E. Lewis and Penny Stempel, *Cult TV: The Comedies* (San Francisco: Bay Books, 1998).

53. Gerard Jones, *Honey, I'm Home! Sitcoms: Selling the American Dream* (New York: Grove Weidenfeld, 1992), 70.

54. Douglas, *Television Families,* 142.

55. Douglas, *Television Families,* 142.

56. Douglas, *Television Families,* 142–43.

57. Bishetta Merritt and Carolyn A. Stroman, "Black Family Imagery and Interactions on Television," *Journal of Black Studies* 23 (1993): 492–98.

58. Douglas, *Television Families,* 147.

59. Douglas, *Television Families,* 147; see also Richard Butsch, "Class and Gender in Four Decades of Television Situation Comedy: Plus ça Change . . . ," *Critical Studies in Mass Communication* 9 (1992): 387–99.

60. See Sut Jhally and Justin Lewis, *Enlightened Racism: The Cosby Show, Audiences, and the Myth of the American Dream* (Boulder, Colo.: Westview, 1992); Leslie B. Inniss and Joe R. Feagin, "The Cosby Show: The View from the Black Middle Class," *Journal of Black Studies* 25 (1995): 692–711.

61. Jhally and Lewis, *Enlightened Racism,* 74.

62. "My Wife and Kids," ABC Television, 2004, www.abc.go.com/prime time/mywifeandkids/show.html (accessed January 1, 2004).

63. "Malcolm in the Middle," TV Tome, 2003, www.tvtome.com/Mal colmintheMiddle (accessed December 30, 2003).

64. "Malcolm in the Middle," FOX.com, 2004, www.fox.com/malcolm/jour nal/404.htm (accessed January 2, 2004).

65. "Malcolm in the Middle," FOX.com.

66. John G. Nettles, "Malcolm in the Middle," *Popmatters: Television,* 2003, popmatters.com/tv/reviews/m/malcolm-in-the-middle.html (accessed December 30, 2003).

67. Nettles, "Malcolm in the Middle," 2.

68. Croteau and Hoynes, *Media/Society,* 79.

69. Butsch, "Class and Gender in Four Decades of Television Situation Comedy."

70. Croteau and Hoynes, *Media/Society.*

71. Uchitelle, "Bottom's Up," WR1.

72. Uchitelle, "Bottom's Up," WR1.

73. Uchitelle, "Bottom's Up," WR1.

74. Lee Clifford, "Getting Malled," *Fortune,* November 25, 2001.

75. Bob Herbert, "Shaking the House of Cards," *New York Times,* October 3, 2003, A27.

76. Bob Herbert, "Caught in the Credit Card Vise," *New York Times,* September 22, 2003, A19, "Caught in the Squeeze," *New York Times,* May 29, 2003, A27, and "Living on Borrowed Money," *New York Times,* November 10, 2003, A23.

77. Herbert, "Caught in the Credit Card Vise," A19.

78. Herbert, "Caught in the Credit Card Vise," A19.

79. Herbert, "Caught in the Credit Card Vise," A19.

80. Herbert, "Caught in the Credit Card Vise," A19.

81. Herbert, "Living on Borrowed Money," A23.

82. Herbert, "Living on Borrowed Money," A23.

83. Herbert, "Living on Borrowed Money," A23.

84. Herbert, "Living on Borrowed Money," A23.

85. Christine Dugas, "Middle Class Barely Treads Water," *USA Today,* September 14, 2003, www.usatoday.com/money/perfi/general/2003-09-14-middle cover_x.htm (accessed December 31, 2003).

86. "'Why Middle Class Mothers and Fathers Are Going Broke,'" MSNBC .com, 2003, msnbc.msn.com/Default.aspx?id=3079221&p1=0 (accessed December 29, 2003).

87. Elizabeth Warren and Amelia Warren Tyagi, *The Two-Income Trap: Why Middle Class Mothers and Fathers Are Going Broke* (New York: Basic Books, 2003), as quoted in "'Why Middle Class Mothers and Fathers Are Going Broke.'"

88. Warren and Warren Tyagi, *The Two-Income Trap,* as quoted in "'Why Middle Class Mothers and Fathers Are Going Broke.'"

89. See, for example, Sharon Epperson, "How to Escape the 'Two-Income Trap,'" MSNBC, 2003, msnbc.msn.com/id/3087477 (accessed December 29, 2003).

90. Uchitelle, "Bottom's Up."

91. Quoted in Uchitelle, "Bottom's Up."

92. Constance L. Hays, "The Middle Class Spends Its Way to Recovery," *New York Times,* November 2, 2003, WK1.

93. Stephanie Strom, "For Middle Class, Health Insurance Becomes a Luxury," *New York Times,* November 16, 2003, A25.

94. Strom, "For Middle Class, Health Insurance Becomes a Luxury," A25.

95. Quoted in Strom, "For Middle Class, Health Insurance Becomes a Luxury," A25.

96. Bill Moyers, "Politics and Economy: Transcript—Middle Class Squeeze," PBS.org, December 13, 2002, www.pbs.org/now/transcript/transcript_middleclass .html (accessed December 31, 2003).

97. Edmund L. Andrews, "Plan Gives Most Benefits to Wealthy and Families," *New York Times*, January 8, 2003, A17.

98. Quoted in Andrews, "Plan Gives Most Benefits to Wealthy and Families," A17.

99. Andrews, "Plan Gives Most Benefits to Wealthy and Families," A17.

100. "Caught in the Squeeze," *New York Times*, May 29, 2003, A27.

101. David Cay Johnston, "Tax Analysis Says the Rich Still Win," *New York Times*, July 14, 2002, BU10.

102. Ben Sargent, "Oh, Yeah? Well, Now They're Talking . . . ," *Austin American-Statesman*, March 26, 2003, A16.

103. Ben Sargent, "Don't Mind Howard . . . , *Austin American-Statesman*, August 29, 2003, A16.

104. Daniel Kadlec, "They're Getting Richer!" *Time*, August 18, 2003, 49.

105. Kadlec, "They're Getting Richer!" 49.

106. Signe Wilkinson, "The Corporate Card Shoppe" *Austin American-Statesman*, September 16, 2003, A11.

107. "Your Honor, my client . . . ," cartoon. *New Yorker*, March 25, 2002, 69.

108. Bob Herbert, "Bracing for the Blow," *New York Times*, December 26, 2003, A35.

109. Bob Herbert, "The White-Collar Blues," *New York Times*, December 29, 2003, A21.

110. Bob Herbert, "Education Is No Protection," *New York Times*, January 26, 2004, A27.

111. Herbert, "Bracing for the Blow," A35.

112. Leslie Haggin Geary, "Guess Which Jobs Are Going Abroad," CNN/Money, January 5, 2004, money.cnn.com/2003/12/30/pf/offshorejob/ (accessed January 25, 2004).

113. Bob Herbert, "The White-Collar Blues," *New York Times*, December 29, 2003, A21.

114. Mary E. Tyler, "Exporting Jobs and Our Way of Life: Letter to the Editor," *New York Times*, December 31, 2003, A20.

115. John Young, "White-Collar Jobs, Too," *Waco Tribune-Herald*, January 22, 2004, www.wacotrib.com/news/newsfd/auto/feed/news/2004/01/22/1074752927 .26609.8057.2758.html (accessed January 28, 2004).

116. Setha Low, *Behind the Gates: Life, Security, and the Pursuit of Happiness in Fortress America* (New York: Routledge, 2003), 12.

117. Edward J. Blakely and Mary Gail Snyder, *Fortress America: Gated Communities in the United States* (Washington, D.C.: Brookings Institution Press, 1997).

118. Low, *Behind the Gates.*

119. Low, *Behind the Gates,* 11.

120. Haya El Nasser, "Gated Communities More Popular, and Not Just for the Rich," 2002, *USA Today,* www.usatoday.com/news/nation/2002-12-15-gated-usat_x.htm (accessed January 28, 2004).

121. Jonathan Yardley, "Book Review: *Behind the Gates,*" *Washington Post,* May 8, 2003, CO2.

122. Low, *Behind the Gates,* 10–11.

123. Bradford McKee, "Fortress Home: Welcome Mat Bites," *New York Times,* January 22, 2004, F1.

124. Leslie Eaton, "From Middle Class to the Shelter Door: In a Trend, New Yorkers Face Poverty after Last Unemployment Check," *New York Times,* November 17, 2002, A37.

125. Geraldine Fabrikant, "From Wall Street to Mean Street," *New York Times,* August 24, 2003, BU1, BU9.

126. Eaton, "From Middle Class to the Shelter Door," A37.

127. Kim Horner, "Anywhere but Here: Library Tells Homeless to Move Along," *Dallas Morning News,* October 8, 2003, 1B.

128. Horner, "Anywhere but Here," 1B.

129. See Ben Clarke, "S.F. Daily Papers Pit Middle Class against Homeless," 2000, www.media-alliance.org/mediafile/19-1/homeless.html (accessed October 12, 2003).

130. Clarke, "S.F. Daily Papers Pit Middle Class against Homeless."

131. "Homeless Shelter Plan Attacked, Porero Hill Neighbors Worry about Property Values." *San Francisco Chronicle,* August 6, 1999.

132. "Showdown over Shelter: A Gritty Little Neighborhood Fights S.F. Plan for Homeless," *San Francisco Examiner,* August 12, 1999.

133. John W. Fountain, "Chicago Looks for Home for Shelter for Homeless," *New York Times,* May 15, 2003, A26.

134. Elizabeth Pezzullo, "Shelter's Plan Not a Popular Move," *Free Lance-Star,* June 7, 2002, www.fredericksburg.com/?News/FLS/2002/062002/06072002/631644 (accessed January 25, 2004).

135. Mike Holmes, "Shelter Will Bring Only Crime," 2003, Fredericksburg .com, www.fredericksburg.com/?News/FLS/2003/04182003/936435.html (accessed January 25, 2004).

136. Harold A. Morse, "Please Don't Let Shelter Ruin Our Neighborhood," Fredericksburg.com, 2003, www.fredericksburg.com/?News/FLS/911/2003/012003/01072003/834032.html (accessed January 25, 2004).

137. Tawny Browne, "There's No Reason to Fear the Poor Residents of a Shelter," Fredericksburg.com, 2002, www.fredericksburg.com/?News/FLS/2002/062002/06192002/637549.html (accessed January 25, 2004).

138. Michael Middleton, "L.A. Confidential: A Well-Run Shelter Suppresses Crime," Fredericksburg.com, 2003, www.fredericksburg.com/?News/FLS/2003/042003/04072003/921809.html (accessed January 25, 2004).

139. Shanto Iyengar, "Framing Responsibility for Political Issues: The Case of Poverty," *Political Behavior* 12 (March 1990): 20.

140. Blakely and Snyder, *Fortress America,* 176.

141. Blakely and Snyder, *Fortress America,* 177.

142. Barry Glassner, *The Culture of Fear: Why Americans Are Afraid of the Wrong Things* (New York: Basic Books, 1999).

143. Quoted in John Sanford, "Fueling Irrational Fears, Media Make Money, Boost Careers, Panel Says," *Stanford Report,* August 6, 2003, news-service.stanford .edu/news/2003/august6/fear-86.html (accessed February 1, 2004).

7

FRAMING CLASS, VICARIOUS LIVING, AND CONSPICUOUS CONSUMPTION

"The Simple Life 2"—the second season of the reality show, on which the celebutante Paris Hilton and her Best Friend Forever, the professional pop-star-daughter Nicole Richie, are set on a cross-country road trip—once again takes the heaviest of topics and makes them as weightless as a social X-ray.[1]

This statement by television critic Choire Sicha in her review of FOX TV's reality-based entertainment show *The Simple Life,* sums up a recurring theme of *Framing Class:* The media typically take "the heaviest of topics," such as class and social inequality, and trivialize it. Rather than providing a meaningful analysis of inequality and showing realistic portrayals of life in various social classes, the media either play class differences for laughs or sweep the issue of class under the rug so that important distinctions are rendered invisible. By ignoring class or trivializing it, the media involve themselves in a social construction of reality that rewards the affluent and penalizes the working class and the poor. In real life, Paris Hilton and Nicole Richie are among the richest young women in the world; however, in the world of *The Simple Life,* they can routinely show up somewhere in the city or the country, pretend they are needy, and rely on the kindness of strangers who have few economic resources.

The Simple Life is only one example of many that demonstrate how class is minimized or played for laughs by the media. Throughout this book, I have provided many examples of how class is framed in the media and what messages those framing devices might convey to audiences. In this chapter, I will look at the sociological implications of how framing contributes to our understanding of class and how it leads to vicarious living and excessive consumerism by many people. I will also discuss reasons why prospects for change in how journalists and television writers portray the various classes are limited. First, we look at two questions: How do media audiences understand and act upon popular culture images or frames? Is class understood differently today because of these frames?

MEDIA FRAMING AND THE PERFORMANCE
OF CLASS IN EVERYDAY LIFE

In a mass-mediated culture such as ours, the media do not simply mirror society; rather, they help to shape it and to create cultural perceptions.[2] The blurring between what is real and what is not real encourages people to emulate the upper classes and shun the working class and the poor. Television shows, magazines, and newspapers sell the idea that the only way to get ahead is to identify with the rich and powerful and to live vicariously through them. From sitcoms to reality shows, the media encourage ordinary people to believe that they may rise to fame and fortune; they too can be the next American Idol. Constantly bombarded by stories about the lifestyles of the rich and famous, viewers feel a sense of intimacy with elites, with whom they have little or no contact in their daily lives.[3] According to the social critic bell hooks, we overidentify with the wealthy, because the media socialize us to believe that people in the upper classes are better than we are. The media also suggest that we need have no allegiance to people in our own class or to those who are less fortunate.[4]

Vicarious living—watching how other individuals live rather than experiencing life for ourselves—through media representations of wealth and success is reflected in many people's reading and viewing habits and in their patterns of consumption. According to hooks, television promotes hedonistic consumerism:

> Largely through marketing and advertising, television promoted the myth of the classless society, offering on one hand images of an American dream fulfilled wherein any and everyone can become rich and on the other suggesting that the lived experience of this lack of class hierarchy was expressed by our *equal right to purchase anything we could afford*.[5]

As hooks suggests, equality does not exist in contemporary society, but media audiences are encouraged to view themselves as having an "equal right" to purchase items that somehow will make them equal to people above them in the social class hierarchy. However, the catch is that we must actually be able to afford these purchases. Manufacturers and the media have dealt with this problem by offering relatively cheap products marketed by wealthy celebrities. Paris Hilton, an heir to the Hilton Hotel fortune, has made millions of dollars by marketing products that give her fans a small "slice" of the good life she enjoys. Middle- and working-class people can purchase jewelry from the Paris Hilton Collection—sterling silver and Swarovski crystal jewelry ranging in price from fifteen to a hundred dollars—and have something that is "like Paris wears." For less than twenty dollars per item, admirers can purchase the Paris Hilton Wall Calendar; a "Paris the Heiress" Paper Doll Book; Hilton's autobiography, *Confessions of an Heiress;* and even her dog's story, *The Tinkerbell Hilton Diaries: My Life Tailing Paris Hilton.* But Hilton is only one of thousands of celebrities who make money by encouraging unnecessary consumerism among people who are inspired by media portrayals of the luxurious and supposedly happy lives of rich celebrities. The title of Hilton's television show, *The Simple Life,* appropriates the image of simple people, such as the working class and poor, who might live happy, meaningful lives, and transfers this image to women whose lives are anything but simple as they flaunt designer clothing and spend collectively millions of dollars on entertainment, travel, and luxuries that can be afforded only by the very wealthy.[6]

How the media frame stories about class *does* make a difference in what we think about other people and how we spend our money. Media frames constitute a mental shortcut (schema) that helps us formulate our thoughts.

THE UPPER CLASSES:
AFFLUENCE AND CONSUMERISM FOR ALL

Although some media frames show the rich and famous in a negative manner, they still glorify the material possessions and lifestyles of the upper classes. Research has found that people who extensively watch television have exaggerated views of how wealthy most Americans are and what material possessions they own. Studies have also found that extensive television viewing leads to higher rates of spending and to lower savings, presumably because television stimulates consumer desires.[7]

For many years, most media framing of stories about the upper classes has been positive, ranging from *consensus framing* that depicts members of the upper class as being like everyone else, to *admiration framing* that portrays them as generous, caring individuals. The frame most closely associated with rampant consumerism is *emulation framing,* which suggests that people in all classes should reward themselves with a few of the perks of the wealthy, such as buying a piece of Paris's line of jewelry. The writers of television shows such as ABC's *Life of Luxury,* E!'s *It's Good to Be . . .* [a wealthy celebrity, such as Nicole Kidman], and VH1's *The Fabulous Life* rely heavily on admiration and price-tag framing, by which the worth of a person is measured by what he or she owns and how many assistants constantly cater to that person's whims. On programs like FOX's *The O.C.* and *North Shore* and NBC's *Las Vegas,* the people with the most expensive limousines, yachts, and jet aircraft are declared the winners in life. Reality shows like *American Idol, The Billionaire, For Love or Money,* and *The Apprentice* suggest that anyone can move up the class ladder and live like the rich if he or she displays the best looks, greatest talent, or sharpest entrepreneurial skills. It is no wonder that the economist Juliet B. Schor finds that the overriding goal of children age ten to thirteen is to get rich. In response to the statement "I want to make a lot of money when I grow up," 63 percent of the children in Schor's study agreed, whereas only 7 percent disagreed.[8]

Many adults who hope to live the good life simply plunge farther into debt. Many reports show that middle- and working-class American consumers are incurring massive consumer debts as they purchase larger houses, more expensive vehicles, and many other items that are beyond their means. According to one analyst, media portrayals of excessive consumer spending and a bombardment of advertisements by credit-card companies encourage people to load up on debt.[9] With the average U.S. household now spending 13 percent of its after-tax income to *service* debts (not pay off the principal!), people with average incomes who continue to aspire to lives of luxury like those of the upper classes instead may find themselves spending their way into the "poor house" with members of the poverty class.

THE POOR AND HOMELESS:
"NOT ME!"—NEGATIVE ROLE MODELS IN THE MEDIA

The sharpest contrasts in media portrayals are between depictions of people in the upper classes and depictions of people at the bottom of the class structure. At best, the poor and homeless are portrayed as deserving of our sympathy on holidays or when disaster strikes. In these situations, those in the bottom classes are depicted as being temporarily down on their luck or as working hard to get out of their current situation but in need of public assistance. At worst, however, the poor are blamed for their own problems; stereotypes of the homeless as bums, alcoholics, and drug addicts, caught in a hopeless downward spiral because of their *individual* pathological behavior, are omnipresent in the media.

For the most part, people at the bottom of the class structure remain out of sight and out of mind for most media audiences. *Thematic framing* depicts the poor and homeless as "faceless" statistics in reports on poverty. *Episodic framing* highlights some problems of the poor but typically does not link their personal situations concerns to such larger societal problems as limited educational opportunities, high rates of unemployment, and jobs that pay depressingly low wages.

The poor do not fare well on television entertainment shows, where writers typically represent them with one-dimensional, bedraggled characters standing on a street corner holding cardboard signs that read "Need money for food." When television writers tackle the issue of homelessness, they often portray the lead characters (who usually are white and relatively affluent) as helpful people, while the poor and homeless are depicted as deviants who might harm themselves or others. Hospital and crime dramas like *E.R., C.S.I.,* and *Law & Order* frequently portray the poor and homeless as "crazy," inebriated in public, or incompetent to provide key information to officials. Television reality shows like *Cops* go so far as to advertise that they provide "footage of debris from the bottom tiers of the urban social order."[10] Statements such as this say a lot about the extent to which television producers, directors, and writers view (or would have us view) the lower classes.

From a sociological perspective, framing of stories about the poor and homeless stands in stark contrast to framing of stories about those in the upper classes, and it suggests that we should distance ourselves from "those people." We are encouraged to view the poor and homeless as the *Other,* the outsider; in the media we find little commonality between our lives and the experiences of people at the bottom of the class hierarchy. As a result, it is easy for us to buy into the dominant ideological construction that views poverty as a problem of individuals, not of the society as a whole, and we may feel justified in our rejection of such people.[11]

THE WORKING CLASS: HISTORICAL RELICS AND JOKES

As we have seen, the working class and the working poor do not fare much better than the poor and homeless in media representations. The working class is described as "labor," and people in this class are usually nothing more than faces in a crowd on television shows. The media portray people who *produce* goods and services as much less interesting than those who *excessively consume* them, and this problem can only grow worse as more of the workers who produce the products are thousands of miles away from us, in nations like China, very remote from the typical American consumer.[12]

Contemporary media coverage carries little information about the working class or its problems. Low wages, lack of benefits, and hazardous working conditions are considered boring and uninteresting topics, except on the public broadcasting networks or an occasional television "news show" such as *60 Minutes* or *20/20,* when some major case of worker abuse has recently been revealed. The most popular portrayal of the working class is *caricature framing,* which depicts people in negative ways, such as being dumb, white trash, buffoons, bigots, or slobs. Many television shows featuring working-class characters play on the idea that the clothing, manners, and speech patterns of the working class are not as good as those of the middle or upper classes. For example, working-class characters (such as Roseanne, the animated Homer Simpson, and *The King of Queens'* Doug) may compare themselves to the middle and upper classes by saying that they are not as "fancy as the rich people." Situation comedy writers have perpetuated working-class stereotypes, and now a number of reality shows, such as *The Swan* and *Extreme Makeover,* try to take "ordinary" working-class people and "improve" them through cosmetic surgery, new clothing, and different hairstyles.

Like their upper-class celebrity counterparts, so-called working-class comedians like Jeff Foxworthy have ridiculed the blue-collar lifestyle. They also have marketed products that make fun of the working class. Foxworthy's website, for example, includes figurines ("little statues for *inside* the house"), redneck cookbooks, Games Rednecks Play, and calendars that make fun of the working class generally. Although some people see these items as humorous ("where's yore sense of humor?"), the real message is that people in the lower classes lack good taste, socially acceptable manners, and above all, middle-class values. If you purchase "redneck" merchandise, you too can make fun of the working class and clearly distance yourself from it.

MIDDLE-CLASS FRAMING AND KIDDY-CONSUMERISM

Media framing of stories about the middle class tells us that this economic group is the value center and backbone of the nation. *Middle-class values framing* focuses on the values of this class and suggests that they hold the nation together. Early television writers were aware that their shows needed to appeal to middle-class audiences, who were the targeted consumers for the advertisers' products, and middle-class values of honesty, integrity, and hard work were integral ingredients of early sitcoms. However, some contemporary television writers spoof the middle class and poke fun at values supposedly associated with people in this category. The writers of FOX's *Malcolm in the Middle* and *Arrested Development,* for example, focus on the dysfunctions in a fictional middle-class family, including conflicts between husband and wife, between parents and children, and between members of the family and outsiders.

Why do these shows make fun of the middle class? Because corporations that pay for the advertisements want to capture the attention of males between ages eighteen and thirty-nine, and individuals in this category are believed to enjoy laughing at the uptight customs of conventional middle-class families. In other shows, as well, advertisers realize the influence that their programs have on families. That is why they are happy to spend billions of dollars on product placements (such as a Diet Coke can sitting on a person's desk) in the shows and on ads during commercial breaks. In recent research, Schor examined why very young children buy into the consumerism culture and concluded that extensive media exposure to products was a key reason. According to Schor, "More children [in the United States] than anywhere else believe that their clothes and brands describe who they are and define their social status. American kids display more brand affinity than their counterparts anywhere else in the world; indeed, experts describe then as increasingly 'bonded to brands.'"[13]

Part of this bonding occurs through constant television watching and Internet use, as a steady stream of ads targets children and young people. Schor concludes that we face a greater problem than just excessive consumerism. A child's well-being is undermined by the consumer culture: "High consumer involvement is a significant cause of depression, anxiety, low self-esteem, and psychosomatic complaints."[14] Although no similar studies have been conducted to determine the effects of the media's emphasis on wealth and excessive consumerism among adults, it is likely that today's children will take these values with them into adulthood if our society does not first reach the breaking point with respect to consumer debt.

The issue of class in the United States is portrayed in the media not through a realistic assessment of wealth, poverty, or inequality but instead through its patterns of rampant consumerism. The general message remains, one article stated, "We pledge allegiance to the mall."[15]

MEDIA FRAMING AND OUR
DISTORTED VIEW OF INEQUALITY

Class clearly permeates media culture and influences our thinking on social inequality. How the media frame stories involving class constitutes a *socially constructed reality* that is not necessarily an accurate reflection of the United States. Because of their pervasive nature, the media have the symbolic capacity to define the world for other people. In turn, readers and viewers gain information from the media that they use to construct a picture of class and inequality—a picture that becomes, at least to them, a realistic representation of where they stand in the class structure, what they should (or should not) aspire to achieve, and whether and why they should view other people as superior, equal, or inferior to themselves.

Because of the media's power to socially construct reality, we must make an effort to find out about the objective nature of class and evaluate social inequality on our own terms. Although postmodern thinkers believe that it is impossible to distinguish between real life and the fictionalized version of reality that is presented by the media, some sociologists argue that we can learn the difference between media images of reality and the actual facts pertaining to wealth, poverty, and inequality. The more we become aware that we are not receiving "raw" information or "just" entertainment from the media, the more we are capable of rationally thinking about how we are represented in media portrayals and what we are being encouraged to do (engage in hedonistic consumerism, for example) by these depictions. The print and electronic media have become extremely adept at framing issues of class in a certain manner, but we still have the ability to develop alternative frames that better explain who we are and what our nation is truly like in regard to class divisions.

THE REALITIES OF CLASS

What are the realities of inequality? The truth is that the rich are getting richer and that the gulf between the rich and the poor continues to widen in the United States. Since the 1990s, the poor have been more likely to stay poor, and the affluent have been more likely to stay affluent. How do we know this? Between 1991 and 2001, the income of the top one-fifth of U.S. families increased by 31 percent; during the same period, the income of the bottom one-fifth of families increased by only 10 percent.[16] The chasm is even wider across racial and ethnic categories; African Americans and Latinos/Latinas are overrepresented among those in the bottom income levels. Over one-half of African American and Latino/Latina households fall within the lowest income categories.

Wealth inequality is even more pronounced. The super-rich (the top 0.5 percent of U.S. households) own 35 percent of the nation's wealth, with net assets averaging almost nine million dollars. The very rich (the next 0.5 percent of households) own about 7 percent of the nation's wealth, with net assets ranging from $1.4 million to $2.5 million. The rich (9 percent of households) own 30 percent of the wealth, with net assets of a little over four hundred thousand dollars. Meanwhile, everybody else (the bottom 90 percent of households) owns only 28 percent of the nation's wealth. Like income, wealth disparities are greatest across racial and ethnic categories. According to the Census Bureau, the net worth of the average white household in 2000 was more than ten times that of the average African American household and more than eight times that of the average Latino/Latina household. Moreover, in 2002, almost thirty-five million people lived below the official government poverty level of $18,556 for a family of four, an increase of more than one million people in poverty since 2001.[17]

THE REALITIES OF HEDONISTIC CONSUMERISM

Consumerism is a normal part of life; we purchase the things that we need to live. However, hedonistic consumerism goes beyond all necessary and meaningful boundaries. As the word *hedonism* suggests, some people are so caught up in consumerism that this becomes the main reason for their existence, the primary thing that brings them happiness. Such people engage in the self-indulgent pursuit of happiness through what they buy. An example of this extreme was recently reported in the media. When Antoinette Millard was sued by American Express for an allegedly past-due account, she filed a counterclaim against American Express for having provided her with a big-spender's credit card that allowed her to run up bills of nearly a million dollars in luxury stores in New York.[18] Using the "victim defense," Millard claimed that, based on her income, the company should not have solicited her to sign up for the card. Although this appears to be a far-fetched defense (especially in light of some of the facts),[19] it may be characteristic of the lopsided thinking of many people who spend much more money than they can hope to earn. Recent studies have shown that the average American household is carrying more than eight thousand dollars in credit-card debt and that (statistically speaking) every fifteen seconds a person in the United States goes bankrupt.[20] Although fixed costs (such as housing, food, and gasoline) have gone up for most families over the past thirty years, these debt-and-bankruptcy statistics in fact result from more people buying items that are beyond their means and cannot properly use anyway. Our consumer expectations for ourselves and our children have risen as the media have continued to attractively portray the "good life" and to bombard us with ads for something else that we *must* have.

Are we Americans actually interested in learning about class and inequality? Do we want to know where we really stand in the U.S. class structure? Although some people may prefer to operate in a climate of denial, media critics believe that more people are finally awakening to biases in the media, particularly when they see vast inconsistencies between media portrayals of class and their everyday lives. According to the sociologists Robert Perrucci and Earl Wysong, "It is apparent that increasing experiences with and knowledge about class-based inequalities among the nonprivileged is fostering a growing awareness of and concerns about the nature and extent of superclass interests, motives, and power in the economic and political arenas."[21] Some individuals are becoming aware of the effect that media biases can have on what they read, see, and hear. A recent Pew Research Center poll, for example, reflects that people in the working class do not unquestioningly accept media information and commentary that preponderantly support the status quo.[22]

Similarly, Perrucci and Wysong note that television can have a paradoxical effect on viewers: It can serve both as a pacifier and as a source of heightened class consciousness. Programs that focus on how much money the very wealthy have may be a source of entertainment for nonelites, but they may also produce antagonism among people who work hard and earn comparatively little, when they see people being paid so much for doing so little work (e.g., the actress who earns seventeen million dollars per film or the sports star who signs a hundred-million-dollar multiyear contract). Even more egregious are individuals who do not work at all but are born into the "right family" and inherit billions of dollars.

Although affluent audiences might prefer that the media industry work to "reinforce and disguise privileged-class interests,"[23] there is a good chance that the United States will become more class conscious and that people will demand more accurate assessments of the problems we face if more middle- and working-class families see their lifestyles continue to deteriorate in the twenty-first century.

IS CHANGE LIKELY?
MEDIA REALITIES SUPPORT THE STATUS QUO

Will journalists and entertainment writers become more cognizant of class-related issues in news and in television shows? Will they more accurately portray those issues in the future? It is possible that the media will become more aware of class as an important subject to address, but several trends do not bode well for more accurate stories and portrayals of class. Among these are the issues of media ownership and control.

MEDIA OWNERSHIP AND SENIOR MANAGEMENT

Media ownership has become increasingly concentrated in recent decades. Massive mergers and acquisitions involving the three major television networks (ABC, CBS, and NBC) have created three media "behemoths"—Viacom, Disney, and General Electric—and the news and entertainment divisions of these networks now constitute only small elements of much larger, more highly diversified corporate structures. Today, these media giants control most of that industry, and a television network is viewed as "just another contributor to the bottom line."[24] As the media scholar Shirley Biagi states, "The central force driving the media business in America is the desire to make money. American media are businesses, vast businesses. The products of these businesses are information and entertainment. . . . But American media are, above all, profit-centered."[25]

Concentration of media ownership through chains, broadcast networks, cross-media ownership, conglomerates, and vertical integration (when one company controls several related aspects of the same business) are major limitations to change in how class is represented in the news and entertainment industry. Social analysts like Greg Mantsios are pessimistic about the prospects for change, because of the upper-class-based loyalties of media corporate elites:

> It is no wonder Americans cannot think straight about class. The mass media is neither objective, balanced, independent, nor neutral. Those who own and direct the mass media are themselves part of the upper class, and neither they nor the ruling class in general have to conspire to manipulate public opinion. Their interest is in preserving the status quo, and their view of society as fair and equitable comes naturally to them. But their ideology dominates our society and justifies what is in reality a perverse social order—one that perpetuates unprecedented elite privilege and power on the one hand and widespread deprivation on the other.[26]

According to Mantsios, wealthy media shareholders, corporate executives, and political leaders have a vested interest in obscuring class relations not only because these elites are primarily concerned about profits but because—being among the "haves" themselves—they do not see any reason to stir up class-related animosities. Why should they call attention to the real causes of poverty and inequality and risk the possibility of causing friction among the classes?

Media executives do not particularly care if the general public criticizes the *content* of popular culture as long as audiences do not begin to question the superstructure of media ownership and the benefits these corporations derive from corporate-friendly public policies. According to the sociologist Karen Sternheimer,

> Media conglomerates have a lot to gain by keeping us focused on the popular culture "problem," lest we decide to close some of the corporate tax loopholes to fund more social programs. . . . In short, the news media promote media phobia because it doesn't threaten the bottom line. Calling for social programs to reduce inequality and poverty would.[27]

Although the corporate culture of the media industry may be set by shareholders and individuals in the top corporate ranks, day-to-day decisions often rest in the hands of the editor-in-chief (or a person in a similar role) at a newspaper or a television executive at a local station. Typically, the goals of these individuals reflect the profit-driven missions of their parent companies and the continual need to generate the right audiences (often young males between eighteen and thirty-five years of age) for advertisers. Television commentator Jeff Greenfield acknowledges this reality: "The most common misconception most people have about television concerns its product. To the viewer, the product is the programming. To the television executive, the product is the audience."[28] The profits of television networks and stations come from selling advertising, not from producing programs that are accurate reflections of social life.

Recent trends in the media industry—including concentration of ownership, a focus on increasing profits, and a move toward less regulation of the media by the federal government—do not offer reassurance that media representations of class (along with race, gender, age, and sexual orientation) will be of much concern to corporate shareholders or executives at the top media giants—unless, of course, this issue becomes related to the bottom line or there is public demand for change, neither of which seems likely. However, it does appear that there is a possibility for change among some journalists and entertainment writers.

JOURNALISTS: CONSTRAINTS AND OPPORTUNITIES

Some analysts divide journalists into the "big time" players—reporters and journalists who are rich, having earned media salaries in the millions and by writing best-selling books (e.g., ABC's Peter Jennings)—and the "everyday" players, who are primarily known in their local or regional media markets.[29] Elite journalists in the first category typically are employed by major television networks (ABC, CBS, and NBC), popular cable news channels (such as CNN and FOX News), or major national newspapers such as the *Wall Street Journal, New York Times,* or *USA Today.* These journalists may be influential in national media agenda-setting, whereas the everyday media players, beat reporters, journalists, and middle- to upper-level managers at local newspapers or television stations at best can influence local markets.

Some of these individuals—at either level—are deeply concerned about the state of journalism in this country, as one recent Pew Research Center for the People and the Press study of 547 national and local reporters, editors, and executives found.[30] One of the major concerns among these journalists was that the economic behavior of their companies was eroding the quality of journalism in the United States. By way of example, some journalists believe that business pressures in the media industry are making the news "thinner and shallower."[31] Journalists are also concerned that the news media pay "too little attention . . . to complex issues."[32] However, a disturbing finding in the Pew study was that some journalists believe that news content is becoming more shallow because that is what the public *wants*. This cynical view may become a self-fulfilling prophecy that leads journalists to produce a shallower product, based on the mistaken belief that the public cannot handle anything else.[33]

Despite all this, some opportunities do exist in the local and national news for *civic journalism*—"a belief that journalism has an obligation to public life—an obligation that goes beyond just telling the news or unloading lots of facts."[34] Civic journalism is rooted in the assumption that journalism has the ability either to empower a community or to help disable it. Based on a civic journalism perspective, a news reporter gathering information for a story has an opportunity to introduce other voices beyond those of the typical mainstream spokesperson called upon to discuss a specific issue such as the loss of jobs in a community or the growing problem of homelessness. Just as more journalists have become aware of the importance of fair and accurate representations of people based on race, gender, age, disability, and sexual orientation, it may be possible to improve media representations of class. Rather than pitting the middle class against the working class and the poor, for example, the media might frame stories in such a way as to increase people's awareness of their shared concerns in a nation where the upper class typically is portrayed as more important and more deserving than the average citizen.

The process of civic journalism encourages journalists to rethink their use of frames. Choosing a specific frame for a story is "the most powerful decision a journalist will make."[35] As journalists become more aware that the media are more than neutral storytelling devices, perhaps more of them will develop alternative frames that look deeply into a community of interest (which might include the class-based realities of neighborhoods) to see "how the community interacts with, interrelates to, and potentially solves a pressing community problem." By asking "What is the essence of this story?" rather than "What is the conflict value of this story?" journalists might be less intent, for example, on pitting the indigenous U.S. working class against more recent immigrants or confronting unionized workers with their nonunionized counterparts. Stories that stress conflict have winners and losers, victors and villains; they suggest that people must compete, rather than cooperate, across class lines.[36] An exploration of other types of framing devices might produce better results in showing how social mobility does or does not work in the U.S. stratification system—highlighting, for example, what an individual's real chances are for moving up the class ladder (as is promised in much of the jargon about the rich and famous).

Advocates of civic journalism suggest that two practices might help journalists do a better job of framing in the public interest: *public listening* and *civic mapping*. Public listening refers to "the ability of journalists to listen with open minds and open ears; to understand what people are really saying."[37] Journalists engaged in public listening would be less interested in getting "superficial quotes or sound bites" and instead would move more deeply into the conversations that are actually taking place. Journalists would use open-ended questions in their interviews, by which they could look more deeply into people's hopes, fears, and values, rather than asking closed-ended questions to which the only allowable response choices are "yes/no" or "agree/disagree"—answers that in effect quickly (and superficially) gauge an individual's opinion on a topic. When journalists use civic mapping, they seek out underlying community concerns through discussions with people. They attempt to look beneath the surface of current public discourse on an issue. Mapping helps journalists learn about the ideas, attitudes, and opinions that really exist among diverse groups of people, not just "public opinion" or politicians' views of what is happening.

By seeking out *third places* where they can find "other voices" and hear "different stories," journalists may learn more about people from diverse backgrounds and find out what they are actually thinking and experiencing.[38] A "third place" is a location where people gather and often end up talking about things that are important to them. According to the sociologist Ray Oldenburg, the third place is "a great variety of public places that host the regular, voluntary, informal, and happily anticipated gatherings of individuals beyond the realms of home and work."[39] If the first place is the home, and the second place is the work setting, then the third place includes such locations as churches, community centers, cafes, coffee shops, bookstores, bars, and other places where people informally gather. As journalists join in the conversation, they can learn what everyday people are thinking about a social issue such as tax cuts for the wealthy. They can also find out what concerns people have and what they think contributes to such problems as neighborhood deterioration.

In addition to listening to other voices and seeking out different stories in third places, journalists might look more systematically at how changes in public policies—such as in tax laws, welfare initiatives, or policies that affect publicly funded child care or public housing—might affect people in various class locations. What are the political and business pressures behind key policy decisions like these? How do policies affect the middle class? The working class? Others? For example, what part does class play in perceptions about local law enforcement agencies? How are police officers viewed in small, affluent incorporated cities that have their own police departments, as compared to low-income neighborhoods of the bigger cities? While wealthy residents in the smaller cities may view police officers as "employees" who do their bidding (such as prohibiting the "wrong kind of people" from entering their city limits at night), in some low-income sectors of larger cities the police may be viewed as "oppressors" or as "racists" who contribute to, rather than reduce, problems of lawlessness and crime in the community. Journalists who practice civic journalism might look beyond typical framing devices to tell a more compelling story about how the intersections of race *and* class produce a unique chemistry between citizens and law enforcement officials. In this way, journalists would not be using taken-for-granted framing devices that have previously been employed to "explain" what is happening in these communities.

Given current constraints on the media, including the fact that much of the new investment in journalism today is being spent on disseminating the news rather than on collecting it,[40] there is room for only cautious optimism that some journalists will break out of the standard reflexive mode to explore the microscopic realities of class at the level where people live, and at the macroscopic level of society, where corporate and governmental elites make important decisions that affect everyone else.

Some media analysts believe that greater awareness of class-related realities in the media would strengthen the democratic process in the United States. According to Mantsios, "A mass media that did not have its own class interests in preserving the status quo would acknowledge that inordinate wealth and power undermine democracy and that a 'free market' economy can ravage a people and their communities."[41] It remains to be seen, however, whether organizations like the Project for Excellence in Journalism and the Committee of Concerned Journalists will be successful in their efforts to encourage journalists to move beyond the standard reflexive mode so that they will use new frames that more accurately reflect class-based realities.

Like journalists, many television entertainment writers could look for better ways to frame stories. However, these writers are also beleaguered by changes in the media environment, including new threats to their economic security from reality shows that typically do not employ in-house or freelance writers like continuing series do. As a result, it has become increasingly difficult for entertainment writers to stay gainfully employed, let alone bring new ideas into television entertainment.[42]

We cannot assume that most journalists and television writers are in a position to change media portrayals of class and inequality; however, in the final analysis, the responsibility rests with each of us to evaluate the media and to treat it as only one, limited, source of information and entertainment in our lives. For the sake of our children and grandchildren, we must balance the perspectives we gain from the media with our own lived experiences and use a wider sociological lens to look at what is going on around us in everyday life. Some analysts believe that the media amuse and lull audiences rather than stimulating them to think, but we must not become complacent, thinking that everything is all right as our society and world become increasingly divided between the "haves" and the "have nots."[43] If the media industry persists in retaining the same old frames for class, it will behoove each of us as readers and viewers to break out of those frames and more thoroughly explore these issues on our own.

NOTES

1. Choire Sicha, "They'll Always Have Paris," *New York Times,* June 13, 2004, AR31 [emphasis added].

2. Tim Delaney and Allene Wilcox, "Sports and the Role of the Media," in *Values, Society and Evolution,* ed. Harry Birx and Tim Delaney, 199–215 (Auburn, N.Y.: Legend, 2002).

3. bell hooks [Gloria Watkins], *Where We Stand: Class Matters* (New York: Routledge, 2000), 73.

4. hooks, *Where We Stand,* 77.

5. hooks, *Where We Stand,* 71 [emphasis added].

6. hooks, *Where We Stand,* 72.

7. Juliet B. Schor, *Born to Buy: The Commercialized Child and the New Consumer Culture* (New York: Scribner, 2004).

8. Schor, *Born to Buy.*

9. Joseph Nocera, *A Piece of the Action: How the Middle Class Joined the Money Class* (New York: Simon and Schuster, 1994).

10. Karen De Coster and Brad Edmonds, "TV Nation: The Killing of American Brain Cells," Lewrockwell.com, 2004, www.lewrockwell.com/decoster/decoster78.html (accessed July 7, 2004).

11. Judith Butler ("Performative Acts and Gender Constitution: An Essay in Phenomenology and Feminist Theory," in *Performing Feminisms: Feminist Critical Theory and Theatre,* ed. Sue-Ellen Case [Baltimore: Johns Hopkins University Press. 1990], 270) has described gender identity as performative, noted that social reality is not a given but is continually created as an illusion "through language, gesture, and all manner of symbolic social sign." In this sense, class might also be seen as performative, in that people act out their perceived class location not only in terms of their own class-related identity but in regard to how they treat other people, based on their perceived class position.

12. See Thomas Ginsberg, "Union Hopes to Win Over Starbucks Shop Workers," *Austin American-Statesman,* July 2, 2004, D6.

13. Schor, *Born to Buy,* 13.

14. Schor, *Born to Buy,* 167.

15. Louis Uchitelle, "We Pledge Allegiance to the Mall," *New York Times,* December 6, 2004, C12.

16. Carmen DeNavas-Walt and Robert W. Cleveland, "Income in the United States: 2002," *U.S. Census Bureau: Current Population Reports,* P60-221 (Washington, D.C.: U.S. Government Printing Office, 2003).

17. Bernadette D. Proctor and Joseph Dalaker, "Poverty in the United States: 2002," *U.S. Census Bureau: Current Population Reports,* P60-222 (Washington, D.C.: U.S. Government Printing Office, 2003).

18. Antoinette Millard, also known as Lisa Walker, allegedly was so caught up in hedonistic consumerism that she created a series of false identities (ranging from being a Saudi princess to being a lawyer, a model, and a wealthy divorcee) and engaged in illegal behavior (such as trying to steal $250,000 from an insurance company by reporting that certain jewelry had been stolen, when she actually had sold it). See Vanessa Grigoriadis, "Her Royal Lie-ness: The So-Called Saudi Princess Was Only One of the Many Identities Lisa Walker Tried On Like Jewelry," *New York Metro,* www.newyorkmetro.com/nymetro/news/people/columns/intelligencer/n_10418 (accessed December 18, 2004); Samuel Maull, "Antoinette Millard Countersues American Express for $2 Million for Allowing Her to Charge $951,000," credit suit.org/credit.php/blog/comments/antoinette_millard_countersues_american_ex press_for_2_million_for_allowing (accessed December 18, 2004).

19. Steve Lohr, "Maybe It's Not All Your Fault," *New York Times,* December 5, 2004, WR1.

20. Lohr, "Maybe It's Not All Your Fault."

21. Robert Perrucci and Earl Wysong, *The New Class Society,* 2nd ed. (Lanham, Md.: Rowman & Littlefield, 2003), 199.

22. Perrucci and Wysong, *The New Class Society.*

23. Perrucci and Wysong, *The New Class Society,* 284.

24. Committee of Concerned Journalists, "The State of the News Media 2004," www.journalism.org (accessed June 17, 2004).

25. Shirley Biagi, *Media Impact: An Introduction to Mass Media* (Belmont, Calif.: Wadsworth, 2003), 21.

26. Gregory Mantsios, "Media Magic: Making Class Invisible," in *Privilege: A Reader,* ed. Michael S. Kimmel and Abby L. Ferber, 99–109 (Boulder, Colo.: Westview, 2003), 108.

27. Karen Sternheimer, *It's Not the Media: The Truth about Pop Culture's Influence on Children* (Boulder, Colo.: Westview, 2003), 211.

28. Quoted in Biagi, *Media Impact,* 170.

29. One study identified the "typical journalist" as "a white Protestant male who has a bachelor's degree from a public college, is married, 36 years old, earns about $31,000 a year, has worked in journalism for about 12 years, does not belong to a

journalism association, and works for a medium-sized (42 journalists), group-owned daily newspaper" (Weaver and Wilhoit 1996). Of course, many journalists today are white women, people of color, non-Protestants, and individuals who are between the ages of 45 and 54 (Committee of Concerned Journalists, "The State of the News Media 2004").

30. Pew Center for Civic Journalism, "Finding Third Places: Other Voices, Different Stories," 2004, www.pewcenter.org/doingcj/videos/thirdplaces.html (accessed July 6, 2004).

31. Bill Kovach, Tom Rosenstiel, and Amy Mitchell, "A Crisis of Confidence: A Commentary on the Findings," Pew Research Center for the People and the Press, 2004, www.stateofthenewsmedia.org/prc.pdf (accessed July 6, 2004), 27.

32. Kovach, Rosenstiel, and Mitchell, "A Crisis of Confidence," 29.

33. Kovach, Rosenstiel, and Mitchell, "A Crisis of Confidence."

34. Pew Center for Civic Journalism, "Finding Third Places."

35. Steve Smith, "Developing New Reflexes in Framing Stories," Pew Center for Civil Journalism, 1997, www.pewcenter.org/doingcj/civiccat/displayCivcat.php?id=97 (accessed July 3, 2004).

36. Richard Harwood, "Framing a Story: What's It Really About?" Pew Center for Civic Journalism, 2004, www.pewcenter.org/doingcj/videos/framing.html (accessed July 3, 2004).

37. Smith, "Developing New Reflexes in Framing Stories."

38. Pew Center for Civic Journalism, "Finding Third Places."

39. Ray Oldenburg, *The Great Good Place: Cafés, Coffee Shops, Bookstores, Bars, Hair Salons and Other Hangouts at the Heart of a Community* (New York: Marlowe, 1999), 16.

40. Committee of Concerned Journalists, "The State of the News Media 2004."

41. Mantsios, "Media Magic," 108.

42. "So You Wanna Be a Sitcom Writer?" soyouwanna.com, 2004, www.soyouwanna.com/site/syws/sitcom/sitcom.html (accessed July 7, 2004).

43. Sternheimer, *It's Not the Media.*

BIBLIOGRAPHY

Aesop. "The Fox and the Grapes." www.pagebypagebooks.com/Aesop/Aesops_Fables/The_Fox_and_the_Grapes_p1.html (accessed December 4, 2003).

"Alabama: Mobile A Prostrate City, Alarming Decline in the Value of Real Estate, Two Hundred and Fifty Stores without Occupants, Poverty and Depression Some of the Causes." *New York Times,* October 21, 1874, 1.

"All in the Family." Classicsitcoms.com, 2004. classicsitcoms.com/shows/family .html (accessed March 21, 2004).

"All in the Family." TVLand.com, 2004. www.tvland.com/shows/aitf (accessed March 21, 2004).

Andrews, Edmund L. "Plan Gives Most Benefits to Wealthy and Families." *New York Times,* January 8, 2003, A17.

"A New Kind of Poverty." *Newsweek,* November 22, 2003. www.msnbc.msn .com/id/3540672 (accessed April 2, 2004).

Archibold, Randal C. "A Nation Challenged: St. Patrick's: City Celebrates Its Heroes and Grieves Over Their Loss." *New York Times,* September 18, 2001, B8.

Ard, Ben J., Jr. "Are All Middle Class Values Bad?" *Family Coordinator* 21 (1972): 223–24.

Arenson, Karen W. "Gates to Create 70 Schools for Disadvantaged." *New York Times,* March 19, 2002, A16.

Armour, Stephanie. "Homelessness Grows as More Live Check-to-Check." *USA Today,* August 12, 2003, A1.

Arnett, Alison. "Counter Culture." *Austin American-Statesman,* December 18, 2003, E1, E10.

Aristotle. *Aristotle's Poetics.* Translated by S. H. Butcher. Introduction by Francis Fergusson. New York: Hill and Wang, 2000.

"Arrested Development." FOX.com, 2003. fox.com/schedule/2003/ad.htm (accessed January 10, 2004).

Associated Press. "New Poverty Guidelines Unveiled." KATU News, Portland, Oregon, February 13, 2004. www.katu.com/news/story.asp?ID=64558 (accessed February 29, 2004).

Banerjee, Neela, David Barboza, and Audrey Warren. "At Enron, Lavish Excess Often Came before Success." *New York Times,* February 26, 2001, C1, C6.

Barber and Associates. "Robin Leach." www.barberusa.com/pathfind/leach_robin .html (accessed November 20, 2003).

Barnes, Michael. "An Inside Look at the New Long Center." *Austin American-Statesman,* February 13, 2001, A1, A9.

"Barton Sees Crisis for Middle Class." *New York Times,* June 26, 1938, 3.

Baudrillard, Jean. *Simulations.* New York: Semiotext(e), 1983.

Benford, Robert D., and David A. Snow. "Framing Processes and Social Movements: An Overview and Assessment." *Annual Review of Sociology* 26 (2000): 611–39.

Bennett, James T., and Jason E. Taylor. "Unions Work Selves Out of Job." *USA Today,* August 28, 2003, A13.

Berger, Peter L., and Thomas Luckmann. *The Social Construction of Reality: A Treatise in the Sociology of Knowledge.* New York: Anchor/Doubleday, 1967.

Bernstein, Jared. "Who's Poor? Don't Ask the Census Bureau." *New York Times,* September 26, 2003, A25.

Best, Steven, and Douglas Kellner. *Postmodern Theory: Critical Interrogations.* New York: Guilford, 1991.

Bhetnagar, Parija. "Over-the-Top Gifts for Junior." CNNMoney. money.cnn.com/ 2003/11/20/news/companies/expensive_toys/index.htm (accessed December 1, 2003).

Biagi, Shirley. *Media Impact: An Introduction to Mass Media.* Belmont, Calif.: Wadsworth, 2003.

"Big Labor Day Parade: Thirty Building Trades Unions to Be Represented. Forty Bands to Play in the Procession—Preparations to Handle Holiday Crowds." *New York Times,* August 31, 1902, 24.

Bird, S. Elizabeth, and Robert W. Dardenne. "Myth, Chronicle and Story: Exploring the Narrative Qualities of News." In *Social Meaning of News: A Text Reader,* edited by Daniel A. Berkowitz, 333–50. Thousand Oaks, Calif.: Sage, 1997.

Blakely, Edward J., and Mary Gail Snyder. *Fortress America: Gated Communities in the United States.* Washington, D.C.: Brookings Institution Press, 1997.

"Blames Union Labor for Work Shortage." *New York Times,* October 2, 1921, 1.

Blasi, Gary. "And We Are Not Seen: Ideological and Political Barriers to Understanding Homelessness." *American Behavioral Scientist* (February 1994): 563–87.

Blumenthal, Ralph. "As Levi's Work Is Exported, Stress Stays Home." *New York Times,* October 19, 2003, A14.

Blumenthal, Ralph, and Carol Vogel. "Ex-Chief of Sotheby's Gets 3-Year Probation and Fine." *New York Times,* April 30, 2002, A27.

Bourdieu, Pierre. *Distinction: A Social Critique of the Judgement of Taste.* Translated by Richard Nice. Cambridge, Mass.: Harvard University Press, 1984.

Bovino, Arthur. "Offering a Hand, and Hope, in a Year of Record Homelessness in New York." *New York Times,* November 2, 2003, A25.

Broder, John M. "California Supermarket Strike Deters Shoppers." *New York Times,* October 14, 2003, A12.

Brooks, David. *Bobos in Paradise: The New Upper Class and How They Got There.* New York: Simon and Schuster, 2000.

———. "The Americano Dream." *New York Times,* February 24, 2004, A27.

Brown, Francis. "What Is the Middle Class and What Does It Want?" *New York Times,* December 22, 1935, BR6.

Browne, Tawny. "There's No Reason to Fear the Poor Residents of a Shelter." Fredericksburg.com, 2002. www.fredericksburg.com/?News/FLS/2002/062002/06192002/637549.html (accessed January 25, 2004).

Bruni, Frank. "Bush Campaign Turns Attention to Middle Class." *New York Times,* September 18, 2000, A1.

———. "Bush Says Rival's Tax-Cut Plan Fails Middle Class." *New York Times,* August 25, 2000, A22.

Bunis, William K., Angela Yancik, and David Snow. "The Cultural Patterning of Sympathy toward the Homeless and Other Victims of Misfortune." *Social Problems* (November 1996): 387–402.

Butler, Judith. "Performative Acts and Gender Constitution: An Essay in Phenomenology and Feminist Theory." In *Performing Feminisms: Feminist Critical Theory and Theatre.* Edited by Sue-Ellen Case. Baltimore: Johns Hopkins University Press, 1990.

Butsch, Richard. "Class and Gender in Four Decades of Television Situation Comedy: Plus ça Change . . ." *Critical Studies in Mass Communication* 9 (1992): 387–99.

———. "Ralph, Fred, Archie and Homer: Why Television Keeps Recreating the White Male Working-Class Buffoon." In *Gender, Race and Class in Media,* edited by Gale Dines and Jean M. Humez, 403–12. Thousand Oaks, Calif.: Sage, 1995.

———. "A Half Century of Class and Gender in American TV Domestic Sitcoms." *Cercles* 8 (2003): 16–34. www.cercles.com/pasteach.html (accessed March 20, 2004).

Cable, Mary. *Top Drawer: American High Society from the Gilded Age to the Roaring Twenties.* New York: Atheneum, 1984.

Cantor, George. "Middle-Class Livonia Turns into Wayne County Power." *Detroit News,* January 26, 2002. www.detnews.com/2002/editorial/0201/28/d07-400393.htm (accessed February 18, 2004).

Carr, David. "Condé Nast Redesigns Its Future: Newhouse Plans a Transition but Tightens His Grip." *New York Times,* October 26, 2003, BU1, BU12.

———. "The Powering Up of the Power Lunch." *New York Times,* December 10, 2003, D1, D4.

Castillo, Juan. "U.S. Payday Is Something to Write Home About." *Austin American-Statesman,* December 14, 2003, J1.

"Cause of Mr. Hilsen's Suicide: His Capital Exhausted and Poverty Staring Him in the Face." *New York Times,* January 25, 1883, 8.

"Changing a City: Philanthropist Believes in Building Bridges." DallasNews.com, 2003. www.dallasnews.com/opinion/editorials/stories/121003dnedimcdermott98208.html (accessed December 12, 2003).

Clarke, Ben. "S.F. Daily Papers Pit Middle Class against Homeless," 2000. www.me dia-alliance.org/mediafile/19-1/homeless.html (accessed October 12, 2003).

Clemetson, Lynette. "Census Shows Ranks of Poor Rose by 1.3 Million." *New York Times,* September 3, 2003, A1.

Clifford, Lee. "Getting Malled." *Fortune,* November 25, 2001. www.fortune.com/ fortune/investing/articles/0,15114,373012,00.html (accessed September 29, 2003).

Cohen, Jeff, and Norman Solomon. "On Local TV News, If It Bleeds It (Still) Leads." *Media Beat,* December 13, 1995. www.fair.org/media-beat/951213.html (accessed February 29, 2004).

Coleman, Richard P., and Lee Rainwater. *Social Standing in America: New Dimensions of Class.* New York: Basic, 1978.

Committee of Concerned Journalists. "The State of the News Media 2004." www .journalism.org (accessed June 17, 2004).

"The Consumers: Fate of the Middle Classes. By Walter G. Cooper" *New York Times,* November 18, 1905, BR774.

Cookson, Peter W., Jr., and Caroline Hodges Persell. *Preparing for Power: America's Elite Boarding Schools.* New York: Basic Books, 1985.

Cowley, Geoffrey. "They've Given Away $24 Billion. Here's Why. Bill's Biggest Bet Yet." *Newsweek,* February 4, 2002, 44–52.

Croteau, David, and William Hoynes. *Media/Society: Industries, Images, and Audiences.* 3rd edition. Thousand Oaks, Calif.: Pine Forge, 2003.

"Customer Review of *Poor Little Rich Girl: The Life and Legend of Barbara Hutton,* by C. David Heymann." Amazon.com, 2003. www.amazon.com/exec/obidos/ search-handle-form/ref=s_sf_b_as/002-5171433-1616062 (accessed December 7, 2003).

D'Angelo, Paul. "News Framing as a Multiparadigmatic Research Program: A Response to Entman." *Journal of Communication* 52 (2002): 870–88.

Danziger, Jeff. "Mr. and Mrs. Lay Start Their Four Thousand Hours of Volunteer Work." *New York Times,* February 3, 2002, WK5.

Danziger, Sheldon, and Peter Gottschalk. *America Unequal.* Cambridge, Mass.: Harvard University Press, 1995.

Dao, James. "Hardships and Damage Linger after Hurricane." *New York Times,* October 2, 2003, A18.

Dean, Wally, and Lee Ann Brady. "Local TV News Project—2002: After 9/11, Has Anything Changed?" Journalism.org, 2004. www.journalism.org/resources/re search/reports/localTV/2002/postsept11.asp (accessed February 29, 2004).

DeBaise, Colleen. "Newest 'Tyco Gone Wild' Video Is Out, and Jurors See $6,000 Shower Curtain." *Wall Street Journal,* November 26, 2003, C1, C7.

De Coster, Karen, and Brad Edmonds. Lewrockwell.com, 2003. "TV Nation: The Killing of American Brain Cells." www.lewrockwell.com/decoster/decoster78 .html (accessed July 7, 2004).

Delaney, Tim, and Allene Wilcox. "Sports and the Role of the Media." In *Values, Society and Evolution,* edited by Harry Birx and Tim Delaney, 199–215. Auburn, N.Y.: Legend, 2002.

DeMott, Benjamin. *The Imperial Middle: Why Americans Can't Think Straight about Class.* New York: William Morrow, 1990.

DeNavas-Walt, Carmen, and Robert W. Cleveland. "Money Income in the United States: 2001." *U.S. Census Bureau: Current Population Reports,* P60-218. Washington, D.C.: U.S. Government Printing Office, 2002.

———. "Income in the United States: 2002." *U.S. Census Bureau: Current Population Reports,* P60-221. Washington, D.C.: U.S. Government Printing Office, 2003.

DeParle, Jason. "In Rising Debate on Poverty, the Question: Who Is Poor?" *New York Times,* September 3, 1990, A1.

"Destitution in New Orleans: The Existing Poverty and Its Causes—Lotteries and Beer Shops." *New York Times,* May 7, 1875, 10.

Dionne, E. J., Jr. "Handing Out Hardship." *Washington Post,* September 16, 2003, A19.

"Distressing Case of Poverty and Suicide." *New York Times,* January 1, 1855, 4.

Domhoff, G. William. *The Higher Circles.* New York: Random House, 1970.

———. "The Women's Page as a Window on the Ruling Class." In *Hearth and Home: Images of Women in the Mass Media,* edited by Gaye Tuchman, Arlene Kaplan Daniels, and James Benet, 161–75. New York: Oxford University Press, 1978.

"Double Dutch." *Joan of Arcadia.* TV Tome, 2004. www.tvtome.com/tvtome/servlet/EpisodeReviewPage/showid-17466/epid-282012/bl (accessed February 29, 2004).

Douglas, William. *Television Families: Is Something Wrong in Suburbia?* Mahwah, N.J.: Lawrence Erlbaum, 2003.

"Down among the Lowly: The Sights That One Sees in the Fourth Ward." *New York Times,* May 7, 1871, 8.

"Driven to Suicide by Poverty." *New York Times,* February 25, 1884, 8.

Dubner, Stephen J. "Suddenly Popular." *New York Times Magazine,* June 8, 2003, 68–71.

Duffy, Michael. "What Did They Know and When Did They Know It?" *Time,* January 28, 2002, 16–22.

Duffy, Michael, and John F. Dickerson. "Enron Spoils the Party." *Time,* February 4, 2002, 19–25.

Dugas, Christine. "Middle Class Barely Treads Water." *USA Today,* September 14, 2003. www.usatoday.com/money/perfi/general/2003-09-14-middle-cover_x.htm (accessed December 31, 2003).

Duke, Pony, and Jason Thomas. *Too Rich: The Family Secrets of Doris Duke.* New York: HarperCollins, 1996.

Durkheim, Emile. *Suicide.* New York: Free Press, 1951 [1897].

Eakin, Emily. "The Cities and Their New Elite." *New York Times,* June 1, 2002, A15, A17.

Eastman, Susan. "White Trash: America's Dirty Little Secret." *Ace Magazine,* 1998. www.aceweekly.com/acemag/backissues/980916/cb2_980916.thml (accessed March 14, 2004).

Eaton, Leslie. "From Middle Class to the Shelter Door: In a Trend, New Yorkers Face Poverty after Last Unemployment Check." *New York Times,* November 17, 2002, A37.

"Economy among the Middle Classes." *New York Times,* November 9, 1868, 4.

Ehrenreich, Barbara. *Fear of Falling: The Inner Life of the Middle Class.* New York: HarperPerennial, 1990.

———. "The Silenced Majority: Why the Average Working Person Has Disappeared from American Media and Culture." In *Gender, Race and Class in Media,* edited by Gale Dines and Jean M. Humez, 40–42. Thousand Oaks, Calif.: Sage, 1995.

———. *Nickel and Dimed: On (Not) Getting By in America.* New York: Metropolitan, 2001.

Eisenberg, Daniel. "Ignorant & Poor?" *Time,* February 11, 2002, 37–39.

Elder, Larry. "'White Trash' Is Politically Correct," 2000. www.townhall.com/columnists/larryelder/le200084.shtml (accessed March 14, 2004).

Ellin, Abby. "'Survivor' Meets Millionaire, and a Show Is Born." *New York Times,* October 19, 2003, BU4.

Elliott, Larry. "Everyday Heroes: Firefighters." abc12.com, May 5, 2003. abclocal.go.com/wjrt/news/050503_NW_r2_heroes_firefighters.html (accessed March 13, 2004).

El Nasser, Haya. "Gated Communities More Popular, and Not Just for the Rich," 2002. *USA Today.* www.usatoday.com/news/nation/2002-12-15-gated-usat_x.htm (accessed January 28, 2004).

Entman, Robert M. "Framing: Toward Clarification of a Fractured Paradigm." *Journal of Communication* 43 (1993): 51–58.

Entman, Robert M., and Andrew Rojecki. *The Black Image in the White Mind: Media and Race in America.* Chicago: University of Chicago Press, 2000.

Epperson, Sharon. "How to Escape the 'Two-Income Trap.'" MSNBC, 2003. msnbc.msn.com/id/3087477 (accessed December 29, 2003).

Epstein, Helen. "Enough to Make You Sick?" *New York Times Magazine,* October 12, 2003, 75–81, 98, 102–106.

Erickson, Christopher L., and Daniel J. B. Mitchell. "Information on Strikes and Union Settlements: Patterns of Coverage in a 'Newspaper of Record.'" *Industrial and Labor Relations Review* (April 1996): 395–407.

Fabrikant, Geraldine. "From Wall Street to Mean Street." *New York Times,* August 24, 2003, BU1, BU9.

Fagan, Kevin. "Shame of the City: Homeless Island." *San Francisco Chronicle,* November 30, 2003. www.sfgate.com (accessed April 11, 2004).

"A Father's Awful Crime: Shooting His Three Little Girls. Why John Remmler, of Holyoke, Killed His Children—Poverty and a Fear for Their Future His Reasons." *New York Times,* June 22, 1879, 7.

Federal Bureau of Investigation. "Organized Crime Section: Labor Racketeering." www.fbi.gov/hq/cid/orgcrime/lcn/laborrack.htm (accessed March 22, 2004).

"Feeding the City's Poor: Giving Bountiful Dinners to Children and Poverty-Stricken People." *New York Times,* November 28, 1884, 3.

Feuer, Alan. "Bronx Girl Follows Vision: A Future Far from Home." *New York Times,* October 4, 2003, A1, A14.

Feuer, Jack. "Miner Chord: Is a Working-Class Hero Still Something to Be?" *AD-WEEK Southwest,* August 5, 2002, 9.

Firestone, David. "4 Dead and 9 Missing in a Pair of Alabama Mine Blasts." *New York Times,* September 25, 2001, A14.

Fiske, John. *Television Culture.* New York: Methuen, 1987.

Fitzgerald, F. Scott. "The Rich Boy." In *The Short Stories of F. Scott Fitzgerald,* edited by Mathew J. Brucoli, 317–49. New York: Scribner, 1995 [1926 in *Redbook* magazine].

Florida, Richard. *The Rise of the Creative Class: And How It's Transforming Work, Leisure, Community and Everyday Life.* New York: Basic, 2002.

Fountain, John W. "Chicago Looks for Home for Shelter for Homeless." *New York Times,* May 15, 2003, A26.

Franklin, Nancy. "Sunny Money: Fox Heads Down the Coast from 90210." *New Yorker,* August 18, 25, 2003, 144–45.

Freudenheim, Milt, and Eric Lichtblau. "Former HealthSouth Chief Indicted by U.S." *New York Times,* November 5, 2003, C1, C8.

Gamson, William A. "News as Framing: Comments on Graber." *American Behavioral Scientist* 33 (1989): 157–61.

Gamson, William A., David Croteau, William Hoynes, and Theodore Sasson. "Media Images and the Social Construction of Reality." *Annual Review of Sociology* 18 (1992): 373–93.

Gandy, Oscar H., Jr., Katharina Kopp, Tanya Hands, Karen Frazer, and David Phillips. "Race and Risk: Factors Affecting the Framing of Stories about Inequality, Discrimination, and Just Plain Bad Luck." *Public Opinion Quarterly* 61 (Spring 1997): 158–82.

Gándara, Ricardo. "Thanks, Austin!" *Austin American-Statesman,* February 1, 2004, K1, K12.

Gans, Herbert. *Deciding What's News.* New York: Pantheon Books, 1979.

Geary, Leslie Haggin. "Guess Which Jobs Are Going Abroad." CNN/Money, January 5, 2004. money.cnn.com/2003/12/30/pf/offshorejob (accessed January 25, 2004).

Geewax, Marilyn. "HealthSouth Founder Is Indicted in Fraud Case." *Austin American-Statesman,* November 5, 2003, D1, D6.

Gesalman, Anne Belli. "Cliff Was Climbing the Walls." *Newsweek,* February 4, 2002, 24.

Gilbert, Dennis. *The American Class Structure in an Age of Growing Inequality.* 6th edition. Belmont, Calif.: Wadsworth, 2003.

Gilbert, Dennis, and Joseph A. Kahl. *The American Class Structure: A New Synthesis.* Homewood, Ill.: Dorsey, 1982.

Gilens, Martin. *Why Americans Hate Welfare: Race, Media, and the Politics of Antipoverty Policy.* Chicago: University of Chicago Press, 1999.

Ginsberg, Thomas. "Union Hopes to Win Over Starbucks Shop Workers." *Austin American-Statesman,* July 2, 2004, D6.

Gitlin, Todd. *The Whole World Is Watching.* Berkeley: University of California Press, 1980.

———. *Media Unlimited: How the Torrent of Images and Sounds Overwhelms Our Lives.* New York: Henry Holt, 2003.

Glassner, Barry. *The Culture of Fear: Why Americans Are Afraid of the Wrong Things.* New York: Basic Books, 1999.

Goffman, Erving. *Frame Analysis: An Essay on the Organization of Experience.* Boston: Northeastern University Press, 1974.

Goldman, Victoria. "The Baby Ivies." *Education Life: New York Times,* January 12, 2003, 22–41.

Goodrum, Charles, and Helen Dalrymple. *Advertising in America: The First 200 Years.* New York: Harry N. Abrams, 1990.

Gootman, Elissa. "Publicist Gets Jail Sentence and Scolding." *New York Times,* October 24, 2002, A28.

Graff, E. J. "Bobos in Paradise: The New Upper Class and How They Got There." *American Prospect,* May 22, 2000, 52.

Grant, Lorrie. "Retail Giant Wal-Mart Faces Challenges on Many Fronts: Protests, Allegations Are Price of Success, CEO Says." *USA Today,* November 11, 2003, B1.

Greenhouse, Steven. "Scandals Affirm New York as Union Corruption Capital." *New York Times,* February 15, 1999, B1.

———. "Middlemen in the Low-Wage Economy." *New York Times,* December 28, 2003, WK10.

———. "If You're a Waiter, the Future Is Rosy." *New York Times,* March 7, 2004, WK5.

———. "Labor Raises Pressure on California Supermarkets." *New York Times,* February 10, 2004, A12.

———. "Workers Assail Night Lock-Ins by Wal-Mart." *New York Times,* January 18, 2004, A1.

Greenhouse, Steven, and Charlie LeDuff. "Grocery Workers Relieved, if Not Happy, at Strike's End." *New York Times,* February 28, 2004, A8.

Grigoriadis, Vanessa. "Her Royal Lie-ness: The So-Called Saudi Princess Was Only One of the Many Identities Lisa Walker Tried On Like Jewelry." *New York Metro.* www.newyorkmetro.com/nymetro/news/people/columns/intelligencer/n_104 18 (accessed December 18, 2004).

Grindstaff, Laura. *The Money Shot: Trash, Class, and the Making of TV Talk Shows.* Chicago: University of Chicago Press, 2002.

Groer, Annie, and Ann Gerhart. "The Reliable Source." *Washington Post,* June 2, 1997, D3.

Gross, Jane. "No Talking Out of Preschool." *New York Times,* November 15, 2002, A22.

Haas, Nancy. "Off and Running for the Silk Stockings." *New York Times,* October 6, 2002, ST2.

Habiby, Margot, and Jim Kennett. "Ex-Enron Executive Killed Self, Police Say." *Austin American-Statesman,* January 26, 2002, A1, A4.

Hakim, Danny. "Auto Deal or Bust: Was Anyone Taken for a Ride in the U.A.W.–Big 3 Contract Talks?" *New York Times,* September 23, 2003, C2.

Hamill, Pete. "In Defense of Honest Labor." *New York Times,* December 31, 1995, SM18.

Harbaugh, Pam. "Dreamers Battle for Home in Harmony." *Florida Today,* January 4, 2004. www.floridatoday.com/!NEWSROOM/peoplestoryP0105DREAM.htm (accessed February 2, 2004).

Harwood, Richard. "Are Journalists 'E-l-i-t-i-s-t'?" *American Journalism Review* (June 1995): 26–30.

———. "Framing a Story: What's It Really About?" Pew Center for Civic Journalism, 2004. www.pewcenter.org/doingcj/videos/framing.html (accessed July 3, 2004).

Hays, Constance L. "The Middle Class Spends Its Way to Recovery." *New York Times,* November 2, 2003, WK1.

"Help for the Working Poor." *New York Times,* April 22, 1869, 4.

Hemphill, Clara. "Admissions Anxiety." *New York Times,* November 17, 2002, WK11.

Henneberger, Melinda. "Testing of a President: The Accuser; The World of Paula Jones: A Lonely Pace Amid Clamor." *New York Times,* March 12, 1998, A1.

Herbert, Bob. "Bracing for the Blow." *New York Times,* December 26, 2003, A35.

———. "Caught in the Credit Card Vise." *New York Times,* September 22, 2003, A19.

———. "Caught in the Squeeze." *New York Times,* May 29, 2003, A27.

———. "Living on Borrowed Money." *New York Times,* November 10, 2003, A23.

———. "Locked Out at a Young Age." *New York Times,* October 20, 2003, A19.

———. "Shaking the House of Cards." *New York Times,* October 3, 2003, A27.

———. "The White-Collar Blues." *New York Times,* December 29, 2003, A21.

———. "Education Is No Protection." *New York Times,* January 26, 2004, A27.

———. "We're More Productive. Who Gets the Money?" *New York Times,* April 5, 2004, A25.

Hermann, William. "Treating the Homeless Where They Live," August 9, 2000. www.cnn.com/2000/LOCAL/pacific/08/09/azc.homeless.medical/index.html (accessed February 8, 2004).

"Heroes amid the Horror." *New York Times,* September 15, 2001, A22.

Heymann, C. David. *Poor Little Rich Girl: The Life and Legend of Barbara Hutton.* New York: Random House, 1984.

Himmelstein, Hal. *Television Myth and the American Mind.* Westport, Conn.: Praeger, 1994.

Hochschild, Jennifer L. *Facing Up to the American Dream: Race, Class, and the Soul of the Nation.* Princeton, N.J.: Princeton University Press, 1995.

Hollingsworth, Skip. "Hi, Society!" *Texas Monthly* (September 2002): 164–67, 194–204.

Holmes, Mike. "Shelter Will Bring Only Crime," Fredericksburg.com, 2003. www.fredericksburg.com/?News/FLS/2003/04182003/936435.html (accessed January 25, 2004).

Holtzman, Linda. *Media Messages: What Film, Television, and Popular Music Teach Us about Race, Class, Gender, and Sexual Orientation.* London: M. E. Sharpe, 2000.

"Homeless Children." *New York Times,* December 22, 1856, 4.

"Homeless Shelter Plan Attacked, Potrero Hill Neighbors Worry about Property Values." *San Francisco Chronicle,* August 6, 1999.

"Homeless Woman Arrested for Threatening Postal Worker." KFMB.com, January 16, 2003. www.kfmb.com (accessed February 2, 2004).

"The Honeymooners." TVLand.com, 2004. www.tvland.com/shows/honeymoon ers (accessed March 20, 2004).

hooks, bell [Gloria Watkins]. *Where We Stand: Class Matters.* New York: Routledge, 2000.

Horkheimer, Max, and Theodor W. Adorno. *Dialectic of Enlightenment.* Translated by John Cummings. New York: Continuum International, 2002 [1944].

Horner, Kim. "Anywhere but Here: Library Tells Homeless to Move Along." *Dallas Morning News,* October 8, 2003, 1B.

———. "Losing Their Cart Blanche." *Dallas Morning News,* January 14, 2004, 1B.

"How the Rich Kids Live." CNN.com, 2003. www.cnn.com/2003/SHOW BIZ/TV/10/27/apontv.bornrich.ap/index.html (accessed October 27, 2003).

Howlett. Debbie. "Stay Upwind in Windy City: Foul-Smelling Trash Keeps Piling Up as Hauler's Strike Enters Day 7." *USAToday,* October 7, 2003, A3.

Hughes, Kristine. "Foundation Offers Help to Working Poor: Organizers Say Many Need Mentoring to Quit Welfare Dependency." *Dallas Morning News,* July 3, 2003, 1S.

"Hungry Families in U.S. on the Rise." MSNBC.com, 2003. www.msnbc .msn.com/id/3341630/ (accessed February 10, 2004).

"If Only the Spirit of Giving Could Continue" (editorial). *Los Angeles Times,* December 25, 1988, 16.

IGT. "Lifestyles of the Rich and Famous® Video Slots." www.igtonline.com/mega jackpots/new_games/lifestyles.html (accessed November 30, 2003).

Inniss, Leslie B., and Joe R. Feagin. "The Cosby Show: The View from the Black Middle Class." *Journal of Black Studies* 25 (1995): 692–711.

"It would never work out . . ." Cartoon. *New Yorker,* March 25, 2002, 75.

Iyengar, Shanto. "Framing Responsibility for Political Issues: The Case of Poverty." *Political Behavior* 12 (March 1990): 19–40.

———. *Is Anyone Responsible? How Television Frames Political Issues.* Chicago: University of Chicago Press, 1991, 1994.

Janjigian, Robert. "A Learjet? You Shouldn't Have!" *Austin American-Statesman,* November 4, 2002, E1.

Jhally, Sut, and Justin Lewis. *Enlightened Racism: The Cosby Show, Audiences, and the Myth of the American Dream.* Boulder, Colo.: Westview, 1992.

Johnston, David Cay. "Tax Analysis Says the Rich Still Win." *New York Times,* July 14, 2002, BU10.

———. "Top 1% in '01 Lost Income, but Also Paid Lower Taxes." *New York Times,* September 27, 2003, B1, B2.

Jones, Gerard. *Honey, I'm Home! Sitcoms: Selling the American Dream.* New York: Grove Weidenfeld, 1992.

Kadlec, Daniel. "They're Getting Richer!" *Time,* August 18, 2003, 49.

Kahl, Joseph A. *The American Class Structure.* New York: Rinehart, 1957.

Kaufman, Jonathan. "Covering Race, Poverty and Class in the New Gilded Age." *Nieman Reports* (Spring 2001): 25.

Kaufman, Leslie. "Millions Have Left Welfare, but Are They Better Off? Yes, No and Maybe." *New York Times,* October 20, 2003, A16.

———. "Welfare Wars: Are the Poor Suffering from Hunger Anymore?" *New York Times,* February 23, 2003, WK4.

———. "Amid Manhattan's Wealthiest, a Beggar Found Open Hearts." *New York Times,* February 14, 2004, A1, A14.

Kaufman, Leslie, and Constance L. Hays. "Blue Lights or Not, Martha Stewart Remains Calm." *New York Times,* January 26, 2002, B1.

Kavaler, Lucy. *The Private World of High Society.* New York: David McKay, 1960.

Keefe, Bob. "Grocery Strike Wearing on Customers, Workers." *Austin American-Statesman,* February 6, 2004, C1, C3.

Kellner, Douglas. *Media Spectacle.* New York: Routledge, 2003.

Kendall, Diana. *The Power of Good Deeds: Privileged Women and the Social Reproduction of the Upper Class.* Lanham, Md.: Rowman & Littlefield, 2002.

Kennedy, Randy. "For Middle Class, New York Shrinks as Home Prices Soar." *New York Times,* April 1, 1998, A1.

Kerbo, Harold R. *Social Stratification and Inequality.* 5th edition. Boston: McGraw-Hill, 2003.

"The King of Queens: Wild Cards." TV Tome, 2004. www.tvtome.com/tvtome/servlet/GuidePageServlet/showid-239/epid-1637 (accessed April 18, 2004).

Kingston, Paul W. *The Classless Society.* Stanford, Calif.: Stanford University Press, 2000.

Kirchhoff, Sue, and Barbara Hagenbaugh. "Immigration: A Fiscal Boon or Financial Strain? Debate Heats Up over Impact on Economy." *USA Today,* January 22, 2004, B1.

Kleinfield, N. R. "Golden Years, on $678 a Month." *New York Times,* September 3, 2003, B1.

Kossan, Pat. "Man Overcomes Homelessness, Will Graduate from ASU." *Arizona Republic,* May 2, 2003. www.azcentral.com (accessed February 28, 2004).

Kovach, Bill, Tom Rosenstiel, and Amy Mitchell. "A Crisis of Confidence: A Commentary on the Findings." Pew Research Center for the People and the Press, 2004. www.stateofthenewsmedia.org/prc.pdf (accessed July 6, 2004).

Kuczynski, Alex. "For the Elite, Easing the Way to Prison." *New York Times,* December 9, 2001, ST1, ST2.

———. "Lifestyles of the Rich and Red-Faced." *New York Times,* September 22, 2002, ST1, ST8.

———. "When Home Is a Castle and the Big House, Too." *New York Times,* August 18, 2002, ST1, ST7.

Kuczynski, Alex, and Andrew Ross Sorkin. "Canapés and Investment Tips Are Served to Well-Heeled." *New York Times,* July 1, 2002, A1, A17.

Kunerth, Jeff. "One Number Can't Measure Poverty." *Austin American-Statesman,* October 5, 2003, E4.

"Labor Unions." *New York Times,* August 26, 1868, 4.

Lacayo, Richard. "Take This Job and Starve." *Time,* February 16, 2004, 76–77.

Lambert, Pam, Alicia C. Shepard, and Sharon Cotliar. "Making Herself at Home: Even behind Bars, Martha Stewart Shows That Living Well May Indeed Be the Best Revenge." *People,* December 13, 2004.

Law & Order. NBC.com, 2003. www.nbc.com/Law_&_Order/about/index.html (accessed December 22, 2003).

Lawrence, Jill. "Values, Votes, Points of View Separate Towns—and Nation." *USA Today,* February 18, 2002, A10.

"Lay Away Plan." *People,* June 10, 2002, 76.

Lee, Felicia R. "Q&A: Welcome to the Working Class!" *New York Times,* July 13, 2003, A15.

Leibman, Nina C. *Living Room Lectures: The Fifties Families in Film and Television.* Austin: University of Texas Press, 1995.

Lester, Paul Martin, ed. *Images That Injure: Pictorial Stereotypes in the Media.* Westport, Conn.: Praeger, 1996.

"Letter to the Editor: Tribulations of the Middle Class." *New York Times,* November 20, 1906, 8.

"Letters to the Editor." *New York Times,* May 23, 2002, F10.

Lewis, Jon E., and Penny Stempel. *Cult TV: The Comedies.* San Francisco: Bay Books, 1998.

"The Life of Riley: U.S. Situation Comedy." Museum.tv.com, 2004. www.museum.tv/archives/etv/L/htmlL/lifeofriley/lifeofriley.htm (accessed March 13, 2004).

Lind, Rebecca Ann, and Colleen Salo. "The Framing of Feminists and Feminism in News and Public Affairs Programs in U.S. Electronic Media." *Journal of Communication* 52 (2002): 211–28.

Linkins, Kim Fulcher. "Midwest Lures Family-Based IT." CNN.com, 1999. www.cnn.com/TECH/computing/9906/11/midwest.idg/index.html (accessed February 17, 2004).

Lipton, Michael A., and Steve Barnes. "Just How Real Was *The Simple Life?* Take a Gander." *People,* December 15, 2003, 68.

"Living Costs Disturb Middle Class, Barton Cautions House in Speech: Warning Crop Plan Means Higher Food and Clothing Prices, He Asserts New Yorkers Ask: 'Why Do We Always Foot the Bill?'" *New York Times,* December 4, 1937, 7.

Lobb, Annelena. "Gifts for Kids Who Have It All." CNN/Money, 2002. money.cnn.com/2002/11/26/pf/saving/holiday_haveitall.index.htm (accessed December 5, 2002).

"Lodging-House for Homeless Girls a New Project of the Children's Aid Society. *New York Times,* May 25, 1862, 3.

"A Lodging-House for the Homeless in the Thirteenth Ward." *New York Times,* February 21, 1868, 5.

Low, Setha. *Behind the Gates: Life, Security, and the Pursuit of Happiness in Fortress America.* New York: Routledge, 2003.

Lule, Jack. *Daily News, Eternal Stories: The Mythological Role of Journalism.* New York: Guilford, 2001.

Lyman, Rick. "For the Ryder Trial, a Hollywood Script." *New York Times,* November 3, 2002, ST1, ST8.

Maher, John. "What's in a Name?" *Austin American-Statesman,* June 28, 2003, C1, C8.

"Malcolm in the Middle." TV Tome, 2003. www.tvtome.com/MalcolmintheMiddle (accessed December 30, 2003).

"Malcolm in the Middle." FOX.com, 2004. www.fox.com/malcolm/journal/404.htm (accessed January 2, 2004).

"Managing Labor Interests: Harmonizing Rival Unions and Concluding to Do without Prayers." *New York Times,* June 11, 1883, 8.

Manoff, Robert K. "Writing the *News,* by Telling the 'Story.'" In *Reading the News,* edited by Robert K. Manoff and Michael Schudson, 197–229. New York: Pantheon, 1987.

Mantsios, Gregory. "Media Magic: Making Class Invisible." In *Privilege: A Reader,* edited by Michael S. Kimmel and Abby L. Ferber, 99–109. Boulder, Colo.: Westview, 2003.

Marc, David. *Comic Visions: Television Comedy and American Culture.* 2nd edition. Malden, Mass.: Blackwell, 1997.

Marchand, Michele. "On the Air and Outside: Homelessness on TV." www.anitra.net/books/activist/mm_on_the_air.html (accessed February 28, 2004).

Mason, Christopher. "Where Everybody Has a Name." *New York Times,* October 26, 2003, ST1, ST2.

Massing, Michael. "Take This Job and Be Thankful (for $6.80 an Hour)." *New York Times,* February 18, 2004, B8.

Maull, Samuel. "Jurors in Tyco Case See Edited Tape of Lavish Party." *Austin American-Statesman,* October 29, 2003, C1, C5.

———. "Antoinette Millard Countersues American Express for $2 Million for Allowing Her to Charge $951,000." creditsuit.org/credit.php/blog/comments/antoinette_millard_countersues_american_express_for_2_million_for_allowing (accessed December 18, 2004).

Maynard, Micheline. "If a Name Is Tarnished, but Carved in Stone." *New York Times,* December 9, 2001, BU4.

"The Mayor's Remarks: 'You're All My Heroes.'" *New York Times,* September 17, 2001, A7.

"McDonald's Features Donald Trump in New Ad Campaign Launching Dollar-Priced Big N' Tasty and McChicken Sandwich." McDonalds.com, 2002. www.mcdonalds.com/countries/usa/whatsnew/pressrelease/2002/10032002_a (accessed December 16, 2003).

McIntee, Michael Z. "The Wahoo Gazette: Wednesday, July 31, 2002—Show #1852," 2002. www.cbs.com/latenight/lateshow/exclusives/wahoo/archive/2002/07/archive31.shtml (accessed March 13, 2003).

McKee, Bradford. "Fortress Home: Welcome Mat Bites." *New York Times,* January 22, 2004, F1.

McLarin, Kimberly J. "Poverty Rate Is the Highest in 16 Years, a Report Says." *New York Times,* July 14, 1995, B3.

"Meeting of Front Bricklayers: A Union of Capital and Labor Advocated." *New York Times,* August 30, 1860, 8.

"Melancholy Case of Suicide: Pride and Poverty the Cause." *New York Times,* March 20, 1873, 1.

Merritt, Bishetta, and Carolyn A. Stroman. "Black Family Imagery and Interactions on Television." *Journal of Black Studies* 23 (1993): 492–99.

"The Middle of the Middle Class." *New York Times Magazine,* June 9, 2002, 74–80.

"Middle Class Finds Homes in Suburbs: Demolition of Private Dwellings in the City Drives Residences to Other Localities." *New York Times,* September 1, 1929, RE2.

Middleton, Michael. "L.A. Confidential: A Well-Run Shelter Suppresses Crime." Fredericksburg.com, 2003. www.fredericksburg.com/?News/FLS/2003/042003/04072003/921809.html (accessed January 25, 2004).

Min, Eungjun, ed. *Reading the Homeless: The Media's Image of Homeless Culture.* Westport, Conn.: Praeger, 1999.

Mishell, Lawrence, Jared Bernstein, and John Schmitt. *The State of Working America, 1998–99.* Ithaca, N.Y.: Cornell University Press, 1999.

Misra, Joya, Stephanie Moller, and Marina Karides. "Envisioning Dependency: Changing Media Depictions of Welfare in the 20th Century." *Social Problems* 50 (2003): 482–504.

Morse, Harold A. "Please Don't Let Shelter Ruin Our Neighborhood." Fredericksburg.com, 2003. www.fredericksburg.com/?News/FLS/911/2003/012003/01072003/834032.html (accessed January 25, 2004).

"Most Expensive Gated Communities in America." Forbes.com, 2003. www.forbes.com/maserati/cx_bs_1114home.html (accessed December 8, 2003).

"Move to the Head of Your Class" (advertisement). *Texas Monthly* (October 2003): 137.

Moyers, Bill. "Politics and Economy: Transcript—Middle Class Squeeze." PBS.org, December 13, 2002. www.pbs.org/now/transcript/transcript_middleclass.html (accessed December 31, 2003).

Muhammad, Richard. "Archie Bunker Lives!" 2001. www.blinks.net/magazine/channels/issues/doc_page5.html (accessed March 14, 2003).

"My Wife and Kids." ABC Television, 2004. www.abc.go.com/primetime/mywifeandkids/show.html (accessed January 1, 2004).

Napolitano, Jo. "As Garbage, and Smell, Rise in Chicago, Striking Trash Haulers Reject a Raise Offer." *New York Times,* October 6, 2003, A9.

———. "Chicago Strike Leaves Garbage Piling Up." *New York Times,* October 3, 2003, A18.

National Coalition for the Homeless. "How Many People Experience Homelessness?" NCH Fact Sheet 2, 2002. www.nationalhomeless.org/numbers.html (accessed February 14, 2004).

Nettles, John G. "Malcolm in the Middle." *Popmatters:Television,* 2003. popmatters
.com/tv/reviews/m/malcolm-in-the-middle.html (accessed December 30, 2003).

Nocera, Joseph. *A Piece of the Action: How the Middle Class Joined the Money Class.*
New York: Simon and Schuster, 1994.

Noer, Michael, and Dan Ackman. "The Forbes Fictional Fifteen." *Forbes,* September 13, 2002. www.forbes.com/2002/09/13/400fictional_10.html (accessed December 7, 2003).

Norris, Pippa. *Women, Media, and Politics.* New York: Oxford University Press, 1997.

Norris, Pippa, and Susan J. Carroll. "The Dynamics of the News Framing Process:
From Reagan's Gender Gap to Clinton's Soccer Moms." ksghome.harvard
.edu/~.pnorris.shorenstein.ksg/acrobat/carroll.pdf (accessed August 27, 2003).

Norris, Pippa, Montague Kern, and Marion Just. *Framing Terrorism:The News Media,
the Government and the Public.* New York: Routledge, 2003.

"Not Able to Earn a Living: The Letter of a Sewing Woman to the Central Labor
Union." *New York Times,* February 16, 1885, 5.

"Notebook: The New Homeless." *Time,* February 11, 2002, 15.

Novak, Shonda. "Austin Mansion Sale's a Stunner." *Austin American-Statesman,* September 25, 2003, A1, A17.

Novak, Shonda, Lori Hawkins, and Amy Schatz. "Overheard in Austin." *Austin
American-Statesman,* February 22, 2002, D1.

Nunberg, Geoffrey. "Keeping Ahead of the Joneses." *New York Times,* November 24,
2002, WK4.

"*The O.C.*" Forums.about.com, 2003. forums.about.com/n/mb/message.asp?
webtag=ab-tvschedules&msg=2794.15 (accessed December 8, 2003).

Oldenburg, Ray. *The Great Good Place: Cafés, Coffee Shops, Bookstores, Bars, Hair Salons and Other Hangouts at the Heart of a Community.* New York: Marlowe, 1999.

Olsen, Eric. "Down and Out in Santa Monica." Blogcritics.org, 2003. www.blog
critics.org/archives/2003/01/06/200033.php (accessed February 22, 2004).

"Organized Crime and the Labor Unions." AmericanMafia.com, 2004. www.amer
icanmafia.com/Crime_and_Labor.html (accessed March 22, 2004).

Pakulski, Jan, and Malcolm Waters. *The Death of Class.* Thousand Oaks, Calif.: Sage,
1996.

———. "The Reshaping and Dissolution of Social Class in Advanced Society." *Theory and Society* 25 (1996): 667–91.

Parenti, Michael. *Inventing Reality:The Politics of the Mass Media.* New York: St. Martin's, 1986.

Parr, Jan, and Ted Shen. "The Richest Chicagoans: Who's Up, Who's Down?"
Chicago (February 2002): 48–55, 76–81.

Partlow, Joshua. "At River's Edge, Left With an 'Empty Feeling.'" *Washington Post,*
September 25, 2003, SM3.

Pear, Robert. "A Proposed Definition of Poverty May Raise Number of U.S. Poor."
New York Times, April 30, 1995, A1.

Peppard, Alan. "Charity Co-Chair Steps Down over Shoplifting Charge." www.dal
lasnews.com (accessed September 29, 2003).

Perrucci, Robert, and Earl Wysong. *The New Class Society.* 2nd edition. Lanham, Md.: Rowman & Littlefield, 2003.

"Perspectives." *Newsweek,* February 4, 2002, 17.

Pew Center for Civic Journalism. 2004, "Finding Third Places: Other Voices, Different Stories." www.pewcenter.org/doingcj/videos/thirdplaces.html (accessed July 6, 2004).

Pew Research Center for the People and the Press. "Bottom-Line Pressures Now Hurting Coverage, Say Journalists." www.stateofthenewsmedia.org/prc.pdf (accessed July 6, 2004).

Peyser, Marc. "Martha's Mess: The Insiders." *Newsweek,* July 1, 2002, 38–43.

Peyser, Marc, and B. J. Sigesmund. "Heir Heads." *Newsweek,* October 20, 2003, 54–55.

Pezzullo, Elizabeth. "Shelter's Plan Not a Popular Move." *Free Lance-Star,* June 7, 2002. www.fredericksburg.com/?News/FLS/2002/062002/06072002/631644 (accessed January 25, 2004).

"Philanthropy: Enriching Our Communities through Giving." *Austin American-Statesman,* January 1, 2002, A11.

Polgreen, Lydia. "An Aging Population, a Looming Crisis." *New York Times,* November 4, 2003, A25.

———. "As Jobs Vanish, the Sweet Talk Could Turn Tough." *New York Times,* October 12, 2003, A26.

Poniewozik, James. "The New Class Action." *Time,* September 29, 2003, n.p.

"Poor Whites in the South: Their Poverty and Principles." *New York Times,* May 13, 1877, 5.

Porter, Eduardo. "What Unions Can Gain from Immigration." *New York Times,* March 28, 2004, BU3.

"Poverty and Charity." *New York Times,* November 8, 1870, 2.

"Poverty Leading to Suicide: Another Body of a Woman Found at New Haven." *New York Times,* September 3, 1881, 2.

"Poverty Leading to Suicide." *New York Times,* April 23, 1883, 8.

Powell, Michael. "First Good Preschool, Then Harvard." *Austin American-Statesman,* November 24, 2002, K3.

Primack, Phil. "We All Work, Don't We?" *Columbia Journalism Review* (September–October 1992): 56.

Proctor, Bernadette D., and Joseph Dalaker. "Poverty in the United States: 2002." *U.S. Census Bureau: Current Population Reports,* P60-222. Washington, D.C.: U.S. Government Printing Office, 2003.

Puette, William J. *Through Jaundiced Eyes: How the Media View Organized Labor.* Ithaca, N.Y.: ILR, 1992.

"Put It on My Tab." *Austin American-Statesman,* September 22, 2002, H1.

Rashbaum, William K. "U.S. Indicts Gottis, Saying They Operated Dock Rackets." *New York Times,* June 5, 2002, B1.

"Reds Plotted Country Wide Strike. Arrests Exceeded 5,000, 2,635 Held; 3 Transports Ready for Them." *New York Times,* January 4, 1920, 1.

Reese, Stephen D., Oscar H. Gandy, Jr., and August E. Grant, eds. *Framing Public Life: Perspectives on Media and Our Understanding of the Social World.* Mahwah, N.J.: Lawrence Erlbaum, 2003.

Rich, Frank. "State of the Enron." *New York Times,* February 2, 2002, A29.

———. "When You Got It, Flaunt It." *New York Times,* November 23, 2003, AR1, AR34.

Rich Girls: Welcome to the World of Rich Girls. MTV, 2003. www.mtu.com/onair/rich_girls (accessed October 22, 2003).

Robbins, Tom. "Working-Class Heroes: Towering Losses, Towering Deeds." *Village Voice* (September 26–October 2, 2001). www.villagevoice.com/issues/0139/robbins.php (accessed March 4, 2004).

Rothman, Robert A. *Inequality and Stratification: Race, Class, and Gender,* 5th edition. Upper Saddle River, N.J.: Prentice Hall, 2005.

Rucker, Allen. *The Sopranos: A Family History.* New York: New American Library, 2001.

"A Sad Case of Poverty: A Woman Commits Suicide, Her Husband at the Point of Death." *New York Times,* July 13, 1874, 5.

"A Sad Life Story: Reduced from Wealth to Poverty and Dying almost without Friends." *New York Times,* August 6, 1883, 5.

Salkin, Allen. "Homes, Sweet Homes: Michael Bloomberg's Real-Estate Holdings Are Fairly Modest—for a Multibillionaire." *New York Magazine,* April 15, 2002, 23.

Sanford, John. "Fueling Irrational Fears, Media Make Money, Boost Careers, Panel Says." *Stanford Report,* August 6, 2003. news-service.stanford.edu/news/2003/august6/fear-86.html (accessed February 1, 2004).

Sargent, Ben. "Don't Mind Howard . . . ," *Austin American-Statesman,* August 29, 2003, A16.

———. "Oh, Yeah? Well, Now They're Talking . . . ," *Austin American-Statesman,* March 26, 2003, A16.

Savan, Leslie. "In Defense of Martha." *New York Times,* June 27, 2002, A27.

"Save Middle Class, Congress Is Urged." *New York Times,* October 21, 1942, 1.

"Says Middle Class Needs Salvation: Martin Asks National Support of Republican Drive to Avert Its 'Ruin' by New Deal." *New York Times,* August 27, 1939, 5.

Scheibal, Stephen. "Long Center Asks City for $25 Million." *Austin American-Statesman,* February 1, 2003, A1, A10.

Scheufele, Dietram A. "Framing as a Theory of Media Effects." *Journal of Communications* 49 (1999): 103–22.

Schmidt, Diane E. "Public Opinion and Media Coverage of Labor Unions." *Journal of Labor Research* 15 (Spring 1993): 151–64.

"School Cooks Win over $95 Million in Powerball." *Dallas Morning News,* October 28, 2003, 5A.

Schor, Juliet B. *Born to Buy: The Commercialized Child and the New Consumer Culture.* New York: Scribner, 2004.

Schwarz, John E., and Thomas J. Volgy. *The Forgotten Americans.* New York: Norton, 1992.

Seelye, Katharine Q. "Gore Offers Vision of Better Times for Middle Class." *New York Times,* September 7, 2000, A1.

Sellers, Patricia. "The Business of Being Oprah." *Fortune,* April 1, 2002. www.fortune.com (accessed March 30, 2002).

"Senate Vote Voided Veto of Labor Bill." *New York Times,* June 24, 1947, 1.

"Sensible Chic." HGTV.com, 2003. www.hgtv.com/hgtv/shows_sec (accessed November 30, 2003).

Shanahan, Gerry. "You Say House Arrest, I Say Paradise." *New York Times,* May 2, 2002, F1, F7.

Sharp, Deborah, Paul Davidson, and Tom Kenworthy. "Employers Praise Bush's 'Guest Worker' Plan: They See Lots of Cheap Labor; Migrant Advocates Skeptical." *USA Today,* January 8, 2004, A3.

Shipler, David K. "A Poor Cousin of the Middle Class." *New York Times Magazine,* January 18, 2004, 22–27.

———. *The Working Poor: Invisible in America.* New York: Knopf, 2004.

"Shop Till You Get Caught." *D Magazine,* November, 2003, 20.

"Showdown over Shelter: A Gritty Little Neighborhood Fights S.F. Plan for Homeless." *San Francisco Examiner,* August 12, 1999.

Shulman, Beth. *The Betrayal of Work: How Low-Wage Jobs Fail 30 Million Americans and Their Families.* New York: New Press, 2003.

Sicha, Choire. "They'll Always Have Paris." *New York Times,* June 13, 2004, AR31, AR41.

Silverstein, Michael J., and Neil Fiske (with John Butman). *Trading Up: The New American Luxury.* New York: Portfolio, 2003.

Smith, Chris. "Can This Man Save Martha?" *New York Magazine,* December 15, 2003, 34–39.

Smith, Steve. "Developing New Reflexes in Framing Stories." Pew Center for Civil Journalism, 1997. www.pewcenter.org/doingcj/civiccat/displayCivcat.php?id=97 (accessed July 3, 2004).

Snow, David A., and Leon Anderson. *Down on Their Luck: A Case Study of Homeless Street People.* Berkeley: University of California Press, 1993.

Snow, David A., E. Burke Rochford, Steven K. Worden, and Robert D. Benford. "Frame Alignment Processes, Micromobilization, and Movement Participation." *American Sociological Review* 51 (1986): 464–81.

Sorkin, Andrew Ross. "Birthday Party Video Takes Center Stage at Kozlowski Trial." *New York Times,* October 29, 2003, C4.

"So You Wanna Be a Sitcom Writer?" soyouwanna.com, 2004. www.soyouwanna.com/site/syws/sitcom/sitcom.html (accessed July 7, 2004).

Spencer, Miranda. "Making the Invisible Visible." *Extra!* (January–February 2003). www.fair.org/extra/0301/poverty.html (accessed February 29, 2004).

St. John, Warren. "Advice from Ex-Cons to a Jet-Set Jailbird: Best Walk on Eggs." *New York Times,* July 13, 2003, ST1, ST2.

———. "Sorrow So Sweet: A Guilty Pleasure in Another's Woe." *New York Times,* August 24, 2002, A15, A17.

Stanley, Alessandra. "All in the (Rich, Dysfunctional) Family." *New York Times,* October 31, 2003, B1, B33.

———. "Focusing on Residents of Gilded Cages." *New York Times,* October 27, 2003, B8.

———. "With a Rich Girl Here and a Rich Girl There." *New York Times,* December 2, 2003, B1, B5.

———. "TV Weekend—Bullies, Bears and Bullets: It's Round 5." *New York Times,* March 5, 2004, E1.

Stanley, Alessandra, and Constance L. Hays. "Martha Stewart's To-Do List May Include Image Polishing." *New York Times,* June 23, 2002, A1, A24.

Stanley, Alessandra, and Jim Yardley. "Lay's Family Is Financially Ruined, His Wife Says." *New York Times,* January 29, 2002, C1, C6.

Stein, Joel. "The Real Face of Homelessness." CNN.com, January 13, 2003. www.cnn/2003/ALLPOLITICS/01/13/timep.homelessness.tm/index.html (accessed February 11, 2004).

Stein, Nicholas. "The Question Authority: Exploding Myths about the Poor." *Fortune,* September 16, 2003. www.fortune.com/fortune/0,15935,487013,00.html (accessed September 29, 2003).

Steinhauer, Jennifer. "Bloomberg's Salon, Where the Powerful Mix over Meatloaf." *New York Times,* May 8, 2002, A1, A29.

Sternheimer, Karen. *It's Not the Media: The Truth about Pop Culture's Influence on Children.* Boulder, Colo.: Westview, 2003.

Stout, David. "A Great Equalizer: Isabel Was Her Name." *New York Times,* September 26, 2003, A17.

Strom, Stephanie. "For Middle Class, Health Insurance Becomes a Luxury." *New York Times,* November 16, 2003, A25.

Sullivan, Teresa A., Elizabeth Warren, and Jay Lawrence Westbrook. *The Fragile Middle Class: Americans in Debt.* New Haven, Conn.: Yale University Press, 2000.

Suskind, Ron. "Can't Win for Losing." *New York Times Book Review,* February 15, 2004, 7.

Swartz, Mimi. "An Enron Yard Sale." *New Yorker,* May 6, 2002, 50–51.

Sweeney, Gael. "The King of White Trash Culture: Elvis Presley and the Aesthetics of Excess." In *White Trash: Race and Class in America,* edited by Matt Wray and Annalee Newitz, 249–66. New York: Routledge, 1997.

"Tarnish, Anyone?" *People,* July 8, 2002, 44–45.

Taylor, LaTonya. "The Church of O." *Christianity Today,* April 1, 2002, 38–45.

Television without Pity. "Here Comes Santa Claus." televisionwithoutpity.com/story.cgi?show=&&story=5940&page=5 (accessed February 28, 2004).

———. "The Hunger Artist." televisionwithoutpity.com/story.cgi?show=15&story=3487&page=2 (accessed February 28, 2004).

"Terrible Tragedy: An Insane Mother Kills Her Daughter." *New York Times,* July 6, 1872, 2.

Thomas, Cathy Booth. "Enron Takes a Life." *Time,* February 4, 2002, 20–21.

Thomas, Evan, and Andrew Murr. "The Gambler Who Blew It All." *Newsweek,* February 4, 2002, 24.

Thomas, Landon, Jr. "Dismantling a Wall Street Club." *New York Times,* November 2, 2003, BU1, BU11.

Truppin, Andrea. "How Much Is That View in the Window?" *New York Times,* September 18, 2003, D4.

Tsao, Amy. "The Two Faces of Wal-Mart." *Business Week,* January 28, 2004. www.businessweek.com/bwdaily/dnflash/jan2004/nf20040128_6990_db014.ht ml (accessed February 2, 2004).

Tuchman, Gaye. *Making News: A Study in the Construction of Reality.* New York: Free Press, 1978.

Tyler, Mary E. "Exporting Jobs and Our Way of Life: Letter to the Editor." *New York Times,* December 31, 2003, A20.

Uchitelle, Louis. "Bottom's Up: The Middle Class—Winning in Politics, Losing in Life." *New York Times,* July 19, 1998, WR1.

———. "Blacks Lose Better Jobs Faster as Middle-Class Work Drops." *New York Times,* July 12, 2003, A1.

———. "We Pledge Allegiance to the Mall." *New York Times,* December 6, 2004, C12.

"Unable to Endure Poverty." *New York Times,* June 2, 1884, 2.

Vane, Sharyn Wizda. "Martha's Dirty Laundry." *Austin American-Statesman,* April 20, 2002, D1, D13.

Veblen, Thorstein. *The Theory of the Leisure Class.* Introduction by Robert Lekachman. New York: Penguin, 1994 [1899].

Vicini, James, and Verna Gates. "HealthSouth's Founder Hit with Criminal Charges." Reuters News, 2003. aolscv.news.aol/news/article.adp?id =20031105051809990002 (accessed November 5, 2003).

"A Violinist in Despair: Domenico Mariani on the Verge of Suicide, Seized as He Was about to Jump from a Hoboken Dock—Poverty in His Old Age Unbearable." *New York Times,* August 30, 1885, 12.

Waldman, Amy. "A Nation Challenged: Reporters Notebook—'Dear Mr. or Mrs. Fireman.'" *New York Times,* September 18, 2001, B8.

"Walks among the New York Poor: Homeless Children." *New York Times,* May 4, 1854, 6.

"Walks among the Poor." *New York Times,* January 30, 1870, 6.

"Wallace Sees All in a Middle Class: Picturing Future, He Asserts the 'Horatio Alger' Spirit Will Never Die Here." *New York Times,* January 25, 1943, 1.

"The Wal-Martization of America." *New York Times,* November 15, 2003, A26.

Warner, W. Lloyd, and Paul S. Lunt. *The Social Life of a Modern Community.* New Haven, Conn.: Yale University Press, 1941.

Warren, Elizabeth, and Amelia Warren Tyagi. *The Two-Income Trap: Why Middle Class Mothers and Fathers Are Going Broke.* New York: Basic Books, 2003.

Weaver, David H., and G. Cleveland Wilhoit. *The American Journalist in the 1990s.* Mahwah, N.J.: Lawrence Erlbaum, 1996.

Weber, Max. *From Max Weber: Essays in Sociology.* Edited by H. H. Gerth and C. Wright Mills. New York: Oxford University Press, 1946.

Wecter, Dixon. *The Saga of American Society: A Record of Social Aspiration 1607–1937.* New York: Scribner, 1937.

Whang, Insung, and Eungjun Min. "Blaming the Homeless: The Populist Aspect of Network TV News." In *Reading the Homeless: The Media's Image of Homeless Culture,* edited by Eungjun Min, 121–33. Westport, Conn.: Praeger, 1999.

"'Why Middle Class Mothers and Fathers Are Going Broke.'" MSNBC.com, 2003. msnbc.msn.com/Default.aspx?id=3079221&p1=0 (accessed December 29, 2003).

Wilkinson, Signe. "The Corporate Card Shoppe" *Austin American-Statesman,* September 16, 2003, A11.

Williams, Maureen. "From Incendiary to Invisible: A Print-News Content Analysis of the Labor Movement." *Labor Center Review* 10 (1988): 23–27.

Williams, Robin M., Jr. *American Society: A Sociological Interpretation.* 3rd edition. New York: Knopf, 1970.

Witchel, Alex. "Tacos, Stir-Fries and Cake: The Junior League at 102." *New York Times,* October 15, 2003, D1, D6.

"Working Men on Parade: An Orderly Labor Demonstration—Ten Thousand Men in Line." *New York Times,* September 6, 1882, 8.

"The Working Men's Views: President Jarrett before the Senate Committee." *New York Times,* September 8, 1883, 8.

Wray, Matt, and Annalee Newitz, eds. *White Trash: Race and Class in America.* New York: Routledge, 1997.

Wrolstad, Mark. "An Unfashionable Turn for Stylish HP Socialite." *Dallas Morning News,* October 25, 2003, 1A, 10A–11A.

Wyatt, Edward, and David M. Halbfinger. "Clark and Kerry Offering Plans to Help Middle Class." *New York Times,* January 6, 2004, A17.

Yardley, Jonathan. "Book Review: *Behind the Gates.*" *Washington Post,* May 8, 2003, CO2.

Yardley, William. "The Last Grain Falls at a Sugar Factory." *New York Times,* January 31, 2004, A13.

Young, John. "White-Collar Jobs, Too." *Waco Tribune-Herald,* January 22, 2004. www.wacotrib.com/news/newsfd/auto/feed/news/2004/01/22/1074752927 .26609.8057.2758.html (accessed January 28, 2004).

"Your Honor, my client . . ." Cartoon. *New Yorker,* March 25, 2002, 69.

Zeller, Tom. "The Nation: Calculating One Kind of Middle Class." *New York Times,* October 29, 2000, WR5.

———. "Of Fuzzy Math and 'Food Security.'" *New York Times,* January 11, 2004, WK16.

Zweig, Michael. *The Working Class Majority: America's Best Kept Secret.* Ithaca, N.Y.: Cornell University Press, 2001.

INDEX

ABOUT THE AUTHOR

Diana Kendall is professor of sociology at Baylor University where her research and teaching interests include social theory, social stratification, and sociology of media. She is the author of *The Power of Good Deeds: Privileged Women and the Social Reproduction of the Upper Class* (Rowman & Littlefield, 2002) and several widely used textbooks, including *Sociology in Our Times* and *Social Problems in a Diverse Society*.